International Studies in Human Rights

VOLUME 95

# Cultural Human Rights

*Edited by*

Francesco Francioni

Martin Scheinin

MARTINUS
NIJHOFF
PUBLISHERS

LEIDEN • BOSTON
2008

# 1
# Culture, Heritage and Human Rights: An Introduction

*Francesco Francioni*

## 1. Cultural rights as human rights

In more than half a century of development in the legal doctrine and practice of human rights, cultural rights have attracted much less attention and conceptual elaboration relative to the other more familiar categories of civil-political rights and social-economic rights.[1] This may be due, in part, to the paucity of specific legal provisions in the relevant international instruments. The text of the 1948 Universal Declaration, for instance, contains only two articles[2] on the subject, as does the 1966 Covenant on Economic, Social and Cultural Rights.[3] The European Convention on Human Rights and the American Convention, on the other hand, entirely ignore cultural rights, a gap only partly filled by subsequent protocols.[4] In

---

1 One of the few comprehensive and interdisciplinary works on the subject, *Les droits culturels* (P. Meyer. Bisch ed., Friburg, 1993), significantly carries the sub-title '*une categorie sous-developée des droits de l'homme*'. More recent contributions have addressed the interplay between economic regulation and cultural identity in the context of European law, see, in particular, R. Crauford Smith (ed.), *Culture and European Union Law* (Oxford, 2004), and the theoretical question whether a liberal theory of the State is compatible with the recognition of collective rights to groups or minorities, see W. Kymlicka, *Multicultural Citizenship* (Oxford, Oxford University Press, 1995).

2 Article 26 on the right to education and Article 27 on the right to participate in cultural life and in scientific progress.

3 Article 13 on the right to education and article 15 on artists' rights, cultural participation and the right to benefit from scientific progress.

4 See Article 2 of the *Protocol to the Convention for the Protection of Human Rights and Fundamental Freedoms*, signed in Paris, 20 March 1952, and entered into force 18 May 1954, 213 UNTS 262; and the *Additional Protocol to the American Convention on Human Rights in*

Francioni and Scheinin (eds), *Cultural Human Rights*, 1–15
 ISBN 978 90 04 16294 5. Printed in the Netherlands.

legal doctrine, contributions to the analysis and reconstruction of cultural rights occupy a minuscule space in the vast panorama of human rights literature.[5]

At the same time, if we look beyond the narrow confines of human rights instruments we can see that there is no shortage of legal texts dealing with culture and cultural rights. UNESCO alone has produced a considerable number of soft law instruments on the subject. Beginning with the 1966 Declaration of the principles of international cultural cooperation and the 1976 Recommendation on participation by the people at large in cultural life, UNESCO has developed several discrete areas of cultural rights and policy, such as the right to education,[6] linguistic rights,[7] traditional culture and folklore,[8] and cultural diversity.[9] Binding treaties relevant to cultural cooperation and cultural rights have been promoted by UNESCO and include the 1950 Florence Agreement on educational, scientific and cultural materials,[10] the 1961 Convention for the Protection of Performers, Producers of Phonograms and Broadcasting Organizations[11] and the 1996 Lisbon Convention on the recognition of higher education titles.[12] In addition to these instruments is the considerable number of UNESCO cultural property conventions, which have evolved toward more expansive forms of cultural heritage protection, inclusive of living cultures, as is witnessed by the two most recent conventions on the safeguarding of intangible heritage (2003)[13] and on the protection and promotion of the diversity of cultural expressions.[14]

---

*the Area of Economic, Social and Cultural Rights* (Protocol of San Salvador) of 17 November 1988, entered into force 16 November 1999.

5 Among the remarkable contributions to the theory of cultural rights and worthy of mention: P. Meyer. Bisch (ed.), *cit. supra* note 1; H. Niec (ed.), *Cultural Rights and Wrongs* (UNESCO, 1998); and J. Simonides, 'Cultural Rights', in J. Simonides (ed.), *Human Rights: Concept and Standards* (UNESCO, 2000), p. 175 ff.

6 See the *World Declaration on Education for All*, adopted in March 1990 in Jomtien, Thailand. Article 1 proclaims that 'every person – child, youth and adult – shall be able to benefit from educational opportunities designed to meet their basic learning needs'.

7 1996 Barcelona Declaration. On this category of rights see the chapter in this book by De Witte and Mancini.

8 See the 1989 Declaration of the same title.

9 2001 *Declaration on Cultural Diversity*.

10 Which states that 'the free exchange of ideas and knowledge and, in general, the widest possible dissemination of the diverse forms of self-expression used by civilizations are vitally important both for intellectual progress and international understanding, and consequently for the maintenance of world peace'.

11 12 U.S.T. 2377, 496 U.N.T.S. 43.

12 Lisbon Convention, *CETS* No. 165.

13 *Convention for the Safeguarding of the Intangible Cultural Heritage*, 2003, available at: <www.unesco.org>.

14 *Convention on the Protection and Promotion of the Diversity of Cultural Expressions*, 2005, *ibid.*

Faced with this wealth of international law sources, how can we explain that cultural rights remain inadequately developed and rather problematic as a specific category of human rights? An easy explanation can be traced to the familiar argument that cultural provisions contained in the existing legal instruments do not establish real rights, with corresponding precise and unconditional obligations, but rather political commitments of a programmatic character that create at most legitimate expectations but not true rights. This explanation is partly correct, if we take into account the very abstract content of the relevant treaty provisions and the difficulty in conceptualizing specific obligations to the rights in question. However, quite apart from the fact that this observation would also apply to economic and social rights, it is the practice of domestic courts and international bodies that shows how cultural rights can be treated as true enforceable rights.[15]

There are, therefore, more complex reasons for the elusiveness and underdeveloped status of cultural rights in international human rights law. These reasons will be amply illustrated in the specific contributions to this book. Nonetheless, by way of a preliminary assessment and introduction, it is of use to highlight the fundamental antinomy that cultural rights pose in their being antagonistic to other human rights or to some established principles and doctrines of international law.

The first type of antagonism is inherent to the peculiar nature of cultural rights as claims to *exclusivity*. Unlike other human rights such as civil, political, economic and social rights, which are premised on the fundamental notion of shared humanity and dignity among all members of the human family, cultural rights hinge on the perceived uniqueness of the legacy that binds a group or community to a shared memory upon which the powerful sentiment of belonging and identity is built. Historically this sense of uniqueness and exclusivity has provided the ideological support for national hegemonic expansionism – the *mission civilisatrice,* the 'white man's burden' or the 'manifest destiny' as legitimating factors in empire building, territorial conquest and the consequent readiness to destroy other cultures – an endeavour that unfortunately continues unabated today with the misconceived myth of 'democracy' export and the salvific mission of regime change by the use of force. On a smaller scale, and in a less dramatic context, exclusivity may nourish a sense of separation and thus hinder cultural exchange and development for fear of 'contamination' of a jealously guarded tradition.[16]

---

15 See *infra* note 18.

16 Sometimes this obsession with exclusivity may be totally divorced from history and border on pure imagination of common tradition, which in turn leads to the 'invention' of a culture totally divorced from reality. This is the case of some political movements such as the Italian Northern League which draws its inspiration from the invention of the mythical country of 'Padania', a region South of the Alps trans-versed by the Po river, inhabited by populations of diverse cultural traditions, and which tries to exploit as a unifying element the sense of dislike for the central government and xenophobic sentiment against immigration.

The second type of conflict is that between individual rights and group rights. If we conceptualize cultural rights as group or community rights, as the majority of commentators tend to do,[17] the collective right of the group may sooner or later attempt to override the rights of its individual members. Practice shows that the right of the group to exist and develop as such may conflict with the right of an individual member to leave, to marry a person of her/his choice outside the group, and, perhaps, to return at a time in the future.[18] If, on the contrary, we construe cultural rights as individual rights and thus consistent with international human rights, then we uphold the individual member's freedom to leave, to marry, to speak and work outside the community and to return, unavoidably at the risk of undermining the group's fundamental interest in the preservation of its social and cultural cohesion and, in the long term, its inherent ability to survive as a distinct cultural society.

Cultural rights or claims are also liable to come into conflict with other established and generally recognized individual rights. Typical of this is the right to property or the right to free speech. A state may assert a cultural claim to the return of antiquities or artistic heritage unlawfully removed from its territory and transferred to another state only to find out that its claim is barred by property rights acquired by the purchaser of the object under the law of the forum or other applicable foreign law. Dealers in cultural objects are keenly aware of this opportunity and tend to choose the law best suited to their transaction so as to maximize the protection of property rights at the expense of the cultural rights of other communities and nations. Treaties have been adopted at the global level[19] and specific legislative measures have been enacted in the European Union[20] to ensure that the abstract guarantee of property rights does not stand in the way of restitution or the return of the cultural object to the community unlawfully dispossessed of it. As for free speech, it is sufficient to recall here that the perverted effect of extremist claims to respect for religious symbols have led to calls for murder in the case of Salman Rushdie, to actual murder

---

[17] See, for instance, R. Stavenhagen, 'Cultural Rights and Universal Human Rights', in A. Eide et al. (eds.), *Economic Social and Cultural Rights* (Dordrecht, 1995), p. 63 ff.; F. Shyllon, 'The Right to a Cultural Past: African Viewpoints', in L.V. Prott, *Cultural Rights & Wrongs* (Institute of Art and Law, UNESCO Publishing, Paris, 1998), p. 103 ff.

[18] See the *Lovelace* case, UN Human Rights Committee, decision of 18 July 1978, concerning communication No. R. 6/24, and chapter by F. Lenzerini in this volume.

[19] I refer here to the 1970 UNESCO *Convention on the Means of Prohibiting and Preventing the Illicit Import, Export and Transfer of Ownership of Cultural Property* (available at: <www.unesco.org>) and to the 1995 UNIDROIT *Convention on Stolen or Illegally Exported Cultural Objects* (available at: <www.unidroit.org/english/conventions/1995culturalproperty/1995culturalproperty-e.htm>).

[20] I refer to the Council Regulation No. 3911/1992 of 9 December 1992 on export of cultural goods (*Official Journal* L395 of 31 December 1992, p. 1) and to the Council Directive 93/7/EEC of 15 March 1993 on the return of cultural objects unlawfully removed from the territory of a Member State (*Official Journal* L074 of 27 March 1993, p. 74).

in the case of Dutch film maker Van Gogh, and to widespread mass violence in the case of the Danish cartoons, perceived by fundamentalists as an intolerable offence against the symbols of the religion and culture of Islam.[21]

At a more technical legal level, cultural rights are likely to come into conflict with generally accepted policy objectives and legal doctrines of the international community. Take for example the present debate concerning the preservation of cultural diversity, and the consequent right to protect such diversity with economic support and with measures restricting the inflow of foreign cultural products or services. Clearly this right may be necessary in order to counteract the excessive standardization and commodification of culture, but its exercise can result in trade restrictive measures which are inconsistent with the international obligations undertaken under WTO agreements and with its underlying liberal principle that the free flow of goods, services and ideas is essential to human development and good governance.

Finally, a word about minority rights and the rights of indigenous peoples. There is no doubt that a powerful movement is underway to secure a safe anchorage of such rights to international law. These rights are largely cultural, in so far as they tend to guarantee the survival of the language, religion, specific social structures and distinct way of life of groups or peoples. The safeguarding of such cultural rights, though, may come into conflict with internationally accepted human rights standards, such as those that prohibit discrimination against women, the protection of children, free speech or the pursuit of scientific research, to the extent that communal values and embedded social or religious traditions are incompatible with the fundamental idea of individual liberty. These strains may become laden with emotional overtones and degenerate into dangerous conflicts, as we are experiencing today in Europe, particularly with the radical and alienated fringes of ethnic and religious minorities. As far as indigenous peoples are concerned, their right to maintain their distinct existence as a group and to safeguard, retain and develop traditional practices essential to the preservation of their cultural identity has been recognized in a number of international instruments, including ILO conventions,[22] the bio-diversity convention,[23] the recent UN Declaration on indigenous peoples,[24] and the UNIDROIT convention on the return of cultural

---

21 The libel case brought by Muslim groups against the Danish paper which had published the controversial cartoons of the Prophet Mohammad was rejected by a Danish court in Aarhus, see BBC Press report regarding Danish cartoons case, City Court of Aarhus dismissal of libel action October 2006.

22 See, in particular, *Convention No. 169 Concerning Indigenous and Tribal Peoples in Independent Countries*, 1989, available at: <www.ilo.org/ilolex/english/convdisp.1.htm>.

23 See *Convention on Biological Diversity*, 1992, Article 8(j), available at: <www.biodiv.org/convention/articles.asp>.

24 Adopted by the UN Human Rights Council in the summer 2006. See Resolution No. 2006/2; U.N. Doc. A/HRC/1/L.10 of 30 June 2006, p. 58 ff.

objects.[25] The latter contains specific provisions for facilitating the restitution of ceremonial objects removed from indigenous communities in violation of their cultural rights. This is a noble move toward providing long overdue redress to indigenous communities for the unspeakable wrongs perpetrated against them in the colonial period by those who conquered their land by force and plundered much of their heritage. However, even in this delicate field, strains may arise in the relations between indigenous peoples' cultural rights and competing rights under international law. The restitution of cultural objects may run counter to the rights of researchers to access such objects for archaeological or anthropological study; or it may even entail the loss of the cultural object in the event of the indigenous community's religious belief or ceremonial practices requiring the destruction or the delivery to mother earth of the returned object, as has happened in practice.[26]

These are some of the strains and contradictions that one has to face when attempting to identify the place of cultural rights in the general context of human rights.

Against this background, I will now examine the issues raised by the specific topic of this chapter; that is, the interplay between cultural heritage and human rights.

## 2. The concept and meaning of cultural heritage

The term 'cultural heritage' today represents the totality of cultural objects, traditions, knowledge and skills that a given nation or community has inherited by way of learning processes from previous generations and which provides its sense of identity to be transmitted to subsequent generations. In international legal terminology, the expression is rather recent. Early treaties adopted under the impulse of UNESCO after World War II did not use the term 'heritage' but rather the more neutral expression 'cultural property'. So goes the title of the 1954 Hague convention on the protection of 'cultural property' in the event of war, as well as the title of the 1970 Paris Convention on the prevention of illicit traffic in 'cultural property'. In 1972 the term 'heritage' was officially adopted by UNESCO in the Convention on the Protection of the World Cultural and Natural Heritage.[27] This change was required by the necessity of bringing under a single conceptual umbrella both cultural properties and natural sites of outstanding universal value. In subsequent international instruments, however, the term 'heritage' has continued to be used. An important example is the 2001 underwater heritage convention[28] where the concept of heritage has become emancipated from that of property so as

25 See, in particular, Article 3(8), Article 5(3)(d) and Article 7(2).

26 See L.V. Prott, *cit. supra* note 17, p. 161, at p. 170.

27 Available at: <www.unesco.org>.

28 See 2001 *Convention on the Protection of the Underwater Cultural Heritage, ibid.*

to acquire the connotation of 'historical or artistic legacy' whose value and whose safeguarding are necessary in view of the protection of a public interest irrespective of ownership. Similarly, with the 2003 UNESCO Convention for the Safeguarding of Intangible Cultural Heritage,[29] the concept of 'heritage' has been expanded beyond built and material cultural objects on which property rights exist to encompass the practices, traditions and skills that represent the common legacy of a community and a fundamental component of its living culture.

This incremental expansion of the concept of cultural heritage in the practice of international law has had the consequence of strengthening the conceptual link between heritage and cultural rights. I will explore this link in the following sections. However, it must be pointed out at the outset that in so far as cultural heritage represents the sum of practices, knowledge and representations that a community or group recognize as part of their history and identity, it is axiomatic that members of the group, individually and collectively, must be entitled to access, perform and enjoy such cultural heritage as a matter of right. Furthermore, the dynamic evolution of the concept of heritage from a mere historical-artistic object to intangible heritage entails that even cultural objects or places must be understood in the function and role they perform in a given society as indispensable tools for the exercise of certain fundamental rights and freedoms, such as the right of association or religious freedom.

## 3. Cultural heritage and human rights

Given this very broad definition of cultural heritage, one can imagine an infinite variety of implications that the concept may have for human rights. For example, to the extent that property rights are recognized as human rights, as in the European Convention system, an individual may claim such a right against a state which asserts some form of eminent domain or pre-emption over a cultural object. The increasing value of art works and antiquities, and their non-fungible character, may add economic relevance to such claims, as is shown by the well-known case of *Beyeler v. Italy*, decided by the European Court of Human Rights on 5 January 2000.[30] Conversely, claims to cultural heritage may be framed in terms of human rights in order to trump competing claims to intellectual property rights, as is

---

29 See *supra* note 13.

30 European Court of Human Rights, Case of *Beyeler v. Italy*, Application No. 33202/96, Judgment of 5 January 2000, Grand Chamber. In this case the Court found that Italy had violated Article 1 of Protocol 1 by way of a forced purchase of a Van Gogh painting at a price that did not reflect the market value of the property. It is interesting that the Court reached this conclusion despite the clear letter of Italian law, which permits the foreclosure of ownership over artworks that are notified by the applicant.

happening today in the field of traditional knowledge of local communities and which provides the useful lead-up to the commercial development of new foods and drugs. At the level of collective rights, cultural heritage may have important implications for the right to development, understood both as economic development induced by a rational and sustainable use of a state's cultural patrimony, and human and cultural development sustained by a society's sense of identity and continuity with its past.

Bearing this in mind, we can identify three distinct legal aspects of the interplay between cultural heritage and human rights: 1) the emergence of the principle according to which the international community as a whole has an interest in the conservation and protection of cultural heritage as part of the safeguarding of human dignity and of the contribution that each people gives to the culture of the world; 2) the assimilation of serious violations of international cultural heritage law to grave violations of human rights entailing the international criminal responsibility of the offender; and 3) the concern with the preservation of the diversity of cultures and heritage as part of the safeguarding of the rich variety of living cultures of the world.

## 4. Cultural heritage, human dignity, and the common heritage of humanity

Although the UN Charter does not contain any specific provision connecting cultural heritage to human rights, and although the UN General Assembly rejected the notion of 'cultural genocide' in the drafting of the 1948 Convention, it is clear that the original conception and the later development of human rights law were not extraneous to the notion of cultural rights and cultural heritage.

First of all the adoption in the Universal Declaration of Human Rights of the central notion of 'human dignity'[31] shows how the drafters intended to safeguard peoples entitlement to the respect of their culture as part of their identity, history, and thus dignity. This concept runs deep throughout the Universal Declaration: Article 18 refers to freedom of conscience and religion, a fundamental component of culture in every society, and Article 22 provides that 'everyone, as a member of society … is entitled to the realization, through national efforts and international cooperation … of … cultural rights indispensable for his dignity';[32] Article 27 proclaims the '… right freely to participate in the cultural life of the community'.

---

[31] 'Whereas recognition of the inherent dignity and of the equal and inalienable rights of all members of the human family is the foundation of freedom, justice and peace in the world', first paragraph of the Preamble of the *Universal Declaration of Human Rights*, U.N. CAOR, 6th Comm. 83rd mtg. U.N. Doc. A/C.6/SR.83 (1948).

[32] *Ibid.*

These rights have been confirmed in the 1966 Covenant on Economic, Social and Cultural Rights. Article 15 addresses the right to take part in cultural life and the right to enjoy the benefits of scientific progress and its applications. For its part, the Covenant on Civil and Political Rights contains the important provision of Article 27 concerning the right of persons belonging to ethnic, linguistic or religious minorities to enjoy their own culture, in the community with other members of the group.[33] These provisions have a significant impact on cultural heritage. First of all they entail a negative obligation of all states to abstain from conduct aimed at the destruction, damage, alteration or desecration of cultural objects or spaces that are of significant importance for the practice and enactment of a people's culture, be it a library, a temple, a civic monument or a sacred site for indigenous peoples. Second, they also entail a positive obligation to take steps to protect cultural groups and communities against the risk of destruction or damage to religious or historical property that is indispensable for those communities' cultural practices and, indeed, for their continuing existence as a cultural group. The dramatic events of the war in the Balkans, which saw the intentional destruction of mosques, churches, historical bridges and libraries, provide grim evidence of the close relationship between the cleansing of cultural heritage and egregious human rights violations. This relationship is aptly stressed by the Special Rapporteur of the Commission on Human Rights, Mazowiecki, in his report on the human rights situation in Yugoslavia in 1992, where we can read:

> Although the conflict in Bosnia and Herzegovina is not a religious one, it has been characterized by the systematic destruction and profanation of mosques, Catholic churches and other places of worship, as well as other sites of cultural heritage. This has been reported to be the case particularly in areas currently or previously under the control of Serb forces... Some Orthodox churches have been destroyed in areas of central Bosnia and Herzegovina which were or are under the control of the Government and/or Croat forces.[34]

After this report, the destruction continued, with devastating effects on the landscape of the Balkan region. Even after NATO's armed intervention in Kosovo, ethnic tensions have re-ignited the violence and we have witnessed attacks on and vandalization of orthodox monasteries and churches, now the target of reverse ethnic-cultural cleansing by the victims of former violence and discrimination.[35]

---

33 This provision has been interpreted by the Human Rights Committee in such a way so as to ensure special entitlement of minorities and indigenous people to have access to natural resources: *Lubicon Band v. Canada*, Communication No. 167/1984 (26 March 1990).

34 Report prepared pursuant to Resolution 1992/S-1 of 14 August, 1992.

35 This has led to the adoption of specific legislation by the interim administration of Kosovo on the safeguarding of cultural property and heritage as part of the project of building

A second consideration in support of the linkage between cultural heritage and human rights is the exponential growth of international cultural heritage law of the past 40 years, which is premised upon the reiterated principle that cultural heritage forms part of the general interest of the international community because it is the expression of our diversified and shared humanity. This principle has evolved both in the context of armed conflict and in peacetime. As far as armed conflicts are concerned, the 1954 Hague Convention, now ratified by 114 states and de facto applied by many non-parties as an expression of the general principles of international law,[36] recognizes that '… damage to the cultural property belonging to any people whatsoever means damage to the cultural heritage of all mankind, since each people makes its contribution to the culture of the world'.[37] In peacetime, the 1972 World Heritage Convention, whose parties now represent the near totality of the world community,[38] confirms the same principle with regard to cultural and natural heritage of outstanding universal value and requires that states recognize such heritage as '… world heritage for whose protection it is the duty of the international community as a whole to cooperate'.[39] Similarly, the public interest and the importance of cultural heritage as an integral part of the general interest of humanity 'as a particularly important element in the history of peoples, nations and their relations with each other concerning their common heritage', has been proclaimed in the 2001 UNESCO Convention on the Protection of Underwater Cultural Heritage.

A further step toward the consolidation of the principle according to which cultural heritage is part of the general interest of humanity has been taken by the 2003 UNESCO Declaration on Intentional Destruction of Cultural Heritage. This Declaration was the result of the sense of outrage and indignation felt by the international community as a whole at the senseless and gratuitous destruction of the Buddhas of Bamyian by the Taliban regime in Afghanistan. This was not a case of cross-border destruction; the Buddhas of Bamyian were located in the territory

---

understanding and cooperation between the hostile communities of the Albanian majority and the Serb and other minorities.

36 The United States, whose ratification has been pending in the Senate for more than several years, applies the Hague Convention in its military manuals which treat the rules as norms of international law. The United Kingdom, for its part, has abandoned its long standing policy of aloofness with regard to international treaties concerning the protection of cultural heritage and, after acceding to the 1970 Paris Convention on illicit traffic of cultural property, has now officially announced its decision to accede to the Hague Convention following a preparatory consultation on the most suitable way to meet the Convention's obligations. Consultation was to be completed by 2 December 2005.

37 Preamble of the Convention.

38 The number of Contracting Parties to the World Heritage Convention has reached 183. See at: <portal.unesco.org/la/convention.asp?KO=13637&language=E> (last visited on 12 January 2007).

39 Article 6, para. 1, 1037 UNTS 151.

of Afghanistan. They formed part of the Afghan historical heritage. Nevertheless their destruction became an international case. The United Nations, UNESCO, the European Union, as well as most Islamic states[40] first mobilized to prevent the destruction and then protested and condemned it once it was accomplished. Condemnation was articulated not only in moral or political terms but was couched in legal terms, precisely as a violation of the duty incumbent upon all members of the international community to preserve and protect cultural heritage of significant importance for humanity. In the above case, the destruction was decried as an attack on a religious symbol and as a discriminatory act against the tangible expression of a cultural tradition, in violation of the principle of equal rights and dignity of all human beings.[41] The adoption by unanimous vote of the UNESCO General Conference of the Declaration on Intentional Destruction[42] provides formal recognition of the ongoing process of internationalization of the concern for preservation and protection of cultural heritage. Akin to what has happened with human rights, the way in which a state deals with cultural heritage is not any longer automatically relegated to the domain of 'domestic jurisdiction'. Under appropriate circumstances – particularly in relation to the importance of the cultural object, the discriminatory intent, and the violence employed – an act of destruction or damage to such an object may constitute a breach of the obligation to preserve and protect a cultural object as an element of the common heritage of humanity, and would thus entail international responsibility toward the international community as a whole.

## 5. 'Crimes' against culture

A hallmark of the development of human rights law is the internationalization of individual criminal responsibility for serious human rights abuses and the corresponding emergence of the category of international crimes including genocide, war crimes, crimes against humanity and crimes against peace.[43] Today, international law provides for the criminalization of serious offences against cultural heritage. This is another manifestation of the increasingly important connection between cultural heritage and human rights.

---

40 For illustration of this practice, see F. Francioni and F. Lenzerini, 'The Destruction of the Buddhas of Bamiyan and International Law', *EJIL* (2003), p. 619, and R. O'Keefe, 'World Cultural Heritage: Obligations to the International Community as a Whole?', *ICLQ* (2004), p. 189, at pp. 195-202.

41 See the second sentence in the Preamble of the United Nations Charter.

42 Available at: <www.unesco.org>.

43 A comprehensive coverage of this topic can be found in A. Cassese, *International Criminal Law* (Oxford, 2003).

The starting point in the evolution of this connection is the 1954 Hague convention on the protection of cultural property in the event of armed conflict,[44] whose article 28 requires states parties to 'undertake ... all necessary steps to prosecute and impose penal or disciplinary sanctions upon those persons, of whatever nationality, who commit or order to be committed a breach of the present Convention'. This was a rather weak provision that left states parties free to implement the commitment to prosecute '... within the framework of their ordinary criminal jurisdiction', thus adding nothing to the existing, and possibly inadequate, reach of national jurisdiction and scope of penal law. A specific provision on the prosecution of offences against cultural heritage is also contained in the 1977 Protocol 1 additional to the Geneva Conventions, which limits prosecution and the duty thereof to cases of 'extensive destruction' of cultural property to which special protection has been accorded within the framework of a competent international organization.[45] The most advanced and detailed regime of individual criminal responsibility for offences against cultural heritage was introduced by the 1999 Protocol 2 additional to the 1954 Hague Convention.[46] The Protocol, which entered into force on 9 March 2004, applies in its entirety to international and non-international armed conflicts; introduces the principle of universal jurisdiction over the most 'serious violations' of the norms protecting cultural heritage; and obliges the party in whose territory the offender is present to prosecute or extradite that person regardless of nationality or location of the offence committed.

A significant stimulus for the development of a principle of individual criminal responsibility for attacks and damage done to cultural heritage also stems from the practice of international criminal tribunals. Building upon Article 3(d) of its Statute, the Criminal Tribunal for Former Yugoslavia (ICTY) has established individual criminal responsibility for intentional destruction or damage to cultural property in a variety of situations. First, the Tribunal has adopted a narrow interpretation of the exception of military necessity and has rejected the plea that the mere vicinity of the religious or cultural institutions to a military objective would justify their attack.[47] Second, the Tribunal has recognized attacks on cultural property as independent counts of criminal liability under the laws and customs of war.[48] Third, the destruction of cultural property with discriminatory intent toward a culturally distinct group has been charged as a crime against humanity, and more specifically

44 The text of the Convention is available at: <www.unesco.org>.

45 Article 85(4)(d) Protocol 1, 1125 UNTS 3.

46 See *Second Protocol to the Hague Convention of 1954 for the Protection of Cultural Property in the Event of Armed Conflict*, 1999, available at: <www.unesco.org>.

47 *Naletilic* case, Trial Chamber, 31 March 2003, para. 604 ff., available at: <www.un.org/icty>.

48 *Jokic* case, Judgment of the Trial Chamber, 18 March 2004, *ibid.*

as a crime of persecution within the meaning of Article 5(h) of the ICTY Statute.[49] Finally, the Tribunal has recognized that acts of destruction or wilful damage to cultural property dedicated to religion are now '... criminalized under customary international law'.[50]

Another important manifestation of the intersection between cultural heritage and human rights is the finding of the ICTY that deliberate and systematic destruction of the cultural heritage of a given ethnic group may provide evidence of the *mens rea* element required for the commission of the crime of genocide.[51] This provides a perspective in which the existence of a group is not appreciated in purely biological terms, but also in social and cultural terms, and consequently that the systematic destruction of the symbolic buildings and spaces for the practice of religion and culture is capable of revealing, under appropriate circumstances,[52] the specific intent to destroy in whole or in part such a group within the meaning of the 1948 Genocide Convention.[53]

The jurisprudence of the ICTY influenced the drafting of the Statute of the International Criminal Court, which contains specific provisions imposing criminal liability for the destruction and wilful damage of cultural heritage.[54]

Of course, developments in international practice with regard to the criminalization of attacks against cultural heritage present certain limits. Firstly, the legal instruments and case law referred to above concern situations of armed conflict, where the protection of cultural property is part and parcel of humanitarian law and a consequence of the fundamental distinction between military and non-military objectives. The second limit relates to the difficulty of establishing the threshold of importance of an item of cultural heritage in order for it to become the object of

---

49 See especially the *Kordic* & *Cerkez* case, Judgment of 26 February 2001, *ibid.*, para. 207.

50 *Ibid.*, paras. 206-207, where the Tribunal, in addressing the acts of deliberate destruction of ancient mosques in Bosnia, held that '... When perpetrated with the requisite discriminatory intent, [the destruction] amounts to an attack on the very religious identity of the people. As such, it manifests a nearly pure expression of the notion of "crimes against humanity" for all humanity is indeed injured by the destruction of a unique religious culture and its concomitant cultural objects.'

51 *Krstic* case, Judgment of the Trial Chamber, 2 August 2001, affirmed by the Appellate Chamber, 19 April 2004.

52 The *Krstic* case was an easy one since it concerned the massacre of Srebrenica where the material element of the crime of genocide was present beyond any reasonable doubt in the extermination of thousands of innocent civilians simply because of their belonging to a specific ethnic group.

53 For a similar socio-cultural approach to genocide, see the decision of 12 December 2000 of the German BundesVerfassungsgerichthof.

54 Articles 8(2)(b)(ix) and 8(2)(e)(iv), concerning war crimes, other than 'grave breaches' under the Geneva Conventions, committed in both international and non-international armed conflicts.

international concern and thus entail international criminal liability in the event of its destruction or wilful damage. Yet these limits may gradually be overcome. As regards the first, it is worth remembering that gross violations in peacetime of the international obligation to respect cultural heritage, such as the destruction of monuments of exceptional universal importance, is now covered by the 2003 UNESCO Declaration on intentional destruction of cultural heritage,[55] applicable in time of war and peace. This declaration is a soft-law instrument, not a binding treaty. However, it provides a text for the evaluation of the legality of acts of wilful destruction of cultural heritage of importance to humanity and it is the first step in the gradual evolution of an *opinio iuris* of the international community concerning the unacceptable character of such acts also in peacetime. As for the second limit, we must remember that there are now several lists, registers and inventories established by competent international organizations – notably, UNESCO – which provide objective parameters for the appreciation of the international significance of a cultural object. The recent decision of the ICTY in the *Strugar*[56] case has found that the inscription of the historical city of Dubrovnik in the World Heritage List was a decisive factor in imposing criminal liability upon those military leaders who ordered or knowingly allowed its bombardment during the Balkan conflict.

## 6. Cultural heritage and cultural diversity

The analysis carried out in the preceding sections shows that the protection of cultural heritage in international law cannot be separated from the social function it performs as a symbolic element of a society's continuity, beyond its biological existence. The recognition of this human dimension has implications for the further expansion of the concept of 'heritage' beyond the material products of creativity to the more complex concept of 'living culture', which include the traditions, social structures and processes that permit the production, evolution and transmission of cultural heritage from one generation to another. This expansion of the concept of heritage to encompass living culture is underway in contemporary international law and has so far produced two important results: the adoption of the 2003 UNESCO Convention for the Safeguarding of Intangible Cultural Heritage[57] and the conclusion in 2005 of the difficult negotiations for the new Convention on the Protection and Promotion of the Diversity of Cultural Expressions.[58] The adoption of the Convention on intangible cultural heritage is of great relevance for the topic of this chapter, because its rationale

---

55 See *supra* note 42.

56 *Strugar* case Judgment of the Trial Chamber, 31 January 2005, available at: <www.un.org/icty>.

57 See *supra* note 13.

58 See *supra* note 14.

lies in the idea that the protection of cultural heritage must not only go beyond built and material cultural objects, but that it must also transcend the traditional notion of cultural heritage as a component of the nation state and an element of national sovereignty. In the new Convention, intangible cultural heritage is defined as 'the practices, representations expressions, knowledge, skills ... that *communities*, *groups* and, in some cases, *individuals* recognize as part of their cultural heritage'.[59] The focus of the convention, therefore, is not on states, but on the communities, groups and individuals who create, maintain and enact the oral and intangible traditions that contribute to forming their identity while at the same time provide 'a mainspring of cultural diversity'.[60] This entails an epistemological reversal of the perspective, from a state-oriented approach which sees the nation as a whole under the mantle of sovereignty, to a bottom-up approach, which places the community or group that creates and maintains the heritage to be safeguarded at its centre.

The negotiations for the new convention on the protection of diversity of cultural expressions signified the logical evolution in recognizing the intangible cultural heritage as a concern of the international community as a whole. Yet while the concept of intangible cultural heritage opens up the traditional sphere of national sovereignty to the legal claim of communities and groups to the protection of their living culture under international law, the 2005 UNESCO Convention on the diversity of artistic content and cultural expressions takes the process even further and recognizes cultural diversity as the common concern of humanity. In this context, the notion of cultural heritage becomes inseparable from human rights in two different ways. First, because the defence and promotion of cultural diversity cannot be divorced from the commitment to the fulfilment of human rights and fundamental freedoms of minorities, groups and indigenous peoples; and second, because cultural diversity may not be invoked as an excuse to infringe upon, or limit the scope of, human rights guaranteed under international law.

The agenda for the international protection of cultural diversity is just beginning to unfold. The problem of reconciling such an agenda with existing international obligations under the WTO and TRIPS is real. The dissenting voices that emerged at the time of the Convention's adoption – notably, the United States and Israel – signal the necessity of harmonizing the new instrument with the existing obligations under the global trade system. At the same time, the adoption of the Convention provides the important recognition that human creativity, while it benefits from the free flow of ideas, nevertheless builds upon the roots of cultural traditions. If humanity neglects to safeguard the diversity of cultural traditions and artistic expressions, there may be nothing in the future to exchange as a product and record of the infinite variety of the human experience.

---

59 Emphasis added. This definition was elaborated by a UNESCO group of independent experts, chaired by the author, who met in Grinzane Cavour, Turin, Italy in March 2001.

60 Preamble of the Convention.

# 2
# The Cross-Cultural Legitimacy of Universal Human Rights: Plural Justification across Normative Divides*

*Tore Lindholm*

## Introduction

In our present-day shrinking world of abundant and irrevocable cultural diversity our cultural divides may be bridged – yet not adulterated – if people everywhere in the world embrace human rights. In this chapter I shall defend the view that, to this end, we need to elaborate a plurality of differing but culturally well-grounded endorsements of universally applicable human rights; or briefly, we should embrace *plural justification* of human rights.

In what I call 'plural justification', justificatory reasoning, when spelled out, proceeds from a plurality of justifying grounds, each of which differing from and being perhaps incompatible with any of the others. My advocacy of plural justification of human rights neither presupposes nor implies acceptance of cultural relativism (the view that all ethical justification is relative to non-justified and arbitrary normative traditions) and it is compatible with, but does not imply, moral realism (broadly, the view that in ethics there is something to be wrong about).

Why is a plurality of justificatory grounds called for? A plurality of justificatory grounds for universal rights, in the sense indicated, is required to facilitate internally well-grounded endorsements of human rights in differing, more or less rivalling, and perhaps incompatible normative traditions (religions, life stances, comprehensive doctrines, philosophies, ideologies etc). Of course, internally well-grounded support for human rights is not forthcoming from the adherents of each

* This chapter builds upon the same author's earlier writings on plural justification of rights; most recently in T. Lindholm, 'Ethical Justification of Universal Rights Across Normative Divides', in G. Bexell and D.-E. Andersson (eds.), *Universal Ethics: Perspectives and Proposals from Scandinavian Scholars* (The Hague, Martinus Nijhoff Publishers, 2002), pp. 63-83.

Francioni and Scheinin (eds), *Cultural Human Rights*, 17–39

and every normative tradition that impinges on the practice of human rights in the present-day world. A given normative tradition may be in irreparable conflict with human rights principles. Or else, the circumstances or inclinations of most of its adherents may be detrimental to the thorny task of reinterpretation and reform of their tradition(s) or doctrine(s). Yet, in all major normative traditions in the present-day world, knowledgeable adherents offer plausible claims to the effect that there are good grounds, within her or his tradition, for principled endorsements of human rights.[1] A set of such justificatory endorsements of human rights amounts to a *plural justification of human rights just to the extent that adherents of each tradition reasonably may hold human rights to be well supported across the normative divides that separate the traditions in question.*

We may ask: How can coherent substantive justification of rights proceed from a plurality of diverse and perhaps mutually incompatible sets of premises? How is plural justification at all pertinent to universal human rights? And why should reasonable people bother with such seemingly perverse options and not rather assess 'head on' competing justificatory arguments in order to elaborate, to the best of their ability, the 'one and only' reasonable grounding of human rights?

Once we accept the public desideratum that universally applicable human rights norms be embraced across abiding cultural divides, on a plurality of internally legitimate but differing grounds, their normative justification is no simple matter.

In this paper I shall address *three hurdles* that come naturally to mind:

- First, one might think that prospects are slight for having adherents of rivalling comprehensive doctrines, religions, life stances, or ideologies in the present-day world *agree* on one normative system of human rights (section 3).
- Second, the fact, if it were a fact, that adherents of rivalling normative traditions do agree on a set of universally applicable public norms should hardly count as normative *justification* of those norms (section 4).
- And third, a set of arguments in support of human rights, each argument internally well-grounded in a given normative tradition, hardly constitutes *reasonable* justification once we admit it may well be based on mutually incompatible premises (section 5).

The logical structure of a plural justification is, I submit, in itself no insurmountable obstacle. It is a fact about deductive reasoning that a specific conclusion may be validly derived from incompatible sets of premises. My favourite simplistic case is this: the true conclusion C 'All whales have lungs' may be derived validly from

1 For the case of major religions in the present-day world, see J. Runzo, N.M. Martin and A. Sharma (eds.), *Human Rights and Responsibilities in the World Religions* (Oxford, Oneworld Publications, 2003).

premise set (I): $P_i1$ 'All whales are mammals' and $P_i2$ 'All mammals have lungs', but also from premise set (II): $P_{ii}1$ 'All whales are fishes' and $P_{ii}2$ 'All fishes have lungs'. – The point is that a true conclusion may be validly derived from, and *in this sense* be equally well supported by, incompatible sets of premises (such that if one set of premises is true then the other set is not true). Moreover, adherents of each of these two incompatible sets of premises (I) and (II) cannot but concede (arguing 'tongue in cheek' in my simplistic case) that adherents of the rivalling set of premises have strong grounds for embracing the conclusion C.

Hence, in reasoning about the normative justification of rights we are not required by the force of logic to rule out that universal human rights may be equally well supported – equally well supported, that is, with respect to the logical force of arguments – by several sets of premises each of which may be incompatible with other sets.

Holding – with regard to the social circumstances of irreversible cultural divisiveness – that an adequate justification of universally applicable human rights must be plural justification, in the sense indicated above, I shall first present arguments for thinking that human rights not only admit of but *call for* such validation across normative divides (section 2). Once the call for plural justification is shown to have initial plausibility, my task is to explain how the idea of plural justification of universally binding human rights may overcome the three main hurdles indicated above (sections 3 through 5).

The term 'human rights' as used in this chapter refers to the complex system of general individual and group rights inaugurated by the 1948 Universal Declaration of Human Rights (UDHR) and subsequently spelled out and codified in binding international human rights law. In this modern concept, human rights are *publicly grounded* in a shared practical commitment to heed the inherent freedom and equal dignity of every human being. This public freedom-and-dignity doctrine in support of human rights puts the burden of proof on the shoulders of human rights adversaries, as it were. But the status and import of this doctrine is not obvious, and part of my task is to spell out its relation to the plurality of differing normative traditions impinging on human rights (section 1).

## 1. A practical commitment to safeguard the inherent freedom and equal dignity of every human being: The public grounds for support of human rights in the present-day world

Drawing on the text and the drafting history of the Universal Declaration (UDHR) I submit that the very concept of human rights includes a minimal outline of their *publicly shared moral grounds*,[2] to wit: the doctrine of the inherent and equal dignity of every human being. This doctrine, solemnly enunciated in the Preamble of the Charter of United Nations, was adopted and espoused by the authors of the UDHR and has been abundantly reaffirmed by subsequently codified international human rights instruments.[3]

I hold the quality of the deliberations of the founding mothers and fathers of the UDHR during 1947 and 1948 to be, most of the time, amazingly high. In particular, the thinking behind Article 1 of the UDHR, first by the Commission on Human Rights and then by the Third Committee of the General Assembly, is impressive for being at once innovative, simple, and cogent.[4]

If we pay heed to the outcome of the protracted discussions conducted in the organs of the United Nations about the moral grounds of human rights norms, the *public justificatory rationale* for human rights can be spelled out as a piece of practical reasoning. Basically, the moral argument supplied by the founding mothers and fathers to underpin the political resolve of peoples organized as state parties under the Charter of United Nations to establish a worldwide regime for the protection of human rights proceeds from *two main premises*. The first is an

---

2 The public moral grounds of universally binding rights, elaborated 1947-48 by United Nations Human Rights bodies, I have earlier referred to as 'a justificatory prototheory of human rights' (T. Lindholm, 'Prospects for Research on the Cultural Legitimacy of Human Rights', in A.A. An-Na'im (ed.), *Human Rights in Cross-Cultural Perspectives* (Philadelphia, University of Pennsylvania Press, 1992), pp. 387-426, at pp. 395-397). Incidentally, knowledge of the Universal Declaration of Human Rights – its content, intellectual background, and political context – is often surprisingly shallow. Opinions, however, are plentiful. A careful study of the text and its background is recommended. Good guidance may be found in M.A. Glendon, 'Knowing the Universal Declaration of Human Rights', *Notre Dame Law Review* (1998), pp. 1153-1176; J. Morsink, 'World War Two and the Universal Declaration', *Human Rights Quarterly* (1993), pp. 357-405; J. Morsink, *The Universal Declaration of Human Rights: Origins, Drafting, and Intent* (Philadelphia, University of Pennsylvania Press, 1999); G, Alfredsson and A. Eide (eds.), *The Universal Declaration of Human Rights: A Common Standard of Achievement* (The Hague, Martinus Nijhoff Publishers, 1999).

3 Most prominent are the two 1966 United Nations Human Rights Covenants. See *Human Rights: A Compilation of International Instruments*, United Nations, New York (several editions; available at: <www2.unog.ch/intinstr/uninstr.exe?language=en>). See also the perspicuous and not much heeded 1986 General Assembly Resolution *Setting International Standards in the Field of Human Rights* (GAR 41/120 4 December 1986) available at: <www.un.org/documents/ga/res/41/a41r120.htm>; quoted in T. Lindholm, 'The Emergence and Development of Human Rights: An Interpretation with a View to Cross-Cultural and Interreligious Dialogue', Paper for the Diyarbakir International Conference on Human Rights, 26–28 September 1997 (Oslo, The Norwegian Institute of Human Rights, Working Paper 1997), pp. 3-14.

4 I am somewhat amazed when people acting as political representatives of governments produce better philosophy than most philosophers acting in their professional capacity. See T. Lindholm, 'Article One', in G. Alfredsson and A. Eide (eds.), *cit. supra* note 2, pp. 41-73, at pp. 67-70 *et passim*.

anthropological *value premise* P1, and the second is a sociological *diagnostic premise* P2 connecting the value premise P1 with a factual interpretation of contemporary societies as being modern or modernizing, internally plural and conflict-disposed, and interdependent:

P1: Every human being is born free and equal in dignity; human beings are, furthermore, presumed to be sufficiently reasonable and conscientious to observe a decent public order defined in terms of human rights (from UDHR Article 1, and in light of Article 29)

P2: If peoples organized as sovereign states, under such global circumstances for human freedom and dignity as prevail now and in the foreseeable future, are not to disregard their moral commitment proclaimed in P1 they must seek to agree on and establish an international regime for the domestic protection of people's freedom and dignity everywhere in the world, by means of legal rights to be called 'human rights' (from UDHR Preamble and other UN sources)[5]

Some comments: concerning the value premise P1 it is just as important to note *what it does not say* as it is important to note *what it says.*

Article 1 of UDHR pronounces a public practical commitment to *the inherent freedom and equal dignity of every human being* to be *in the present-day world* the proximate and more or less freestanding value premise of human rights.[6] Also, Article 1 in conjunction with UDHR Article 29 gives voice to the crucially important presumption that people, whatever their cultural tradition, religion, or ideology, are capable of sufficient moral knowledge and effective motivation to observe a decent global order, defined in terms of observance of human rights. Note that Article 1 does *not* spell out the grounds of the cosmopolitan doctrine of freedom and dignity; in particular it neither entails nor bars the view that the freedom and dignity of all human beings spring from their being 'endowed with reason and

5 To make the structure of the above piece of practical reasoning explicit the two premises and the conclusion would have to be put in the first person plural, giving voice to the reasoning of governments as representatives of their peoples, as in the Charter of the United Nations: 'We the peoples of the United Nations ... hold P1 and P2 and we therefore agree on and resolve to establish ...' Of course, the argument is still elliptical; in particular, the globally prevailing social circumstances of human rights are not spelled out. See below note 9 and text to note 9.

6 The term 'freestanding' is borrowed from J. Rawls, *Political Liberalism* (New York, Columbia University Press, 1993), p. 10 *et passim*. The idea of a public moral rationale of rights that is freestanding, in the sense that it bridges while inviting support from a plurality of more comprehensive but also more controversial underpinnings, is pioneered, to my knowledge, by the originators of the international human rights regime after World War II. For the pertinent notion of human dignity, see below note 18.

conscience' – (the presumptive anthropological features that ground the human duties specified in Article 29).

Article 1's commitment to the inherent freedom and equal dignity of every human being is *not a commitment to an individualism at odds with people's legitimate attachments to community.* It is, rather, a public moral principle of non-exclusive, mutual solidarity encompassing all human beings in the present-day world, bridging our cultural, ethnic, religious and ideological divides, everyone recognizing, as it were, the equal public moral status of everyone else as a fellow human being, as institutionalized in the global regime for domestic protection of human rights.

In the same vein, though human rights are designed to protect the freedom and dignity of individual human beings, *human rights do not celebrate individual autonomy*: Article 1 does not imply support of comprehensive individualist philosophies such as those propounded by Immanuel Kant or John Stuart Mill nor, for that matter, do human rights support more vulgar individualist ideologies.[7]

Lastly, the universalist notion of equal human dignity is very far from perfectionist. It indicates, rather, a minimum threshold level of decency, a protective floor below which a human being should not have to sink. Claiming ethical validity for the system of universally applicable human rights, therefore, emphatically does not imply a claim to a comprehensive system of morality; very many moral questions and concerns are manifestly *not* addressed by modern human rights norms.

From the records of the United Nations we know that more profound but, inevitably, also more controversial grounding principles of human rights were seriously and in some cases persistently advanced, both in the Commission on Human Rights and later in the Third Committee of the General Assembly. Among theological, metaphysical and anthropological grounds in support of human rights seriously discussed in 1947 and 1948 were *God*, *Reason*, *Nature*, and *Human Nature* (just to mention four catch phrases). However, after long discussions (and a number of preliminary votes!) recourse to deep but irreparably controversial grounds of universal human rights was *not* included in the UDHR.[8]

The overriding reasoning behind this *exercise of foundational restraint* by the founding mothers and fathers of modern human rights was that they conceived the UDHR to be morally binding on all reasonable and conscientious human beings *across existing, and publicly legitimate cultural, religious, ethical and ideological divides.*[9]

---

7 For the purposes of plural justification a minimally determinate conception of human rights is of course mandatory. Due to the popular successes of flawed conceptions and perceptions of modern human rights it is also urgent to spell out what human rights are not. See T. Lindholm, *cit. supra* note 3, pp. 15-17.

8 These votes took place first in the Commission on Human Rights and subsequently in the Third Committee of the General Assembly. See T. Lindholm, *cit. supra* note 4, pp. 42-63.

9 T. Lindholm, *cit. supra* note 4. See also the assessment by Jacques Maritain (quoted in text to note 12 below) of the apparent paradox of partaking in a self-consciously pluralist support

This foundational restraint does not of course imply a denial of the legitimacy, or a rejection of the practical urgency, of devising authentic support of the public principles of inherent freedom and equal dignity in greater depths, on a variety of *different and even rivalling* religious, metaphysical, or other more comprehensive normative grounds. But, the authors of the UDHR left unresolved the analysis of plural human rights justification across normative divides. What was rejected by the founding mothers and fathers of modern human rights was to include such divisive foundations of human rights in a text designed so as to be normatively binding on all.

In a word: a practical commitment to heed the inherent freedom and equal dignity of every human being, supplemented by the general presumption for the requisite moral capacity and motivation, is proclaimed as the official public gateway to principled normative support of human rights across the divides of culture, religion or ideology; it is an open gate to be entered by adherents of any doctrine or conviction who, in each case, are invited to draw on the precepts and resources of their own normative tradition *as they see fit* (and, as I would want to add, preferably after internal discussion and dialogue across normative divides; cf. sections 4 and 5).

How about the diagnostic premise P2? This premise of the public argument for human rights hints at the epochal modern transformations, worldwide, of the *circumstances* for respecting the freedom and equal dignity of all humans – including conditions for the general public recognition of these values. The Preamble of the UDHR points to socially produced threats and challenges to, as well as to opportunities and promises for, accommodating freedom and dignity, circumstances that prevail in the present-day world and the presence of which have become practically irreversible. These are the *societal circumstances of universally binding human rights* in the sense that they tend to make human rights institutionally feasible and morally pertinent 'everywhere in the world'.[10]

So much for the idea of the public moral grounds of human rights embodied in the UDHR. Public normative justification of human rights proceeds by way of a practical commitment to heed the inherent freedom and equal dignity of all human beings, in tandem with a diagnosis of prevailing, or evolving, societal circumstances worldwide, and it concludes that human rights are morally mandatory legal and

---

for universal human rights. A similar foundational constraint, though not fully heeded, apparently bedevilled the task for the authors of the now defunct draft *Treaty establishing a Constitution for Europe* (see Preamble, first two points).

10 I elaborate on the modern circumstances of human rights in sections 3 and 4 of Lindholm, *cit. supra* note 3, and more extensively in T. Lindholm, 'Kultur, verdier og menneskerettigheter' ['Culture, values, and human rights'], in T. Hylland Eriksen (ed.), *Flerkulturell forståelse* (Oslo, Tano Aschehoug, 1997), pp. 67-89, at pp. 69-80.

political measures for safeguarding, up to a minimum threshold level, that human beings may live in freedom and dignity 'everywhere in the world'.[11]

## 2. Why human rights call for plural justification

I shall submit first a prudential and then a moral argument for thinking that once we are committed to the universal *application and observance* of human rights, including the human rights precepts of freedom of religion or belief and of non-discrimination, we cannot but call for universal *acceptance* of human rights. Hence we are bound to crave, so I now want to argue, for plural justification of human rights.

Once we recognize the recalcitrant fact of religious, philosophical and ideological plurality and rivalry within and between present-day societies it is obvious, I submit, that universal and worldwide application and observance of human rights would significantly benefit from human rights being also endorsed and embraced on solid internal grounds by adherents of rivalling normative traditions whether religious, philosophical or ideological. Unforced and stable endorsement of human rights could surely serve such peaceful social coexistence as is facilitated by the general application and observance of human rights. So, given the goal of universal application and observance of human rights, the goal of ecumenical endorsement of human rights on internal grounds has strong *prudential* support.

Normative plurality and rivalry within and between present-day societies has come to stay. The fact of plurality and rivalry has public legitimacy, within the generous bounds circumscribed by modern human rights. Hence, the fundamental human rights to freedom of thought and conscience, religion and belief and to non-discrimination on any grounds including religion, belief or opinion, more than intimate that bolstering unforced endorsement of human rights across existing normative divides ought to be a universally shared public goal. Granted the public commitment to the inherent freedom and equal dignity of every human being, as enounced by Article 1 of the Universal Declaration, that goal also becomes a morally mandatory *public desideratum*: mutual recognition of the equal and inviolable dignity and the inherent freedom of every human being would be pragmatically incoherent, among adherents of differing and more or less rivalling religions or beliefs, if the parties were to shrink from committing themselves to the pursuit of the goal of unforced 'trans-doctrinal', cross-cultural and inter-religious justification of human rights – provided, of course, that this goal or ideal is not itself logically or pragmatically defective on other counts.

---

[11] The immense importance of World War II for the authors of the Universal Declaration – and for the political possibility of reaching internationally binding agreements on a global human rights regime – is convincingly documented and analyzed in J. Morsink (1993), *cit. supra* note 2 and, in much greater detail, J. Morsink (1999), *cit. supra* note 2, pp. 36-91.

## 3. Prospects for consensus on human rights across normative divides in the present-day world

Can the goal of unforced endorsement of human rights across existing normative divides be realized or even significantly approximated? Is the project of consensus on rights across cultural divides feasible? On these issues two interesting voices in the fierce debates about human rights nearly 60 years ago may provide us with some initial guidance.

Jacques Maritain, in his introduction to a 1947 UNESCO report inquiring into the foundations of an international declaration of human rights, put the predicament of plurality versus universality in the following terms:

> This book then is devoted to the rational interpretation and justification of those rights of the individual which society must respect and which [it] is desirable for our age to strive to enumerate more fully. Many schools of thought are represented, each of which brings to the whole its particular view and justification of individual rights, leaning in various degrees towards the classical, or the revolutionary, interpretation: it is not the first time that expert witnesses have quarreled among themselves. The paradox is that such rational justifications are at once indispensable, and yet powerless to bring about agreement between minds. They are indispensable because each one of us believes instinctively in the truth, and will only assent to what he himself has recognized as true and based on reason. They are powerless to bring about a harmony of minds because they are fundamentally different, even antagonistic ... The very diversity of the interpretations and justifications put forward in the essays in this book is in itself an important object lesson for the reader ... Is there anything surprising in systems antagonistic in theory converging in their practical conclusions?[12]

Also in 1947, the American Anthropological Association issued its well-known words of warning against the monopolization of human rights by any single normative culture, authored by Melville Herskovits:

> Standards and values are relative to the culture from which they derive so that any attempt to formulate postulates that grow out of the belief or moral codes of one culture must to that extent detract from the applicability of any Declaration of Human Rights to mankind as a whole. ... The rights of

[12] UNESCO, with an Introduction by J. Maritain, *Human Rights: Comments and Interpretations* (London and New York, Alan Wingate, 1949), pp. 9 and 12. When submitted to the Commission on Human Rights late in summer 1947 this UNESCO report bore the title *The Bases of an International Bill of Human Rights: Report submitted by the UNESCO Committee on the Philosophical Principles of Human Rights to the Human Rights Commission of the United Nations*. Note the use of the plural in the title of the 1947 UNESCO report.

> Man in the Twentieth Century cannot be circumscribed by the standards of any single culture or be dictated by the aspirations of any single people. Such a document will lead to frustration, not realization of the personalities of vast numbers of human beings.[13]

Herskovits seems to accept a version of the philosophical doctrine called cultural relativism, i.e. the view that normative validity of public norms and precepts is relative to existing and non-justified cultural frameworks. While cultural relativism is an absurd position – it amounts, in effect, to unwitting cultural absolutism[14] – Herskovits makes a pertinent and valid point: universal standards of rights cannot be *dictated* by the aspirations of any single people or through exclusive implementation of their particular normative tradition(s); at least (we would want to add) not without the unforced consent of all parties, each party reasoning in light of their differing normative traditions. And such unforced consent to and endorsement of human rights, when achieved, will have to be conditioned by the parties' social circumstances and informed by their political purposes, it will take much discussion, and it will hardly ever terminate in all parties accepting what was, before discussion, the aspirations and standards of any one party. The construction of the UDHR was, I have argued, an early demonstration of this general point.[15]

On the possibility of building unforced consent to human rights across entrenched normative divides, Maritain's interpretation of his own experience in the UNESCO group is most instructive: cross-cultural, inter-religious, political and plain philosophical discussion about moral foundations does not, at least not always and not even normally, eliminate all pre-existing differences among parties with respect to their fundamental normative principles and authorities. Far from it: the more we discuss, even when circumstances are favourable for untrammelled conversation about the basic grounds of human rights, the more we may discover that we disagree, and why we disagree, about fundamental principles and normative authorities.

However, such a recalcitrance of peoples' commitments to their basic normative traditions is, I submit, neither irrational nor generally unreasonable. To the contrary, it is hardly ever reasonable, nor feasible, to suspend one's entire system of cognitive and normative beliefs, values, attitudes, sensibilities and loyalties. Reasonable change of beliefs and values must, most of the time, be piecemeal, and particularly if it is to be facilitated by the force of the better argument. It is not reasonable to expect agreement, all the way down, among reasonable people about the deepest grounds of their positions on human rights.

---

13 *American Anthropologist* 49, No. 4 (1947), pp. 539-43.

14 R. Howard, 'Cultural Absolutism and the Nostalgia for Community', *Human Rights Quarterly* (1993), pp. 315-338.

15 T. Lindholm, *cit. supra* note 4.

But genuine and unforced consensus about the normative validity of human rights, as codified in the Universal Declaration, may nevertheless be a realistic goal of dialogues – and practical cooperation – across tradition-based normative divides, and that far beyond the small circles of human rights experts and human rights activists. Such unforced consensus about the normative validity of human rights as has been realized, 60 years after the Universal Declaration was proclaimed, include competent and authentic adherents of numerous differing, and in other respects more or less rivalling normative traditions, including most major contemporary world religions, non-religious worldviews, and political ideologies. In my own studies of the interrelationship between human rights norms and politically significant normative traditions in the present-day world I have found convincing cases of internally legitimate support of human rights on the most diverse grounds ranging, say, from His Holiness the Dalai Lama via Norwegian representatives of atheistic humanism to the Sudanese law professor and reform thinker Abdullahi An-Na'im to His Holiness Pope John XXIII.[16]

My point here is not to provide conclusive factual evidence for the broad extent or the steady increase of cross-cultural support for human rights, nor to deny the significant extent and force of purportedly culture-based critique and rejection of the universalist normative claims of human rights. Moreover, tradition-based support of human rights principles is often internally contestable. My point is, rather, to indicate the potential and the dynamics of ongoing processes of intra-cultural and cross-cultural of human right validation. Building well-grounded and stable support of universal human rights in a given normative tradition necessarily takes *protracted discussion* and perhaps *a lot of heated debate*, it may need *much time* and require reasonably *favourable circumstances* for the reinterpretation and reconstruction of a community's authoritative sources and shared commitments. Pioneering individuals and groups have at times been propelled by provoking experiences: for instance, slavery, racial discrimination, genocide or destructive war, in order for them to be able to undertake a recasting of their normative tradition with respect to its support of human rights.

---

16 Address by the 14th Dalai Lama to New York Lawyers Alliance for World Security and the Council on Foreign Relations 27 April 1994, as quoted in J. Powers, 'Human Rights and Cultural Values: The Political Philosophies of the Dalai Lama and the People's Republic of China', paper presented to Seventh East-West Philosopher's Congress, University of Hawaii, January 1995; L. Gunnar Lingås, *Human Rights: In Search for a Universal Human Identity* (Oslo, Human-Etisk Forbund, 1996); A,A. An-Na'im, *Toward an Islamic Reformation: Civil Liberties, Human Rights, and International Law* (Syracuse, Syracuse University Press, 1990); and Pope John XXIII's Encyclical Letter *Pacem in terris*, published in J. Gremillion (ed.), *The Gospel of Peace and Justice: Catholic Social Teaching since Pope John* (Maryknoll, Orbis Books, 1976), pp. 201-241. For Islam I would also recommend studying K. Abou el Fadl, 'The Human Rights Commitment in Modern Islam', in J. Runzo, Nancy M. Martin and Arvind Sharma (eds.), *cit. supra* note 1, pp. 301-364.

Myself a Lutheran, I know of no more instructive case of such doctrinal reconstruction than the reversal in the Roman Catholic Church, between 1791 and 1963, of its position with respect to the normative grounds of human rights.[17]

For obvious reasons, the doctrinal position of the Roman Catholic Church on human rights is the weightiest among Christian churches: there are in excess of 1 billion Catholics in the world! The Catholic position has, over the last 200 years, shifted from outright rejection and condemnation of non-exclusive human rights to unqualified and principled embrace. Pope Pius VI (1775-1799), condemned the doctrine of human rights only two years after they had been proclaimed by the French revolutionaries in 1789. Pius taught that the human rights to freedom of religion and freedom of the press are just as incompatible with Church principles as the declaration of the equal dignity of human beings (!). He was followed by other Popes who in a number of encyclicals repeated and elaborated the rejection by the Church of rights founded on equal human dignity and freedom. Pope Leo XIII in *Rerum novarum* 1889 made a significant move forwards by recognizing the subsidiarity-graded entitlement of wage labourers to certain economic and social benefits – but not as based on their human rights. Only with Pope John XXIII did the Church come up with theologically well-grounded support for the full range of modern human rights norms, *now* based squarely on the doctrine of the sacred, and radically non-exclusivist, dignity of the human person.[18] The encyclical *Pacem*

---

17 The two paragraphs that follow are lifted with minor revisions from T. Lindholm, 'Human Rights in Christianity and in Islam?', in S. Silvennoinen and M. Suksi (eds.), *Human Rights and Religion: The Case of the Sudan* (Turku/Åbo, Institute for Human Rights, Åbo Akademi University, 1997). pp. 67-99.

18 We may note that the historical roots of the now crucially important public doctrine of human dignity are not specifically Christian. The doctrine was imported by Ficino and Pico della Merandola into early modern Western anthropological discourse from what was held to be a decidedly non-Christian 'Hermes Trismegistos' tradition hailing from Egyptian and pre-Christian Greek roots. The oldest preserved source of the pertinent doctrine of human dignity is a philosophical work by M. Tullius Cicero, *de Officiis* (written 43 B.C.). For a succinct and competent overview of the historical trajectory of the doctrine, see H. Cancik, '"Dignity of Man" and "Persona" in Stoic Anthropology: Some Remarks on Cicero, *De officis* I 105-107', in D. Kretzmer and E. Klein (eds.), *The Concept of Human Dignity in Human Rights Discourse* (The Hague/London/New York, Kluwer Law International, 2002), pp. 19-39. Of course, here as in other matters of substance historical pedigree is immaterial to questions of validity. Incidentally, the irrelevance of origins is highlighted also by the fact that the chief originator, at the 1945 San Francisco Conference, of the official concern in the United Nations Charter with human dignity was no other than Field Marshall Jan Smuts of South Africa. T. Lindholm, *cit. supra* note 4, p. 44; P.J. Anker, *The Ecology of Nations: British Imperial Science of Nature, 1985-1945* (Dissertations and Thesis No. 2/99) (Cambridge, Mass., Harvard University, 1999), pp. 203-214.

*in terris* April 1963,[19] and the 1965 Vaticanum II declaration *Dignitatis humanae personae* as well as the pastoral constitution *Gaudium et spes* mark invaluable steps in the piecemeal incarnation of universalist human rights principles in Christian doctrine.

A Catholic theological anthropology of religious freedom and equal dignity had, we may add, been available much earlier, most prominently perhaps in St. Thomas Aquinas' doctrine that non-believers may possibly have an inculpably erroneous conscience, which – when properly identified – is morally binding and must be respected, as such, by the Church. Hence non-believers and heretics may have a moral duty to follow their conscience, even when in grave religious error.[20] But neither St. Thomas nor other Church authorities were able to draw out the pertinent moral and canonical implications of this doctrine so as to help legitimate not only religious toleration but Church protection of equal dignity and freedom.[21]

Having for some years studied the potential grounding of human rights in various normative traditions I have also examined obstacles to internal support of human rights in major religious or secular humanist traditions in the present-day world. In no major religious or belief tradition have I come across impediments that could not conceivably be overcome by reasonable internal reinterpretation or reconstruction, as exemplified by the turnabout of the Roman Catholic Church between 1791 and 1963. This optimistic assessment is reinforced also by recent experience at the 'meso' level of inter-denominational public consensus building in my own country of Norway: a number of extended dialogue projects involving representatives from most religious and life stance communities in this country have addressed hard questions about a common public ethics and, most recently, the issue of a shared understanding of and commitment to human rights by all parties to the dialogue.[22]

Of course, not every normative tradition that has current political impact is amenable to reinterpretation such that adherents become disposed to endorse human rights on internally legitimate grounds. A culture or doctrine that is irreparably racist, or one that is group supremacist in other ways, cannot accommodate human

---

19 Pope John XXIII, knowing he would very soon die, insisted that *Pacem in terris* be promulgated partly in light of the urgent necessity, in his view, of promoting suitable normative foundations for global peaceful coexistence in the aftermath of the very nearly apocalyptic Cuban missile crisis October 1962.

20 St. Thomas Aquinas, *Summa Theologica. Complete English Edition in Five Volumes* (Westminster, Maryland, Christian Classics, 1981), Vol. 2, pp. 674-675 (Pt. I-II, Q. 19 Art 5).

21 See D. Little in D. Little, J. Kelsay and Abdulaziz A. Sachedina, *Human Rights and the Conflict of Cultures: Western and Islamic Perspectives on Religious Liberty* (Columbia S.C., University of South Carolina Press, 1988), pp. 13-17. A more thorough discussion would include several other Catholic voices, most prominently Fray Bartolomé de las Casas (1484-1566).

22 I. Eidsvaag and L. Larsen (eds.), *Religion, livssyn og menneskerettigheter i Norge [Religion, Life Stance and Human Rights in Norway]* (Oslo, Universitetsforlaget, 1997).

rights. Nor is there much hope for a culture or doctrine that obliges adhering insiders to repudiate that outsiders may have the moral capacity and motivation required to observe human rights for the right reasons, i.e. out of respect for the equal and inviolable dignity and freedom of every human being.

Nevertheless we may conclude that a wide-ranging consensus on human rights across tradition-based normative divides in the present-day world appears to be feasible and that the prospects for further advances in this direction are reasonably promising.[23]

## 4. Consensus on rights is not justification of rights: The objection of David Little

David Little has recently authored an instructive and perspicuous review article in which he deals with altogether six major books on human rights published after 1990.[24] This review article (according to Little's introductory note) 'summarizes the present status of the "human rights revolution" that was signaled by the adoption in 1948 of the *Universal Declaration of Human Rights*. It goes on to elaborate and evaluate some of the attempts contained in these books to deal with theoretical and practical controversies surrounding the subject of human rights, particularly the discussion of what to make of "cultural relativism" as far as human rights are concerned.' (151)

Having learned much from Little's review article and sharing most of his assessments, I shall only discuss one of his tenets, with which I am bound to disagree, namely his rejection of the view (as he puts it) that appeal to cross-cultural and inter-religious 'consensus has any independent force as a reason for approving of human rights norms' (160) and his closely related belief that we need 'a tradition-independent moral standard' (164) in order to justify the universal moral validity of human rights norms. I owe Little a response, and a clarification, since a chapter of mine, printed in one of the volumes under review, receives a fair share of his strictures.[25]

---

23 See A.A. An-Na'im (ed.), *Human Rights in Cross-Cultural Perspectives: A Quest for Consensus* (Philadephia, University of Pennsylvania Press, 1992); R. Traer, *Faith in Human Rights, Support in Religious Traditions for a Global Struggle* (Washington DC, Georgetown University Press, 1991); J. Witte Jr and J.D. van der Vyver (eds.), *Religious Human Rights in Global Perspective: Religious Perspectives* (The Hague, Martinus Nijhoff Publishers, 1996), in J. Runzo et al., *cit. supra* note 1.

24 D. Little, 'Rethinking Human Rights: Religion, Relativism, and Other Matters', *Journal of Religious Ethics* (1999), pp. 151-177. In section 4 page references in parentheses refer to D. Little (1999).

25 D. Little, *ibid.*, discusses T. Lindholm, *cit. supra* note 2. As for clarification: Probably due to my infelicitous use of the English language Little reports (158) me to assert that all familiar Western justificatory traditions, including 'a doctrine of natural law or a liberal theory of

Little welcomes *practical efforts* to achieve

> as much agreement as possible concerning the implementation of human rights and other desirable laws and patters of behavior. If different cultures or religions in fact concur with and agree to enforce various rights and freedoms (such as standard prohibitions against discrimination, torture, enslavement, and extrajudicial killing), that is of course of the greatest practical importance for those committed to human rights. The fact of that agreement obviously matters more in 'real-life terms' than the religious or cultural reasons as to why the agreement was reached. On this level, and 'overlapping consensus' makes urgently good sense, and must devoutly be encouraged. (159)

Little objects, however, to the idea of *theoretical justification* of human rights in terms of an overlapping consensus:

> However, it is quite another thing to propose the idea of overlapping consensus as a theoretical justification for human rights. That suggestion continues to face certain difficulties, even in the hands of its most eloquent advocates. At first blush, the fact that several different religions or philosophical positions converge in supporting a given behavioral prescription (e.g. a prohibition on extrajudicial killing such as exists in the human rights instruments) does not prove anything about the rightness or wrongness of that prescription. It simply proves that at a given time x number of positions do in fact approve of a given prescription. In order to move from 'the *is* to the *ought*,' an additional argument would have to be supplied showing in what way *shared beliefs are justified beliefs.*
>
> Positivists and conventionalists typically argue that the fact that moral convictions are shared somehow justifies those convictions. However, among other deficiencies, such claims serious distort the actual character of moral experience (159).

Little goes on to clinch this last objection by reference to actions that are unquestionably and non-controversially morally wrong, such as the massacre of innocent civilians in Srebrenica in 1995. Such actions, he says,

> *are not wrong because there is common agreement about them, but there is common agreement about them (to the degree there is) because they are wrong.*

---

natural rights ... are safely known to be false'. What I tried to say (but obviously failed to say sufficiently clearly) was that though these traditions are *not* safely known to be false (they surely are not!) their proponents tend to ignore 'the novel global problem situation which for strategic as well as moral reasons requires a pluralist, and overlapping, global consensus on universal human rights' (T. Lindholm, *cit. supra* note 2, p. 399).

> Even a more sophisticated and nuanced defense of the overlapping consensus idea, does not, at least as developed so far, succeed in showing that the appeal to consensus has any independent force as a reason for approving human rights norms. (160)

I shall respond to Little in two steps. My first step is to criticize a picture of moral reasonableness that emerges, I believe, from Little's review article. My second step is to indicate how shared beliefs, properly qualified, may constitute justified belief.

*First step*: One reason Little rejects the very idea of appealing to consensus as a reason for approving human rights norms is that he thinks it commits us to a 'procedure' according to which 'one must first consult an existing consensus, including an international consensus – however "overlapping" it may be – in order to determine whether violations of the prohibitions against massacre are morally wrong or not! That procedure places the cart before the horse …' (159-160).

Of course, it would be absurd to try to 'determine' the moral validity of the prohibitions against massacre of innocent civilians by consulting any existing consensus. But the reason such a 'procedure places the cart before the horse' is, I submit, that such a prohibition constitutes a morally fixed point, an uncontroversial 'theorem', as it were, in any justified morality. The very idea of consensual justification of moral norms is not shown to 'distort the actual character of moral experience' by Little's *reductio* argument. What is undermined, rather, the very idea of justifying *all* moral norms solely by departing from some *a priori* established principle – from the Archimedean point of moral theory, as it were.

Let me explain: reasonable people may conceive of the epistemic grounds of moral validity in terms of, for example, maximal overall utility, or God's will, or assent issuing from a stipulated contractual situation. But they would not leave their moral position on the prohibition against massacre of innocent civilians to be decided solely by whatever might follow from what has, hitherto, been their cherished moral theory. For should their theory permit such a massacre, then reasonable people would *not* stick to it unrevised, but seek to improve it (say, its construal of utility maximization, or its interpretation of God's will, or the constraints it puts on the contractual situation, etc.) so as to avoid a morally appalling implication. *What is morally appalling is appalling not just because it is censured by our normative theory; but our moral theory must of course censure what is morally appalling.*

A main reason for elaborating moral theories (there are others) is that we need a justified moral theory to guide our moral policies, actions and judgments in practical situations and predicaments *precisely when what is right and wrong is no longer unquestionable to us and is no longer non-controversial between us.* And so we develop, revise and improve on our moral theories (if we do) by trial and error, much as in other intellectual endeavours: by maximizing coherence and simplicity, by aiming (as suggested by Rawls) at reflective equilibrium both between our construal of moral principles and our more or less unproblematic moral judgments and convictions, and between our moral beliefs and commitments and our overall conceptions of what there is and, perhaps, of God, or of Being. Now, such pursuit of reflective equilibrium is, of course, to engage in justification.

Granted such a view of moral reasonableness, the idea of a consensual justification of moral norms *need* fare no worse than a utilitarian, or a theist, or a contractual justification of moral norms. To hold that one must *first* calculate utilities, or *first* consult one's construal of God's will, or *first* check one's contractual principles, *before* condemning massacres against innocent civilians as morally wrong is, in each case, to place the cart (some moral theory) before the horse (our relatively incontrovertible moral judgments and convictions, always held in light of some more or less elaborate theory or tradition). Moral theories, be they theist, contractualist, utilitarian or consensualist, can and must be tested against fixed points of moral experience, and continually be revised, elaborated and improved so as to better fit relatively settled moral judgments and convictions.

I put the first part of my response to Little this way in order to emphasize the fallible and holistic character of moral reasoning: advance in moral theory proceeds by discussion, criticism, and listening to criticism, by learning from our mistakes in normative and factual judgments, by our discovery of alternatives, and by our invention of new conceptions, and so on. But nowhere do we come across moral principles that are beyond criticism and that need not be tested against more or less settled moral convictions and judgments, and by way of our critical search for counter-examples and weak spots, etc.

The *second step* in my response to Little addresses his strictures against the view that 'the appeal to consensus has any independent force as a reason for approving of human rights norms', respectively his demand that 'an additional argument would have to be supplied showing in what way *shared beliefs are justified beliefs*.' (159)

I agree, of course, that any existing consensus about human rights norms does not *as such* constitute ethical justification of human rights norms; the justificatory authority of any existing moral consensus depends crucially on *how it is qualified.*

However, a cross-culturally assimilated, widely shared public endorsement of human rights norms codified in international law in our present-day world may indicate that human rights are morally sound, provided we take for granted, as we now may, that the establishment and evolving construction and elaboration, during the last 60 years or so, of internationally codified human rights norms have been accompanied, at every major turn, by energetic, inventive and often fierce objections and criticisms, and that the present system of human rights norms is the outcome of a continuous process of critical checks, modifications, compromises and quality control. Though heed of moral truth has not been the only motive of participants in this process, its institutional structure and dynamics make it conducive to the construction of morally well-grounded norms. Examining the various procedural legitimization mechanisms for human rights norms (domestic constitutional, democratic and jurisprudential mechanisms, the workings of the global and regional human rights regimes, scholarly assessments, religious contributions and transnationally operating human rights activist networks) would require more space than I can offer in this paper. But the main defence of internationally codified and recognized human rights is probably this: in spite of the impressive worldwide success of the global human rights movements in terms of public recognition and renown, until now no intellectually successful refutation of the claim to public moral legitimacy for human rights have materialized.

But I would like to make a terminological concession to Little here: the Rawlsian term 'overlapping consensus' may be a misnomer, since the idea, of course, is to refer to cross-cultural, inter-religious, and 'inter-belief' *justifications* of human rights norms. Misled perhaps by overlapping consensus terminology, Little asks adherents of what he takes to be an ethical-justification-by-sheer-convergence view to provide and to 'defend an *additional premise*, namely (again) that *shared beliefs are justified beliefs*.' (160) 'Without … support … from the proponents of the overlapping consensus view [of] this added premise about the special validity of shared beliefs … an overlapping consensus may … represent nothing more than an accidental, selective, and temporary convergence, which even in practical terms many not create a reliable basis for sustained cooperation. … Lindholm does not provide such a defense …' (160)

I believe that here Little has got the relevant options with respect to ethical justification of human rights wrong: 'overlapping consensualists' do not have to choose between sheer factual convergence or a premise (never forthcoming) to the effect that any convergence justifies. The still fledgling global moral consensus on human rights surely has justificatory credentials other than sheer consensus to speak for itself!

Of course, with this last assessment Little has no quarrel. What he misses, and asks for, is a master argument for human rights that furnishes, as he repeatedly puts it, 'a tradition-independent moral standard' by recourse to which it would 'be theoretically possible to censure Hitler, Karadzic and Mladic for violating necessary moral conditions, whether or not they first "implicitly accepted" the terms of moral discourse by willingly participating in the practice.' Little's last remark is directed against Nino who '… in keeping with prevailing relativist fashions … thinks he can and must avoid … a tradition-independent moral standard …' (164) Little goes on to say:

> For the reasons I have tried to sketch out, I, in contrast, believe that without assuming such a standard, a fundamental reason for the continuing appeal and power of the 'human rights revolution' will be surrendered – namely the need to call certain gross moral offenders to account according to a common moral standard, and to do so no matter who in the world they are, what in the world they do or do not agree to, or where in the word they commit their crimes. (164)

We must, I submit, do without a tradition-independent moral standard in support of human rights; there can for general philosophical reasons[26] be no such thing and Little's own elaboration (163-164) of the hedonic principle is, while constituting additional reasonable support of human rights, a far cry from a tradition-independent moral standard. But though ethical justification cannot be independent of normative traditions all ethical justification is not relative to *non-justified and arbitrary normative traditions*. It makes all the difference that our acceptance of moral and political values, principles and norms is *critical acceptance*, acceptance tested and corroborated by the cannons of critical argument and deliberation. And we surely have the arguments it takes to 'censure Hitler, Karadzic and Mladic for violating necessary moral conditions'. First of all: as indicated above no good grounds for grumbles have, to my knowledge, come up against the moral validity of basic human rights in our present-day world, everything taken into account (including feasible normative alternatives). So reason – or good reasons – do not stop us from claiming, and from proclaiming with the Universal Declaration of Human Rights, that a well-tested universally applicable moral standard is already at hand. This standard, moreover, does not depend exclusively on any one moral tradition for its claim to validity. To the contrary: the principle of non-exclusive or cosmopolitan moral solidarity encompassing all human beings in the present-day world, articulated in terms of the inherent freedom and equal dignity of all (as expounded in section 1 above), is supported, today, by many voices speaking reasonably on behalf of differing, mutually rivalling normative traditions. Why is such a globally entrenched public morality not good enough, in Little's eyes?

Is his objection due to the insistence by 'the proponents of the overlapping consensus view'[27] that human rights *ought to be founded on a plurality of differing and perhaps incompatible normative traditions*? Is it due to the acceptance, by 'overlapping consensualists' like myself, of the view that a plurality of rivalling and perhaps incompatible normative traditions are not just challenges to human rights but are also legitimate, and even necessary platforms for a fully adequate demonstration of the cross-cultural legitimacy of universal human rights in the present-day world? I now turn to this last obstacle to the idea of plural justification of rights.

---

26 Beyond the remarks on recalcitrant moral disagreement (text between notes 14 and 15) and on moral reasonableness (first step in my response to Little) I might refer to what Heidegger and his pupils call 'die Endlichkeit im Menschen'; cp. my attempt at making Anglo-Saxon sense of the hermeneutical theory of tradition in T. Lindholm, 'Coming to Terms with Tradition', in H. Høibraaten and I. Gullvåg (eds.), *Essays in Pragmatic Philosophy* (Oslo, Norwegian University Press, 1985), pp. 103-117. Briefly, Little indicates as I read his argument a justificationist approach, whereas I hold to a fallibilist approach to the challenge of intellectual justification – or, as Sir Karl Popper would have put it, to 'corroboration'. Fallibilists have learned to live with the fact that the language of epistemology remains justificationist.

27 Please read: 'plural justification'.

## 5. Why plural justification is mandated by reason: Reasonable disagreement about the grounds of human rights *versus* monopolization of human rights justification

I shall finally defend head on the intellectual legitimacy and practical necessity of justifying human rights on plural grounds and, conversely, I shall criticize particularist public monopolizations of modern human rights by any philosophical, cultural, ideological or religious community, given the circumstances of an irrevocable cultural diversity.

A person's reasons for endorsing the moral validity of human rights norms may be multiple: speaking for myself I believe all human beings (including non-believers) are created by God in His image, and I think this makes it mandatory to accept the public value premise of human rights (as presented in section 1 above. I know, however, that Christian churches during most of their history have manifestly rejected this non-exclusive doctrine on the equal moral status of human beings, which now facilitates Christian support for human rights.) I also adhere to a philosophy of dialogue which implies support of public principles of the equal dignity and inviolable freedom of all human beings. And, third, I think it takes strong moral grounds to repudiate widely accepted, democratically sanctioned, legally binding public precepts. These three complementary grounds for endorsing human rights do not exhaust my reasons for heed of human rights norms. I have high regard for, though I do not fully understand, a number of contemporary moral philosophical doctrines that support human rights principles, such as the discourse ethics of Jürgen Habermas, the Kantian doctrine of Otfried Höffe, and Alan Gewirth's 'transcendental proof' of the moral validity of human rights norms – though the latter clearly does not amount to a proof.[28]

I take it that other people may have a somewhat similar experience and approach with respect the question of the normative validity for human rights norms. But the hard question is how we reasonably should deal with religious, ideological and philosophical doctrines held by other persons and groups to be grounds for justifications of human rights norms, once we hold we have good reasons to reject the claim to truth or normative validity for these other foundational doctrines?

Let me first address rivalling philosophical justifications of human rights norms. It stands to reason, of course, that proponents of philosophical human rights-supportive doctrines may and should propound and defend their position as being true, or as having the better argument, not least by way of fierce criticism

---

[28] J. Habermas, *Faktizität und Geltung: Beiträge zur Diskurstheorie des Rects und Des demokratischen Rechtsstaats* (Frankfurt, Suhrkamp, 1992); J. Habermas, *Die Einbeziehung des Anderen: Studien zur politischen Theorie* (Frankfurt, Suhrkamp, 1996); O. Höffe, 'Moral Reasons for an Intercultural Criminal Law: A Philosophical Attempt', *Ratio Juris* (1998), pp. 206-227; A. Gewirth, *Human Rights: Essays on Justification and Application* (Chicago, University of Chicago Press, 1984).

of rivalling philosophical tenets. But it does not follow, and *neither is it warranted by the state of reasonable discussion*, that philosophers should demand public authorization of their own philosophical doctrine in support of human rights as the *only* reasonable foundation of human rights, say to the point at which adherence to rivalling philosophical doctrines in support of rights is publicly disqualified. Of course, observance of human rights requires of philosophers that they tolerate foundational doctrines they reject. But discursive reasonableness requires more: it is not just, and not mainly, a question of inter philosophical toleration.[29]

Reasonable philosophical discussion, even under favourable circumstances, about the basic normative grounds of human rights is liable, again and again, to terminate not in substantive agreement but in *reasonable disagreement about the foundations of human rights*. Confronted with and made fully aware of all pertinent arguments offered by other parties to the discussion, we may of course reach well-grounded substantive partial or total agreement. But we are more likely to discover that some of our basic foundational disagreements have come to stay. Once we realize that through reasonable discussion, even under favourable circumstances, our disagreement may change and perhaps improve but not vanish or even diminish, we must conclude that our disagreement is ethically and theoretically legitimate, *as far as we can know by way of reasonable discussion*. Once the reasonability of such foundational disagreement is granted, our human rights philosophy, to be adequate, should elucidate why philosophical disagreement about the foundations of human rights has come to stay.[30]

In light of reasonable and recalcitrant philosophical disagreement about the philosophical foundations of human rights philosophers should not announce their favoured philosophical doctrine of human rights to be *the* universal foundation of human rights. Philosophers should of course be persistent both in propounding their own theories and in criticizing that of others, but the provisos called for by the fact of reasonable disagreement about basic doctrinal tenets should be observed. Philosophers who neglect this precept risk perhaps no more than public ridicule.

---

29 I take toleration to imply *unqualified disapproval of/disagreement with* what is tolerated; *reasonable disagreement*, as addressed in the text below, should be publicly qualified by provisos to the effect that such disagreement persists in spite of the reasonability of the disagreeing parties, is due to causes or circumstances beyond their control, and is explicable in terms that are neutral between their rivalling points of view. A lucid philosophical analysis of how to explain recalcitrant but reasonable public disagreement is H. Grimen, 'Neutral Explanation of Disagreement in Liberal Political Thought', in Solveig Bø, Bengt Molander and Brit Strandhagen (eds.), *I første, andre og tredje person: Festskrift for Audun Øfsti* (Trondheim, NTNU Filsofisk institutt, 1999), pp. 111-123.

30 Philosophical analysis of reasonable disagreement is crucial for a proper understanding of pluralist social orders. A pioneering contribution is the analysis of 'the burdens of judgement' in J. Rawls, *cit. supra* note 6, pp. 54-58.

It is potentially a much more serious matter if adherents of a particular religion, normative tradition, culture or ideology advance claims to public monopoly in the grounding of universally applicable human rights norms. Here the precept for philosophers finding themselves in persistent foundational disagreement applies much more strongly: no religion or tradition or group or ideology has a legitimate exclusive claim to ground universally binding human rights norms – not until or unless all parties who endorse human rights on freely adopted and reasonably held grounds do so on *identical* grounds 'all the way down'. But such a situation is utopian and is definitely not ours.

A series of questions raised in the introduction to this chapter can now be answered. The questions were: How can coherent substantive justification of human rights proceed from a plurality of diverse, and perhaps mutually incompatible sets of premises? How is plural justification at all pertinent to universal human rights? And why should reasonable people bother with such seemingly perverse options and not rather assess 'head on' competing justificatory arguments in order to elaborate, to the best of their ability, the 'one and only' reasonable grounding of human rights?

If we are to heed the inherent freedom and equal dignity of all human beings and also realize that our recalcitrant foundational disagreements across cultural, religious, ideological and other normative divides are reasonable, we must accept that substantive justification of universally binding human rights, if successful, cannot conclude other than in plural justification. As a party to the project of human rights justification we may begin with our own best reasons. But we cannot conclude that human rights have fully adequate normative grounding and yet not be concerned with the reasonability of those who propound supportive grounds that differ from and are incompatible with ours. In our shrinking world of abundant and irrevocable cultural diversity our justification project cannot rest unless, and until, we also grapple with how support of human rights proceeding from normative platforms that differ, rival, and are perhaps incompatible with ours may nevertheless be reasonable support of human rights. The prudential rationale is obvious. The public moral rationale is simple: parties mutually recognizing one another in terms of inherent freedom and equal dignity cannot but take seriously the other party's grounds for such recognition and, hence, the other party's grounds for being obliged by *good reasons* to observe human rights as universally binding.

These are my arguments for thinking that a fully adequate normative justification of human rights must – in a plural social order – be justification across reasonably upheld normative divides and, hence, include plural justification of human rights. What then does plural justification require?

Plural justification of the system of human rights is fully realized just to the extent that competent and authoritative adherents of each of a set of rivalling normative traditions reasonably hold universally applicable human rights to be well supported by each of the separate normative traditions in the set; in other words they reasonably hold rights to be arguably well-grounded in each particular normative tradition including their own.

This is admittedly a tall order. For the practical purpose of bridging – without adulterating – irrevocable cultural diversity it suffices if *representative adherents of each of a set of normative traditions reasonably hold universally applicable human rights to be well grounded in their own tradition and have reasonable trust that the other normative traditions in the set bind their respective adherents similarly.*

And perhaps public solidarity across normative divides by way of universal human rights does not even have to be 'theoretical', made explicit, be upheld as discursively available arguments. What counts, we may think, is that the human rights *practice of inclusive solidarity* becomes institutionalized, habitualized, unproblematic, a matter of course that people share across cultural differences and societal divides. An inclusive concern for others, such that a human being is answerable, that certain things are never done to a human being and that other things are always done for a human being, is of course utopian, and yet – in the time of far-reaching and compound globalization – no longer totally farfetched. The modern tradition of human rights is rooted in an emerging worldwide public commitment to heed as inviolable the inherent dignity of every human being. Equal dignity is no longer just a stoic metaphysical idea; it is becoming an entrenched practical value that resonates within and across difference.

One last point: in a proper plural justification of human rights parties to the project of shared validation of rights are not bound to argue 'tongue in cheek' (as was the case when arguing for 'all whales have lungs' from the rivalling premises 'all whales are mammals' and 'all whales are fishes'). To the contrary: while sticking to, or improving on, their own fundamental normative tenets and distinctions people may also appreciate, and learn from, the reasonableness of the corresponding convictions of others. Though situated in the predicament of persistent and reasonable disagreement about normative fundamentals people are free to focus on the coherence and pertinence of arguments in support of human rights offered by others. And, of course, they may simply cultivate reasonable trust that others embrace human rights, too.

I do not want to hide that the idea of plural justification of human rights invites serious public dialogue and debate across existing normative divides. But such public discourse may produce more light than heat, once participants mutually recognize one another as free and equal human beings and also understand they share the predicament of reasonable disagreement.

# 3
# Self-Determination and Cultural Rights

*Ana Filipa Vrdoljak*

## 1. Introduction

Self-determination has broadly two components: one relates to participation and the other concerns identity. Until recently, contemporary discourse on self-determination has largely centred on the former; and usually, the participation of a people as a fully-fledged member of the international community. Yet, from its earliest conceptions, self-determination has been inextricably tied to notions of identity of peoples – and cultural rights. This chapter examines the evolving link between self-determination and cultural rights in modern international law. By detailing their often tandem, sometimes overlapping, development, I argue that the reformulation and reinforcement of self-determination in recent decades has had an accompanying impact upon cultural rights.

Self-determination and cultural rights sit uncomfortably within the classic human rights framework. This has much to do with what they have in common. Both rights can, and are, held and exercised collectively. Both are motivated toward ensuring the perpetuation of the group. This emphasis on the group as opposed to the individual right holder makes it difficult to place them in relation to other human rights; and problematic for states. It also goes some way to explaining why cultural rights are the most neglected category of human rights.[1] Yet, by contrast, self-determination has undergone a significant resurgence. The International Court of Justice has reaffirmed the right of peoples to self-determination – 'a right *erga omnes*', an obligation owed to (and it would appear, an obligation owed by) the community as a whole.[2] Today, the right to self-determination is viewed as a

[1] J. Symonides, 'Cultural Rights: A Neglected Category of Human Rights', 158, *International Social Science Journal* (1998), p. 595.

[2] *East Timor* (*Portugal v. Australia*), Judgment, ICJ Reports (1995), p. 90, at *p.* 102, *para.* 29; and *Advisory Opinion on the Legal Consequences of the Construction of a Wall in the Occupied Palestinian Territory*, ICJ Reports (2004), *paras.* 88 and 89. See also UN Human Rights Com-

Francioni and Scheinin (eds), *Cultural Human Rights*, 41–78

foundational right, with its effective exercise considered crucial for the enjoyment of all human rights, including cultural rights.[3]

It is no coincidence that, in international law, cultural rights have been primarily developed in respect of the most vulnerable groups, including colonized peoples, minorities and indigenous peoples. This is because cultural rights have been elaborated and applied by the international community to groups whose right to self-determination (including secession) they have suppressed or denied. These groups have tested the boundaries of international law and challenged established state practice on self-determination and cultural rights. Colonized peoples, who had the exercise of their right to self-determination perpetually deferred, ensured that the division between self-determination and development was formally put asunder following decolonization. Minorities within states denied the right to self-determination, have been afforded cultural and other rights as an alternative mode of ensuring the protection and preservation of their identities. Indigenous peoples draw on both these traditions and maintain that the right to self-determination and cultural rights can only be enjoyed and exercised effectively in unison.

If self-determination underpins all human rights, this chapter considers what impact this has for cultural rights. Periods of cleavage in international law and relations expose the failings or flaws of existing doctrines or principles and contestation over their possible reform or replacements. I concentrate on three periods of transition for my discussion. First, I analyse the years in the early 20th century when self-determination was a political objective and cultural rights were articulated in the League of Nations' mandate and minorities systems. Next, I examine the decades of decolonization following the Second World War, when self-determination emerged as a right of peoples, exercisable by those subject to colonial occupation or foreign domination; and cultural rights retreated into the framework of human rights. Finally, I consider the redefinition of the right to self-determination following the end of the Cold War and the related re-emphasis on cultural rights through multilateral initiatives in the fields of minority protection and indigenous peoples.

---

mittee stated in its General Comment No. 12 (Self-Determination), UN Doc.A/39/40 and Corr.1 and 2, Annex 3, *para.* 6. It is unclear what the ICJ means when it says it is an obligation *erga omnes*. The Court in the *Wall* Advisory Opinion seems to go beyond the notion of an obligation owed to all states, and argue that is also an obligation on all states to ensure that the right is effectively realized (*para.* 159). Cf. Separate Opinion of Judge Rosalyn Higgins, *para.* 38; and Separate Opinion of Judge Pieter H. Kooijmans, *para.* 45.

3 General Comment No. 12, *ibid.*, at *para.* 1.

## 2. Minorities and mandates under the League of Nations

Any contemporary interpretation of the right to self-determination and its inter-relation with the cultural rights of peoples cannot be understood without reference to the Covenant of the League of Nations (Covenant), the peace treaties negotiated following the First World War and the work of League bodies which interpreted and oversaw these various provisions. This regime, which facilitated the first wave of dismantling of empires, provided legal protection with oversight by the international community of cultural rights which were positive and collective in character. Furthermore, they were articulated at a time when the right to self-determination was little more than a political notion; and human rights as we know them today had not yet entered the public imagination. Nonetheless, these embryonic manifestations of cultural rights shaped the later enunciation of the right to self-determination and human rights generally in the years following the Second World War.

However, these provisions were not of universal application. Rather, this protection of the cultural rights of specific groups was contained in provisions relating to certain minorities in Central and Eastern Europe and mandates covering former German and Ottoman territories. The victorious powers offered this protection as a compromise to those groups whose exercise of self-determination they had denied or deferred. These efforts to enable groups to protect their identities were viewed as crucial to ensuring regional peace and stability.

### *A. Self-determination under the League of Nations*

Although the debate about the definition and application of self-determination originated and evolved with the disintegration of empires within and beyond Europe, it resurfaces whenever a group seeks full participation in the community of states.[4] During the First World War and in its immediate aftermath, both V.I. Lenin and US President Woodrow Wilson advocated the adoption of self-determination of peoples as a principle to guide international relations.[5] Lenin promoted its application to ethnic or national groups; colonial peoples; and populations subject to territorial redistribution.[6] He argued that all ethnic groups, not only those under colonial domination, should be able to freely determine their own fate, either through secession or autonomy within a federation, even through force of arms.

---

4 See N. Berman, 'Sovereignty in Abeyance: Self-Determination in International Law', *Wisconsin International Law Journal* (1988-89), p. 51, at pp. 52 and 58.

5 See A. Cassese, *Self-determination of Peoples: A Legal Reappraisal* (Cambridge, 1995), p. 14 ff.

6 V.I. Lenin, *On the Foreign Policy of the Soviet State* (Moscow, 1968), p. 11 ff.

Similarly, Wilson vowed that peoples should not be 'bartered about ... as though they were mere chattels and pawns in a game'.[7] However, for the US President self-determination was the right of all peoples to choose their form of government, through peaceful, democratic means and not armed struggle.[8] The principle had an essentially internal character and was subject to the principle of territorial integrity. His draft provision on self-determination, to have been included in the Covenant, required future territorial redistributions to be made with full appreciation of racial, social and political considerations and 'pursuant to the principle of self-determination'.[9] Wilson's draft article on self-determination was not inserted into the final text of the Covenant. This result reflected the significant resistance by the victorious powers to the universal application of self-determination. By way of a concession, those groups whose exercise of self-determination was thwarted were provided with other, more limited political, social and cultural rights in the form of minority guarantees.

The relationship between minority rights and self-determination was considered by two commissions established by the League of Nations to examine the legal status of the Åland Islands. The Åland Islanders sought to secede from Finland and unite with Sweden. In their first report, the International Commission of Jurists observed that the principle of self-determination was not mentioned in the Covenant and was not 'a positive rule of the Law of Nations'.[10] They noted that international law did not recognize the right of 'national' groups to secede because it would infringe the state's sovereignty and threaten the stability of the international community.[11] The issue, they said, was usually a purely domestic concern.[12] However, the Commission of Jurists found that because Finland was seeking independence from Russia it was undergoing a process of transformation; consequently, the principle of self-determination was not only an internal matter.[13] The exercise of self-determination, they maintained, needed to be weighed up against other countervailing geo-political considerations. Accordingly, the Jurists proposed a compromise for the Åland

7 Cited in M.O. Hudson, 'The Protection of Minorities and Natives in Transferred Territories', in E.M. House and C. Seymour (eds.) *What Really Happened at Paris: The Story of the Peace Conference, 1918-1919 by American Delegates* (New York, 1921), p. 208.

8 See H.W.V. Temperley (ed.), *History of the Peace Conferences of Paris* (1920-24) (Reprint, vols 6, Oxford, 1924), Vol. 6, p. 539 ff.

9 R. Lansing, *The Peace Negotiations, a Personal Narrative* (Boston, 1921), p. 283; and D. Hunter Miller, *The Drafting of the Covenant* (New York, 1928), Vol. 2, p. 99.

10 Report of the International Commission of Jurists Entrusted by the Council of the League of Nations with the Task of Giving an Advisory Opinion upon the Legal Aspects of the Åland Islands Question, (Larnaude, Huber, Struycken), LNOJ, SS No. 3, October 1920, pp. 5-6.

11 *Ibid.*

12 *Ibid.*

13 *Ibid.* See also M. Berman, *cit. supra* note 4, at pp. 72-76.

Islanders by way of minority guarantees based on the existing League model and 'dictated by the interests of peace'.[14]

The Commission of Jurists found there was 'a common object' between self-determination (that is, the right of a people to form their own state) and the protection of minorities: 'to assure to some national Group the maintenance and free development of its social, ethnical or religious characteristics'.[15] If this purpose was denied the minority, they did not rule out the possible exercise of self-determination by a group within a state. The Jurists found that:

> [I]n affirming these principles, [it did] not give an opinion concerning the question as to whether a manifest and continued abuse of sovereign power, to the detriment of a section of the population of a state, would, if such circumstances arose, give to an international dispute, arising therefrom, such a character that its object should be considered as one which is not confined to the domestic jurisdiction of the state concerned, but comes within the sphere of action of the League of Nations.[16]

While the subsequent report by the Committee of Rapporteurs found that Finland was a properly constituted state and self-determination was therefore a purely domestic concern, they also recommended minority guarantees be imposed upon Finland.[17]

The Committee of Rapporteurs argued that to allow minorities to cede from the state in which they found themselves 'at their good pleasure' would 'destroy order and stability within states and … inaugurate anarchy in international life'.[18] Nevertheless, they reiterated that in exceptional cases the minority may separate from the state as 'a last resort when the state lacks either the will or the power to enact and apply just and effective guarantees'.[19] Indeed, they suggested that if Finland had refused the minority guarantees, they would have recommended that the islanders be afforded a plebiscite to determine their future status. Pursuant to the reports, the Council of the League recognized Finland's sovereignty over the Åland Islands and put in place minority guarantees to protect the islanders' language and identity which remain in force to date, in a varied form.[20]

---

14 *Ibid.*

15 *Ibid.*

16 *Ibid.*

17 Report prepared by a Commission of Rapporteurs at the Council's behest: League of Nations, Report presented to the Council of the League by the Commission of Rapporteurs, Council Doc.B7/21/68/106[VII], 16 April 1921, pp. 27-28.

18 *Ibid.*

19 *Ibid.*

20 Resolution of 24 June 1921, LNOJ SS No. 5, p. 24, at p. 34; and Convention relating to the Status of the Ålands Islands, 20 October 1921, 9 LNTS 212.

The *Åland Islands* case continues to permeate judicial and academic opinions in respect of self-determination, minorities and cultural rights. For James Crawford, it lends support to the principle in international law of *carence de souveraineté,* that is, where a territory is so misgoverned by the state that cessation is permitted.[21] Whereas, for Karen Knop, with their emphasis on minority protection including language and cultural rights as a compromise, the reports go beyond the equation of self-determination with questions of governance and include the protection of group identity.[22] For our purpose, its most telling legacy is the connection made between the two – self-determination and minority protection: their underlying common objective; and that self-determination is the ultimate safeguard protection of identity of particular groups and the cultural rights of their members.

### B. Minority guarantees and cultural rights under the League of Nations

The minority protections recommended for the Åland Islanders was modelled on those already in place for select groups within new or enlarged states in Central and Eastern Europe.[23] These communities had been subject to territorial redistribution, but were denied the opportunity of exercising self-determination, and so were given treaty-based minority guarantees. During the Versailles peace conference, the victorious Allied and Associated powers conceded the potentially destabilizing impact of assimilation policies by making recognition, or entry into the League, conditional for some states upon acceptance of minority guarantees, which included cultural rights.[24]

This inter-war minority protection usually had three elements which reflected the double purpose of ensuring participation within the state; and maintaining and developing the minority's identity. First, members of minorities could choose their nationality pursuant to certain guidelines.[25] Second, applying the principle of non-discrimination, members of the minority were entitled to equal enjoyment of civil and political rights like other nationals. The effectiveness of this provision was assessed by 'the absence of discrimination in fact as well as in law'.[26] Although this

---

21 J. Crawford, *The Creation of States in International Law* (2nd edn., Oxford, 2006), p. 111.

22 K. Knop, *Diversity and Self-Determination in International Law* (Cambridge, 2002), p. 79.

23 The minority guarantee contained in Articles 2, 3, 7 and 8 of the Treaty between the Principal Allied and Associated Powers and Poland, 28 June 1919, 223 Parry's CTS 412 ('Peace Treaty with Poland') were the first such provisions and they became the model for subsequent minority protections imposed on other states seeking recognition or entry into the League.

24 LNOJ, July 1928, p. 942, Minutes of 50th Council. See C.A. Macartney, *National states and National Minorities* (2nd edn., New York, 1968), pp. 296-97; and P. Thornberry, *International Law and the Rights of Minorities* (Cambridge, 1991), p. 41 ff.

25 Article 3, Peace Treaty with Poland, *ibid.*

26 *Rights of Minorities in Upper Silesia (Minority Schools)*, (1928) PCIJ Series A, No. 15, p. 29. See also Articles 2, 7 and 8, Peace Treaty with Poland, *cit. supra* note 23; and *Treatment of*

arm of the guarantees provided for the use of minority languages, the Permanent Court of International Justice (PCIJ) found that their intended purpose was to ensure the equal enjoyment of civil and political rights and 'prevent any unfavourable treatment, and not to grant a special regime of privileged treatment'. They were, it said, of 'a purely negative character in that they were confined to a prohibition of any discrimination'.[27]

Third, these international guarantees provided that minorities should enjoy equal rights to establish, control and manage their own 'charitable, religious and social institutions, schools and other educational establishments, with the right to use their own language and to exercise their religion freely therein'.[28] The relevant state was under a positive obligation to ensure the realization of these rights. In territories where the minority made up a 'considerable proportion of ... nationals', it was required to provide instruction in the minority language in the public education system and an equitable share of public funds to the communities to realize these goals.[29] When interpreting a similar provision in the *Minority Schools in Albania* case, the PCIJ observed that its purpose was 'to ensure for the minority elements suitable means for the preservation of their racial peculiarities, their traditions and their national characteristics'.[30]

The ultimate purpose of the minority guarantees was the subject of extensive disputation especially the provision requiring special treatment of minorities in respect of cultural and social rights. On the one hand, it was clear the Allied powers did not intend to create 'states within states' by granting national groups political autonomy.[31] For this reason, they referred throughout to '"members of minorities" and not simply "minorities"'.[32] Conversely, as H. Black Calderwood pointed out, the inter-war peace treaties 'if they [did] not establish the minorities as collectives, confer[red] rights that [could] only be enjoyed by individuals acting together'.[33] And so, on the other hand, the scheme was viewed as ensuring the perpetuation of the minority's cultural identity within the state but with its members 'living peaceably

*Polish Nationals and other Persons of Polish Origin or Speech in the Danzig territory*, (1932) PCIJ Series A/B, No. 44, pp. 28 and 39.

27 *Ibid.*

28 Article 9, Peace Treaty with Poland, *cit. supra* note 23.

29 *Ibid.* See *Advisory Opinion in the Greco-Bulgarian 'Communities'*, (1930) PCIJ, Series B, No. 17, 33.

30 *Minority Schools in Albania*, (1935) PCIJ, Series A/B, No. 64, p. 4, at p. 17.

31 H. Black Calderwood, 'The Protection of Minorities by the League of Nations', *Geneva Research Information Committee Special Studies* (1931), p. 17, at p. 21. See Report of M. de Mello-Franco, 9 December 1925, LNOJ, 7th year (February 1926), p. 141; and H.W.V. Temperley, *cit. supra* note 8, Vol. 5, p. 121.

32 C.A. Macartney, *cit. supra* note 24, at pp. 282-283.

33 H. Black Calderwood, *cit. supra* note 31, at p. 20.

alongside that population and co-operating amicably with it'.[34] The Permanent Court found that the civil, political and cultural rights contained in the minority guarantees were directed toward the same aim:

> These two requirements are indeed closely interlocked, for there would be no true equality between a majority and a minority if the latter were deprived of its own institutions, and were consequently compelled to renounce that which constitutes the very essence of its being as a minority.[35]

So whilst the international community had denied these groups the right to self-determination, through the compromise of minority guarantees they tried to ensure their cultural autonomy in the shadow of the dominant culture.[36]

In return for their recognition, new or enlarged states in Central and Eastern Europe were required to accept the minority guarantees as fundamental law, which could not be altered by domestic legislation, and their compliance was subject to external oversight. They argued that such conditional recognition impinged on their sovereignty and threatened their internal stability.[37] Clearly, these provisions did undermine the positivists' notion of state sovereignty in the interests of international and regional peace and stability.[38] This development facilitated the rise of human rights discourse after 1945.[39] These inter-war guarantees conceptualized cultural rights as positive obligations. They were also articulated as equal and interrelated to civil and political rights. This interdependence of human rights would be reflected in the 1948 Universal Declaration of Human Rights.[40]

---

34 *Minority Schools in Albania*, (1935) PCIJ, Series A/B, No. 64, p. 4, at p. 19.

35 *Ibid.*

36 See P. Thornberry, *cit. supra* note 24, at pp. 41 ff; Speech of US President Woodrow Wilson on 31 May 1919, in C.A. Macartney, *cit. supra* note 24, at pp. 232-233; and *Advisory Opinion in the Greco-Bulgarian 'Communities'*, (1930) PCIJ, Series B, No. 17, p. 19.

37 H. Black Calderwood, *cit. supra* note 31, at p. 22.

38 See *German-Polish Upper Silesia Convention*, 15 May 1922, in which minorities and their members were entitled to address their petitions directly to the League's Council. See J. Stone, *Regional Guarantees of Minority Rights: A Study of Minorities Procedure in Upper Silesia* (Toronto, 1933); M. St. Korowicz, 'The Problem of the International Personality of Individuals', *AJIL* (1956), p. 533; J.K. Kunz, 'The Present Status of International Law for the Protection of Minorities', *AJIL* (1954), p. 548, at pp. 552-558; J.B. Kelly, 'National Minorities in International Law', *Journal of International Law and Policy* (1973), p. 253, at p. 260; and B. Vukas, 'International Protection of Minorities: Limits to Growth', 23 *Thesaurus Acroasium* (1999), p. 21, at p. 33.

39 See A. Anghie, 'Cultural Difference and International Law: The League of Nations and Its Two Visions of the Nation-State', *ICCLP Review* (2002), 5(2), p. 3, at p. 9.

40 See J. Humphrey, 'The International Law of Human Rights in the Middle Twentieth Century', in International Law Association, *The Present State of International Law and Other Essays* (Deventer, 1973), p. 101.

## C. Mandates, development and cultural rights

The League of Nations' mandate system was the remedial measure meted out to the inhabitants of the former German colonies and Turkish territories whose exercise of self-determination was deferred by the Allied powers. Article 22 of the Covenant was the result of heated politicking between those countries seeking outright annexation and others advocating a form of tutelage.[41] The provision imposed a 'trust' for these peoples who were considered unprepared for self-governance but could exercise self-determination following a period of 'tutelage'.[42]

President Wilson conceded that the rights and interests of the colonized and colonizer had not always coincided nor had they been given equal weight by the international community in the past.[43] The League's mandate system sought to recalibrate relations between colonial peoples and metropolitan powers during the inter-war period. This new relationship was governed by efforts to balance two defining principles: self-determination and equal access to resources and markets. The mandatory power held the territory on double trust: on behalf of the inhabitants of the territory to prepare them for eventual self-governance; and this was balanced against its duty to the international community to ensure its members had equal access to the territory's resources and labour.[44]

Hersch Lauterpacht noted that like its precursor, the dual mandate contained in the Final Act of the 1885 Berlin Conference, Article 22 embodied a clash between 'humanitarian, cultural and cosmopolitan aspects' related to the protection and advancement of the colonized and 'the power principle' equated to the free trade and development agenda of the colonizers.[45] He conceded that Article 22 was groundbreaking because the obligation was included in the Covenant and its oversight

---

41 Versailles, 28 June 1919, LN, LNOJ (February 1920), 1st Yr, No. 1, p. 3; BFSP, Vol. 112, p. 13; (1919) 225 Parry's CTS 195; 13 (supp.) *AJIL* (1919), p. 128. See generally Q. Wright, *Mandates under the League of Nations* (Chicago, 1930); and H. Duncan Hall, *Mandates, Dependencies and Trusteeship* (Washington DC, 1948).

42 See P.B. Potter, 'Origin of the System of Mandates under the League of Nations', *APSR* (1922), 16, pp. 563-583; Q. Wright, 'The United States and the Mandates', 23 *Michigan L. Rev.* (1925), p. 717; D. Hunter Miller, 'The Origin of the Mandates System', 6 *Foreign Affairs* (1928), p. 277; and A. Margalith, *The International Mandates* (Baltimore, 1930), p. 35 ff.

43 H.W.V. Temperley, *cit. supra* note 8, Vol. 6, p. 500. See H. Rolin, 'Le systemé des mandats coloniaux', 3-4 *Revue de droit international* (1920), p. 344; Wilson's Four Principles of 11 February 1918, reproduced in Lansing, No. 9, at p. 286; J.C. Smuts, *The League of Nations: a practical suggestion,* (New York, 1919), p. 11; and M. Pomerance, 'The United States and Self-Determination: Perspectives on the Wilsonian Conception', *AJIL* (1976), p. 1.

44 See Advisory Opinion on the International Status of South West Africa, ICJ Reports (1950), pp. 131-132.

45 H. Lauterpacht, 'The Mandate under international law in the Covenant of the League of Nations', in E. Lauterpacht (ed.), *International Law: Being the Collected Papers of Hersch Lauterpacht* (Cambridge, 1977), p. 29, at pp. 39-41.

was guaranteed by the international community.[46] He, nonetheless, observed that while 'the nucleus of this cultural-ethical requirement [had] been retained' it was only achieved with significant deference to political and economic interests of the colonial powers.[47] Given the political and economic upheaval generated by colonial rivalry during the nineteenth and early 20th century, its concession was viewed as essential for peace and stability under the League.[48]

This compromise was complicated further by the underlying premise of the 'sacred trust of civilization'; that is, because of their political, social, economic and cultural structures, colonized peoples were 'not yet able to stand by themselves under the strenuous conditions of the modern world.'[49] It was the duty of the mandatory power to foster the 'development' of these structures to the stage of advancement determined by external standards as necessary for their eventual exercise of self-determination and full sovereignty.[50] Even the 'cultural-ethical requirement', or duty owed to the inhabitants, often entailed the suppression of certain cultural, religious or social practices deemed 'backward' by the mandatory power.[51]

In addition, the cultural rights of inhabitants in mandated territories were affected by the mandatory state's duty to 'secure equal opportunities for the trade and commerce of other Members of the League', which applied with equal force to the cultural 'resources' of mandated territories.[52] For example, the Treaty of Peace with Turkey of 1920 covering territories of the former Ottoman Empire required the passage of legislation which was strictly defined to ensure equal treatment for archaeological research and excavations to the nationals of all member states.[53] It was the mandatory power, under the supervision of the League, which balanced the interests of the international community against those of colonized peoples in their own cultural heritage. Despite its humanitarian rationale, by reaffirming this division between self-determination and development and assigning them to different beneficiaries, the League's mandate system necessarily continued to adversely impact their rights to their cultural heritage and to maintaining their identity.[54]

---

46 E. Lauterpacht, *cit. supra* note 45, at pp. 40.

47 *Ibid.*

48 *Ibid.*.

49 Article 22, Covenant of the League of Nations, *cit. supra* note 41.

50 See A. Anghie, *Imperialism, Sovereignty and the Making of International Law* (Cambridge, 2004), pp. 168-178; and A, Anghie, 'Nationalism, Development and the Postcolonial State: The Legacy of the League of Nations', *Texas ILJ* (2006), p. 447, at p. 454 ff.

51 *Ibid.*

52 See N. de Mattos Bentwich, *The Mandate System* (New York, 1930), pp. 41-43.

53 Article 421 and Annex, Treaty of Peace with Turkey, Sèvres, 10 August 1920, not ratified, Cmd 964 (1920); BFSP, Vol. 113, p. 652; 15 (supp.) *AJIL* (1921), p. 179.

54 See A. Anghie, *cit. supra* note 50, at p. 168 ff.

## 3. Decolonization and human rights

While the Covenant of the League of Nations made no explicit reference to the principle of self-determination, the Charter of the United Nations (UN Charter), the body which replaced the League after the Second World War, not only incorporates the principle but extends it to include cultural development.[55] The Charter confirms that self-determination is applicable to 'peoples'.[56] Yet, during the Cold War, its exercise was almost exclusively confined to inhabitants of territories under (European) colonial occupation or foreign domination.

Whereas during the inter-war period, select new or enlarged states were subject to minority guarantees, there was not such requirement for states emerging following decolonization. Instead, member states of the United Nations are required to 'reaffirm faith in fundamental human rights' and respect 'the principle of equal rights and self-determination of peoples'.[57] With the downgrading of minority protection on the international agenda, cultural rights became subsumed within the human rights framework and were to be enjoyed by the individual right holder.

### *A. Right to self-determination and cultural development*

It is generally accepted that there was no legally recognized right to self-determination prior to the finalization of the UN Charter in 1945.[58] The Charter incorporates it as an aim and purpose of the new organization and its Member States (Articles 1(2) and 55); in respect of former mandated territories (Chapter IX and XIII); and all 'colonial' territories' (Chapter XI). Despite these developments, there was still significant resistance to its metamorphosis into a legally binding principle.[59]

---

55 Charter of the United Nations, San Francisco, 26 June 1945, in force 24 October 1945, UNCIO XV, 335; amendments by General Assembly Resolutions in UNTS 557.

56 The drafting committee deliberately rejected efforts to amend the reference of 'peoples' to 'states' or 'nations': see United Nations Conference on International Organization, Doc.I/1/16; and A Cristescu, The Historical and Current Development of the Right to Self-Determination on the basis of the Charter of the United Nations and Other Instruments adopted by United Nations Organs, with particular reference to the Promotion and Protection of Human Rights and Fundamental Freedoms, Preliminary Report, UN Doc.E/CN.4/Sub.2/L.625, *paras.* 54-60 (1975).

57 Preamble and Article 1(2), UN Charter, *cit. supra* note 55.

58 See Report of the International Commission of Jurists on the Åland Islands, *cit. supra* note 10; A. Cassese, *cit. supra* note 5, at p. 37 ff; and J. Crawford, 'Right to Self-Determination in International Law: Its Development and Future', in P. Alston (ed.), *Peoples' Rights* (Oxford, 2001), p. 7, at p. 14. Cf. J. Crawford, *cit. supra* note 21, at p. 111.

59 *South West Africa* (*Ethiopia v. South Africa*; *Liberia v. South Africa*), Second Phase, ICJ Reports (1966), p. 6; and G. Fitzmaurice, 'The Future of Public International Law and the International Legal System in the Circumstances of Today', in Institut de droit international, *Evolution et perspectives du droit international* (Paris, 1973), p. 196, at p. 233.

While there were early indicators that it was the objective of the international community that self-determination would be of universal application,[60] there was an equal presumption that there would be a continuing need for certain territories to be administered by other states to facilitate their populations' eventual exercise of this principle and the attainment of statehood. Nevertheless, for the first time in an international instrument, the interests of colonized peoples were given precedence. Under the Declaration regarding Non-Self-Governing Territories contained in Chapter XI, administering states were required to 'ensure, with due respect for the culture of the peoples concerned, their political, economic, social and educational advancement, their just treatment and their protection against abuses'.[61]

Self-determination had its most enduring impact when it was summoned by those striving for decolonization. Colonized peoples, and socialist countries, promoted its interpretation as independence from the relevant metropolitan power. The Universal Declaration of Human Rights (UDHR) which was approved by the UN General Assembly in 1948 does not specifically refer to a right to self-determination.[62] This occurred with the 1960 Declaration on the Granting of Independence to Colonial Countries and Peoples (UNGA Res.1514 (XV)). It states in part:

> All peoples have the *right to self-determination*; by virtue of that right they freely determine their political status and freely pursue their economic, social and *cultural development*.[63]

Successive United Nations General Assembly (UNGA) resolutions and their gradual endorsement by the International Court of Justice facilitated the articulation of self-determination as a justiciable right.[64]

Only in the aftermath of these developments was self-determination defined as a legally-binding, 'human' right. Common Article 1 of the International Covenant

---

60 Doc.2G/7(c), UNCIO.

61 Article 73, Chapter XI, Charter of the United Nations, *cit. supra* note 55 (covered colonial territories not previously encompassed by the Mandate system).

62 Paris, UNGA Res.217A(III), 10 December 1948, UN Doc.A/810, 71; 43 (supp.) *AJIL* (1949), p. 127. See also UNGA Res.545(VI), 5 February 1952 regarding the insertion an article stating 'All peoples shall have the right to self-determination' should be included in the International Covenant on Human Rights.

63 UNGA Res.1514 (XV), 14 December 1960, 15 UN GAOR Supp. (No. 16), p. 66, 40 UN Yearbook (1960), Article 2 (emphasis added). See Declaration on Principles of International Law concerning Friendly Relations and Co-operation among states in Accordance with the Charter of the United Nations, UNGA Res.2625(XXV), 24 October 1970, 25 UN GAOR Supp. (No. 18), p. 122; 9 ILM (1970), p. 1292, Principle (e).

64 *Legal Consequences for states of the Continued Presence of South Africa in Namibia* (South West Africa) (1970) Advisory Opinion, ICJ Reports (1971), p. 16, at p. 31; and *Western Sahara*, Advisory Opinion, ICJ Reports (1975), p. 12, at pp. 31-33; and *Wall* Advisory Opinion, *para.* 88.

of Civil and Political Rights (ICCPR) and the International Covenant of Economic, Social and Cultural Rights (ICESCR) was approved by the UN General Assembly in 1966.[65] Article 1 of the two International Covenants replicates the wording of UNGA Res.1514(XV). With its inclusion in the International Bill of Rights, the right of self-determination (so-defined) moved away from the narrow colonial context, and apparently became of universal application to all peoples.[66]

Given the history of colonization, it was no coincidence that the articulation of the legal right to self-determination during the 1960s and 1970s was firmly tied to development and control of natural resources. New states actively campaigned for the broadening of self-determination beyond a political act that was extinguished upon independence. Proponents of the New International Economic Order advocated a new international order that would also lead to a new international cultural order.[67] The reconfiguration of colonial relations from the mid-20th century led for the first time to the vesting of the right to self-determination and development in the same peoples. No longer would the rights and interests of 'colonized' peoples be subordinated to the interests of other states in their resources, including cultural 'resources'.[68]

These new states maintained that self-determination was an ongoing process in which they endeavoured to attain equality with other states. From the outset, it was clear that the right to self-determination was not confined to the right of peoples to freely determine 'by and for themselves' their political status, but extended to include economic, social and *cultural* matters.[69] Sovereign equality, that is, the reversal of the legacies of colonialism, they argued, would only be achieved through development – not only economic development, but social and *cultural*

---

65 International Covenant on Civil and Political Rights, New York, 16 December 1966, in force 23 March 1976, UNGA Res.2200A(XXI), 21 UN GAOR Supp. (No. 16), p. 52; 999 UNTS 171; 6 ILM (1967), p. 368; and International Covenant on Economic, Social and Cultural Rights, New York, 16 December 1966, in force 3 January 1976, UNGA Res.2200A(XXI), 21 UN GAOR Supp. (No. 16), p. 49; 993 UNTS 3; 6 ILM (1967), p. 360. For discussion of the *travaux préparatoires* of common Article 1: M.J. Bossuyt, *Guide to the 'Travaux Préparatoires' of the International Covenant on Civil and Political Rights* (Boston, 1987), pp. 19-48.

66 *Wall* Advisory Opinion, Separate Opinion of Judge Rosalyn Higgins, *paras.* 29-30; and J. Crawford, *cit. supra* note 58, at pp. 27-28.

67 See UN Doc.A/CN.4/322, *para.* 46; and E/CN.4/Sub.2/404, *para.* 599. See Declaration on the Establishment of a New International Economic Order, UNGA Res.3201(S-VI), 1 May 1974; 13 ILM (1974), p. 720; 68 *AJIL* (1974), p. 798; and M. Bedjaoui, *Towards a New International Economic Order* (New York, 1979).

68 See United Kingdom, Foreign Office, *A Commentary on the Charter of the United Nations signed at San Francisco on 26th June 1945*, Cmd.6666 (London, 1945), *para.* 58.

69 UN ECOSOC OR, 14th Session, Supp. No. 4, (E/2256), 252nd – 266th meetings, *para.* 20-74; and UN Doc.E/CN.4/Sub.2/L.625, *para.* 103.

development.[70] In his report on the historical and current development of the right to self-determination, UN Special Rapporteur Aureliu Cristescu suggested that the right to self-determination as it referred to cultural matters is the 'right of peoples to choose their cultural system and freely pursue their cultural development' and 'regain, enjoy and enrich their cultural heritage'.[71] He observed that the right to self-determination was 'an insurance and safeguard of the cultural development of peoples' and hoped that 'cultural' decolonization would revive, strengthen and extend cultural human rights.[72] Cristescu argued that the realization of this right was crucial because 'all cultures, in their rich variety, multiplicity, diversity and interaction, form part of the common heritage of all mankind'.[73]

This move was combined with the assertion contained in Common Article 1(2) of the International Covenants that 'all peoples may, for their own ends, freely dispose of their natural wealth and resources'. Cultural heritage, tangible and intangible movable and immovable, became a cultural resource, exploited by these states to develop a *national* cultural identity. During the decolonization period, several initiatives were promoted as being essential to a people's cultural development and exercise of the right to self-determination. The first demand concerned the restitution of cultural resources removed as a direct result of the often unfettered and unauthorized exploitation during colonial occupation.[74] Next, there was an insistence on the present need for technical and financial assistance to preserve and develop their cultures and cultural heritage.[75] Finally, they called for the international

70 Preservation and Further Development of Cultural Values, Note by the Secretary-General, 24 August 1976, UN Doc.A/31/111, *para.* 66 (emphasis added). See also *paras.* 7 and 25; and UNESCO, *Moving towards change: some thoughts on the new international economic order* (Paris, 1976), pp. 25-26. It was further elaborated upon in Article 1, Declaration on the Right to Development, UNGA Res.41/128, annex, 4 December 1986; 41 UN GAOR Supp. (No. 53), p. 186.

71 UN Doc.E/CN.4/Sub.2/L.625, *para.* 31. See also Article 1, Charter of Economic Rights and Duties of States, UNGA Res.3281 (XXIX), 12 December 1974; 29 UN GAOR Supp. (No. 31), p. 50; 14 ILM (1975), p. 251; 69 (supp.) *AJIL* (1975), p. 484, Chapter II.

72 A. Cristescu, The Historical and Current Development of the Right to Self-Determination on the basis of the Charter of the United Nations and Other Instruments adopted by United Nations Organs, with particular reference to the Promotion and Protection of Human Rights and Fundamental Freedoms, Final Report, 3 July 1978, UN Doc.E/CN.4/Sub.2/404, *para.* 584.

73 UN Doc.E/CN.4/Sub.2/L.625, *para.* 48.

74 See UN Doc.A/31/111, para. 62, and UN Doc.A/33/157, *paras.* 56 ff. See Third Congress of the International Association of Art Critics in Kinshasa-N'Sele, 1973, Resolution of the Fourth Conference reproduced in part in UN Doc.A/9199, 2; and Fifth Conference of Heads of state or Government of Non-Aligned Countries, Colombo, 1976, UN Doc.A/31/1976, Annex IV, UN Doc.A/9199, 2; and UN Doc.A/9330 and Corr.1, *para.* 18.

75 *Ibid*, *paras.* 57-60 and 64. See UN Doc.A/34/PV.51(1979), *para.* 60 (Ecuador).

regulation of the ongoing illicit export, import and transfer of cultural objects.[76] This legislative framework was finally realized with the Convention on the Means of Prohibiting and Preventing the Illicit Import, Export and Transfer of Ownership of Cultural Property (1970 UNESCO Convention).[77]

With its strong emphasis on the role of states, the 1970 UNESCO Convention is a document of its time. The *travaux* had defined the Convention's purpose as controlling the illicit transfer of the cultural heritage of 'peoples'.[78] The preamble of the preliminary draft had specifically referred to Article 27 UDHR (the right to freely participate in cultural life) which meant that 'it [was] incumbent upon states to protect the cultural property existing within their territory'.[79] Drafted when there was an emphasis in international law on the protection of national cultures by the states and individual human rights, it is not surprising that this preambular recital was deleted from the final text.[80]

Although defined as 'people's rights', for decades, self-determination and cultural development were rights confined to states and national cultures. Participation referred to independence and membership of the international community; and identity was defined by the national boundaries of the state. The principles of state sovereignty and territorial integrity outweighed any application of the right to external self-determination beyond the inhabitants of territories of formerly colonized European countries. New states feared the assertion of multiple (and competing) cultural identities would have a destabilizing effect on national unity.[81] Yet, there is an inherent problem in defining 'people's rights' as being held by all the inhabitants of a state. As Crawford has noted, human and peoples' rights are usually violated by the home state and 'it is the violations at home which the government of the home state is likely to be least willing to address ...'.[82]

---

76 *Ibid*, *paras.* 61 and 63.

77 Paris, 14 November 1970, in force 24 April 1972, 823 UNTS 231; 10 ILM (1971), p. 289.

78 UNESCO Doc.SHC/MD/3, *para.* 10.

79 *Ibid.*, Annex.

80 The United States opposed this interpretation of Article 27 and successfully negotiated its deletion from the final text: UNESCO Doc.SHC/MD/5, Annex 1, 22. However, during the 1990s, the UN Committee on Economic, Social and Cultural Rights confirmed that Article 15(1)(a) of the ICESCR, which translated this right into treaty form, encompasses a positive duty to protect such heritage from theft and deliberate destruction: UN Docs.E/1991/23, *para.* 79; E/1992/23, *paras.* 310, 312; E/1993/22, *para.* 186; and E/1995/22, *para.* 136. See also R. O'Keefe, The '"Right to Take Part in Cultural Life" under Article 15 of the ICESCR', *ICLQ* (1998), p. 904 ff., at p. 909.

81 UN Doc.E/CN.4/Sub.2/404, *para.* 596.

82 J. Crawford, *cit. supra* note 58, at p. 22; J. Crawford, 'The Rights of Peoples: "Peoples" or "Governments"?' in J. Crawford (ed.), *The Rights of Peoples* (Oxford, 1988), p. 55.

UNESCO instruments and UN human rights bodies have gradually enabled non-state groups to have a voice in national and transnational decision-making processes affecting their enjoyment of cultural rights and cultural heritage. Indeed, in the same year that the international human rights covenants were finalized, the UNESCO General Conference proclaimed the Declaration of the Principles of International Cultural Cooperation. The Declaration enunciated principles concerning the right (and duty) of *peoples* to develop their culture.[83] Article 1 recognizes that each culture must be respected and preserved because all cultures form part of the 'common heritage belonging to all mankind.'[84]

### B. Human rights and cultural rights

The conceptualization and promotion of cultural rights has been tied inextricably to the fluctuating fortunes of minority protection in international law. The new states recognized following the dismantling of Europe's overseas empires in the post-1945 era were not subject to minority protection. Instead of a framework of minority guarantees, the international community enunciated a system of human rights with universal application.[85] Cultural rights became human rights held by every individual human being. It was argued that non-discrimination and the effective realization of human rights would ensure that members of minorities in new and existing states would also have their rights protected, including their cultural rights.

By the closing decades of the 20th century, this argument was no longer sustainable nor accepted. It was apparent that individual human rights alone could not operate as an effective bulwark against a state hostile to groups on its territory. Gradually,

---

83 See B. Boutros-Ghali, 'The right to culture and the Universal Declaration of Human Rights', in UNESCO, *Cultural Rights as Human Rights* (Paris, 1970), p. 73.

84 4 November 1966, UNESCO Doc.16C/Resolution 8. The preamble referred to the Universal Declaration of Human Rights, the Declaration on the Granting of Independence to Colonial Countries and Peoples, and the UN Declaration on the Elimination of all Forms of Racial Discrimination. See also Article 22, African Charter on Human and Peoples' Rights (Banjul Charter), Adopted 27 June 1981, in force 21 October 1986, OAU Doc.CAB/LEG/67/3, rev.5; 1520 UNTS 217; 21 *ILM* (1982), p. 58.

In 1995, the World Commission on Culture and Development presented its report, 'Our Creative Diversity' to the UNESCO General Conference and UN General Assembly. It recommended that the International Law Commission (ILC) at the instruction of the UN General Assembly draft a list of cultural rights not currently protected by treaty law and various methods to render cultural rights justiciable. While most UNESCO Member states responded favourably to the drawing up of a list of cultural rights there was little support for the remaining recommendations. See World Commission on Culture and Development, *Our Cultural Diversity* (Paris, 1995).

85 The UN Secretariat found the League of Nations minorities protection were terminated following the Second World War: see UN Doc.E/CN.4/367 (1950). Cf. S. Rosenne, 'Minorities and Human Rights', in Y. Dinstein and M. Taboy (eds.), *The Protection of Minorities and Human Rights* (Dordrecht, 1992).

certain existing human rights, particularly cultural rights, were reinterpreted as having a 'collective' dimension; and the question of special measures for protection of minorities re-emerged in international and regional fora.

### 1. *Cultural rights as individual rights: Articles 27 UDHR and 15 ICESCR*

The right to participate in cultural life contained in Article 27 of the UDHR and Article 15 of the International Covenant on Economic, Social and Cultural Rights has been flagged frequently in reference to the cultural dimension of the right to self-determination.[86] And like the interpretation of the right to self-determination, this right has until recently been strictly limited to participation in the 'national culture' by the individual right holder. Nonetheless, the inclusion of Article 27 in the UDHR meant that this right was to be enjoyed by every human being and it was a right equal to and indivisible from all other rights contained in the Declaration.[87]

While the UDHR is a non-binding declaration, this human right's subsequent inclusion in the ICESCR renders it legal binding on states parties. During the ICESCR drafting process, UNESCO had provided two proposed formulations of Article 15. Its preliminary draft would have required states parties to 'encourage[e] the free cultural development of racial and linguistic minorities'.[88] UNESCO's committee of experts called to elaborate upon this right observed that a distinction needed to be made 'between different types of communities, to which any given individual may belong at one and the same ... may run counter to, or at least differ considerably from, those of the national community ...'.[89] UNESCO provided an alternative briefer draft Article which borrowed heavily from Article 27 of the UDHR.[90] However, UNESCO's recommendation to include the additional wording: 'to take part in the cultural life of the communities to which he belongs', was dropped from the final text.[91] The focus remained squarely on participation in the national culture.

However, in the decades since the adoption of the International Covenants, there has been a reconfiguration of the boundaries of the right to take part in cultural life that has slowly encompassed UNESCO's original interpretation. The 1976 UNESCO Recommendation, which elaborates upon the right contained in Article 15 ICESCR, obliges state parties to ensure that minorities have 'full opportunities for gaining

---

86 See successive UNGA resolutions entitled 'Preservation and further development of cultural values', from UNGA Res.3148(XXVIII), 14 December 1973.

87 UNESCO Doc.UNESCO/DG/188, 6 October 1952.

88 UN Doc.E/CN.4/541, 18 April 1951.

89 CUA/42, p. 17.

90 UN Doc.E/CN.4/541, Rev.1, p. 3. Chile submitted this draft version to the Commission: UN Doc.E/CN.4/613. May 1953.

91 UN Doc.A/C.3/SR.797, October 1957, p. 178; and UN Doc.A.C.3/SR.799, October 1957, pp. 190-191.

access to and participating in the cultural life … in order to enrich [the relevant country] with their specific contributions, while safeguarding their right to preserve their cultural identity.'[92] The revised guidelines for state parties reporting their implementation of the Covenant adopted in 1990 require them to provide information about the 'promotion of awareness and enjoyment of cultural heritage of national ethnic groups and minorities and of indigenous peoples'.[93] The UN Committee for Economic, Social and Cultural Rights, the body which monitors the implementation of this treaty obligation, has repeatedly stated that Article 15 guarantees minority and indigenous peoples the freedom to practise and promote awareness of their cultures.[94] This position is reinforced by the committee's endorsement of a broader understanding of culture that covers its individual and collective dimensions and accepts that it 'reflects … the community's way of life and thought'.[95]

### *2. Cultural rights as collective rights: Article 27 ICCPR*

Often cited as an example of the backlash against the perceived failures of the League of Nations' guarantees, the UDHR does not include a provision dedicated to minority protection. During deliberations of the draft Universal Declaration, the UN Sub-Commission on the Prevention of Discrimination and Protection of Minorities and UN Secretary-General distinguished between non-discrimination provisions and a regime of minority protection.[96] They noted that minority protection implied a permanent set of arrangements to protect the identity of the community by placing a positive obligation on the state to establish institutions for non-dominant groups to protect and develop their language, culture and religion.[97] The Sub-Commission prepared a draft provision that largely replicated the inter-war minority guarantees

---

92 Article 4(f), 1976 UNESCO Recommendation, adopted on 26 November 1976 by UNESCO General Conference, 19th session, Nairobi.

93 Revised Guidelines regarding the Form and Contents of Reports to be Submitted by states Parties under Articles 16 and 17 of the International Covenant on Economic, Social and Cultural Rights, UN Doc.E/C.12/1991/1. See UN Doc.E/1991/23, *para.* 79; and E/1992/23, *para.* 310.

94 See General Discussion on the Right to Take Part in Cultural Life as recognised in Article 15 of the International Covenant on Economic, Social and Cultural Rights, UN Doc.E/1993/22, Chapter VII, *para.* 205; Revised Guidelines, *para.* 1(d); E/1992/23, *para.* 153, 162; and E/1997/22, *para.* 302.

95 *Ibid., paras.* 204, 209, 210 and 213.

96 UN Doc.E/CN.4/Sub.2/8, 29 October 1947.

97 See F. Capotorti, 'The Protection of Minorities under Multilateral Agreements on Human Rights', IYIL (1976), pp. 2, 3; and UN Doc.E/CN.4/Sub.2/384/Add.5, (Capotorti), 20 June 1977, *paras.* 29 ff.

but would have been of universal application.[98] The draft provision was not included in the final text of the UDHR.

The Universal Declaration does not contain explicit protection for minorities but does provide for the principle of non-discrimination.[99] During its negotiation, states with significant migrant and indigenous populations, like the United States, championed individual human rights over the revival of minority guarantees.[100] They argued that the equal and effective realization of human rights norms for individuals would safeguard the identity of the members of minority groups.[101] In addition, these states maintained that cultural rights in the form of collective rights could threaten the unity and the stability of their existing national structures.[102] In response to such arguments, Lauterpacht invoked the reasoning of the Permanent Court. He countered that the cultural unity of the state must not trump the rights of minorities and thereby deny the equality intended by the principle of non-discrimination, which they championed.[103]

Article 27 of the International Covenant on Civil and Political Rights (ICCPR) is the first provision for the protection of minorities of universal application (to states parties to the Covenant).[104] Unlike the UDHR, the ICCPR includes provisions covering self-determination and the cultural rights of minorities. The ambiguous relationship that Articles 1 and 27 have with the remaining rights contained in the Covenants is partly explained by the fact that self-determination and minority protection pre-date the International Bill of Rights. Article 27 evolved from the UN General Assembly Resolution on the Fate of Minorities adopted on the same day as the Universal Declaration.[105] Its purpose is: 'towards ensuring the survival

---

98 UN Doc.A/CN.4/AC.1/3.

99 Arts. 2 and 7, UDHR, *cit. supra* note 62.

100 See UN Doc.A/C.3/SR.162, 723.

101 Some contemporary legal scholars argue that non-discrimination (Article 26, ICCPR), freedom of association (Articles 21 and 22, ICCPR), the right to take part in cultural life (Article 15, ICESCR), and other substantive rights if protected and promoted fully would make a specialist minority provision redundant. See C. Tomuschat, 'Protection of Minorities under Article 27 of the International Covenant on Civil and Political Rights', in *Völkerrecht als Rechtsordnung Internationale Gerichtsbarkeit Menschenrechte: Festschrift für Hermann Mosler* (Berlin, 1983), p. 952; and N.S. Rodley, 'Conceptual Problems in the Protection of Minorities: International Legal Developments', 17 *Human Rights Quarterly* (1995), p. 48, at pp. 54-59.

102 See P. Thornberry, *cit. supra* note 24, at p. 122; and I.L. Claude, *National Minorities: An International Problem* (Cambridge, 1955), p. 167.

103 H. Lauterpacht, *International Law and Human Rights* (London, 1950), pp. 352-353.

104 Article 5(1)(c), UNESCO Convention against Discrimination in Education, 14 November 1960, Paris, in force 22 May 1963, 429 UNTS 93, is the first binding provision of universal application for the protection of the cultural rights of persons belonging to minorities of universal application.

105 UNGA Res.217C(III), 10 December 1948, UN Doc.A/810.

and continued development of the cultural, religious and social identity of the minorities concerned ….'[106] It is a right granted over and above other rights contained within the two International Covenants, including the provisions relating to non-discrimination.[107] Although Article 27 is riddled with provisos, since its inclusion in the Covenant, it has played a crucial role in defining the cultural rights held by minorities and indigenous peoples in international law.

In an effort to limit the reach of the protection Article 27 afforded, several states insisted on the inclusion of the words: '[i]n those states in which ethnic, religious or linguistic minorities exist'.[108] However, as the Permanent Court observed in a series of inter-war decisions, the existence of a minority is a question of fact not law.[109] To allow states to define a minority group could effectively render such legal protections illusory. In its General Comment No. 23, the Human Rights Committee (HRC) which oversees the implementation of the ICCPR states that the existence of a minority within 'a given state party does not depend upon a decision by that state party but requires to be established by objective criteria'.[110]

The inclusion of the minority protection within the international human rights framework reinforced the presumption that the right holder is an individual and not the group.[111] Indeed, Article 27 refers to 'persons belonging to such minorities' and not 'minorities' *simpliciter*. In addition, the complaint mechanism contained in the Optional Protocol to the ICCPR provides standing to states or individuals but not to 'communities'.[112] The concession to the collective aspect of minority rights came with the words 'in community with other members of their group'. The HRC has repeatedly affirmed that the right of enjoyment of culture, practice of religion, or use of language can only be realized meaningfully when exercised 'in a community', that

---

106 Human Rights Committee, General Comment No. 23, UN Doc.HRI/GEN/1/Rev.1, 38 (1994), *para.* 9.

107 General Comment No. 23, *paras.* 4, 5(1) and 9.

108 See UN Doc.A/C.3/SR.1104, *para.* 23.

109 See *supra* note 26.

110 General Comment No. 23, *para.* 5(2). See also *Lovelace v Canada*, No. 24/1977, 30 July 1981, *para.* 14; and *Kitok v. Sweden*, No. 197/1985, UN Doc.A/43/40, p. 221 (1988), *para.* 9(7).

111 See UN Doc.E/CN.4/Sub.2/384/Add.2, *paras.* 125 ff.; and General Comment No. 23, *para.* 1.

112 Optional Protocol to the International Covenant on Civil and Political Rights, UNGA Res.2200A(XXI), 16 December 1966, in force 23 March 1976, 21 UN GAOR Supp. (No. 16), p. 59; UN Doc.A/6316 (1966); 999 UNTS 302; and 6 *ILM* (1967), p. 368. Nonetheless, the Committee has noted that 'in principle, [there is] no objection to a group of individuals, who claim to be similarly affected, collectively to submit a communication about the alleged breaches of their rights': *Howard v. Canada* No. 879/1999 Doc.CCPR/C/84/D/879/1999, *para.* 8.3; *Lubicon Lake Band (Bernard Ominayak) v. Canada*, No. 167/1984, UN Doc.A/45/40, Pt.2, p. 1 (1990), *para.* 32(1). Cf. J. Crawford, *cit. supra* note 58, at pp. 36-37, fn.78.

is as a group.[113] General Comment No. 23 states that Article 27 protects 'individual rights' but that the obligations owed by states are collective in nature.[114]

By contrast, the Human Rights Committee has reaffirmed consistently that the right to self-determination is held collectively.[115] In *Lubicon Lake Band (Bernard Ominayak) v. Canada*, the Committee confirmed that a people's right to self-determination and disposal of their resources was 'an essential condition for the effective guarantee and observance of individual human rights'.[116] It has also stated that effective participation in decisions relating to land and resources may be integral to protecting the right to a 'way of life' under Article 27 ICCPR.[117] But the HRC added in *Lubicon Lake Band*, that the complainant as an individual could not bring a claim under the Optional Protocol alleging that he or she was a victim of the denial of the right contained in Article 1, because self-determination was a right conferred upon peoples.[118]

There had been significant deliberation about the inclusion of the right to self-determination (and cultural development) prior to its insertion in the International Covenants. Proponents of its inclusion maintained that it was 'the cornerstone of the whole edifice of human rights'.[119] It was viewed as an essential prerequisite for other human rights, 'since there was no genuine exercise of individual rights without the realisation of the right to self-determination'.[120] Conversely, even at this early stage, it was clear that its inclusion in an instrument covering human rights would not deter its interpretation as a collectively held right. Certain members of the Third Committee maintained that the 'community itself consisted of individuals and any encroachment on its collective rights could be tantamount to a breach of fundamental freedoms'.[121]

The *travaux préparatoires* of the International Covenants reflect the notion that the right to self-determination operates on two levels: internally, it signified a

113 See *Kitok v. Sweden, cit. supra* note 110; *Lubicon Lake Band (Bernard Ominayak) v. Canada, cit. supra* note 113; and *I. Länsman v. Finland*, No. 511/1922, UN Doc.CCPR/52/D/511/1992, and No. 671/1995, UN Doc.CCPR/C/58/D/671/1995.

114 General Comment No. 23, *para.* 6(2).

115 *Ibid.*, *para.* 3(1).

116 *Lubicon Lake Band (Bernard Ominayak) v. Canada, cit. supra* note 113, at *para.* 13(3).

117 General Comment No. 23, *paras.* 3(2) and 7.

118 *Lubicon Lake Band (Bernard Ominayak) v. Canada, cit. supra* note 113, at *para.* 13(3).

119 UN GAOR, 6th session, Third Committee, 366th meeting, *para.* 26, 397th meeting, *para.* 4, and 399th meeting, *para.* 50. See J. Crawford, *cit. supra* note 58, at p. 16.

120 *Ibid.*; and UN Doc.E/CN.4/Sub.2/L.625, *paras.* 72 and 112.

121 UN GAOR, 5th session, Third Committee, 310th meeting, *para.* 35; and 311th meeting, *para.* 37.

people's right to self-government; and externally, it related to right to secession.[122] However, the drafters of the Covenants were firm in their view that the UN Charter did not extend the right of self-determination to minorities.[123] They noted that while the protection of minorities was important to international peace and security it must not 'destroy the unity of a nation or … impede the creation of that unity, in violation of national sovereignty'.[124] This position was reiterated constantly by states emerging from colonial rule and is reflected in the Declaration on Principles of International Law concerning Friendly Relations and Co-operation among states (1970 Declaration on Friendly Relations).[125]

Likewise, the Human Rights Committee has continually reiterated that 'a distinction [must be drawn] between the right to self-determination and rights protected under Article 27'..[126] Yet, in order to sidestep argument that the denial of individual claims for self-determination renders Article 1 non-justiciable, the Committee has suggested that the same facts which have been used to bring a complaint about the violation of the right to self-determination could be examined on their merits, under Article 27, in respect of denial of enjoyment of culture, language or religion of the community to which they belong.[127] The relegation of such claims from Article 1 covering self-determination to Article 27 concerning protection of minorities means they are subject to its various inbuilt qualifications.

The right contained in Article 27 is negatively conferred, with the addition of the words 'shall not be denied the right'.[128] However, UN Special Rapporteur Francesco Capotorti argued that, even if it was contained in the ICCPR, Article 27 resembled the 'economic and social' rights contained in the ICESCR that require a state to act proactively on behalf of the right holders.[129] Furthermore, he stressed that states have a responsibility to encourage and assist the cultural development

---

122 UN GAOR, 6th session, Third Committee, 397th meeting, *para.* 5; and UN Doc.E/CN.4/Sub.2/L.625, *para.* 80.

123 UN GAOR, 6th session, Third Committee, 366th meeting, *para.* 29; and UN Doc.E/CN.4/Sub.2/L.625, *para.* 77.

124 UN GAOR, 6th session, Third Committee, 397th meeting, *para.* 6; and 399th meeting, *paras.* 6 and 22.

125 1970 Friendly Relations Declaration, *cit. supra* note 63, principle (a).

126 General Comment No. 23, *para.* 3(1).

127 *Lubicon Lake Band (Bernard Ominayak) v. Canada, cit. supra* note 113, at *paras.* 32(2) and 33; and *Kitok v. Sweden, cit. supra* note 110, at *para.* 6(3).

128 UN Doc.E/447, *para.* 55; UN Doc.E/CN.4/Sub.2/351, 13-14; UN Doc.E/CN.4/Sub.2/SR.647, 158; UN Doc.E/CN.4/Sub.2/384/Add.2, *paras.* 130 ff.

129 UN Doc.E/CN.4/Sub.2/384/Add.2, *paras.* 130-136, 160-161; and UN Doc.E/CN.4/Sub.2/384/Add.5, *paras.* 24-30. See General Comment No. 23, *paras.* 6(1) and 6(2).

of minorities.[130] General Comment No. 23 also endorses the position that Article 27 imposes positive obligations on states parties.[131] In reality, the words 'shall not be denied the right' are a limitation not placed on the right to self-determination contained in Common Article 1. For instance, the HRC has held that states parties pursuing economic development which may have 'limited' impact upon the way of life of members of a minority 'will not necessarily [be in] violation of Article 27'.[132] As noted below, the potential for conflict between the national development objectives and protection of the group identity is an issue which continues to plague indigenous peoples.

## 4. Self-determination and cultural rights after 1989

The end of the Cold War forced the international community to reconsider the exclusivity it placed on the exercise of the right to self-determination and the utility of minority protection in international law. In its 2004 *Wall* Advisory Opinion, the ICJ described the right to self-determination of peoples as 'irreproachable'.[133] In support of this statement, the Court drew a trajectory from Article 22 of the Covenant of the League of Nations to Common Article 1 of the International Covenants and its own decisions from the 1970s onwards.[134] Mindful that several new states had entered the international community since 1989, the ICJ for the first time recognized 'self-determination beyond colonialism'.[135] The term 'peoples' was no longer restricted to the entire population of a given state. This development was facilitated by the proliferation of instruments concerning minorities and indigenous peoples that have reshaped the definition of the right to self-determination and rendered it more flexible and inclusive.

---

130 UN Doc.E/CN.4/Sub.2/384/Add.5, *paras.* 22-23, 34, 39 and 41. See Article 1, UNESCO Declaration of the Principles of Cultural Co-operation, adopted 4 November 1966, UNESCO Doc.14C/Resolutions, and UNESCO, *Cultural Rights as Human Rights* (Paris, 1970), p. 123.

131 General Comment No. 23, *paras.* 6(1), 6(2) and 9. Cf. R. Cholewinski, 'State Duty towards Ethnic Minorities: Positive or Negative?', 10 *Human Rights Quartelry* (1988), p. 344, at pp. 346-359.

132 *Länsman v. Finland, cit. supra* note 114 See also Separate Opinion of Mr N Ando in *Chief of the Lubicon Lake Band v Canada, cit. supra* note 113.

133 *Wall* Advisory Opinion, *cit. supra* note 2, at para. 88.

134 See *Namibia* Advisory Opinion, *cit. supra* note 64, at pp. 16, 31; *Western Sahara* Advisory Opinion, *cit. supra* note 64, pp. 12, 31-33; and *East Timor*, Judgment, *cit. supra* note 2, at p. 102, *para.* 29.

135 Separate Opinion of Judge Higgins, in *Wall* Advisory Opinion, *cit. supra* note 2, at *paras.* 29-30 (though she lamented that it was done 'without any particular legal analysis').

Except in very limited (yet-to-be delineated circumstances), the right of self-determination of peoples has become the right to internal self-determination.[136] Once again, a 'compromise' is offered by the international community to these groups whose right to self-determination is not recognized as including secession. Significantly, this has entailed the negotiations of various types of autonomy arrangements with the relevant state. These agreements invariably enumerated cultural rights to ensure that the group can maintain and develop its identity.

### *A. Minorities*

The large-scale human tragedy and instability caused by various conflicts during the 1990s led to a growing acceptance that dependence on the universal application of individual human rights alone failed to protect victims targeted because of their membership of a particular ethnic or religious community. In response, new instruments which incorporated cultural rights were finalized at the international and regional level to protect minorities. The most significant of these are the United Nations' 1992 *Declaration on the Rights of Persons Belonging to National or Ethnic, Religious and Linguistic Minorities* (UN Minorities Declaration); and the Council of Europe's 1994 *Framework Convention for National Minorities* (CE Framework Convention). On their face, these documents largely reflect the interpretative changes of existing rights which was already occurring within UN and regional human rights bodies and courts. However, peripheral documentation and related discourse has reconsidered the interrelationship between self-determination and cultural rights.

#### *1. Cultural rights and internal self-determination*

Ironically, Yugoslavia had originally co-sponsored the decades-long effort to formulate an instrument within the UN system dedicated to minority protection. The UN Minorities Declaration was finally realized in 1992, partly in response to the dismemberment of that state.[137] In its Preamble, the Declaration notes that it is inspired rather than based on Article 27 ICCPR, and therefore, is not restricted by the provision.[138] Its 2005 commentary advises that the Declaration augments other international human rights instruments 'by strengthening and clarifying

---

[136] J. Crawford, *cit. supra* note 58, at p. 25; and J. Crawford, *cit. supra* note 21, at pp. 120-121.

[137] Declaration on the Rights of Persons Belonging to National or Ethnic, Religious and Linguistic Minorities, UNGA Res. 47/135, 18 December 1992, UN Doc.A/Res/47/135; 32 *ILM* (1993), p. 911.

[138] Fourth recital, Preamble, UN Minorities Declaration, *ibid.* See P. Thornberry, 'The UN Declaration on the Rights of Persons Belonging to National or Ethnic, Religious and Linguistic Minorities: Background, Analysis, Observations and an Update', in A. Phillips and A. Rosas (eds.), *Universal Minority Rights* (Helsinki, 1995), p. 37.

those rights which make it possible for persons belonging to minorities to preserve and develop their group identity'.[139] Unlike the protection of minorities provided by the League of Nations, the UN Declaration is of universal application. However, whilst the League guarantees were legally binding, the United Nations' provisions are only declaratory.

The UN Minorities Declaration reproduces the classic binary contained in minority protection. It covers effective participation of members of the group within the relevant state; and maintenance and development of the group's identity.[140] First, it reaffirms the principle of non-discrimination and effective participation of its members in public and political life.[141] Second, cultural rights of the group are accommodated by the restatement of the wording of Article 27 ICCPR, but it does so as a positive rather than negative obligation.[142] In addition, according to the Declaration, special measures designed to meet these obligations will not prima facie offend the principle of equality contained in the UDHR.[143] The commentary insists that the safeguarding and promotion of the identity of minorities and the effective realization of their cultural rights will often require protective and proactive measures by the state.[144] Pursuant to the Declaration, states must create favourable conditions to enable members of a minority to 'express their characteristics' and 'develop their culture, language, religion, traditions and customs' where they do not violate national or international law.[145] Importantly, the 2005 commentary suggests that equitable distribution of resources, particularly state funding, must be deployed to minorities to achieve these aims.[146] This reformulation reclaims ground laid down for the protection of the cultural rights of minorities under the League of Nations abandoned after 1945.

The UN Declaration privileges individual rather than collective rights by referring to the rights of 'persons belonging to minorities'.[147] Nonetheless, it does provide

---

[139] Commentary of the Working Group on Minorities to the United Nations Declaration on the Rights of Persons Belonging to National or Ethnic, Religious and Linguistic Minorities, 4 April 2005, UN Doc.E/CN.4/Sub.2/AC.5/2005/2.

[140] The 2005 commentary notes that minority protection is based on four requirements: protection of existence; non-exclusion; non-discrimination; and non-assimilation: *ibid.*, *para.* 23.

[141] First and third recitals, Preamble and Articles 2, 3 and 4(1), 1992 UN Minorities Declaration, *cit. supra* note 138.

[142] Article 2(1), UN Minorities Declaration, *cit. supra* note 137.

[143] Article 8(3), UN Minorities Declaration, *cit. supra* note 137.

[144] UN Doc.E/CN.4/Sub.2/AC.5/2005/2, p. 8, *para.* 33.

[145] Article 4(2), UN Minorities Declaration, *cit. supra* note 137. See also UN Doc.E/CN.4/Sub.2/AC.5/2005/2, pp. 7-8, *paras.* 28-29.

[146] UN Doc.E/CN.4/Sub.2/AC.5/2005/2, p. 13, *para.* 56.

[147] Article 2, UN Minorities Declaration, *cit. supra* note 137.

a bridge between the individual right and its exercise in the collective context.[148] While the rights are granted to individuals, the duties of states extend to minorities as groups.[149] The commentary also stipulates that 'the state cannot fully implement them without ensuring adequate conditions for the existence and identity of the group as a whole'.[150]

The reluctance of states to afford minorities recognition of collective rights is driven by the same trepidation which encircles the question of self-determination. The Declaration reiterates the principles of sovereign equality, territorial integrity and political independence of states and is deliberately silent on the right to self-determination.[151] Indeed, the 2005 commentary reiterates the distinction between the right of persons belonging to minorities and the rights of peoples to self-determination.[152] It also reaffirms that the right to self-determination contained in Common Article 1 of the International Covenants 'does not apply to persons belonging to minorities'.[153]

Yet, the UN Minorities Declaration arguably lends support for the argument that minorities have a right to internal self-determination – particularly in respect of cultural and economic development.[154] Indeed, the 2005 commentary suggests that the duties of states to protect the identity of these groups are often most effectively achieved through negotiated autonomy agreements.[155] It notes that while these agreements vary from state to state, what is required are legal, administrative and territorial conditions which permit 'peace and constructive group accommodation based on equality in dignity and rights of all and which allow[] for the necessary pluralism to enable the persons belonging to the different groups to preserve their

---

148 Article 3, UN Minorities Declaration, *cit. supra* note 137. The first two drafts of the Declaration did contain collective rights in the first article covering respect for and promotion of their national, cultural linguistic and other characteristics: UN Doc.E/CN.4/L.1367/Rev.1, 2 March 1978; and UN Doc.E/CN.4/Sub.2/L.734, 2 July 1980.

149 Article 1, 1992 UN Declaration on Minorities, *cit. supra* note 138; and UN Doc.E/CN.4/Sub.2/AC.5/2005/2, p. 4, *para.* 14.

150 UN Doc.E/CN.4/Sub.2/AC.5/2005/2, p. 5, *para.* 14.

151 Article 8(4), UN Minorities Declaration, *cit. supra* note 137.

152 UN Doc.E/CN.4/Sub.2/AC.5/2005/2, p. 5, *para.* 15.

153 *Ibid.*

154 Articles 2(3) and (4) and 6, UN Minorities Declaration, *cit. supra* note 137.

155 UN Doc.E/CN.4/Sub.2/AC.5/2005/2, p. 6, *para.* 20. The UN Working Group on Minorities is currently preparing a General Comment on the relationship between autonomy and self-determination. See Report of the Working Group on Minorities on its Ninth Session, UN Doc.E/CN.4/Sub.2/2003/19, *para.* 39. See Minorities and Self-Determination, Working Paper presented by Jose Bengoa, UN Doc.E/CN.4/Sub.2/AC.5/2004/WP.1 (advocates a diverse approach to exercising the right to self-determination without threatening the fragmentation of existing states).

identity.'[156] It is also important to recall that Article 27 is contained in the International Covenant on Civil and Political Rights. These trends reflect an appreciation that the civil and political, and economic, social and cultural rights must operate effectively and interdependently to ensure the protection of group identity and of the rights of its members. While several states have negotiated such arrangements, the commentary notes that the declaration does not require states to establish them.[157]

Significantly, the 2005 commentary intimates that minorities may be entitled to exercise the right to external self-determination in certain circumstances:

> If participation is denied to a minority and its members, this might in some cases give rise to a legitimate claim to self-determination. ...The Declaration neither limits nor extends the rights to self-determination that peoples have under other parts of international law.[158]

Former Chairperson and Rapporteur of the UN Working Group on Minorities, Asbjørn Eide has noted that if states seek to avail themselves of the principle of state sovereignty and territorial integrity, they must adhere to other elements of United Nations law, including the respect for democracy and human rights inside their states.[159] This view arises from an interpretation of the so-called 'safeguard' clause contained in the 1970 UN Friendly Relations Declaration which reaffirms the applicability of territorial integrity or political unity of states:

> ...conducting themselves in compliance with the principle of equal rights and self-determination of peoples as described above and thus possessed of a government representing the whole people belonging to the territory without distinction as to race, creed or colour.[160]

This wording, in a slightly modified form, was replicated in the final declaration of the United Nations World Conference on Human Rights held in Vienna in 1993; and expanded by the Secretary-General's High Level Panel Report on Threats, Challenges and Change delivered in 2004.[161] In the *Quebec Secession* case, the

---

156 UN Doc.E/CN.4/Sub.2/AC.5/2005/2, p. 4, *para.* 13.

157 *Ibid*, *para.* 20.

158 *Ibid*, pp. 5-6, *paras.* 15, 19 and 20. See also UN Doc.E/CN.4/Sub.2/AC.5/2000/WP.1, *paras.* 18-21, 91.

159 A. Eide, 'United Nations Standards on Minorities and Group Accommodation', 23 *Thesaurus Acroasium* (1999), p. 543, at pp. 545-546.

160 Principle 5, *para.* 7 of the UNGA Res.2625(XXV), Annex, 24 October 1970 (emphasis added). See also K. Knop, *cit. supra* note 22, at pp. 75-79.

161 United Nations World Conference on Human Rights, Vienna Declaration and Programme of Action, 25 June 1993, 32 *ILM* (1993), p. 1661, p. 1665; and Secretary-General's High Level Panel Report on Threats, Challenges and Change, *A More Secure World: Our Shared Responsibility,* 2 December 2004, UN Doc.A/59/565 (2004), *paras.* 29 and 30.

Canadian Supreme Court found that this requirement was 'normally fulfilled through internal self-determination – a people's pursuit of its political, economic, social and cultural development within the framework of an existing state'.[162] The Court also considered that the safeguard clause may justify the exercise of external self-determination or secession 'when a people is blocked from the meaningful exercise of its right to self-determination internally, it is entitled, as a last resort, to exercise it by secession'.[163] Crawford has noted that if self-determination is defined in respect of a process rather than the attainment of independence, then it is usually realized through the enjoyment of civil, political and social rights within a state, which if denied could raise issues of international concern.[164]

The more than faint echo of the *Åland Islands* case is arguably no mere coincidence. The various upheavals experienced during the 1990s put the international community on notice that fragmentation of states and international peace and stability could be threatened by the denial, not the recognition, of the unique identity and cultural rights of minorities.[165] The 1992 UN Minorities Declaration states that the protection of minorities is the concern of the international community and it 'contribute[s] to the political and social stability of states in which they live'.[166] Christian Tomuschat has noted that while state practice does not currently support such a customary rule, the protracted multilateral efforts to resolve the question of Kosovo's final status may break new ground in this area.[167] The possible granting of autonomy to Kosovo may be viewed as a response to the existence of a blockage of the kind described by the Canadian Supreme Court. Equally, the international community will only permit its inhabitants to exercise self-determination on conditional acceptance of minority guarantees including protection of cultural rights and cultural heritage.[168]

### 2. *Conditional recognition revisited*

The acceptance of minority protection into domestic law as a condition of recognition of statehood has had a long and fraught history in international law.[169] Recognition

---

162 (1998) 115 *ILR*, p. 536, at p. 582.

163 *Ibid*, pp. 586-587.

164 J. Crawford, *cit. supra* note 28, at p. 40.

165 J. Symonides, *cit. supra* note 1, at p. 146.

166 Fifth and seventh recitals, Preamble, UN Minorities Declaration, *cit. supra* note 137.

167 C. Tomuschat, 'International Law: Ensuring the Survival of Mankind on the Eve of a New Century: General Course on Public International Law', 281 *Recueil des Cours* (1999), p. 9, at pp. 253-254, *paras.* 19-20.

168 See UN Security Council Resolution 1244 of 10 June 1999; Rambouillet Accords: Interim Agreement for Peace and Self-Government in Kosovo, 7 June 1999, UN. Doc.S/1999/648; and Council of the European Union decision of 30 January 2006 (2005/56/EC).

169 See P. Thornberry, *cit. supra* note 24, at pp. 32-37.

was irrevocable once a state had entered the international community and other principles came into play including non-interference and territorial integrity which stymie criticism of its 'internal' affairs.[170] However, there appears to have been a revival of conditional recognition on a regional level in Europe since the 1990s. Following the dismantling of the USSR and Yugoslavia, the European Community adopted declarations covering conditions for the recognition of the emerging states which included respect for human rights; 'guarantees for the rights of ethnic and national groups and minorities'; and inviolability of territorial boundaries.[171]

The Declaration on 'Guidelines on the Recognition of New States in Eastern Europe and in the Soviet Union' proscribed that the minority guarantees to be adhered to by these states were those set by the Conference on Security and Co-operation in Europe.[172] The Organisation for Security and Cooperation in Europe (OSCE) (formerly the Conference on Security and Co-operation in Europe) in its 1989 Vienna Concluding Document requires participating states to ensure that minorities on their territory can 'maintain and develop their own culture in all its aspects, including language, literature and religion; and that they can preserve their cultural and historical monuments and objects'.[173] It recognizes collective rights and the need to provide different treatment for minorities so they can preserve their identity. Its Copenhagen Document enunciates a broad statement on minority rights which encompasses participation rights, the relations between official and minority languages, the prohibition of forced assimilation, maintenance of organizations and associations, and membership of the group.[174]

---

170 See L. Oppenheim, *International Law: A Treatise*, in R.F. Roxburgh (ed.) (3rd ed, London, 1920), Vol. I, p. 136.

171 Declaration on Yugoslavia, Brussels, 16 December 1991, 31 *ILM* (1992), p. 1485; and Declaration on 'Guidelines on the Recognition of New states in Eastern Europe and in the Soviet Union', Brussels, 16 December 1991, 31 *ILM* (1992), p. 1486. The arbitral commission established by the European Community Conference for Peace in Yugoslavia stated that the new states were subjected to minority protections not because of treaty obligations which they consented to but because they were *jus cogens*: Conference on Yugoslavia, Arbitration Commission, *Opinion No. 1*, 31 *ILM* (1992), p. 1494, at p. 1496; and *Opinion* No. *2*, 31 *ILM* (1992), p. 1497, at p. 1498. The findings of the arbitration commission have been heavily criticised: for summary see K. Knop, *cit. supra* note 22, at p. 175 ff.

172 See T. Grant, 'The Recognition of States: Law and Practice in Debate and Evolution' (Westport, 1999), Chapter 4; V.-Y. Ghebali, 'La CSCE et la question des minorities nationals', in A. Liebich and A. Regler (eds.), *L'Europe Centrale et ses Minorités: vers une solution Européenne?* (Paris, 1993), pp. 51-72; and J. Helgesen, 'Protecting Minorities in the Conference on Security and Cooperation in Europe (CSCE)', in A. Rosas and J. Heglesen (eds.), *The Strength of Diversity* (London, 1992), p. 159-186.

173 CSCE, Concluding Document of the Vienna Meeting, 17 January 1989, *para.* 59.

174 Document for the Copenhagen Meeting of the Conference on the Human Dimension of the OSCE, 1990, *paras.* 32 and 33; 29 *ILM* (1990), p. 1306. See P. Thornberry and M.A. Martín Estébanez, *Minority Rights in Europe: A Review of the Work and Standards of the Council*

Somewhat ironically, the European Union (EU) does not have a legally-binding instrument covering minority rights and does not require its existing members to adhere to such protections. Nonetheless, all members of the Union are signatories to the European Convention on Human Rights and Fundamental Freedoms (ECHR).[175] This Convention does not refer to cultural rights; but it does prohibit discrimination on various grounds.[176] Subsequent efforts to insert some form of minority protection via an additional protocol met with limited success.[177] An initiative to draft an additional protocol covering individual rights in the cultural field has been suspended indefinitely. Nonetheless, with the accession of states from Central and Eastern Europe in the late 1980s and early 1990s, there has been an emphasis on developing minority protection standards to be adhered to by prospective members of Europe's regional organizations. The European Union has developed significant policies on minorities in its external relations particularly with potential new member states.[178] For example, the Copenhagen Criteria for Membership adopted by the European Council in 1993 require candidate countries to show that they have established respect and protection for minorities.[179]

---

*of Europe* (Strasbourg, 2004), p. 17; M.A. Martín Estébanez, 'Minority Protection and the Organisation for Security and Cooperation in Europe', in P. Cumper and S. Wheatley (eds.), *Minority Rights in the New Europe* (The Hague, 1999), pp. 33-34; and the Lund Recommendations on the Effective Participation of National Minorities in Public Life and Explanatory Note, Foundation in Inter-Ethnic Relations, September 1999, available at <www.osce.org/documents/hcnm/1999/09/2698_en.pdf>.

175 Rome, 4 November 1950, in force 3 September 1953, CETS No. 005.

176 Article 14 which refers to 'association with a national minority' was only applicable in combination with another provision of the ECHR until the adoption of Protocol No. 12, on 4 November 2000, in force 1 April 2005, CETS No. 177.

177 CE, Consultative Assembly, Doc.1002, 30 April 1959; and CE, Consultative Assembly, Doc.1299, 26 April 1961. Consultative Assembly Recommendation 285, 28 April 1961 contained the following draft minority provision:

> Persons belonging to a national minority shall not be denied the right, in community with the other members of their group, and as far as compatible with public order, to enjoy their own culture, to use their own language, to establish their schools and receive teaching in the language of their choice or to profess and practise their own religion.

See M. Lannung, 'The Rights of Minorities', in *Mélanges offerts à Polys Modinos, Problèmes des droits de l'homme et de l'unification Européenne* (Paris, 1968), pp. 181-195.

178 See B. Brandtner and A. Rosas, 'Human Rights and the External Relations of the European Community: An Analysis of Doctrine and Practice' *EJIL* (1998), p. 468.

179 See M. Nowak, 'The Copenhagen Political Criteria for Accession to the EU', in P. Alston, M. Bustelo and J. Heenan (eds.), *The EU and Human Rights* (Oxford, 1999), p. 687, at pp. 691-692; A. Biscoe, 'The European Union and Minority Nations', in P. Cumper and S. Wheatley, *Minority Rights in the 'New' Europe* (The Hague, 1999), p. 89, at p. 98; and G. Pentassuglia, *Minorities in International Law* (Strasbourg, 2002), Chapter VII.

The Framework Convention for the Protection of National Minorities, adopted by the Council of Europe on November 1994, is the first binding multilateral instrument dealing exclusively with minority protection.[180] This document is intended to set specific legal standards in respect of minority protection and thereby complement the work of the OSCE.[181] The *travaux* tend to support an interpretation that the document gives rise to positive obligations.[182] However, it is a statement of principles rather than enforceable rights; it is not subject to judicial oversight, instead its implementation is monitored by the Committee of Ministers.[183] Most European states remain reticent about the adoption of legally binding minority guarantees because of their ongoing concerns that claims for cultural autonomy would eventually lead to secession claims.[184] Not surprisingly, the Framework Convention refers to 'persons belonging to national minorities' rather than 'minorities' *simpliciter.* This carries with it a twofold restriction. The explanatory report states that not 'all ethnic, cultural, linguistic or religious differences necessarily lead to the creation of national minorities'.[185] In addition, there was an explicit rejection of the recognition of collective rights.[186] Yet, the Council of Europe had previously adopted a series of recommendations which explicitly recognized that collective rights of minorities 'to maintain and develop their culture'; 'to maintain their own educational, religious and cultural institutions'; and 'to participate fully in decision making about matters which affect the preservation and development of their identity and in the implementation of those decisions'.[187]

### *B. Indigenous peoples*

Indigenous peoples reject their categorization as 'minorities' arguing that their plight is distinguishable because of differing historical circumstances. They stress that their colonial occupation or foreign domination did not cease with decolonization. Yet, the present-day articulation of cultural rights applicable to indigenous peoples

---

180 1 February 1995, in force 1 February 1998, CETS No. 157.

181 Council of Europe, Framework Convention for the Protection of Minorities and Explanatory Report, (Strasbourg, November 1994), H(94) 10, *para.* 4.

182 CE Doc. CAHMIN(94)28, September 1994, p. 28; and CE Doc. Explanatory report, No. 180, at para. 52.

183 CE Doc. Explanatory report, No. 180, at *paras.* 6 and 93-97.

184 See H. Klebes, 'The Council of Europe's Framework Convention for the Protection of National Minorities', *HRLJ* (1995), p. 92; and B. Vukas, 'International Protection of Minorities: Limits to Growth', 23 *Thesaurus Acroasium* (1999), p. 21, at p. 29.

185 CE Doc. Explanatory report, No. 180, at *para.* 43.

186 Article 3(2), Framework Convention, *cit. supra* note 180; and CE Doc. Explanatory Report, No. 180, at p. 201, para. 13; and CE Doc. CAHMIN(94)5, January 1994, p. 3.

187 PACE Recommendation 1134 (1990), *para.* 11. See also PACE Recommendation 1201 (1993), Annex.

in international instruments borrows heavily from Article 27 ICCPR. Since the 1970s, indigenous campaigns have engaged not only minority protection but non-discrimination, human rights, self-determination, historic sovereignty and existing treaties to have their rights recognized at the international and domestic levels.[188] Whatever the basis of these claims, self-determination is usually defined as their 'foundational' premise.[189] While there is greater acceptance of the right of indigenous peoples to self-determination compared to its outright rejection in respect of minorities, what that right entails remains a matter of heated contention and negotiation.

Former Chairperson of the Working Group on Indigenous Populations, Erica-Irene Daes, has argued that: '[I]ndigenous peoples is an important field of study for all ... students of international law and human rights, precisely because it tests the limited assumptions of familiar theories and principles.'[190] Indeed, the negotiations concerning the leading instruments in the field – the International Labour Organization Convention (No. 169 of 1989) concerning Indigenous and Tribal Peoples in Independent Countries (ILO 169) and the draft UN Declaration on the Rights of Indigenous Peoples – have been a lesson in recalibrating the interrelatedness between self-determination and cultural rights in international law.

In its preamble, the International Labour Organization Convention (No. 169 of 1989) concerning Indigenous and Tribal Peoples in Independent Countries recognizes:

> [T]he *aspirations* of these peoples to exercise control over their own institutions, ways of life and economic development and to maintain and develop their identities, languages and religions, *within the framework of the states in which they live.*[191]

The Convention expressly qualifies its use of the term 'peoples' to allay the anxieties of various states by noting that it should not be construed as implying rights under international law, vis-à-vis, external self-determination.[192] ILO 169 presumes that indigenous and tribal peoples will continue as distinctive components of the state, and that governments will deal with them in accordance with the standards laid

---

188 See B. Kingsbury, 'Reconciling Five Competing Conceptual Structures of Indigenous Peoples' Rights in International and Comparative Law', *NYU JIL* & P (2001), p. 189; and General Comment No. 23, *paras.* 3(2) and 7.

189 See S.J. Anaya, *Indigenous Peoples in International Law* (New York, 1996), p. 75 ff.

190 I.-E. Daes, 'The International Protection of Indigenous Peoples at the Regional and Global Levels', 33 *Thesaurus Acroasium* (1994), at p. 70, *para.* 173.

191 Fifth recital, Preamble, ILO No. 169, 27 June 1989, in force 5 September 1991, 1650 UNTS 383; and 28 *ILM* (1989), p. 1382 (emphasis added).

192 Article 1(3), ILO No. 169, *cit. supra* note 189. See K. Knop, *cit. supra* note 22, at pp. 237-242.

down in it. These standards relate largely to economic, social and cultural matters which are within the remit of the International Labour Organization. Unlike the 1992 UN Minorities Declaration, ILO 169 acknowledges the collective right of indigenous and tribal peoples to preserve and develop their cultural identity.[193] Even though it is highly qualified, the Convention is currently the only multilateral treaty to recognize collective rights and therefore continues to be 'the reference for many indigenous peoples, states and intergovernmental organizations'.[194] The Convention together with the ILO implementation mechanisms have been influential in drafting (and in some cases explicitly invoked) in recent agreements between indigenous peoples and various states protecting indigenous identity and guaranteeing cultural rights.[195]

The UN Working Group on Indigenous Populations (WGIP) agreed on the final text of the draft UN Declaration on the Rights of Indigenous Peoples (draft UN Declaration) in 1993.[196] The draft declaration was then renegotiated within the working group established by the Commission on Human Rights and this draft was approved by the UN Council on Human Rights in mid-2006 but is yet to be approved by the General Assembly.[197] The drafts acknowledges the right of self-determination of all peoples in their Preamble; and makes specific reference to the UN Charter and the two International Covenants. For indigenous organizations, the right to self-determination is the foundation of the document.[198] They maintained that the

193 See Articles 2(2)(b) and (c), 4, 5, 7, 23, 26-31, ILO No. 169.

194 Report of the Secretary-General on the preliminary review by the Coordinator of the International Decade of the World's Indigenous Peoples on the activities of the United Nations system in relation to the Decade, 24 June 2004, UN Doc.E/2004/82, *para.* 65.

195 See Actions and Measures for Chiapas: Joint Commitments and Proposals, and related agreements (San Andrés de Larráinzar Agreements), Mex.-Chiapas-Ejército zapaist de liberación nacional (EZLN), 16 February 1996, available at <www.usip.org/library/pa.html>, in particular, Joint Proposals that the Federal Government and the Ezin Agree to Remit to the National Debating and Decision-Making Bodies in Accordance with Paragraph 1.4 of the Rules of Procedure; Agreement on Identity and Rights of Indigenous Peoples, 31 March 1995, Guatemala-URNG, UN Doc.A/49/882-S/1995/256, 36 ILM (1997), p. 285, available at <www.usip.org/library/pa/guatemala/guat_950331.html>; and in respect of the peace agreements between the Government of Nepal and Communist Party of Nepal (Maoist), see O. Gurung and S. Webster (eds.), *Proceedings of the National Dialogue Conference on Promotion of the ILO Convention No. 169 on Indigenous and Tribal Peoples and Peace Building in Nepal* (Nepal, 2005). I am indebted to Christine Bell for providing this information.

196 Approved 26 August 1994, UN Doc.E/CN.4/Sub.2/Res/1994/56; and 34 *ILM* (1995), p. 541.

197 UN Council on Human Rights resolution 2006/2 of 29 June 2006, Annex. On 28 November 2006, the Third Committee deferred its adoption by the General Assembly to 'allow time for further consultation.' See UN Doc.A/61/448, p. 25.

198 UN Doc.E/CN.4/1998/106, pp.9-10, *para.* 44; and S. Pritchard, *Setting International Standards: An Analysis of the UN Declaration on the Rights of Indigenous Peoples and the First Six Sessions of the Commission on Human Rights Working Group* (3rd edn, Sydney, 2001), pp. 52-58.

recognition of their collective right to self-determination is a prerequisite to their full enjoyment of all human rights, including cultural rights.[199]

The consistent apprehension of some national delegations to the application of the term 'indigenous peoples' arises from their concern that the international community may sanction a right to secession, resulting in the fragmentation of existing states.[200] Certain states have reasserted that Article 3 of the 1993 draft, which replicates Common Article 1 of the ICESCR and ICCPR and specifically applies it to indigenous peoples, goes 'beyond existing international and national law and practice in that the right to self-determination had to be placed in the historical context of decolonisation'.[201] While other states, like Australia and the United States, support the inclusion of the right to self-determination in the draft UN Declaration, they argue that indigenous communities – like all other peoples in independent states with representative governments – have a right to self-determination, not a right to statehood.[202] They define this right in a manner consistent with the rights arising under the UN Minorities Declaration. They contend that indigenous peoples have a right to participate in national affairs on an equal basis with other citizens; and the right to preserve and develop their distinct cultural identity 'with a power to take decisions over their own affairs'.[203] Indeed, the US delegation insisted that, because international law recognised individual human rights only, the draft should reflect the terminology of the 1992 UN Minorities Declaration, that is 'persons belonging to indigenous groups' instead of 'indigenous peoples'.[204]

Indigenous peoples have rejected vigorously the application of the term 'minorities' to their communities by states because it downplays the ongoing effects of colonial occupation on their present circumstances.[205] Indigenous representatives

---

199 UN Doc.E/CN.4/1996/84, *para.* 51.

200 *Ibid.*, *paras.* 38 and 44. See also UN Doc.E/CN.4/Sub.2/1993/26/Add.1, *para.* 4. See Special Rapporteur José Martínez Cobo, Study of the Problem of Discrimination against Indigenous Populations, UN Doc.E/CN.4/Sub.2/1986/7/Add.4 *para.* 379.

201 UN Doc.E/CN.4/1996/84, *para.* 43.

202 L.-E. Chávez, Report of the Working Group Established in Accordance with CHR Res.1995/32, Fifth Session, 6 December 1999, UN Doc.E/CN.4/2000/84, *paras.* 49, 50 and 62; Eighth Session, 6 January 2003, UN Doc.E/CN.4/2003/92, *paras.* 22 and 24; Ninth Session, 7 January 2004, UN Doc.E/CN.4/2004/81, *para.* 68; and UN Doc.E/CN.4/2004/WG.15/CRP.1, p. 5. See J. Crawford, *cit. supra* note 21, at p. 7; and M.C. Lâm, 'Indigenous Peoples' Conception of Their Self-Determination in International Law', in C. Lynch and M. Loriaux (eds.), *Law and Moral Action in World Politics* (Minneapolis, 2000), p. 205.

203 UN Doc.E/CN.4/1996/84, *para.* 43; UN Doc.E/CN.4/1999/82, *para.* 40, and E/CN.4/2003/92, *para.* 22 (United States); and, UN Doc.E/CN.4/1995/WG.15/2/Add.2, *para.* 12 (Australia).

204 UN Doc.E/CN.4/1999/82, *para.* 40. See response of indigenous representatives: UN Doc.E/CN.4/2001/85, Annex II.

205 See A. Eide and E.-I. Daes, Working Paper on the Relationship and distinction between the Rights of Persons Belonging to Minorities and Those of Indigenous Peoples, 19 July 2000,

and some states suggest that 'the gaining of national independence by a state through decolonization does not extinguish the applicability of the right of self-determination of indigenous peoples'.[206] Former WGIP Chairperson Erica-Irene Daes observed that self-determination had acquired 'a new meaning in the post-colonial era'.[207] She draws a distinction between internal and external self-determination. She notes that while indigenous claims relate to internal self-determination, the situation would alter when 'a state may abuse … this right of its citizens so grievously and irreparably that the situation is tantamount to classical colonialism, and may have the same legal consequences'.[208] Indigenous representatives reject the term 'internal self-determination' as having no basis in international law.[209] Rather, indigenous organizations viewed self-determination as a process, involving a renegotiation of political, economic, social and cultural arrangements with states to provide an agreed form of autonomy.[210] The 2006 draft includes the right to 'autonomy or self-government in matters relating to their internal and local affairs'.[211] Daes acknowledged that existing states have a duty through constitutional reform to 'accommodate' the aspirations of indigenous peoples for democratic power-sharing.[212] The current draft recognizes that 'indigenous peoples have the right to freely determine their

---

UN Doc.E/CN.4/Sub.2/2000/10; R. Barsh, 'Indigenous Peoples: An Emerging Object of International Law', *AJIL* (1986), p. 369, at pp. 373-374; and H. Hannum, *Autonomy, Sovereignty and Self-Determination: The Accommodation of Conflicting Rights* (Philadelphia, 1990), pp. 88-91.

206 UN Doc.E/CN.4/1996/84, *para.* 43.

207 E.-I. Daes, Explanatory Note concerning the Draft Declaration on the Rights of Indigenous Peoples, 19 July 1993, UN Doc.E/CN.4/Sub.2/1993/26/Add.1, *para.* 23.

208 *Ibid.*, *para.* 23.

209 UN Doc.E/CN.4/2000/84, *paras.* 43-47; UN Doc.E/CN.4/2001/85, *para.* 78; and UN Doc.E/CN.4/2003/92, *para.* 24. See K. Knop, *cit. supra* note 22, at pp. 255-274.

210 See UN Doc.E/CN.4/1996/84, *para.* 43; E.-I. Daes, 'Some Considerations on the Rights of Indigenous Peoples to Self-Determination', *Transnat'l L. & Contemp. Probs.* (1993), p. 3, at p. 5; and B. Kingsbury, 'Reconciling Five Competing Conceptual Structures of Indigenous Peoples' Claims to International and Comparative Law', in P. Alston (ed.), *Peoples' Rights* (Oxford, 2001), p. 69, at p. 87 ff.

211 Article 4, 2006 draft UN Declaration, *cit. supra* note 194. Article 31 of the 1993 draft, *cit. supra* note 196, stated:

> Indigenous peoples, as a specific form of exercising their right to self-determination, have the right to autonomy or self-government in matters relating to their internal and local affairs, including culture, religion, education, information, media, health, housing, employment, social welfare, economic activities, land and resource management, environment and entry by non-members, as well as ways and means for financing these autonomous functions.

212 UN Doc.E/CN.4/Sub.2/1993/26/Add.1, *para.* 25. See Twelfth recital, Preamble, 1993 draft UN Declaration, *cit. supra* note 196.

relationships with States in a spirit of coexistence, mutual benefit and full respect'.[213] Indeed, states like Australia, Canada and the United States which are ambivalent about the inclusion of self-determination in the draft declaration, have adopted various measures granting a measure of autonomy to indigenous peoples within their territory.[214]

Whereas the international community has consistently stated that minority protection is provided as an alternative for those groups which, for whatever reasons, are not afforded the right to self-determination, indigenous peoples inextricably tie such cultural rights to the right to self-determination.[215] Under the 1993 draft, Part III containing Articles 12 to 14 had previously been titled 'cultural rights' and it corresponded to the typology of Article 27 ICCPR:[216] extrapolated to reflect the concerns of indigenous peoples, Article 12 covered enjoyment of culture; Article 13 concerns profession and practise of religion; and Article 14 related to use of language. Transformed into Articles 11 to 13 of the 2006 draft, those parts of the provisions relating to 'self-determination' in respect of these cultural rights were not contested by state delegations. In addition, related provisions covering education, media, land, resources and cultural heritage reinforce these cultural rights and through the inclusion of terms like 'control' strengthen indigenous claims to autonomy with respect to cultural matters.[217]

This trend is further elaborated upon by the draft Principles and Guidelines for the Protection of the Heritage of Indigenous Peoples, presented by Daes in 1995. They state that the protection of indigenous peoples' heritage can only be effective if it is based 'broadly on the principle of self-determination'.[218] Indigenous representatives emphasize the importance of the collective nature of self-determination and development, including cultural development, in reversing 'the impact of racism on the expression of indigenous identity'.[219] This extension of the notion of

---

213 13th preambular recital, 2006 draft Declaration, *cit. supra* note 197.

214 See M. Langton et al. (eds.), *Settling with Indigenous Peoples: Modern Treaty and Agreement Making* (Sydney, 2006); and 'Agreements, Treaties and Negotiated Settlements with Indigenous Peoples in Settler States: Their Role and Relevance for Indigenous and other Australians', available at <www.atns.net.au>.

215 UN Doc.E/CN.4/2001/85, *para.* 151.

216 See Technical Review of the United Nations Draft Declaration on the Rights of Indigenous Peoples: Note by the Secretariat, UN Doc.E/CN.4/Sub.2/1994/2, *para.* 48.

217 See Articles 14, 16, 26 and 31, draft 2006 Declaration, *cit. supra* note 197.

218 Protection of the heritage of indigenous people. Final Report of the Special Rapporteur, Mrs Erica-Irene Daes, UN Doc.E/CN.4/Sub.2/1995/26, Annex. However, Daes explained that: '[P] rinciple 2 did not use the principle of self-determination in the same broad sense as in article 3 of the draft United Nations declaration on the rights of indigenous peoples': UN Doc.E/ CN.4/Sub.2/2000/26, *para.* 19.

219 UN Doc.E/CN.4/2002,98, *para.* 34.

self-determination as a process, which was articulated during the decolonization period, is incorporated in the redrafted Principles and Guidelines on the Heritage of Indigenous Peoples, tabled in 2005. The 2005 draft states that the protection of the cultural heritage of indigenous peoples shall be 'based on the right to self-determination of all peoples, including indigenous peoples, which includes indigenous peoples' right to sovereignty over the natural resources in their territories'.[220] Consequently, it stresses that, like other resources, indigenous peoples' cultural heritage, including traditional knowledge and cultural expressions, must not be exploited without their free, prior and informed consent.[221] This emphasis is reflected in recent UN and UNESCO instruments that provide some measure of participation by indigenous peoples in state decision-making which impacts upon their cultural heritage;[222] and in the reshaping of the UN Millennium Development Goals to incorporate indigenous concerns, including those related to identity.[223]

## 5. Conclusion

Since its emergence in international discourse during the early 20th century, the notion of peoples determining their own fate has gradually and indelibly permeated international law. However, because of the realities on the ground, it has been equally clear from the outset that self-determination did not necessarily mean that the international community would condone secession in each and every case. Rosalyn Higgins wrote in 1963: 'if the international order is not to be reduced to a

---

220 Expanded working paper submitted by Yozo Yokota and the Saami Council on the substantive proposals on the draft principles and guidelines on the heritage of indigenous peoples, UN Doc.E/CN.4/Sub.2/AC.4/2005/3.

221 Review of the draft principles and guidelines on the heritage of indigenous peoples, prepared by Yozo Yokota and the Saami Council, UN Doc.E/CN.4/Sub.2/AC.4/2004/5, *para.* 19. The requirement of free, prior and informed consent is incorporated into Article 16, ILO No. 169. See also Expanded working paper submitted by Mrs. Antoanella-Iulia Motoc and the Tebtebba Foundation offering guidelines to govern the practice of Implementation of the principle of free, prior and informed consent of indigenous peoples in relation to development affecting their lands and natural resources, 14 July 2005, UN Doc.E/CN.4/Sub.2/AC.4/2005/WP.1.

222 Including Article 8(j), Convention on Biological Diversity, Rio de Janeiro, 5 May 1992, in force 29 December 1993, 1760 UNTS 79; 31 *ILM* (1992), p. 818; Article 11(b), Convention for the Safeguarding of the Intangible Cultural Heritage, Paris, 17 October 2003, UNESCO Doc.32C/Resolution 32; and the Revised Operational Guidelines for the Implementation of the World Heritage Convention, 2 February 2005, UNESCO Doc.WHC-05/2.

223 See Information received from the UN System, Note by the Secretariat, Addendum, Indigenous Peoples and the Millennium Development Goals, 28 March 2005, UN Doc.E/C.19/2005/4/Add.13; and International Expert Group Meeting on the Millennium Development Goals, Indigenous Participation and Good Governance, New York, 11-13 January 2006, UNESCO Contribution, PFII/2006/WS.3/6.

fragmented chaos' then the following question needed to be addressed: '[T]o what unit does the concept of self-determination apply?' Her solution was straightforward: '[I]t is necessary to start with stable boundaries and to permit political change within them'.[224] But the international community has been aware that participation in political and civil processes alone is not always an effective protection for the diverse identities of groups within states. Indeed, various 'compromises' have been provided to placate those groups denied statehood and to minimize the potential for 'fragmented chaos.' These compromises have invariably included provisions covering the cultural rights of members of the group.

A legacy of decolonization and the end of the Cold War for international law is an appreciation that self-determination is a process, and not a right extinguished upon independence. This realization has significant implications for its inter-relation with cultural rights, also. If self-determination is a process then it is to be realized through political, civil, social and cultural rights within a state which ensures effective participation of all inhabitants and the distinct identity of its constituent groups. The arrangements may entail the granting of extensive autonomy to groups in respect of economic, social and cultural matters. However, should there be gross violation or denial of these rights, then it becomes a matter of international concern and is no longer confined to the internal affairs of the state. In such cases, the exercise of self-determination as secession becomes the ultimate mechanism for protecting group identity and the cultural rights of its members.

---

[224] R. Higgins, *The Development of International Law through the Political Organs of the UN* (London, 1963), p. 104. See also A. Cassese, 'The International Court of Justice and the Rights of Peoples to Self-Determination', in V. Lowe and M. Fitzmaurice (eds.), *Fifty Years of the International Court of Justice: Essays in Honour of Sir Robert Jennings* (Cambridge, 1996), p. 351.

# 4
# Cultural Rights: A Necessary Corrective to the Nation State

*William K. Barth**

This chapter examines the history of the international minority regime and discusses its implications for normative questions raised by political theorists on multiculturalism. In this chapter, I briefly review how the establishment of nation states sometime antagonizes certain minority groups. I conclude that the minority regime is a necessary corrective for these states.

## 1. Cultural rights

I use the terms cultural rights and minority rights interchangeably. However, some clarification is necessary in order to distinguish the context of these two different terminologies. Cultural rights comprise an aspect of human rights in that they are universal in character and guarantee all persons the right to access their culture. The United Nations' minority regime only grants cultural protection to qualified classes of persons, that is, national, ethnic (inclusive of race), linguistic, and religious minority groups. One of the main UN human rights treaties, namely, the 1966 International Covenant on Civil and Political Rights (ICCPR), identifies three of these particular minority group classifications (not mentioning national minorities) as a response to the prevailing state structures which are controlled by a dominant national group.[1] Because most states maintain a national, as opposed to a civic, character, sub-dominant groups require treaty protection.

---

* This article is based on research for Dr. Barth's D.Phil. thesis in Politics entitled 'On Cultural Rights: The Equality of Nations and the Minority Legal Tradition'.

1 *International Covenant on Civil and Political Rights, 1966,* Article 27, 999 UNTS 171; *Declaration on the Rights of Persons Belonging to National or Ethnic, Religious and Linguistic Minorities,* Resolution by the General Assembly, Forty-Seventh Session, UN Document A/RES/47/135, 3 February 1993. As indicated in the name of the instrument, this declaration also covers national minorities.

Francioni and Scheinin (eds), *Cultural Human Rights*, 79–90
 ISBN 978 90 04 16294 5. Printed in the Netherlands.

The world's states were responsible for two world wars in the 20th century that resulted in human death tolls in excess of 50 million persons, as well as repeated forcible assimilation, denationalization, and genocidal campaigns. This record of state practices provides the UN with justification for establishing a corrective, namely, the minority regime. So, while cultural rights are universal in character, they are applied by international instruments to four sub-dominant classes, that is, national, ethnic, religious, and linguistic minorities. These classifications are related to that aspect of state practices that is responsible for the fact of creating minority groups, namely, control of the state's apparatus by a dominating national group.

Several writers conclude that political thinkers should not accept the structure or existence of the nation state and should reformulate their ideas of statecraft in terms of sub-national and super-national structures so as to develop a form of liberal nationalism.[2] For example, Margaret Canovan writes that theorists 'should acknowledge their reliance upon their idea of the nation-state and not take the nation-state for granted', because nation states are not established by liberal democratic means.[3] Asbjørn Eide, former Chair of the United Nations' Working Group on Minorities, writes that the purpose of a minority regime is to liberalize the nation state

> [into] a civic nation which allows for double identity and loyalty: to the civic nation as a whole, respecting the common legal code with particular emphasis on equality and non-discrimination in the common domain, and at the same time to maintain one's identity to separate ethnic, religious or linguistic groups.[4]

Protecting an individual's access to culture is the essence of a cultural right because it goes to the interiority of personhood. There is no disagreement amongst political theorists that access to culture is necessary to develop the individual capacity for autonomy. Joseph Raz, for example, explains that only by being socialized in a culture can one tap the options that give human life meaning. Individual freedom depends on options that rely on rules which constitute those options. Culture is fundamental to individual autonomy because it provides a conglomeration of interlocking practices which constitute the range of life options open to one who

---

2 M. Canovan, *Nationalism and Political Theory* (Cheltenham, Edward Elgar, 1996), p. 115; Y. Tamir, *Liberal Nationalism* (New Jersey, Princeton University Press, 1993), pp. 75-77: '... state powers should devolve to smaller, autonomous national entities on the one hand, and to larger, regional frameworks on the other'.

3 M. Canovan, *ibid.*, pp. 107, 115.

4 A. Eide, 'Minority Protection and World Order: Towards a Framework for Law and Policy', in A. Phillips and A. Rosas (eds.), *Universal Minority Rights* (Turku/Åbo and London, Åbo Akademi University Institute for Human Rights Minority Rights Group International, 1995), p. 99. The Working Group on Minorities was established in 1995 as a subsidiary organ of the UN Sub-Commission on the Promotion and Protection of Human Rights (previously called the Sub-Commission on Prevention of Discrimination and Protection of Minorities).

is socialized within them.[5] Will Kymlicka defines cultural practices as foundational to personal autonomy. Understanding cultural narratives – language, education, religion, custom, myth, symbols, morals, ethics, history and manners – is a necessary precondition to making intelligent judgments about how to live our lives. Culture provides options through which we identify experiences as valuable. Without culture, individuals would be left to invent everything [including language] in their own lives and all aspects of conduct.[6]

While some authors disagree as to whether culture, a broad and ambiguous concept, is properly recognized as part of international treaty law or domestic law, the United Nations' Human Rights Committee has provided clarification for the administration of cultural protection.[7] When combined with related international treaties, conventions and declarations, it is plain that the protection of minority cultural identity is ensconced as an internationally recognized aspect of the UN's human rights treaty system.[8] Taken together, UN authorities for the protection of culture provide a broad scope of protection requiring states to take positive steps to guarantee individual access to culture.[9]

---

5 J. Raz, 'Multiculturalism: A Liberal Perspective', in *Ethics in the Public Domain: Essays in the Morality of Law and Politics* (Oxford, Clarendon Press, 1995), pp. 175-177. Raz explains that culture is indispensable to charting the life course of successive choices.

6 W. Kymlicka, *Multicultural Citizenship* (Oxford, Oxford University Press, 1995), p. 83. Also see, F. Caporoti, *Study on the Rights of Persons belonging to Ethnic, Religious and Linguistic Minorities* (Geneva, United Nations, Centre for Human Rights, 1991), p. 37. Capotorti cites M. Leiris, *Race and Culture* (Paris, UNESCO, 1951), pp. 20-21.

7 B. Barry, *Culture and Equality An Egalitarian Critique of Multiculturalism* (Cambridge, Polity Press, Blackwell Publishers Ltd., 2001), p. 67; E.W. Metcalfe, 'Are Cultural Rights Human Rights? A Cosmopolitan Conception of Cultural Rights', (diss., University of Oxford 2000), p. 2.

8 H. Niemi, *National Implementation of Findings by United Nations Human Rights Treaty Bodies, A Comparative Study* (Finland, Institute for Human Rights, Åbo Akademi University, 2003), p. 1.

9 *Convention on the Prevention and Punishment of the Crime of Genocide, 1946*, Articles 1 and II, 78 UNTS 277 (existence); *International Covenant On Civil and Political Rights, 1966*, Articles 1, 2 and 27, 999 UNTS 171 (self-determination and cultural development); *International Covenant on Economic and Social and Cultural Rights, 1966*, Articles 13 and 15, 993 UNTS 3 (education and access to cultural life); *International Convention on the Elimination of All Forms of Racial Discrimination*, Article 2 (2) *1966*, 660 UNTS 195 (social and cultural development); *Declaration On the Elimination of All Forms of Intolerance and of Discrimination Based on Religion or Belief, 1981*, Article 5 UN doc. A/36/684 (1981) (religious education; this article is frequently applied in conjunction with Article 18 of the *International Covenant on Civil and Political Rights, 1966*, on religious practice and belief); *International Convention on the Suppression and Punishment of the Crime of Apartheid, 1973*, Article II. Gen. Assembly Resolution 2068 (life and liberty); *Convention on the Rights of the Child, 1989*, Articles 4, 8, 20, 23, 29, 30, 31 UN Doc. A/44/49 (1989) (child cultural development, identity, and nationality); UNESCO *Convention Against Discrimination In Education, 1960*, Articles 1, 3, 4, 5, 429 UNTS

## 2. Definitions

> Nothing, I venture to say, is more likely to disturb the peace of the world than the treatment which might, in certain circumstances, be meted out to minorities.
>
> — Woodrow Wilson[10]

The minority question has troubled world peace and international goodwill for centuries.[11] The normative literature on the subject of minority rights covers a range of polarizing contemporary issues such as affirmative action, desegregation, bilingual education, religious exemptions, immigration reform, and multiculturalism. The debate evokes great passion from those who support or oppose the idea of special rights for individuals who are members of minority groups. However, treatment of minorities as a historical subject differs from the modern literature, because the topic is portrayed instead as an international question centring on the relationship between different states. The minority problem has a distinctly international character since the subject involves the relationship between different national groups who generally emigrate from different countries.[12] Disputes between states and internal state conflicts about minorities have served as a justification for war as well as for other forms of violence between national groups, including World War I.[13] The minorities question is a subject that also lends itself to international law exercised through the treaty-making power of states, since treaty law is the vehicle by which different states govern their formal relationships.

The modern nation, an abstract concept, makes it difficult to produce a clear definition of the term minority. Definitions of the nation, as well as of minority

93 (non-discrimination, minority schools and cultural education); *International Convention on the Protection of the Rights of All Migrant Workers and Members of their Families, 1990*, Articles 12, 16, 17, 18, 31, UN General Assembly Resolution 45/158 (the migrant worker's cultural rights and identity); UNESCO *Declaration of the Principles of International Cultural Co-operation, 1966* (cultural life, value and development).

10 Wilson's address to the eighth plenary session of the European peace conference in Versailles on 31 May 1919. See P. Thornberry, *International Law and the Rights of Minorities* (Oxford, Clarendon Press, 1991), pp. 40-41. Thornberry cites J. Robinson et al., *Were The Minorities Treaties a Failure?* (New York, Institute of Jewish Affairs, 1943), p. 21.

11 F. Capotori, *cit. supra* note 6, p. 6.

12 P. Thornberry, *cit. supra* note 10, p. 3. A minority may also have formerly constituted an independent nation (tribal organization); been part of a nation living under its own state, which was segregated from this jurisdiction and annexed to another state; be a regional or scattered group that has not reached a minimum degree of assimilation with the predominant group.

13 C.A. Macartney, *National States and National Minorities* (London, OUP,1934), p. 181: An immediate cause of WWI was the Sarajevo murder of Archduke Franz Ferdinand as well as the ethnic group conflict in the Balkan states.

groups, must be treated as two aspects of the same topic, because so-called minority groups are produced by the grant of sovereignty to the nation state, which is itself controlled by different national groups. Therefore, to define a minority we must also find a definition for the nation. Some scholars maintain that attempts to define a minority group are futile, since the idea of a minority is an inherently ambiguous concept lacking definitive characteristics. Some states unsuccessfully argue that they have no minorities.[14] Legal scholars maintain that a state's failure to recognize the existence of its minority groups does not exempt it from fulfilling treaty obligations requiring the state's recognition for the existence and identity of minority groups.[15] United Nations Special Rapporteur Francesco Capotorti's 1991 study on the rights of minorities explains that, in recommending international minority rights standards, the United Nations Human Rights Committee (HRC) 'did not consider it necessary to define the term minority ... [because] the only point at issue ... is whether an indisputable objective core (religious, linguistic, ethnic, national) can be widened or restricted'.[16] Instead, the United Nations identifies four groups – national, ethnic (inclusive of race), linguistic and religious – as entitled to legal protection. Although the UN has not formalized a definition for the term minority, Francesco Capotorti has produced what Patrick Thornberry concludes is the most accepted definition:[17]

> ... a group numerically inferior to the rest of the population of a State, in a non-dominant position, whose members – being nationals of the State – possess ethnic, religious or linguistic characteristics differing from

---

14 M. Castan, S. Joseph, and J. Schultz, *The International Covenant on Civil and Political Rights, Cases, Materials, and Commentary* (Oxford, OUP, 2000), p. 574; C. Anderson, *Eyes Off The Prize, The United Nations And The African American Struggle For Human Rights, 1944-1955* (Cambridge, Cambridge University Press, 2003), p. 75. Anderson illustrates the American position against recognition of minority existence: 'there are probably no national minorities in the U.S.' quoting a US State Department statement in support of formation of the UN Sub-Commission on the Protection of Minorities during the 1950's; P. Thornberry, *cit. supra* note 10, p. 116: 'In the kind of world for which we fight, there must cease to exist any need for the use of that accursed term, racial or religious minority'. The quote is a statement made by the Roosevelt Administration's Secretary of State during the UN Genocide Convention; *Adarand Constructors, Inc. v Pena*, 515 U.S. 200 (1995) US Chief Justice Antony Scalia recently found that 'in the eyes of the [US] government, we are just one race here. It is American'; I.L. Claude Jr., *National Minorities An International Problem* (Cambridge, Harvard University Press, 1955), p. 82. Claude describes how Hawaii statehood was delayed until its racial groups had been Americanised.

15 See Articles 1 and 27, *International Covenant on Civil and Political Rights, 1966*, 999 UNTS 171.

16 F. Capotorti, *cit. supra* note 6, pp. 6, 8, 95.

17 *Ibid.*, pp. 5, 6. Capotorti warns, however, that there is still no generally accepted definition of the term 'minority'.

> those of the rest of the population and show, if only implicitly, a sense of solidarity, directed towards preserving their culture, traditions, religion or language.

The prospect of expanding categories of minority classifications ad infinitum results in criticism of special rights for minorities. Some authors favour the alternative remedy of equal opportunity and universalized protection from invidious forms of discrimination for members of groups who suffer inequality.[18] However, anti-discrimination and equal opportunity guarantee only the protection of individuals, and do not protect minorities as groups. Illustrating the failure of anti-discrimination laws to protect African-Americans, for example, Sandra Fredman explains:[19]

> As surely as the law has outlawed racial discrimination, it has affirmed that Black Americans can be without jobs, have their children in all black, poorly funded schools, have no opportunities for decent housing and have very little political power, without any violation of anti-discrimination law.

## 3. State-sponsored violence

> The greatest adversary of the rights of nationality is the modern theory of nationality. By making the state and nation commensurate with each other in theory, it reduces practically to a subject condition all other nationalities that may be within the boundary. … The co-existence of several nations under the same state … indicates a state of greater advancement than the national unity which is the ideal of modern liberalism.
>
> — John Emerich Edward Dalberg-Acton, First Baron.[20]

The evolution of the nation state is important to the subject of cultural rights because it helps us to understand the origins for the modern concept of a minority. For example, E.J. Hobsbawn concludes that the term minority belongs exclusively to a 'particular, and historically recent period … [and] a certain kind of modern territorial state'[21] namely, the nation state. For Hobsbawn, the terms

---

18 D. Miller, *On Nationality* (New York, OUP, 1995), p. 154. Miller writes '[the] principle of nationality is resistant to special rights for groups, over … what equal treatment requires …'

19 S. Fredman, 'Discrimination', in P. Cane and M. Tushnet (eds.), *Oxford Handbook of Legal Studies* (Oxford, Oxford University Press, 2003), p. 220.

20 J.E.E. Dalberg-Acton, *The History of Freedom and Other Essays*, J. Neville Figgis and R. Vere Laurence (eds.) (New York, Books for Libraries Press, 1907), pp. 290, 297.

21 E.J. Hobsbawn, *Nations and Nationalism since 1780* (Cambridge, Cambridge University Press, 1990), p. 9.

*nation state, nation, nationality, and minority* are all 'intertwined and sides of the same coin'.[22]

After the fall of the Roman Empire, *Christendom* replaced Europe and the Roman Empire as the name for the better part of the continent. Christendom was governed by a sovereign authority. From the 11th century onwards, the Pope alone was free to decree what was right or in the public interest.[23] *De Systematibus Civitatum* is Martin Wight's seminal writing that traces the evolution of the modern nation states system from the *Treaty of Westphalia* in 1648. The peace established by the Congress of Westphalia became the legal basis of the modern state system and marks the transition from religious to secular politics, that is, from Christendom back to Europe.[24] More than 300 part-sovereign states were recognized by the Peace of Westphalia.[25] Wight explains how Western Christendom or *Respublica Christiana* was a system of universal jurisdiction *in temporalibus* based on unity and hierarchy, ruling through a bureaucratic distribution of power among multiple government units. Some of these units became *civitates et reginae* or a 'perfect community' that gave birth to the idea of sovereign states.[26] The states emerged out of the schism that divided Latin Christendom between two to three rival popes. The medieval international papal monarchy was replaced by a system of secular powers as well as kings and churches organized according to nation states that included Italy, France, Germany, England and Spain. The Holy Roman Empire was transformed into an Italian great power. Each state had its own national sentiment based upon a common religion, *cuius regio, eius religio*.[27] Later, the doctrine evolved into the more contemporary idea of the national identity derived from its particular ruler, *cuius regio eius natio*.[28]

Wight concludes that most state systems end up in a universal empire with jurisdiction over all the states of the system. This is because sovereign state systems, in contrast to universal empires, must rely upon a balance of power between them

22 *Ibid.*

23 F.H. Hinsley, *Sovereignty* (Cambridge, Cambridge University Press, 1986), p. 54.

24 M. Wight, *Systems of States*, in H. Bull (ed.) (New Jersey, Leicester University Press, 1977), p. 113.

25 P.J. Baker, 'The Doctrine of Legal Equality', *The British Year Book of International Law* (1923-1924), p. 9.

26 J. Bodin, *On Sovereignty* (Cambridge, Cambridge University Press, 1992). Bodin (1576) was the first man to state the theory behind the word sovereignty.

27 *Cuius regio, eius religio* meaning that the faith of the ruler becomes the religion of the state or, like king, like religion; M. Wight, *cit. supra* note 24, pp. 26, 27, 28, 44, 131, 151.

28 *Cuius regio eius natio* meaning that the nation has the same identity as the ruler or that national identity derives from the ruler. Also meaning, like king, like nation; I.L. Claude, *cit. supra* note 14, p. 90.

that leads to a monopoly of power.[29] Inevitably, the sovereign states of Europe formulated into the Central Powers and Allied Powers (Triple Alliance) balance of power alliances that degenerated into World War I resulting, by some estimates, in 15 million deaths. The death toll from the state-system battles in WWI was higher than that from all wars fought between the years 1793-1914.[30] The resulting carnage motivated United States President Woodrow Wilson to support the creation of a League of Nations to serve as a universal organization for the collective peace and security of states and peoples. His objective was to prevent another great war that had ravaged not only the states of Europe but also the peoples of the world.

National culture, like that of the nation, is also a vague concept. Authors on the subject of culture and national identity maintain that characteristics of culture can be separated into two groups: firstly, higher-order culture represented by artistic, literary, scientific and intellectual work that tends to be the preserve of the elite; and second, an anthropological type of culture reflected in a people's characteristics, including not merely language, religion, and education but also myth, symbols, icons, dress, customs, habits and morals.[31] Anthony Smith explains that the basis of prejudice in the 20th century is not physical (racial) – rather it is cultural. Smith postulates that the problem of nationalism is found in its ethnocentrism or belief of the centrality, rightness and superiority of one's own community and a corresponding denial of the value of other communities. Throughout the 20th century, stronger nations often attacked subordinate and weaker national groups and their cultures, often by means of war, population transfer, denationalization and genocide.

Totalitarian states resulted from nationalist-inspired campaigns throughout Europe as well as Asia, and include: Germany's National Socialism and the Third Reich under Adolf Hitler 1933-1945; Greece's Third Hellenic Civilization under Greek General Joannis Metexas 1936-1941; Spain's Great Spanish Empire of the Golden Century under Francisco Franco Falangists 1939-1975; Italy's Facists under Mussolini 1922-1943; Japan's Land of the Rising Sun under Emperor Hirohito, 1936-1945; Russian Pan-Slavism, from the 1867 Pan-Slav Congress to the Bolshevik revolution and continuing by way of the defeat of Hitler's Pan-Germanism campaign, up to 1949; the Young Turks of the Committee of Union Progress (CUP), and Pan-Turkism under the Ottoman Empire, 1908-1918.[32]

---

29 M. Wight, *cit. supra* note 24, pp. 43, 44, 149.

30 A. Shaw (ed.), *The Messages and Papers of Woodrow Wilson*, Vol. 1 (New York, The Review of Reviews Corporation, 1924), pp. 926, 927.

31 T. Eagleton, *The Idea of Culture* (Oxford, Blackwell Publishers Ltd., 2000), p. 118; A. Spiliopoulou Akermark, *Justifications of Minority Protection In International Law* (The Hague, Kluwer Law International, 1997), p. 81.

32 A.D.S. Smith, *Nationalism In The Twentieth Century* (Oxford, Martin Robertson and Co., 1979), pp. 88, 90, 91 Smith maintains that physical anthropologists divide the human species into the following broad racial categories: Mongoloid, Negroid, Caucasian, Australoid, American

This chapter does not attempt to provide a comprehensive analysis of nationalism. However, the record of state practices when inspired by the ideology of nationalism is bound to the justification for the minority regime. That is, the minority regime is established as a corrective to the record of atrocity caused by state coercive assimilation campaigns inspired by the ideology of nationalism. The historical record of coercive assimilation campaigns used against minority groups is not incidental. Rather, state-sponsored violence used against minority groups in the 20th century shocks the moral conscience.

Denationalization campaigns that took place against subordinate national groups and weak national states resulted in such large humanitarian disasters that it is difficult to understand how nationalism survived as a legitimate ideology upon which to base the existence of a state. These campaigns include the Turkish government's systematic murderous campaign against Armenians lasting from 1894 through WWI and resulting in over 1.4 million Armenian deaths, in the first contemporary genocide by a nation state against one of its subordinate national groups.[33] In addition to denationalisation efforts, other techniques such as the transfer of entire populations out of the country were implemented as a means to eliminate ethnically different subordinate national groups and purge nation states of minorities. These actions resulted in no less than 17 migratory movements in Macedonia alone from 1912-1925. The Lausanne Convention Concerning the Exchange of Greek and Turkish Populations of 30 January 1923 allowed for the forcible expulsion of 2 million Greek-Orthodox Catholics from Turkey to Greece and 500,000 Moslem residents in Greece to Turkey.[34]

Germany's denationalisation campaign in the 20th century resulted in the genocide of over six million European Jews and half a million Roma.[35] Population

---

Indian or Hottentot; W. Kymlicka, *Politics In The Vernacular, Nationalism, Multiculturalism and Citizenship* (New York, Oxford University Press, 2001), p. 230, cites French Government coercion of Breton and Basque groups, Slovak government actions against ethnic Hungarians, and Latvian government activity against Ethnic Russians; H. Kohn, *Nationalism, Its Meaning and History* (Princeton, D.Van Nostrand Co., Inc., 1955), p. 80; H. Kayali, *Arabs and Young Turks: The Ottoman Empire 1908-1918* (Berkeley, University of California Press, 1997).

33 L.P. Mair, *The Protection of Minorities, The Working and Scope of the Minorities, Treaties Under the League of Nations* (London, Christophers, 1928), p. 217; V.N. Dadrian, *The History of Armenian Genocide, Ethnic Conflict from the Balkans to Anatoli to Causasus* (Providence, Berghan Books, 1997), Introduction.

34 *Ibid.*, p. 728; also see R. Hirschon, *Heirs of the Greek Catastrophe, The Social Life of Asia Minor Refugees in Priaeus* (New York, OUP, 1999), p. 36.

35 A. Hitler, *Mein Kampf* (My Struggle) (London, Radius Books/Hutchinson and Co. Ltd., 1936), pp. 356, 357. Hitler exploits German culture to promote totalitarianism writing 'the state ... is the necessary basis for the formation of a higher culture ... The highest end of the national (*Volkish*) state is to see the preservation of those social elements which give out culture, and create the beauty and dignity of a higher humanity'.

transfer, denationalization, and genocide continued after WWII and included the flight of 12 million Hindus and Moslems into India or Pakistan respectively after the 1949 partition of India, as well as the migration of 425,000 Jews to Israel by 1952. Genocide of national minority groups after WWII continued to be used by nation states as a tool to annihilate weaker national groups. A more recent example is the murder of 800,000 Tutsi tribe members by Hutu nationalist troops in Rwanda.[36]

## 4. Normative consequences

*Fiat iustitia, ruat caelum* (Let justice be done though the heavens fall)

— Latin Proverb

Minority protections are founded on the international system of states that developed after the Treaty of Westphalia, 1648. Legal scholarship and historical literature bases the justification for the minority regime in the concept of the nation, the ideology of nationalism, and the structure of the nation state. Normative discussions generally resist the challenge to analyse multiculturalism as a question about the structure of states. The minority regime challenges the tendency to accept the nation state's structure as a given. It establishes an obligation for all states to comply with human rights standards, irrespective of the state's national bias or majority sentiment.

Legal scholarship explains the minority regime as a corrective for a multi-national system of states based upon the control exercised by powerful nations of the state's administrative apparatus. Proper understanding of the justification for the minority regime is important because, in this writer's opinion, it reduces the intensity as well as the necessity for a normative debate on multiculturalism. The minority regime creates a paradigm shift from the domestic polity into the international sphere. Within the domestic context, minority rights appear as a regime that qualifies only certain groups for exemptions, as well as differential or special treatment. The international perspective changes the paradigm. The international perspective demands that all nations, as well as minority groups, be afforded equal treatment by the world's states. Human rights also require the application of equality for all minority groups, irrespective of their power relationship within any particular state. The minority regime requires that all domestic states recognize, as well as provide equality to minority groups, especially those who maintain unequal positions.

It is the international character of the minority regime that provides the most significant contribution to normative questions raised about multiculturalism.

---

36 S. Power, *A Problem From Hell* (New York, New Republic Books, 2002), p. 91; B. Harff and T.R. Gurr, 'Toward Empirical Theory of Genocides and Politicides: Identification and Measurement of Cases Since 1945', *International Studies Quarterly* (1988), p. 370. Harff and Gurr estimate that since 1945 there are 7-16 million human victims of genocide.

The minority regime was established at the supra-state, regional and international levels, and encourages domestic regimes to implement the equal treatment of minority groups. The minority regime is an effort to implement a system that recognizes the multi-national (and multicultural) nature of states; also, to prescribe guidance on how states conduct their recognition of groups emigrated, descended, or incorporated from different nations. That is, the minority regime is a regime of universal human rights that attempts to harmonize inter-state and intra-state relations by permitting individuals, in community with other members of her or his group, access to culture.

Differential or special treatment recognizing the unique characteristics of minority groups in the domestic sphere is now an established jurisprudential principle necessary for ensuring equality for minority groups. This precedent was established by the League of Nations' Permanent Court of International Justice in the *Minority Schools in Albania*, Advisory Opinion of 6 April 1935[37] which found that perfect equality requires states to 'attain a result which establishes an equilibrium between different situations'. That is, to guarantee equality, states must grant to minorities 'suitable means for the preservation of their racial peculiarities, their traditions and their characteristics'.[38] The concept of differential treatment for persons whose situations are significantly different was reaffirmed by the European Court of Human Rights in the *Case of Thlimmenos v. Greece* (6 April 2000), over half a century after the PCIJ *Minority Schools in Albania* decision.[39]

## 5. The Balkanization Effect

In this final section, I discuss the normative claim that minority rights damage common citizenship and national unity, resulting in what I describe as a Balkanization of the state, or division of the state along ethnic lines. My research revealed the opposite of the claim that special rights for minorities damages common citizenship and divides the state into competing ethnical groups. State regimes of forced assimilation, migration, segregation and apartheid that divide states into separated population groups, preceded the establishment of the minority regime. Such discriminatory regimes tend to remain entangled within states' established patterns of tradition, custom, and social mores, which will be perpetuated by intergenerational transmission long after the elimination of the regimes' discriminatory provisions.

---

37 *Minority Schools in Albania, Advisory Opinion of 6 April 1935*, Series E.-No. 11, Eleventh Annual Report of the Permanent Court of International Justice (15 June 1934-15 June 1935), Leyden, A.W. Sijthoff's Publishing Co. 138.

38 *Ibid.*

39 *Thlimmenos v. Greece* (ECHR, 6 April 2000, No. 34369/97).

The international minority regime does not foster so called Balkanization but, instead, offers new terms for group integration into the state based upon respect for human rights. The normative claim that minority protections result in competing, tribal, ghettoized, or illiberal parochial groups who have survived centuries of subjugation and persecution, is in error. Such assumptions merely provide a theoretical foundation for the continuation of regimes that violate human rights because they undermine the application of minority protections. The minority regime restores national unity and common citizenship by granting historically segregated groups just terms upon which they can base their reintegration into the civic life of the national state.

The minority regime also contains Rousseauian obligations from minority groups toward their respective states. Minority regimes, starting with the League of Nations' minority protection treaty system, through to the current UN regime, include requirements for minority group responsibility as regards the state's territorial unity, national loyalty and solidarity, guarantees against irredentism, and citizenship obligations. By itself, the minority regime contains no obstacle to the state's citizenship requirements for language proficiency, military conscription, jury-duty, voting, taxation, civics education, and citizenship training. On this question, it works more as a shield than a sword, in that its objective is to prevent state-building campaigns from engaging in coercive assimilation or other violent practices that target members of minority groups.

# 5
# Protecting Peoples' Cultural Rights: A Question of Properly Understanding the Notion of States and Nations?

*Matthias Åhrén*

## 1. Introduction

In 1956, Ivor Jennings suggested that the notion that the people shall decide is ridiculous, since one must then first decide who constitutes a people.[1] Half a century ago, Jennings' categorical dismissal of the notion of a people's right to culture, for instance, was not controversial. However, over the last few decades legal theorists have increasingly questioned the traditional state-individual dichotomy developed by conventional individual liberalism, asserting that one must add peoples into the equation to achieve an adequate protection of cultural rights. International law has seen a similar trend. This article aspires to give a brief overview of the parallel developments within legal theory and international law respectively, aspiring to answer whether these developments have resulted in Jennings' assertion no longer being correct, or whether it rather is true, as Waldron has phrased it responding to calls for protection of indigenous peoples' cultures: engaging in the traditions of an indigenous community in the modern world is like living in Disneyland and believing that one's surroundings epitomize what it is for a culture to really exist, at the same time demanding the funds to live in Disneyland as well as the protection from modern society for the boundaries of Disneyland.[2] Finally, reacting to claims that there exists no such thing as peoples' human rights proper, the article will

1 I. Jennings, *The Approach to Self-government* (1956), p. 56.

2 J. Waldron, in W. Kymlicka: *Multicultural Citizenship: A Liberal Theory of Minority Rights* (Oxford, Oxford University Press, 1995), p. 101.

Francioni and Scheinin (eds), *Cultural Human Rights*, 91–118
 ISBN 978 90 04 16294 5. Printed in the Netherlands.

offer some views on what relevance this claim has to the protection of collective cultural rights.[3]

## 2. The emergence of human rights and the nation state

The modern nation state emerged in Europe in the second half of the 17th century, underpinned by the belief that free government is only possible in the presence of cultural unity within the state.[4] Simultaneously, the notion of human rights of individuals emerged in England, and quickly spread to France and the United States.[5] England was at that time a relatively homogeneous country, and the human rights evolving did not include any norms on ethnic minorities.[6] These theories acknowledged the rights of the individual on one hand, and the sovereignty of the total social collective, on the other.[7] According to liberal individualism, the ideal of democracy corresponds to a belief in individual human rights. Interestingly, the legal theories initially included the sovereignty of the people as a central element, but the role of the people was quickly transformed into the fictional idea of a state.[8] The state was perceived to be formed by a social contract between a number

---

3 The term 'cultural rights' is not self-explanatory. Cultural rights can be divided into many kinds of sub-groups, depending on need. For instance, the mass of cultural rights can be split up based on who is the subject of the right. Some claim that only individuals can be subject to cultural human rights. Others hold that also collectives such as peoples can be the subject of cultural human rights proper. If accepting this argument, cultural rights can be divided into individual and collective rights. The individual cultural rights can in turn be divided into two sub-sets of rights. First, there are those individual rights that are truly individual in nature, in that they can be meaningfully exercised independently, without direct interaction with other members of the group. Other rights on the other hand, even though *strictu sensu* individual, only make sense in a collective context, in that it is not possible to exercise them in a meaningful manner outside the context of the group the individual belongs to. If not explicitly stated otherwise, with 'cultural rights' in this article are understood collective cultural rights proper. These too can, however, be divided into two quite distinct sets of rights, that to some extent contradict each other. First, with a collective cultural right can be understood a people's right to control its culture, and prevent non-members from access elements thereof. But with a collective cultural right could also be understood quite the opposite; a right for a people to have information diffused to it and to take part in the general development. This article only addresses the first category of rights.

4 M. Walzer, in W. Kymlicka, *cit. supra* note 2, p. 140.

5 A. Eide, 'Economic, Social and Cultural Rights as Human Rights', in A. Eide et al. (eds.), *Economic, Social and Cultural Rights, A Textbook* (The Hague, 2001), p. 12.

6 N. Glazer, in W. Kymlicka, *cit. supra* note 2, p. 126.

7 J. Anaya, *Indigenous Peoples in International Law* (2nd ed., Oxford, 2004), p. 13.

8 A. Eide, *cit. supra* note 5, p. 13.

of men.[9] Liberalism emerged with the modern state, and presupposes it.[10] The concept of the nation state was hence based on European models of political and social organization.[11] These individual liberal theories of human rights, states and peoples were still dominant when the young United Nations elaborated a human rights system in the aftermath of the Second World War.[12]

## 3. Criticism of the state-individual dichotomy

Hence, liberal individualism corresponds well to the traditional understandings of democracy and justice resting on implicit assumptions about the cultural make-up of the state. The term 'democracy' does not explain, however, in what manner the membership of the group that composes the democratic process should be defined, i.e. what is a society and how should the boundaries around it be drawn. Conventional liberal individualism takes for granted that the boundaries around a community have already been settled.[13] In other words, one people – per definition – make up one state.[14] In the real world, however, two or more different ethnic groups often

---

9 V. Van Dyke, in W. Kymlicka, *cit. supra* note 2, p. 34.

10 J. Carens, in W. Kymlicka, *cit. supra* note 2, p. 342.

11 J. Anaya, *cit. supra* note 7, p. 15.

12 In the years that followed the emergence of the liberal individualism, one attempt was made to break away from the state-individual dichotomy. The League of Nation, established in the wake of the World War I, actively promulgated a minority rights system that contained a number of minority rights guarantees, see B. Kingsbury, 'Reconciling Five Competing Conceptual Structures of Indigenous Peoples' Claims in International Law', in P. Alston (ed.), *Peoples' Rights* (Oxford, 2001), p. 78. The focus on minority rights chiefly served to address the interests of ethnic groups that had been denied the right to independence. A number of treaties were entered into with the aim to protect ethnic minorities, see J. Crawford, 'The Right of Self-Determination in International Law: Its Development and Future', in P. Alston, *cit. infra*, pp. 14-15. It could also be mentioned that in this era in an advisory opinion, the Permanent Court on International Justice also confirmed ethnic groups' right to cultural integrity. The Court stated that an ethnic minority group has the right to preserve the traditions and national characteristics which distinguish it from the majority, see *Minority Schools in Albania*, Advisory Opinion, 1935 P.C.I.J. (Ser. A/B) No. 64. The World War II did, however, again make the world community adverse to minority rights, chiefly due to Nazi-Germany's use of German minorities in neighbouring countries as an excuse to wage war against these countries. In addition, it did not help that the minority protection system established under the League of Nations had broke down. Instead, a belief surfaced that an effective protection for individual rights would indirectly – yet adequately – also protect groups, see J. Crawford, *cit. infra*, pp. 14-15 and B. Kingsbury, *cit. infra*, p. 78.

13 W. Kymlicka, *cit. supra* note 2, pp. 1-2.

14 M. Walzer, in Kymlicka, *cit. supra* note 4, p. 138; W. Kymlicka, *ibid.*, p. 4.; and D. Johnston, in W. Kymlicka, *cit. supra* note 2, p. 185.

cohabit a state. Similarly, sometimes the traditional territory of one ethnic group stretches across national borders. Liberal political theorists have essentially been blind to this reality.[15]

Since the late 1970s, however, legal theorists have increasingly come to argue that conventional liberal individualism, recognizing only the rights of individuals, is inadequate. In 1977, Van Dyke asserted that the liberal–individualistic conception is unduly limited. He claimed that human needs exist at various levels, at the level of the individual, at the level of the community, and at the level of peoples. Reasonably, the existence of such needs implies a right also to meet them.[16] In 1978, Bay criticized individual liberalism for cutting the citizen off from the person and constructed a cripple of a man, lacking moral or political nature, without roots.[17]

In 1983, Garet asserted that existence constitutes something intrinsically good and submitted that a human being is composed of both personhood and communality. He claimed that groupness constitutes a fact of our lives of unfathomable value. Life not subject to the call of groupness is, Garet argues, as difficult to imagine as life not subject to the call of personhood. He refused to admit that collective rights can be reduced to individual rights, and rather insisted that personhood, communality and sociality are neither derivative from each other nor conceptually ordered. Garet further justified the existence of collective human rights proper by arguing that if there is a right to a good that only a collective can have and exercise, then the right must reasonably also belong to the collective as such.[18]

In 1989, Kymlicka asserted that liberals could embrace cultural rights without in any way denouncing liberalism's individualist premises. Culture is, he claimed, important because the range of options open to us to choose is determined by our cultural heritage. It is cultural structures that provide us with 'a context of choice'. According to Kymlicka, membership in a cultural collective may be a relevant criterion for distributing the benefits and burdens which are the concern of a liberal theory of justice. It is only through having a rich and secure cultural structure that individuals can become aware of the options available to them. Concerns for cultural structures consequently accord, rather than conflict with, liberal concern for freedom to judge the value of various options in our life.[19]

---

15 In other words, liberal theorists have failed to accept the fact 'well known to great masses of people for a long time but not to generations of elite humanist scholars …: namely, that our tribal separateness is hear to stay', see H.R. Isaacs, *Idols of the Tribe: Group Identity and Political Change* (New York, 1975), p. 216.

16 V. Van Dyke, in W. Kymlicka, *cit. supra* note 9, pp. 31 and 37.

17 C. Bay, 'From Contract to Community: Thoughts on Liberalism and Postindustrial Society', in F.R. Dallmayr (ed.), *From Contract to Community* (New York, 1978), p. 30.

18 R.R. Garet, 'Communality and Existence: The Rights of Groups', *South California Law Review* (1983).

19 W. Kymlicka, *Liberalism, Community, and Culture* (Oxford, 1989), p. 167.

In 1990, Dunn questioned whether, if the concept of the state no longer describes a reality, there is any sense in supposing that for every state there is just one community or society to which individuals own their being and allegiance.[20] In 1992, Waldron, referring to Dunn, repeated the same question.[21] Anaya has referred to the traditional Western theoretical conception of the term peoples – that limits humanity to two categories, the individual and the state – as 'flawed', in that it simply ignores the complex, multiple overlapping spheres of community and ethnic groups that actually exists in human socicty.[22]

Further in 1990, Margalit and Raz submitted that individual well-being depends on successful pursuit of worthwhile goals and relationships that are culturally determined. Those goals are the products of culture, dependent on the sharing of patterns of expectations, on traditions preserving implicit knowledge of how to do what, of tacit conventions regarding what is part of that enterprise, what is appropriate, and what is valuable. Membership of the group is of fundamental importance to individual well-being, since it affects one's opportunity and ability to engage in relationships and pursuits marked by the culture.[23]

Kymlicka's interest in the issue continued and it seems that what really came to intensify the debate on whether there exists such a thing as collective rights proper, was the release of his *Multicultural Citizenship: A Liberal Theory of Minority Rights*, in 1995. Many scholars that have engaged in the debate since then have done so by responding to *Multicultural Citizenship*. In this book, Kymlicka asserts that there is a clear trend in legal thinking towards accommodating for group interests, carving out a new space for ethnic and racial groups, in between those of states and individuals.[24] He thus challenges liberal theory's traditional position that accepting the existence of collective cultural rights is intrinsically incoherent with liberal theory. Kymlicka concludes the case for a recognition of a collective right to culture with that since groups interests cannot be reduced to individual interests; groups, in addition to individuals, must also be able to hold human rights. Once we recognize that individuals' well-being is tied up with the group to which they belong, what is the rationale, he argues, for not recognizing the existence of certain collective rights, including the right to self-preservation, which are not reducible to individual rights?[25]

---

20 J. Dunn: *Interpreting Political Responsibility* (1990), p. 124.

21 J. Waldron, *cit. supra* note 2, pp. 95-96.

22 J. Anaya, *cit. supra* note 7, p. 78. Also Shachar has submitted that today, state-centred perceptions are clearly under increased scrutiny, see A. Scachar, *Multicultural Jurisdictions: Cultural Differences and Women's Rights* (Cambridge, 2001), p. 9.

23 A. Margalit and J. Raz, in W. Kymlicka, *cit. supra* note 2, pp. 86 ff.

24 W. Kymlicka, *Multicultural Citizenship: a Liberal Theory of Minority Rights* (Oxford, 1995), and compare A. Scachar, *cit. supra* note 22, p. 1 and 22.

25 W. Kymlicka, *cit. supra* note 2, p. 13.

It has further been argued that liberal individualism is not as neutral as it purports to be. Members of the dominant culture possess an institutional advantage over members of the minority.[26] Thus, individualism in fact provides an advantage to members of the dominant group. Members of the majority group tend to obtain disproportionate representation in the various cultural elites.[27] Kymlicka argues that cultural minorities suffer a disadvantage since they face inequalities that are not a result of their choice, but of decisions by people outside their society.[28] What is labelled non-discriminatory, neutral, state, is thus often, in effect, a system of 'group rights' that supports the majority language, history, culture and calendar.[29] If a particular people has greater economic and political power, that people's point of views and cultural assumptions is likely to become the norm. Allegedly culturally neutral liberal individualism, hence, in reality promotes assimilation.[30] Individualism is in fact implicitly biased towards the needs and interests of the majority group, excluding members of the minority culture. All cultures do not enjoy an equal chance of survival. A multicultural state will inevitably, at least partially favour one culture, and state legislation and other norms will be based on that culture.[31]

A strong case has thus been made for recognizing peoples' right to culture, and few seem to question this notion today. However, as outlined above, legal theorists such as Kymlicka also want to qualify such peoples' right to culture as human rights proper. This assertion has not been uncontested, however. Hartney claims that only good to individual human beings is of ultimate value, wherefore collective entities derive their value only from the contributions to the good of individual human beings.[32] His argument is, even though it calls for the protection of collectives, a liberal individualistic one.[33] The difference from conventional liberal individualism is a denouncement of the perception that all goods are enjoyed individually.[34] Also Kukathas subscribes to this view, acknowledging that individuals undeniably are members of collectives that shape their identity. He asserts that it is not that collectives do not matter. Rather, there is no need to depart from liberal individualism

---

26 B. Walker, 'Plural Cultures, Contested Territories: a Critique of Kymlicka', *Canadian Journal of Political Science* (1997), pp. 211-234.

27 V. Van Dyke, in Kymlicka, *cit. supra* note 9, p. 50.

28 W. Kymlicka, *cit. supra* note 19, p. 190.

29 W. Kymlicka, *cit. supra* note 2, p. 10.

30 I.M. Young, in Kymlicka, *cit. supra* note 2, pp. 162 ff.

31 A. Shachar, *cit. supra* note note 22, pp. 23 and 73, and R. Stavenhagen, *Cultural Rights: A Social Science Perspective*, in A. Eide et al. (eds.), *cit. supra* note 5, p. 96.

32 M. Hartney, in W. Kymicka, *cit. supra* note 2, p. 206.

33 W. Kymlicka, *cit. supra* note 19, p. 165.

34 M. Hartney, in W. Kymlicka, *cit. supra* note 32, p. 208.

to protect them.[35] Buchanan too, associates himself with these theories, asserting that cultures are valuable because of their contribution to its members, rather than in themselves.[36] In conclusion, these scholars recognize that peoples are morally important, but denounce that they have cultural human rights in their own capacity, i.e. that they are beneficiaries of human moral rights proper.[37]

Hartney questions whether it makes any sense to claim that a collective as such can have an interest in sustaining and growing in situations where it would be better for most of the members if it ceased to exist. He hence claims that a collective as such has no interest in surviving; that such an interest is merely conditional to the interest of the individual members of the collective. Hartney and Kukathas argue that a collective as such can not have an interest that is not reducible to an interest of its individual members, even if the interest is in a participatory good that can reasonably only be enjoyed in community with others. Whether the contribution to the well-being of individuals is joint or separate is irrelevant to the fact that it is individuals' lives that are enriched by it.[38] The conclusion is that there is no such thing as morally relevant collective interests; whatever interest there is in the survival of a group, it is a derivative interest, derived from the aggregate interest of its members in the survival.[39]

## 4. Early international law

As demonstrated above, liberal individualism, at least in its traditional form, is reluctant to recognize rights and obligations for other subjects than states and individuals. As has also been elaborated upon above, however, in more recent times human rights legal theory has seen a movement away from state-centred positivism. The question is then: Has this shift in legal theory been reflected in international law?

---

35 C. Kukathas, in W. Kymlicka, *cit. supra* note 2, pp. 231-232.

36 A. Buchanan, in W. Kymlicka, *cit. supra* note 2, p. 355.

37 M. Hartney, in W. Kymicka, *cit. supra* note 32, p. 208; and C. Kukathas in W. Kymlicka *loc. cit.* (note 35), p. 232.

38 M. Hartney, in W. Kymlicka, *cit. supra* note 32, p. 209; and C. Kukathas, *ibid.*, pp. 233 ff.

39 M. Hartney, in W. Kymlicka, *cit. supra* note 32, p. 209 ff. One should note that what Hartney is analyzing is the existence of moral, and not legal, rights. Legal rights differ from moral rights in that they depend ultimately and merely on the acts of an authority, such as a legislator. Since a legislator can create duties for all sorts of reasons, one could have a legal right to something completely unimportant. A moral right, on the other hand, implies a good sufficiently important that it warrants protection against others. In other words, there are no unimportant moral duties. An estimate of the importance of the good is key to the evaluation of a moral right exists. Hartney hence does not question that collectives cannot hold legal rights. It is 'merely' a question of a competent authority conferring such rights to the collective, see M. Hartney, in W. Kymlicka, *cit. supra* note 2, pp. 210-215.

Proponents of peoples' rights sometimes point out that already the UN Charter Articles 1(2) and 55 proclaim the equal right of all peoples to self-determination. Still, even though the Charter refers to peoples' right to self-determination, it is normally claimed that the provisions should be understood as referring to a state right, or, rather, as a right of the sum of the inhabitants of a state.[40] According to Cassese, the right to self-determination embedded in the UN Charter was merely an obligation on states to grant, as far as possible, self-government for communities over which they exercised jurisdiction.[41]

One must understand the notable absence of provisions protecting the rights of collectives in the Universal Declaration on Human Rights[42] (UDHR) of 1948 – as well as in regional human rights instruments adopted during the early years of the UN, such as the European Convention for the Protection of Human Rights and Fundamental Freedoms (ECHR)[43] and the American Declaration of the Rights and Duties of Man (ADRDM)[44] – against the background of the adverse attitudes towards minority rights following the wake of the Second World War, as explained above.[45] Article 13(2) of the ADRDM, adopted in 1948, declares only individuals' right to protection for their intellectual creations and Article 23 proclaims an individual right to property.[46] Also adopted in 1948 was the Genocide Convention.[47] The right mirrored in the Genocide Convention is clearly a collective one, and proponents of collective cultural rights consequently often rely on the Genocide Convention when claiming a collective right to culture. Alston claims, however, that the Genocide Convention does not make a very strong case for the existence

---

40 P. Alston, in P. Alston, *cit. supra* note 12, p. 260, and A. Cassese, *Self-Determination of Peoples* (1995), pp. 14-23.

41 A. Cassese, *ibid.*, p. 42, and compare J. Crawford, *cit. supra* note 12, p. 16.

42 Adopted and proclaimed by UN General Assembly Resolution 217 A (III) of 10 December 1948.

43 Concluded at Rome, 4 November 1950. Entered into force 3 September 1953, E.T.S. 5; 213 U.N.T.S. 221. On 20 March 1952, the European states agreed on a Protocol No. 1 to the ECHR, proclaiming an individual right to property.

44 Adopted by the Ninth Conference of American States, Bogotá, 30 March – 2 May 1948. O.A.S. Res. XXX, reprinted in Basic Documents Pertaining to Human Rights in the Inter-American System, OAS/Ser.L/V/I.4 Rev. 9 (2003).

45 See B. Kingsbury, *cit. supra* note 12, p. 78.

46 Below the article will describe that at least the latter provision has later been understood to protect also the collective rights of peoples.

47 See The Convention on the Prevention and Punishment of the Crime of Genocide, 78 United Nations Treaty Series 277.

of collective human rights, mainly because it stipulates states' obligations rather than proclaiming rights.[48]

Shortly after the UN member states had agreed on the UDHR, the world community commenced crafting two legally binding human rights covenants – the International Covenant on Civil and Political Rights[49] (ICCPR) and the International Covenant on Economic, Social and Cultural Rights[50] (ICESCR). In 1950, the Soviet Union proposed that a provision on self-determination be included in the Covenants, with the aim of addressing the situation of ethnic minorities. The proposal to include a reference to self-determination in the Covenants met resistance, but in the debate that followed, increasingly gained momentum. The Covenants' Common Article 1 was approved in 1955, notably with a clear understanding that it applies also beyond a colonial context.[51] In the same breath, however, several states were concerned that the article would confer the right to self-determination also to ethnic minorities, which would, in their opinion, disrupt sovereign states. Several states declared that in their opinion, the article was not intended to cover such situations. Cassese thus asserts that with the term 'peoples' in Common Article 1 of the 1966 Covenants, the drafters of the Covenants meant the sum of the population of a state or a territory. Cassese claims that the right to self-determination at that time applied merely to three different groups of individuals; (i) the sum of the population of an independent and sovereign state, (ii) the entire population of territories that have not yet attained independence, and (iii) populations living under foreign military occupation.[52] Similarly, ILO Convention No. 107, agreed upon in 1957, took an assimilation approach, and did not protect indigenous peoples as distinct ethnic entities. In the 1950s and 1960s, self-determination was forcefully invoked within the United Nations to call for the independence of the colonies.[53] As history tells, the call was successful. The decolonization movement is one of the strongest in world

---

48 See P. Alston, in P. Alston, *cit. supra* note 12, pp. 261-262. See, however, also R. Stavenhagen, *cit. supra* note 31, who referring to T. Buergenthal, asserts that the Genocide Convention recognizes the right of groups to exist as groups, which he asserts amounts to the most fundamental of human rights, *cit. supra* note 31, p. 87.

49 Adopted and opened for signature, ratification and accession by UN General Assembly resolution 2200A (XXI) of 16 December 1966.

50 Adopted and opened for signature, ratification and accession by UN General Assembly resolution 2200A (XXI) of 16 December 1966.

51 See J. Crawford, *cit. supra* note 12, pp. 17 and 27-29.

52 A. Cassese, *cit. supra* note 40, pp. 47-53, 59 and 61-62. Note, however, that in the same breath, Cassese argues against the assertion that peoples should not hold legal rights proper pursuant to the common Article 1. He makes this conclusion chiefly based on a semantic interpretation of the term 'peoples' in Article 1. Cassese underlines that the drafters of the Covenants carefully choose between the terms 'peoples' and 'states', when crafting Article 1, see *infra* , pp. 143-144, 242 and 285.

53 A. Cassese, *cit. supra* note 40, p. 71-73.

political history, and is generally regarded as one of the United Nations greatest achievements. However, there are no examples of the right to self-determination that emerged in the decolonization process attaching to groups by virtue of ethnic make-up or historical territorial sovereignty.[54] The dominating view that the right to self-determination did not apply beyond a colonial context largely prevailed during the 1950s and into the 1960s.[55] For Cassese, the fact that the right to self-determination emerging during the decolonization era did not apply to ethnic groups constituting a colonial people was a 'major flaw'.[56]

But even if it should be correct that the early self-determination discourse's view on what groups constitute peoples under international law was a flawed one, the coming shift in focus from the state-individuals paradigm to an interest in peoples' rights appears to a large extent to have been a result of the political and legal debate around the concept of self-determination that followed the adoption of the 1966 Covenants. As Cassese has himself put it; '[Self-determination] has set in motion a restructuring and redefinition of the world community's basic "rules of the game".'[57] Also Alston argues that despite its vagueness and ambiguity, the inclusion of the right to self-determination in the 1966 Covenants encouraged proponents of peoples' rights in general and spurred an increased inclination to recognize the existence of such rights. Along the same line, Crawford asserts that the recognition of the right to self-determination spurred a group of writers to champion a general acceptance of peoples' rights.[58] It would take some 20 more years, however, before international law would come to recognize a right of peoples that has hardly been disputed.

Similar to the UN Charter and Article 1 of the 1966 Covenants, on a first reading, the 1962 UN General Assembly Declaration on Permanent Sovereignty over Natural Resources[59] appears to proclaim a peoples' right to their natural resources. However, again Crawford, for instance, asserts that it is ambiguous as to whether the subject of the right in the Declaration is the people or the state.[60] Clearly, the Declaration was adopted in a colonial context,[61] and mixes references to a state's right to sovereignty over natural resources with that of peoples. The same is true about the right to development, enshrined first and foremost in the UN Declaration on

---

54 J. Anaya, *cit. supra* note 7, p. 78.

55 J. Crawford, *cit. supra* note 12, p. 16.

56 A. Cassese, *cit. supra* note 40, p. 74.

57 *Ibid.*, p. 1.

58 J. Crawford, *cit. supra* note 12, p. 21.

59 See GA Res. 1803 (XVII), adopted on 14 December 1962.

60 J. Crawford, *cit. supra* note 1212, p. 22.

61 A. Cassese, *cit. supra* note 40, p. 100.

the Right to Development.[62] It has consequently often been debated whether these instruments could be invoked when arguing for the existence of peoples' rights.

Further, save for Common Article 1, the 1966 Covenants, on the face of it, proclaim individual cultural rights. ICESCR Article 15(1)(c) elaborates on UDHR Article 27(2), and hence declares that everyone has the right to benefit from the protection of the moral and material interests resulting from any scientific, literary or artistic production of which he is the author. Similarly, Article 27 of the ICCPR proclaims that individuals belonging to a minority group have the right to enjoy their culture. The right is hence clearly an individual one. Still, Article 27 constitutes a step towards minority rights protection compared to the UDHR, which, as pointed out above, contains no such rights but rather underlines the universality of human rights. ICCPR Article 27 affirms that many cultural rights, to be applied in any meaningful manner, must be enjoyed in community with other members of the group.

The International Convention on the Elimination of All Forms of Racial Discrimination (the CERD Convention),[63] also adopted in 1966, prohibits all forms of racial discrimination. The CERD Convention Article 2(1)(a) obliges states not to discriminate against groups in addition to individuals and Article 2(2) stipulates that states shall also take special measures to protect groups from racial discrimination. Further, the rights that the CERD Convention specifically calls on states to safeguard are all formulated as individual rights. Consequently, and since the CERD Convention places obligations on states, rather than proclaims rights, it is perhaps difficult to argue with any strength that the CERD Convention, as understood at the time of its adoption, constituted a decisive argument for the existence of peoples' rights.

In 1969, the OAS concluded the work with an American Convention on Human Rights (ACHR).[64] The ACHR elaborates on the rights contained in the ADRDM and like the ADRDM, encompasses only individual rights, including a right to property in Article 21.

## 5. Some indications of a changed perception of the term 'peoples' in international law

In 1970, the UN General Assembly adopted the Declaration on Friendly Relations, which confers the right of the internal aspect of self-determination to ethnic groups.[65] Cassese holds that the Friendly Relations Declaration only allows such groups a very limited form of internal self-determination. Nonetheless, by entrusting ethnic groups

---

62 See Declaration on the Right to Development, G.A. Res 41/128, 4 December 1986.

63 Concluded at New York 7 March 1966 by General Assembly resolution 2106 A (XX). Entered into force 4 January 1969.

64 Entered into force 18 July 1978. 1144 U.N.T.S. 123; O.A.S.T.S. 36.

65 A. Cassese, *cit. supra* note 40, p. 113.

with even a limited form of self-determination, it is clear that the proponents of the Friendly Relations Declaration did not mean that with the term 'peoples' should necessarily be understood as the sum of the population of a state.

In the 1970s and the 1980s, the International Court of Justice[66] (ICJ) had the opportunity to deliver opinions on cases regarding the right to self-determination on a few occasions, including the *South West Africa Case (Namibia) Case*[67] (1971), the *Western Sahara Case*[68] (1975) and the *Frontier Dispute* (*Burkina Faso v. Mali) Case*[69] (1986). In these cases, the ICJ did not specify what groups constitute a 'people'. Notwithstanding, the positions taken by the ICJ suggest at least that the ICJ was not convinced that with the term 'peoples' should be understood the sum of the inhabitants of a state. Indeed, the ICJ's opinion in the *Frontier Dispute* case suggests that a 'people' must not necessarily mean the sum of the inhabitants of a state or a territory.

Even if the 1960s and 1970s saw some incidental sources that foretold the development to come, it appears difficult to conclude that international law at that time recognized a peoples' right to culture. However, as outlined above, in the late 1970s and early 1980s, some influential legal theorists commenced to submit that the conventional liberal individualism's state-individual dichotomy is arbitrarily limited. Simultaneously, an increased recognition for peoples' cultural rights can be detected within international law.

## 6. International law – later developments

The year 1981 saw the adoption of the African Charter on Human and Peoples' Rights,[70] which, as the title hints, places peoples' rights on the same footing as individual human rights. The African Charter proclaims that peoples have a right to, for instance, existence, self-determination and cultural development.

Indigenous peoples' demand for respect for their human rights, and their focus on the collective aspects of their societies, has been a driving force in the change in international law. In 1986, UN Special Rapporteur José Martinez Cobo presented

---

66 Obviously, decisions by the ICJ are only binding on the state parties concerned. Hence, they do not have the same legal status as the UN Charter or internationally legally binding treaties. Still, the ICJ's interpretation of international law is highly influential also beyond the context of the state parties', see J. Crawford, *cit. supra* note 12, p. 32.

67 See ICJ, Reports (1971), 3.

68 See ICJ, Reports (1975), 33.

69 See ICJ Judgement of 22 December 1986.

70 See 21 *IML* (1982) 58.

a final report on the discrimination against indigenous peoples,[71] concluding that self-governance is an inherent part of indigenous peoples' cultural heritage which has contributed to the maintenance of their cultural tradition. Further, the report asserts that self-determination is a basic pre-condition for indigenous peoples to be able to preserve, develop and pass on to future generations their specific cultural identity. The presentation of the Cobo report sparked one of the strongest movements in the history of the UN. Already before its finalization, the Cobo report resulted in the establishment of a UN Working Group on Indigenous Populations (WGIP) in 1982. Although situated at the lowest possible level in the UN system, from the WGIP would spring a number of institutions, instruments and other initiatives that have been paramount in advancing indigenous rights in the UN system. For instance, both the UN Permanent Forum on Indigenous Issues and the UN Declaration on the Rights of Indigenous Peoples (the Indigenous Declaration) have their roots to the WGIP.

In 1989 the International Labour Organization (ILO) adopted ILO Convention No. 169, which contains a number of provisions that proclaim peoples' cultural rights.[72] Seemingly, these rights are also human rights. The Convention respects the cultures and ways of life of indigenous peoples, with the aim that they shall continue to exist as distinct cultural entities.[73] The ILO Convention No. 169 thus breaks with the individual/state dichotomy that had lingered in dominant conception of the human society since the birth of human rights in the 1800s.[74] Kristian Myntti has

71 See the Study of the Problem of Discrimination against Indigenous Populations, UN Doc.E/CN.4/Sub.2/1986/7.

72 For instance, Article 2(2)(b) proclaims the responsibility of governments to protect the collective cultural rights of indigenous peoples. Pursuant to Article 5(a), the cultural values and practices of indigenous peoples should be protected. Article 7 declares that indigenous peoples have the right to control to the largest extent possible their cultural development. At the same time, one must note Article 1(3), pursuant to which the use of the term 'peoples' in the ILO Convention No. 169 shall be without implications as to what rights attach to that term under international law. In other words, even though ILO Convention No. 169 does contain a number of provisions that spells out cultural rights for indigenous peoples, Article 1(3) could be viewed as rendering it uncertain to what extent the Convention does in fact proclaim rights of peoples. However, the majority of the provisions contained in ILO Convention No. 169 are crafted in such a manner that they could not be reasonably understood in any other way than to proclaim rights to indigenous peoples as collectives. Article 1(3) should therefore probably be understood as underlying that the ILO Convention No. 169 does not take a stand on whether indigenous peoples are entitled to the right to self-determination, rather than as asserting that none of the provisions contained in the Convention contains collective rights.

73 See Indigenous and Tribal Peoples: A Guide to ILO Convention No. 169 (1996).

74 J. Anaya, *cit. supra* note 40, p. 48.

referred to ILO Convention No. 169's view on peoples' rights as mirroring 'ethno political self-government'.[75]

Also in 1989, the UN adopted the Convention on the Rights of the Child (CRC).[76] The subjects of the rights contained in the CRC are undoubtedly individual children. Still, the CRC flirts with some collective dimensions to those rights. For instance, pursuant to Article 5, states shall respect local customs pertaining to child care and respect communities' role in such. In addition, the CRC in its Article 30 includes a clone of ICCPR Article 27, proclaiming indigenous children's and children belonging to an ethnic minority's right to enjoy their culture in community with other members of the group.[77]

The early 1990s saw the adoption of a number of instruments addressing the situation of members of minority groups. Most notably, in 1992, the UN adopted the Declaration on the Rights of Persons Belonging to National or Ethnic, Religious and Linguistic Minorities.[78] Further, in the early 1990s the Conference on Security and Cooperation in Europe declared that national minorities have the right to maintain and develop their culture, and must be free of any attempt of assimilation,[79] and the Council of Europe adopted a couple of instruments aiming to protect linguistic and other cultural rights of members of national and ethnic minorities. The rights these documents proclaim are individual in nature. Nonetheless, they evidence an increased recognition of the need to protect collective cultures. Kymlicka asserts that these instruments are all a result of legal theory claims that individual liberalism renders cultural minorities vulnerable to injustices by the majority.[80]

In 1993, Vienna hosted the UN World Conference on Human Rights, which produced the Vienna Declaration on Human Rights.[81] The Vienna Declaration was a disappointment for proponents of peoples' cultural rights. True, the Vienna Declaration underscored that the right to self-determination applies also beyond a colonial context.[82] In the same breath, however, the Declaration borrows language from the Friendly Relations Declaration, and goes on to state that this should not

---

75 K. Myntti, 'National Minorities, Indigenous Peoples and Various Models of Political Participation', in F. Horn (ed.), *Minorities and their right of Political Participation* (Lapland's University Press, Juridica Lapponica No. 16, Rovaniemi, 1996), p. 24.

76 See General Assembly Resolution 44/25 of 20 November 1989.

77 One should thus note that the CRC Article 30 distinguishes between indigenous peoples and minorities, something that the CCPR Article 27, adopted some 20 years earlier, does not.

78 Adopted by General Assembly Resolution 47/135 of 18 December 2002.

79 See Document of the Copenhagen Meeting of the Conference on the Human Dimension of the CSCE, 29 June 1990, Art. 32.

80 See W. Kymlicka, in W. Kymlicka, *cit. supra* note 2, p. 18.

81 See the United Nations World Conference on Human Rights, Vienna Declaration and Programme of Action, 25 June 1993, 32 ILM (1993) 1661.

82 J. Crawford, *cit. supra* note 12, pp. 30-31.

be construed as authorizing any action that would impair the territorial integrity of states conducting themselves in compliance with the principle of equal rights to self-determination and thus possessed with a government representing the whole people belonging to the territory. The reference to 'people' in singular form indicates that the drafters of the Vienna Declaration understood the term 'people' to mean the sum of the inhabitants of a territory or a state. Despite the shortcomings of the Vienna Declaration, this document did not stop the movement in international law towards an increased recognition of peoples' rights.

Almost immediately after its establishment in 1982, the WGIP set out to draft the Indigenous Declaration. In 1993, the WGIP presented a finalized draft declaration to the UN Sub-Commission on the Prevention of Discrimination and the Protection of Minorities (the Sub-Commission), which contains a number of provisions protecting indigenous peoples' cultural rights. The Sub-Commission endorsed the draft in 1995. This is significant, since the Sub-Commission is composed of a number of renowned human rights experts. Kymlicka asserts that the Indigenous Declaration too, is a result of legal theory responding to the claims that individual liberalism renders cultural minorities vulnerable to injustices by the majority.[83] At the same time, however, a number of states at this stage objected against the idea that the right to self-determination should apply to indigenous peoples.[84]

Not many domestic courts have had to address the question of which groups the right to self-determination applies to. When the Supreme Court of Canada was faced with the question in connection with the issue of whether the province of Quebec had the right to unilaterally secede from Canada, the Court took the matter seriously. The Supreme Court employed a number of international legal experts, predominantly to outline international law's position on secession, but the experts also indirectly came to touch upon which groups the right to self-determination applies to. With the assistance of legal expertise, the Supreme Court concluded that a people may be made up of only a portion of the total population of the state.[85] In other words, the Supreme Court's decision supports the idea that non-state forming peoples can be subject of rights.[86]

Recall that neither the ADRDM nor the ACHR on the face of it recognize peoples' cultural rights. However, since 2001, the Inter-American Court and the Inter-American Commission on Human Rights have reinterpreted these two instruments to encompass also collective rights, at least when applied to indigenous peoples. In 2001, in the *Awas Tingni case* the Inter-American Court of Human Rights articulated that 'property' includes indigenous peoples' communal property, and

---

83 W. Kymlicka, in W. Kymlicka, *cit. supra* note 2, p. 18.

84 B. Kingsbury, *cit. supra* note 12, p. 88.

85 See [1998] 1 SCR 217, at 281 (paras. 123-5).

86 J. Crawford, *cit. supra* note 12, pp. 59-60.

as such is protected as a human right.[87] Subsequently, building on the *Awas Tingni case*, the Inter-American Commission on Human Rights has concluded that Maya communities in the Toledo District in Belize held that indigenous peoples have property rights to their traditional lands and resources under international human rights law. Similar statements have been made by the Commission in the *Raposa Serra do Sol* case (Brazil) and the *Western Shoshone Mary and Carrie Dann* case (United States). As outlined above, the ECHR and its Protocol No. 1 was adopted approximately at the same time as the ADRDM. The European Court on Human Rights has yet to conclude, however, that the property right encompassed in Protocol No. 1 to the ECHR entails in addition to an individual right, also a collective right. Indeed, the ECHR has so far generally taken quite a cautious stand on minority rights issues.[88]

Another initiative to strengthen the protection of peoples' cultural rights in a European context looks more promising, however. In 1986, the Saami Council proposed that the four countries within which the indigenous Saami population today finds itself residing,[89] in cooperation with the Saami people, should agree on a Convention on the rights of the Saami people. After a number of political and legal twists and turns, an Expert Group with the task of crafting a Nordic Saami Convention[90] commenced its work in 2003 and in November 2005 presented a unanimous proposal for a Saami Convention text to the three governments and the three Saami parliaments. The draft Saami Convention contains a number of provisions that clearly underline the Saami people's cultural rights.[91] The Saami Convention remains a draft.[92] Still, having been crafted by some of the Nordic countries' greatest

87 The case *Mayagna (Sumo) Community of Awas Tingni v. Nicaragua*, Inter-Am. Ct. H.R., Sentencia de 31 de agosto de 2001.

88 P. Alston, in P. Alston, *cit. supra* note 12, pp. 275-276.

89 These are Finland, Norway, the Russian Federation and Sweden.

90 In the end, the Russian Federation did not become a party to the project of crafting a Saami Convention.

91 First and foremost, Article 3 proclaims that the Saami people – as a people – have the right to self-determination, pursuant to which they, e.g., have the right to determine their cultural development. The Expert Group explicitly affirms that the right to self-determination that the Saami Convention proclaims is the same right that all peoples enjoy, e.g., under the common Article 1 of the 1966 Covenants, and not a *sui generis* right. Pursuant to Articles 16 and 36, the Saami people through the Saami parliament have the right to veto any activity in the Saami traditional areas that would severely damage the Saami culture. Article 31(1) stipulates that the Saami people have the right to manage their traditional knowledge (TK) and traditional cultural expressions (TCEs).

92 The presidents of the Saami parliaments and the national ministers responsible for Saami affairs met in October 2006. They then decided that during one year, the governments and the Saami parliaments shall jointly endeavour to prepare for an adoption of the Saami Convention in 2007.

experts on international law, it is a relevant barometer for determining where the international legal winds are blowing. Further, in its Northern Dimension Action Plan,[93] the European Union's Council of Ministers declared its position that the right to self-determination applies to indigenous peoples, with the view to protect their cultural rights.

The Human Rights Committee has, in a series of observations and general comments, gradually 'collectivized' the individual right to culture that ICCPR Article 27 proclaims. As pointed out above, ICCPR Article 27 does not, like CRC Article 30, specifically refer to indigenous peoples. Nonetheless, much of the Committee's jurisprudence on Article 27 relates to claims by indigenous groups. In applying Article 27 in the context of indigenous peoples, the Committee has repeatedly underlined the collective dimension of the provision. In the *Kitok* case (1988), the Committee confirmed that reindeer husbandry, as a traditional livelihood of the indigenous Saami people, constitutes such an activity that is protected under Article 27.[94] In *Ominayak v. Canada* (1990), the Committee confirmed its finding in the *Kitok* case and concluded that the exploitation of timber, gas and oil in the aboriginal Lubicon Lake Band's traditional territory amounted to a violation of ICCPR Article 27, since these activities effectively destroyed the Band's traditional hunting and fishing grounds.[95] The applicant in the case was an individual, but it is clear that the beneficiary of the Committee's finding was the Band in its entirety. In 1994, the Committee affirmed that culture manifests itself in many forms, for instance, in the particular way of life of indigenous peoples.[96] The Committee has subsequently repeatedly affirmed that ICCPR Article 27 must be understood to encompass a dimension that protects indigenous peoples' collective culture, for instance, in the two *Länsman* cases[97] (1994 and 1996) and in *Apirana Mahuika*

---

93 See The Second Nordic Dimension Action Plan 2004-2006, Commission of the European Communities, COM(2003) 343 (final), p. 21.

94 See *Ivan Kitok v. Sweden* (Communication No. 197/1985), views adopted 27 July 1988, Report of the Human Rights Committee, GAOR, Forty-third session, Suppl. No. 40 (A/43/40), pp. 221-230.

95 See *Bernard Ominayak, Chief of the Lubicon Lake Band v. Canada* (Communication 167/1984), views adopted 26 March 1990, Report of the Human Rights Committee, GAOR, Thirty-Eighth session, Suppl. No. 40 (A/38/40), pp. 1-30. See also B. Kingsbury, *cit. supra* note 12, p. 80.

96 See HRC General Comment No. 23 (50), reproduced in UN Doc. HRI/GEN/1/Rev.5, pp. 147-150.

97 See *Ilmari Länsman et al v. Finland* (Communication No. 511/1992), views adopted 26 October 1992, Report of the Human Rights Committee, Vol. II, GAOR, Fiftieth session, Suppl. No. 40 (A/50/40), pp. 66-76 and *Jouni E. Länsman et al v. Finland* (Communication No. 671/1995), views adopted 30 October 1996, Report of the Human Rights Committee, Vol. II, UN Doc. No. A/52/40), pp. 191-204.

*et al v. New Zealand*[98] (2000). Still, whilst in effect utilizing Article 27 to protect peoples' cultural rights, the Committee still clarified that the right contained in Article 27 is an individual one. That said, one should note that in *Apirana Mahuik*, the Committee formally recognized the interdependence between ICCPR Articles 27 and 1, and hence the relevance of Article 1, proclaiming a pure peoples' right, when addressing cultural rights claims by peoples falling under Article 27.[99] The Human Rights Committee is thus only one step short of proclaiming that ICCPR Article 27, at least when applied to indigenous peoples, encompasses a collective cultural right of peoples. The Committee has, however, also had the opportunity to offer its opinion on the extent to which non-state forming peoples can hold rights pursuant to ICCPR Article 1, when addressing periodic reports submitted by signatory states that have within their borders indigenous peoples claiming a right to self-determination. The Committee's jurisprudence under Article 1 is perhaps of even greater interest than the case law developed under Article 27, since the right to self-determination is undoubtedly a right of peoples.

Throughout the larger part of the 1990s, the Human Rights Committee only very sporadically addressed the right to self-determination. Only since 1999 has the Committee more systematically addressed the right to self-determination in its country specific reports. Since then, a fairly coherent jurisprudence as to the extent to which the right to self-determination contained in ICCPR Article 1 applies to non-state forming peoples has emerged. Analysing this jurisprudence, it is evident that the Committee has been responsive towards indigenous peoples' claims that they do have a right to self-determination under Article 1. Generally speaking, when an indigenous group is regarded as a people by domestic authorities and asserts the right to self-determination, the Committee has held that it is entitled to such a right.[100]

---

98 See *Apirana Mahuika et al v. New Zealand* (Communication No. 547/1993), views adopted 27 October 2000, Report of the Human Rights Committee, Vol. II, UN Doc. No. A/56/40), pp. 11-29.

99 See *Mahuika, ibid., para.* 9.2, and M. Scheinin, 'Indigenous Peoples' Rights under the International Covenant on Civil and Political Rights', in J. Castellino and N. Walsh (eds.), *International Law and Indigenous Peoples* (Leiden, Martinus Nijhoff Publishers, 2005), p. 9.

100 To give a few examples, in 1999 the Human Rights Committee, with reference to the indigenous peoples of Canada, and to ICCPR Article 1(2), emphasized '*that the right to self-determination requires, inter alia, that all peoples must be able to freely dispose of their natural wealth and resources and that they may not be deprived of their own means of subsistence*', see CCPR/C/79/Add.105. Further in 1999, the Committee expressed that it expected Norway to report on the indigenous Saami people's right to self-determination under Article 1 of the ICCPR, see CCPR/C/79/Add.112. Also in 1999, the Committee called on Mexico to respect the indigenous peoples' collective rights to culture and traditional patterns of living, see CCPR/C/79/Add.109. In 2000, the Committee with reference to ICCPR Article 1(2), called on Australia to allow the indigenous population a stronger role in decision-making over their traditional lands and natural resources, see A/55/40, paras. 498-528. In 2002, the Committee encouraged New Zealand to continue to reinforce its efforts to ensure the full enjoyment

Even though the right invoked in *Gillot et al v. France*[101] was an individual one pursuant to ICCPR Article 25, the case warrants discussion in the context of what groups qualify for the right to self-determination under ICCPR Article 1. The complaint concerned participatory rights in a referendum held in New Caledonia, which was open only to persons with close enough ties to the territory. The Committee interpreted Article 25 in the light of Article 1, and held that due to the issue subject to referendum, it was legitimate to restrict the participation to persons with a close tie to New Caledonia. In other words, the Committee concluded that New Caledonia consists of at least two people, with the right to self-determination, and found it legitimate that, for that right to be effectively exercised, participation in a referendum in the territory be restricted to one people. In conclusion, the Human Rights Committee has clearly established that indigenous groups can constitute such peoples that enjoy the right to self-determination pursuant to ICCPR Article 1. In other words, the term 'peoples' in ICCPR Article 1 can not be understood to mean the sum of the inhabitants of a state.[102]

In its General Comment No. 17, adopted in 2005[103], the Committee on Economic, Social and Cultural Rights (the ESC Committee), the UN body authorized to interpret the ICESCR, stated that ICESCR Article 15(1)(c), even though on the face of it clearly formulated as spelling out an individual right, also safeguards the link between

---

of the Covenant rights by the Maori people, see CCPR/CO/75/NZL. Further in 2002, the Committee, referring to ICCPR Article 1, expressed its concern over at the limited extent to which Sweden allows the Saami people a significant role in decision-making processes on issues affecting their traditional lands and economic activities, see CCPR/CO/74/SWE. In 2004, the Committee regretted that it had not received a clear answer concerning the rights of the Saami as an indigenous people, in the light of ICCPR Article 1, see CCPR/CO/82/FIN. In 2006 the Committee concluded that the extinguishment of inherent aboriginal rights in Canada may in practice amount to extinguishment of aboriginal rights pursuant to ICCPR Article 1, see (CCPR/C/CAN/CO/5). Also in 2006, the Committee commended Norway for entering into an agreement with the Saami parliament, the representative body of the Saami people, as well as for enacting legislation that furthered the Saami people's right to self-determination under ICCPR Article 1, see CCPR/C/NOR/CO/5. Further in 2006, the Committee called on the United States to take further steps in order to secure the rights of all indigenous peoples under ICCPR Articles 1 to exercise greater influence in decision-making affecting, e.g., their culture, see CCPR/C/USA/Q/3/CRP.4.

101 *Marie-Hélèn Gillot et al v. France* (Communication No. 932/2000), Views adopted 15 July 2002, Report of the Human Rights Committee, Vol. II, GAOR, Fifty-Seventh Session, Suppl. No. 40 (A/57/40), pp. 270-293.

102 M. Scheinin, member of the HRC during the period when most of the HRC's jurisprudence pertaining to indigenous peoples' cultural rights was crafted, has affirmed that some groups identifying themselves as indigenous do constitute peoples pursuant to the common Article 1 of the 1966 Covenants, see M. Scheinin, *cit. supra* note 99, p. 3.

103 See General Comment No. 17 (2005). The right of everyone to benefit from the protection of the moral and material interest resulting from any scientific, literary, or artistic production of which he or she is the author (article 15, paragraph 1(c) of the Covenant).

peoples and their collective cultural heritage. The ESC Committee underscores that Article 15(1)(c) calls for recognition of the collective authorship of indigenous peoples to elements of their culture. The ESC Committee recognizes that this new interpretation of the article is a result of the constant progressive development of international law, and admits that the drafters of the ICESCR at that time did not realize that the provision could also apply to collectives.[104]

In 2004, the WGIP set out to elaborate guidelines for the protection of indigenous peoples' cultural heritage.[105] The Guidelines were crafted in a joint project involving the Saami Council and WGIP member Professor Yozo Yokota, who presented a final version of the Guidelines to the WGIP's 2006 session.[106] The Guidelines contain an elaborate set of provisions that extensively protect indigenous peoples' collective cultural rights, for instance, affirming that indigenous peoples have the right to control their own cultural elements and determine their cultural development. The WGIP did not, however, decide to adopt the Guidelines. Rather, the WGIP recommended that a technical workshop should be arranged to further discuss the Guidelines and report back to the next session of the WGIP.[107] It remains unclear whether any relevant UN body will act on the WGIP Guidelines, and even if so, the Guidelines are of a non-legally binding character. Nonetheless, the WGIP Guidelines are in line with the general trend in international law towards a recognition of peoples' cultural rights.

## 7. Similar developments within the field of intellectual property rights

Certainly, the world community shall first and foremost protect cultures as human rights. Nonetheless, developments within non-human rights processes can be of relevance for tracing general trends in international law. Some ten plus UN system organizations currently engage in activities relating to peoples' cultural heritage. Most of those do, however, address these issues from a preservation angle, and do not take any position on who hold rights to elements of peoples' cultures. These

---

104 See CESCR General Comment No. 17, paras. 2, 7, 10 and 32.

105 The WGIP Guidelines build on previous work conducted by the WGIP. In 1993, the then Chair of the WGIP, Mdm. Erica-Irene Daes, undertook a study on the Protection of the Cultural and Intellectual Property of Indigenous Peoples, see U.N. Doc. E/CN.4/Sub.2/1993/28 followed by a draft statement of principles of indigenous cultural heritage, see U.N. Doc. E/CN.4/Sub.2/1994/31, Annex (1994). Having received comments from experts, indigenous and state representatives, Mdm Daes revised the Principles and Guidelines, see U.N. Doc E/CN.4/Sub.2/1995/26 (1995). Mdm. Daes subsequently submitted that her text should serve as basis for a declaration by the UN General Assembly, but the UN system failed to act on her request.

106 See E/CN.4/Sub.2/AC.4/2006.

107 See A/HRC/Sub.1/58/22.

processes are of little relevance to an evaluation of the extent to which international law recognizes peoples' right to culture. The World Intellectual Property Organization (WIPO), on the other hand, addresses protection of elements of cultures from a property, or more precisely intellectual property rights (IPRs), perspective. A brief look at how WIPO is addressing these issues can therefore be of interest.

Traditionally, WIPO addressed elements of indigenous peoples' culture in the same manner as it views all forms of human creativity, i.e. by promoting such protection as individual property rights. The approach is natural since IPRs are, per definition, individual rights. Lately, however, WIPO has broadened its view, and has commenced discussing IPR type rights that protect the collective creativeness of peoples. For instance, WIPO is in the process of developing two sets of draft guidelines that protect traditional knowledge (TK) and traditional cultural expressions (TCEs) respectively.[108] These guidelines contain a number of provisions that grant indigenous peoples a collective right over elements of their culture. Hence, also the WIPO guidelines, even though not yet adopted,[109] highlight a trend in international law towards increased recognition of peoples' cultural rights.

## 8. A more modern view on what constitutes discrimination

As described above, the CERD Convention imposes state obligations rather than proclaims rights, and the rights that states shall specifically protect are individual rights. This mirrors a traditional perception that the subjects proper of the right to non-discrimination are individuals, and that the right applies to groups only indirectly.[110] The approach further sits well with the conventional understanding of non-discrimination as meaning that equal cases be treated equally.

In its General Recommendation No. XXIII (1997),[111] the UN Committee on the Elimination of Racial Discrimination (the CERD Committee), established to oversee state compliance with the CERD Convention, recognized that the fact that indigenous peoples have lost their traditional lands constitutes a specific form of discrimination directed against them. The Committee further called on states to recognize and respect indigenous peoples' distinct cultures and ways of life and ensure that indigenous communities can exercise their right to practise and revitalize their cultural traditions and customs. As mentioned above, the CERD Convention places obligations on states, rather than proclaims rights, which is also reflected

---

108 For the latest version of these guidelines, see WIPO Documents WIPO/GRTKF/IC/9/4 and WIPO/GRTKF/IC/9/5.

109 The Guidelines were discussed at the WIPO Intergovernmental Committee on IPRs, Genetic Resources, TK and Folklore, 30 November – 8 December, 2006.

110 A. Cassese, *cit. supra* note 40, p. 329.

111 General Recommendation No. 23, Indigenous Peoples 18/08/97.

in the wording of the General Recommendation. Hence, one cannot perhaps with complete certainty conclude that the Committee recognizes a people's right to culture. Nonetheless, when calling on states not only to guarantee individuals' right to property as stipulated in CERD Convention's Article 5(v), but also to protect indigenous peoples' collective right to property and culture, it undoubtedly appears that the CERD Committee is of the opinion that indigenous peoples are subjects of cultural rights. The Committee has since 1997 reaffirmed this position in numerous observations and decisions.[112]

The notion that the right to non-discrimination is not only an individual but also a collective right, is mirrored in a changed perception of the content of the right to non-discrimination, firmly established in international law today, namely that the right entails not only that equal cases be treated equally but also that different cases be treated differently.[113] Thus understood, the collective right to non-discrimination appears to have essentially the same content as a people's right to culture. Because what is a right to be treated differently other than a right to defend a minority culture from being absorbed into the majority culture? In other words, the individual cultural right is the right to be treated equally to all other human beings, whereas the corresponding collective cultural right is the right to be treated differently.[114]

## 9. The UN Indigenous Declaration – the final nail in the coffin of those arguing against the existence of collective rights of peoples?

The chapter has described how in the aftermath of World War II, the human rights system that the young UN commenced to elaborate was entrenched in the state-individual dichotomy professed by classical individual liberalism. Correspondingly, during the same era self-determination evolved from being 'merely' a principle to also become a legal right; it might be that the term 'peoples' in the phrase 'all peoples have the right to self-determination' was to be generally understood as the sum of

---

112 See, e.g., recommendations adopted with regard to Mexico, which elaborates extensively on indigenous peoples' cultural rights, CERD/C/MEX/CO 15. See also the recent Early Warning & Urgent Action Procedure initiated against New Zealand, Decision 1 (66), CERD/C/DEC/NZL/1.27/04/2005/ and the United States of America, DECISION 1 (68), CERD/USA/DEC/1, 11 April 2006, that both affirms the Committee's view that the CERD Convention protects indigenous peoples' collective rights.

113 For instance, the European Court on Human Rights has stated that 'The right not to be discriminated against … is also violated when States without an objective and reasonable justification fail to treat differently whose situations are significantly different', see *Thilmmenos v. Greece*, Application No. 34369/97, European Court of Human Rights, Judgement of 6 April 2000.

114 M. Hartney, in W. Kymlicka, *cit. supra* note 32, p. 220, and compare R. Stavenhagen, *cit. supra* note 31, p. 98.

the inhabitants of a state or territory.[115] Similarly, the right to non-discrimination appears to have encompassed merely that equal cases be treated equally.

The chapter has further outlined, however, that during the last 30 years or so, there has undeniably been a trend within both legal theory and international law towards an increased recognition of peoples' cultural rights. This trend took off rather cautiously and modestly, but gained real momentum in the 1990s. The question is then: Has this movement reached its goal? Has it been firmly established that international law recognizes peoples' rights to culture? As mentioned above, the engine for the movement towards an acknowledgment of peoples' rights has been indigenous peoples' claim for recognition of their rights. It is therefore logical to seek the ultimate answer to these questions in the processes that have aspired to define what indigenous peoples' rights are under international law.

Following the Sub-Commission's endorsement of the draft Indigenous Declaration presented by the WGIP, the UN in 1995 established the Ad Hoc Working Group on the Draft UN Declaration on the Rights of Indigenous Peoples (WGDD). Notably, the WGDD commenced its work in the same year as Kymlicka published *Multicultural Citizenship*, which, as mentioned above, jet-fuelled the discussions within legal theory on whether peoples can be the subjects of human rights proper. Further, since the inception of the WGDD, and to the conclusion of its work, the two general questions that dominated the discussions in the WGDD were exactly i) is there such a thing as collective human rights? and ii) can non-state forming peoples have the right to self-determination?

In the early years of the WGDD process, many states were quite reluctant to answer particularly the second question in the affirmative.[116] However, after 11 years of deliberations and text negotiations, the WGDD concluded its work in February 2006. The Human Rights Council subsequently by vote adopted the Indigenous Declaration on 29 June 2006, and passed the Declaration on for final approval by

115 Historically, States' and legal scholars' objection towards a right to self-determination for non-state forming peoples appears often to have been based on an unfunded assumption that with the right to self-determination follows a right to complete political independence, to full sovereignty. For instance, when Cassese on p. 283 (*supra* note 40) asserts that national minorities had to be excluded from the right to self-determination, and that only entire populations of sovereign states should be the beneficiaries of that right, it appears clear that he is talking about a right to secession. Similarly, when on p. 287 asserting that the Helsinki Final Act on does not include any rights for ethnic groups to self-determination, Cassese is referring to the external aspect of self-determination, which to Cassese equals a right to secession. See A. Cassese (*cit. supra* note 40) and compare J. Anaya (*cit. supra* note 7), p. 80, A. Buchanan, in W. Kymlicka, *cit. supra* note 36, p. 352, and J. Crawford (*cit. supra* note 12), p. 39. This is a misconception. International law firmly establishes that the right to self-determination, save in extraordinary circumstances, must be exercised within existing state borders.

116 See P. Alston, in P. Alston, *cit. supra* note 12, p. 278.

the UN General Assembly at its 61st session.[117] The Indigenous Declaration has a strong focus on indigenous peoples' collective rights. As indicated above, the issue of whether the Indigenous Declaration should explicitly express that the rights contained in the Declaration are human rights was, however, highly contentious. The final compromise can be found in Article 1, which declares that 'Indigenous peoples have the right to the full enjoyment, as a collective or as individuals, of all human rights ... recognized in ... international human rights law.' Article 1 is an example of what diplomats like to refer to as 'constructive ambiguity'. The overwhelming majority of the participants in the WGDD were of the position that international law does recognize the existence of collective human rights proper, and a normal understanding of Article 1 seems to verify that position. Still, the provision is arguably unclear enough to leave room for those considerably fewer states that are of the opinion that there are no such thing as collective human rights, to interpret Article 1 their way. In connection with the adoption of the Indigenous Declaration by the Human Rights Council, both Sweden and the United Kingdom held interpretative statements claiming that international law does not acknowledge collective human rights proper.

Regardless of any potential uncertainty with regard to the interpretation of Article 1, however, the Indigenous Declaration is packed with provisions that cannot be understood in any other manner than to proclaim cultural rights of indigenous peoples.[118] Further, Article 3 in the Indigenous Declaration is a clone of the Common Article 1(1) in the 1966 Covenants, hence proclaiming that indigenous peoples have the right to self-determination, by virtue of which they may freely pursue their cultural development. Indeed, things have really changed since the mid 1990s, when, as mentioned earlier, a large number of states objected to the idea that the right to self-determination could apply also to non-state forming peoples.

Prior to the adoption of the Indigenous Declaration, legal scholars questioned whether a UN declaration on the rights of indigenous peoples would ever be adopted

---

117 The Declaration, as contained in UN Document A/61/L.67, was adopted by the General Assembly on 13 September 2007, with 143 against 4, and 11 abstentions.

118 For instance, Article 11(1) declares that indigenous peoples have the right to practice and revitalize their cultural traditions and customs. Pursuant to Article 12(1), indigenous peoples have the right to manifest, practice, develop and teach their spiritual and religious traditions, customs and ceremonies. Article 13 underlines that indigenous peoples have the right to revitalize, use, develop and transmit to future generations their histories, languages, oral traditions, philosophies, writing systems and literatures. Article 15 proclaims that indigenous peoples have the right to the dignity and diversity of their cultures, traditions and histories and pursuant to Article 24, indigenous peoples have the right to their traditional medicines and to the conservation of their vital medical plants, animals and minerals. Article 34 declares that indigenous peoples have the right to promote, develop and maintain their distinct customs, traditions and practices. Article 31 proclaims that indigenous peoples have the right to control, protect, and develop their cultural heritage, including their TK and TCEs.

that affirmed indigenous peoples as beneficiaries of the right to self-determination. The same legal scholars further asserted that if such a declaration were to be adopted, that would fundamentally change the international law position on the right to self-determination in the context of non-state forming peoples. For instance, Alston claimed that adoption by the United Nations of an Indigenous Declaration proclaiming a right to self-determination for indigenous peoples would be the test of whether this right applies also to non-state forming peoples.[119] Also Crawford questioned whether an Indigenous Declaration would ever be adopted containing the language on self-determination found in the original draft.[120]

## 10. Conclusions

If there were any lingering doubt, the Indigenous Declaration signals a final break away from a state-individual dichotomy which has been increasingly viewed as inadequate, and affirms that peoples are subject to cultural rights. Political theory and international law have in parallel moved towards acknowledging that a mere respect for individual human rights is not enough to protect peoples' cultures.[121] As Kingsbury has pointed out, to adequately address the needs and aspirations of groups, there is a need to reinvent international law and add additional concepts that go beyond individual human rights.[122] Universal human rights are simply inadequately defined to protect those that want to be different. Indeed, they risk serving as a vehicle for assimilation.[123] Similarly to accommodate for this recognition, the right to non-discrimination has evolved to entail not only the principle that equal cases be treated equally but also that different cases be treated differently.

In concert with the increased respect for peoples' rights, international law's position on what groups constitutes such peoples that have the right to self-determination has also evolved. The adoption of the Indigenous Declaration, proclaiming that indigenous peoples do have the right to self-determination, reasonably puts an end to the uncertainty expressed by some as to whether the right to self-determination can apply also to non-state forming peoples. The Declaration underscores that the concept of 'peoples' is to be perceived in the normal understanding of the word, and has a much broader meaning, both semantically and legally, than the sum of the inhabitants of a state or territory.[124] This development in international law is in

---

119 P. Alston, in P. Alston, *cit. supra* note12, p. 3.

120 J. Crawford, *cit. supra* note 12, p. 25.

121 *Ibid.*, p. 23 ff.

122 B. Kingsbury, *cit. supra* note 12, p. 78.

123 J. Crawford, *cit. supra* note 12, p. 24.

124 It is fully consistent with international law that the interpretation of international legal provisions evolves over time. Pursuant to Article 31 of the Vienna Convention on the Law of Treaties,

line with arguments made by legal scholars. Crawford has observed that if the right to self-determination is a general right of peoples, it appears that it has to be applied equally to state and non-state forming peoples. Concluding that the 'peoples' that are entitled to self-determination under international law constitute the sum of the inhabitants of the state would render the concept a 'cruel deception'. Crawford hence asserts that the presumption under international law must be the contrary; that also non-state forming peoples must constitute such groups that are entitled to the right to self-determination.[125] Similarly, Anaya argues that 'peoples' should not be defined as the sum of the inhabitants of a state, but by perceived spheres of ethnographic cohesion and historically exercised territorial sovereignty.[126]

Finally, the adoption of the Indigenous Declaration makes a strong case for the principle that peoples' right to culture is not only a collective right, but also a collective human right. However, there are still some objections to the final claim. As mentioned above, a few states will certainly make interpretative statements in connection with the adoption of the Indigenous Declaration, claiming that international law does not acknowledge collective human rights proper. Further, as outlined above, Hartney and others continue to argue that – from a legal theory perspective – human rights proper only apply to individuals. One can of course argue with that assertion, but hardly dismiss it outright. But perhaps one does not have to spend too much time lingering on the question of whether international law recognizes collective human rights. To adequately protect peoples' cultural rights, perhaps it is more fruitful to frame the discussion in terms of redefining the very concepts of state and nation,[127] rather than dwelling on whether, academically speaking, peoples' cultural rights are human rights proper or not. As Parekh has pointed out, requesting non-members of an engulfing society to respect the form of life of the dominating society is to confuse the state with the nation.[128] Or, taking this argument one step further, as Stavenhagen has suggested, referring to Connor,

---

subsequent practice constitutes the primary source when interpreting a provision contained in an international treaty, see United Nations, Treaty Series, vol. 1155, p. 331. Preparatory work before the adoption of a treaty is thus merely a secondary source; it is only relevant to the extent that no subsequent practice exists that can guide the interpretation of a particular provisions.

125 J. Crawford *cit. supra* note 12, pp. 40 and 64.

126 J. Anaya, *cit. supra* note 7, p. 78. And, if faced with this new interpretation of what is meant with a people, perhaps Cassese would re-evaluate his position as to what groups the right to self-determination applies to. Note that Cassese, who, as described above, makes a restrictive interpretation *de lege lata* of the content of the right to self-determination as it applies to ethnic groups, in a *de lege ferenda* argument asserts that a the right to self-determination for such groups should encompass a right to autonomy in, e.g., cultural matters, see A. Cassese, *cit. supra* note 40, pp. 354-355.

127 R. Stavenhagen, *cit. supra* note 31, pp. 96 and 108.

128 See B. Parekh, in W. Kymlicka, *cit. supra* note 2, p. 310.

the development of modern states has resulted more in nation-destroying than of nation-building.

Recall that when ideas of sovereignty of collectives started to emerge, the subject of sovereignty was the people and not a state and that the state superseded the people based on a notion that states are ethnically homogenous. If we now accept that such is not the case, it is reasonable to go back to the starting point, that the sovereign that has cultural rights is not a fictional state but a people founded in reality. The notion that all men somehow consent to the jurisdiction of the state is obviously a fiction. It does not make sense that just a random group of men come together to form a state. It would be more natural that they have some kind of ethnic togetherness. Indeed, the people's right to self-determination must reasonably pre-date statehood, since if a group has a right to form a state, certainly it must also have the right to agree on other forms of arrangements through which to exercise the right to self-determination and control its culture. A people should then, even under the notion of a social contract that is the fundament in individual liberalism, have the right to control its own culture. So, responding to Ivor Jennings' claim that peoples cannot hold cultural rights because one must first then define what constitutes peoples, the same could be said about states.[129]

This approach would also defeat one of the most frequent arguments made against recognizing a people's right to culture. Opponents to recognizing such a right often claim that doing so amounts to the same thing as taking the position of the majority of an ethnic group, against the minority of the minority or against those that otherwise are without power within the group.[130] As outlined above, however, liberal theorists do not only accept but actually presuppose the notion of a state, through which a majority of the citizens can impose decisions on the minority. They fail to explain why such behaviour is acceptable when exercised by a state, but not when exercised by a people, even when the people is operating in accordance with democratic principles. The same concerns that are raised with regard to certain individuals' status if respecting the rights of peoples could be raised against the powers exercised by a state. It is difficult to see why non-state forming peoples should not have the same right as state forming peoples to determine the course of their culture, even when this implies implementing decisions that might not be favoured by all members of the group.[131] If accepting this approach, it is perhaps

---

129 That is particularly so, since it is generally perceived that the formation of a state is a matter of fact and not law, see J. Crawford, *The Creation of States in International Law* (Oxford, 2006), pp. 3-5.

130 C. Kukathas, *cit. supra* note 35, p. 236.

131 V. Van Dyke, *cit. supra* note 9, p. 44. In this context note that also Cassese has observed that the traditional multi-ethnic state has become effete, is gradually losing its authority and legitimacy and is probably doomed to demise, see A. Cassese, *cit. supra* note 40, pp. 339, 349-350 and 262.

not so important whether academia labels peoples' rights to culture human rights proper or not.[132] Indeed, states are not perceived to have human rights. What one has to establish, though, is the relationship between the cultural right of the people and individual members' right to the same, in exactly the same manner that any state has to determine its relationship with its citizens.[133] That will have to be the subject of another chapter, however.

---

[132] As outlined extensively above, Hartney argues against the existence of collective human rights proper. In the next breath, however, Hartney, offers a reformulation of term collective rights. A right could be labelled collective, Hartney asserts, not if it inheres in a group, but because its objective or the interest served or its exercise is collective. In other words, a right is a collective right if it is designed to serve the collective interest of the members of a collective, see M. Hartney, *cit. supra* note 32, pp. 219-220. Hartney further refers to Tarnopolsky, who has expressed this notion somewhat differently. Tarnopolsky distinguishes between rights which individuals possess in virtue of being human beings (individual rights or human rights) and rights which individuals possess in virtue of their membership in an ethnic group (group rights). Hence, the subjects of both sets of rights are individuals. The distinction is rather that the first category is universal, whereas the application of the second category of rights is limited to a group. See W.S. Tarnopolsky, 'The Equality of Rights', in W.S. Tarnopolsky and G.-A. Beaudoin (eds.), *The Canadian Charter of Rights and Freedoms: Commentary* (Toronto, 1982), 395, pp. 437-439.

[133] See R. Stavenhagen, *cit. supra* note 31, p. 108. In this context, note also that Kymlicka, responding to the concern that recognition of group rights might lead to discrimination of vulnerable members of the group, submits that the group's actions should be evaluated as were it a state. W. Kymlicka, *cit. supra* note 24, Ch. 3, and compare Kingsbury, *cit. supra* note 12, p. 84.

# 6
# Indigenous Peoples' Cultural Rights and the Controversy over Commercial Use of Their Traditional Knowledge

*Federico Lenzerini*

## 1. Introduction. The clash between drastically different visions of life: 'holisticism' vs. the logic of economic profit[1]

There are innumerable true stories in the context of indigenous visions of life that better illustrate the importance of plant genetic resources than any theoretical explanation could. One of these stories concerns *ayahuasca*, the sacred beverage of autochthonous communities in the Amazon.

Centuries ago, Amazon peoples received from the 'plant teachers' (superior beings who can only be seen in special states of consciousness and provide human beings with knowledge and power) the knowledge for developing a special beverage – obtained from the mixture of a selection of natural ingredients manipulated and boiled while performing an elaborate set of rituals – called *ayahuasca*.[2] The name *ayahuasca* derives from the combination of the Quechua words *aya* (meaning 'soul' or 'spirit') and *huasca* (meaning 'vine').[3] The knowledge related to the 'vine of the soul' has been transmitted from generation to generation until today, and is held by local shamans. The basic ingredient of *ayahuasca* medicine is the *Banisteriopsis caapi* vine (commonly named ayahuasca itself), mixed with the leaves of *Psychotria viridis* (chacruna), a small jungle tree, or, in alternative, other plants containing

---

1 This section's title has been inspired by an Article written by M.A. Lee, entitled 'Shamanism versus Capitalism. The Politics of the Hallucinogen Ayahuasca', published in the *San Francisco Bay Guardian*, 19 February 2001, available online at <www.jcrows.com/ayahuasca.html> (last visited on 31 August 2005).

2 See M.A. Lee, *cit. supra* note 1.

3 See O. Blanco, 'Sacred Teacher Healer Plants of the Peruvian Amazon', available at <www.biopark.org/peru/four.html> (last visited on 31 August 2005).

Francioni and Scheinin (eds), *Cultural Human Rights*, 119–149

dimethyltryptamine (DMT) or related alkaloid compounds.[4] There are various kinds of *ayahuasca*, characterized by different botanical and functional characteristics.[5] The *ayahuasca* is 'a powerful holistic purgative medicine capable of great healing and transformation … regarded as the supreme holistic plant medicine throughout the western Amazon'.[6] Many rainforest shamans simply refer to it as *el remedio* ('the remedy'),[7] since they attribute to the *ayahuasca* the power of treating a wide range of physical, psychological and spiritual diseases.[8] Its properties are not limited to curative effects, however. *Ayahuasca* also has deep religious and spiritual significance, since it is used by shamans for falling in trance and communicating with divinities. It represents:

> the fount of understanding, the ultimate medium that reveals the mythological origins of life. To drink [it] … is to return to the cosmic uterus, the primordial womb of existence, where the individual 'sees' the tribal divinities, the creation of the universe and humanity, the first couple, the creation of the animals, and the establishment of the social order.[9]

The spiritual significance of *ayahuasca* is thus even greater than its importance as a medicinal treatment. Throughout the centuries it has become a basic element of the anthropologic and cultural identity of the communities that have developed and made use of it.

When the Western world had its first taste of *ayahuasca* in the 17th century, it was derided and then demonized as a 'diabolical potion' by Jesuit missionaries, who considered its hallucinogenic properties a form of possession by demoniac spirits.[10] Despite all the attempts – which have taken different forms with time – aimed at eradicating the practices associated with *ayahuasca*,[11] indigenous shamans have been able to transmit these practices to present generations, and they have eventually been revitalized after the legalization of the sacramental use of *ayahuasca* by the Brazilian government in 1987.[12] In recent years, Western scientists have pragmati-

---

4 See M.A. Lee, *cit. supra* note 1; O. Blanco, *ibid.*

5 See Blanco, *cit. supra* note 3.

6 *Ibid.*

7 See M.A. Lee, *cit. supra* note 1.

8 See O. Blanco, *cit. supra* note 3.

9 See M.A. Lee, *cit. supra* note 1, quoting the anthropologist Gerardo Reichel-Dolmatoff.

10 *Ibid.*

11 For a comprehensive assessment of events characterizing the history of the *ayahuasca* from the seventeenth century to the present time, see M.A. Lee, *cit. supra* note 1.

12 See M.A. Lee, *cit. supra* note 1.

cally identified the hallucinogenic properties of *ayahuasca*,[13] though some of its effects remain unexplained if appraised on the sole basis of scientific reason.[14] At the same time, however, they have confirmed its curative properties.[15] So, when the potential economic profit to be gained from *ayahuasca* was finally perceived, Western firms and corporations tried to appropriate, through patents, the plants and the knowledge used in obtaining the vine. In particular, in 1986 the American citizen Loren Miller obtained for the *International Plant Medicine Corporation* a patent (U.S. patent No. US5751P) for a claimed new variety of *Banisteriopsis caapi*, named *Da Vine*.[16] In 1999, following a re-examination request presented by the Center for International Environmental Law (CIEL), based on the fact that *Da Vine* was neither new nor distinct and actually corresponded to the *Banisteriopsis caapi* (the sacred plant of the indigenous tribes of the Amazon Region), the United States Patent and Trademark Office (USPTO) revoked the patent. Nonetheless, in 2001, following another re-examination request presented by Loren Miller, the USPTO re-granted the patent.[17]

This is only one of many examples of bioprospection followed by unlawful appropriation of indigenous traditional knowledge (TK) and/or related biogenetic resources occurring around the world.[18] It is commonly called 'biopiracy'.

---

13 The hallucinogenic properties of *ayahuasca* are due to the sophisticated combination of its component elements. Although DMT has hallucinogenic properties, it is generally metabolized and neutralized by a particular gastric enzyme. The action of other chemicals contained in *ayahuasca* deactivate the action of this enzyme, however, thereby allowing DMT to circulate in the blood and eventually the brain, where it produces exceptional visions and mystical experiences. *Ayahuasca* has been described by the chemist J. C. Callaway as 'one of the most sophisticated [forms of] drug delivery in existence'. See M.A. Lee, cit. *supra* note 1.

14 For example, it is not explained why the visions triggered by *ayahuasca* often include Amazon jungle animals even when drunk by people from other continents who, possibly, have never seen such animals; see Lee, *supra*, note 1.

15 For example, a project developed by UCLA (the 'Hoasca Project') has confirmed the role of *ayahuasca* as vermifuge treatment for gastrointestinal parasites among Amazon communities; see O. Blanco, *cit. supra* note 3.

16 See <12.espacenet.com/espacenet/viewer?PN=US5751P&CY=ch&LG=en&DB=EPD> (last visited on 30 September 2004).

17 See <www.amazonlink.org/biopiracy/ayahuasca.htm> (last visited on 30 September 2004).

18 For other examples of unauthorized and unregulated taking of biological samples from lands belonging to indigenous peoples and/or related knowledge, see F. Lenzerini, 'Biogenetic Resources and Indigenous Peoples' Rights', in F. Francioni (ed.), *Biotechnologies and International Human Rights* (Hart Publishing, Oxford, 2007), section I and the sources cited therein.

## 2. Cultural rights of indigenous peoples

In a letter sent to James Madison in 1789, the then-US President Thomas Jefferson stated that '[w]hat is true of every member of the society individually, is true of them all collectively, since the rights of the whole can be no more than the sum of the rights of individuals'.[19] Such visions of collective rights as the mere sum of the individual rights of members of the collectivity concerned have inspired international law on human rights until recently. Their main implication is that there is no need to include specific provisions aimed at the protection of collective rights in human rights instruments, since these are automatically safeguarded through the defence of individual rights. No provision on collective rights – with the exception of the right to self-determination established in Common Article 1 – was included in the 1966 UN Covenants on human rights, even with respect to cultural rights. These latter rights, though of clearly paramount collective character, are contemplated by the Covenant on Economic, Social and Cultural rights (ICESCR)[20] solely within the limits of their individual connotation. Thus, they include only certain rights, consisting of taking part in cultural life, enjoying the benefits of scientific progress and benefiting from the protection of intellectual property rights (IPRs).[21] The scope of protection granted to cultural rights by the ICESCR is rather narrow and inadequate in light of their inherent nature; and does not deal with the necessity of safeguarding the right of preserving one's own culture. This right has both an individual and a collective dimension, but it is the latter facet that plays a more significant role.

In this perspective, cultural rights are indeed dependent on the concept of culture, the internationally accepted definition of which shows how inextricably its individual component is linked to its collective element. According to the definition developed in Mexico City in 1982, culture is:

> the whole complex of distinctive spiritual, material, intellectual and emotional features that characterize a society or social group. It includes not only the arts and letters, but also modes of life, the fundamental rights of the human being, value systems, traditions and beliefs.[22]

As is made clear in this definition, all the elements of culture turn on the concept of 'society' or 'social group', which is by nature collective. As a consequence, to the

---

19 See The Letters of Thomas Jefferson: 1743-1826. The Earth Belongs to the Living. To James Madison Paris, Sep. 6, 1789, available at <www.let.rug.nl/usa/P/tj3/writings/brf/jefl81.htm> (last visited on 26 April 2006).

20 *International Covenant on Economic, Social and Cultural Rights*, 1966, 993 *UNTS* 3.

21 See Article 15.

22 See 1982 *Mexico City Declaration on Cultural Policies*, available at: <www.unesco.org/culture/laws/mexico/html_eng/page1.shtml> (last visited on 5 April 2005).

extent that cultural rights derive their *raison d'être* from the concept of culture, they must necessarily be of a collective character, with the exception of certain 'marginal' prerogatives at the edge of the area defining the rights in point. Such prerogatives relate mainly to the individual right of taking part in the enjoyment of benefits deriving from the collective exercise of the above-mentioned rights. This individual right is simply functional or secondary in character, since it is conditioned on the actual enjoyment, by the community concerned, of collective rights on which the group bases its own identity. Putting this theoretical reasoning into practical terms, the individual right to take part in the cultural life of a given community is void when this community is not allowed to enjoy and practise its own culture at the collective level, to the same extent that the right of a believer to practise his/her own religion is void (or, at least, strongly impaired) when the religious congregation of which he/she is part is not allowed to meet in its own consecrated buildings to pray and celebrate religious functions.

The assumption that collective rights correspond to the mere 'sum' of individual rights is thus rather misconceived because – to remain with the example just provided – although the right to participate in religious functions may have an individual nature, other elements essential to such functions make sense only in light of their collective significance. For instance, the 'right' of a Christian priest to consecrate the Host and to distribute it as Christ's Body is not the individual right of the priest, but simply a power he is entitled to exercise on account of his position as the authority entrusted to perform this function on behalf of the Church as a collective institution. To the same extent, the power of the ministers of certain Buddhist communities to cut the hair of the faithful as a sign of subjection to Buddha is not an individual right, but just a function they exercise on behalf of the community as its representatives.

Similarly, the legalization of the sacramental use of *ayahuasca* decreed by the Brazilian government in 1987[23] resulted from recognition of a collective right in favour of the communities concerned, not of an individual right for the members of such communities. This is demonstrated by the fact that use of the drug was authorized only for sacramental purposes, i.e. in the context of the exercise of certain rites whose *raison d'être* is their communal significance.

Similar examples can also be provided from outside the area of religious rights. For instance, the exemption of aboriginal subsistence whaling from the prohibition on whaling imposed by the International Whaling Commission,[24] which is constantly

---

23 See *supra*, text corresponding to note 12.

24 See, *inter alia*, A. Gillespie, 'Aboriginal Subsistence Whaling: A Critique to the Inter-Relationship between International Law and the International Whaling Commission', *Colorado Journal of International Environmental Law and Policy* (2001), p. 77 ff. R.J. Miller, 'Exercising Cultural Self-Determination: The Makah Indian Tribe Goes to Whaling', *American Indian Law Review* (2000/2001), p. 165 ff.

granted not only for nutritional needs, but also for cultural reasons,[25] results from recognition, by the Commission, of a right that is collective (and not individual) in character. It is true that the right to hunt whales may be invoked individually by any member of the community concerned, but the reason why individuals possess this prerogative is not to do with their individual qualities, but exclusively the fact that they are part of the aboriginal community, which, as a collective, is the only owner of the right recognized by the Commission. In other words, the individual right comes to members of the community from, and is inextricably interrelated with, the corresponding collective right granted to the community itself. It is a right conferred for its communal significance, as the Commission clarified in 1982:

> [w]haling and associated activities [represent] perhaps the most important single element in the culture and society of north Alaskan whale hunting communities. It provides a focus for the ordering of social integration, political leadership, ceremonial activity, traditional education, personality, values, and Eskimo identity ... the position of whaling as a pivotal, cultural activity and the extremely high valuation placed on bowhead whale products as food makes [the] replacement [of food deriving from whaling] impossible.[26]

A similar reasoning has been developed by the Human Rights Committee (HRC) in interpreting Article 27 of the International Covenant on Civil and Political Rights (ICCPR).[27] The provision in question affirms that:

> [i]n those States in which ethnic, religious or linguistic minorities exist, persons belonging to such minorities shall not be denied the right, in community with the other members of their group, to enjoy their own culture, to profess and practise their own religion, or to use their own language.

In its General Comment relating to the provision just quoted, the HRC, though affirming that 'Article 27 ... relates to rights conferred on individuals as such',[28] also emphasized that the 'persons designed to be protected [by the article] are those *who belong to a group and who share in common a culture, a religion and/or a language*'.[29] The HRC made it clear that:

---

25 See, on this point, F. Lenzerini, 'The Interplay between Environmental Protection and Human and Peoples' Rights in International Law', *African Yearbook of International Law* (2003), p. 93.

26 See *Report of the International Whaling Commission*, 1982, Special Issue, No. 4, p. 35.

27 *UNTS*, Vol. 993, p. 3.

28 See Human Rights Committee General Comment No. 23, 6 April 1994, 'The rights of minorities (Art. 27)', available at: <www.unhchr.ch/tbs/doc.nsf/(Symbol)/fb7fb12c2fb8bb21c12563ed004df111?Opendocument> (last visited on 5 September 2006), para. 3.1.

29 *Ibid.*, para. 5.1 (emphasis added).

> [t]he right of individuals belonging to a linguistic minority to use their language among themselves, in private or in public, is distinct from other language rights protected under the Covenant. In particular, it should be distinguished from the general right to freedom of expression protected under article 19. The latter right is available to all persons, irrespective of whether they belong to minorities or not.[30]

So, although formally of an individual nature (and enforceable only on an individual basis), the particular right encompassed by Article 27 ICCPR has the purpose of safeguarding a value belonging to the community; it thus loses all importance when disconnected from its communal significance. This is subsequently clarified by the HRC:

> [a]lthough the rights protected under article 27 are individual rights, *they depend in turn on the ability of the minority group to maintain its culture, language or religion.* Accordingly, *positive measures by States may also be necessary to protect the identity of a minority* and the rights of its members to enjoy and develop their culture and language and to practise their religion, *in community with the other members of the group* ... The protection of these rights is directed towards ensuring the survival and continued development of the cultural, religious and social identity of the minorities concerned.[31]

The significance of this reasoning emerges in clear terms when it is translated into practice. For example, in the case of *Ominayak and the Lubicon Lake Band v. Canada*[32] the HRC found that the selling of oil and gas concessions on traditional Lubicon Band lands by the province of Alberta would result in a breach of Article 27, in that

30 *Ibid.*, para. 5.3.

31 *Ibid.*, paragraphs 6.2 and 9 (emphasis added). Para. 9 states that 'article 27 relates to rights whose protection imposes specific obligations on States parties. The protection of these rights is directed towards ensuring the survival and continued development of the cultural, religious and social identity of the minorities concerned, thus enriching the fabric of society as a whole. Accordingly, the Committee observes that these rights must be protected as such and should not be confused with other personal rights conferred on one and all under the Covenant. States parties, therefore, have an obligation to ensure that the exercise of these rights is fully protected and they should indicate in their reports the measures they have adopted to this end'.

32 *Ominayak and the Lubicon Lake Band v. Canada*, Communication No. 167/1984, 26 March 1990, U.N. Doc. A/45/40 (1990). See also, *inter alia*, *Ilmari Länsam et al. v. Finland*, Communication No. 511/1992, 14 October 1993, U.N. doc. CCPR/C/52/D/511/1992 (1994) (though limited quarrying on the slopes of one mountain did not jeopardize applicants' right to culture, in the event that mining activities were to be approved on a large scale and significantly expanded, said activities could give rise to a breach of Article 27); *Apirana Mahuika et al. v. New Zealand*, Communication No. 547/1993, 27 October 2000, available at: <www1.umn.edu/humanrts/undocs/547-1993.html> (last visited on 6 October 2005).

it threatened the way of life and culture of the Band on account of environmental degradation and failure to preserve the Band's cultural relationship with its ancestral lands and resources. In practical terms, the individual claimant acted here as the 'representative' of an interest that was basically collective in character. In fact, the decision of the HRC asserting that the Canadian government could not freely dispose of the Lubicon Lake Band's traditional lands was not based on an individual title of ownership to the lands. On the contrary, it was the Band as a whole, i.e. the *community*, that was recognized as the titleholder of a collective cultural right limiting the freedom of the Canadian government to exploit the lands in question. (Nonetheless, due to the formally individual nature of the right protected by Article 27 and pursuant to the ICCPR system, the right in point may only be enforced on an individual basis, as previously noted).

In this context, while it may be true that the collective rights discussed here may be 'divided' into a number of individual rights corresponding exactly to the number of community members concerned, the contrary is not true. In other words, it is important to emphasize that, while such individual rights derive their *raison d'être* from corresponding collective rights belonging to the community, the latter exist independently of the former, deriving their existence from the communal cultural heritage of the social group to which they belong. Consequently, they cannot in substance be considered the sum of the individual rights in point.

In recent years the scope of the international legal protection of cultural rights has evolved significantly, especially with regard to indigenous peoples. In this sense, it is important to observe that the principle expressed by Article 27 ICCPR is reiterated in Article 30 of the Convention on the Rights of the Child (CRC)[33] with almost identical wording (but of course with reference to children). The only significant additions in Article 30 CRC with respect to Article 27 ICCPR consist of the phrases 'or persons of indigenous origin exist' and 'or who is indigenous' after the words 'minorities' and 'minority', respectively. (This is on account of the fact that indigenous peoples cannot be considered 'minorities' in the proper sense of the word). As a matter of legal coherence, the significance of this provision should be interpreted with an approach equivalent to the HRC reading of Article 27 ICCPR, although no general comment on Article 30 CRC has been adopted by the Committee on the Rights of the Child at the time of writing.[34] For the time being, the strict connection of Article 30 CRC with respect to the integrity of the cultural identity of peoples has been fully perceived by the government of Canada, which

33 1989 *United Nations Convention on the Rights of the Child*, available at: <193.194.138.190/html/menu3/b/k2crc.htm> (last visited on 6 October 2005).

34 See <www.ohchr.org/english/bodies/crc/comments.htm> (last visited on 19 April 2005).

in ratifying the CRC,[35] made a reservation to Article 21 (concerning the regulation of child adoption), declaring:

> with a view to ensuring full respect for the purposes and intent of… article 30 of the Convention, the Government of Canada reserves the right not to apply the provisions of article 21 to the extent that they may be inconsistent with *customary forms of care among aboriginal peoples in Canada.*[36]

Indeed, preservation of the cultural identity of peoples represents the central element and simultaneously the very *ratio* of the protection of cultural rights. The cultural identity of any human being is, in fact, shaped by the collective cultural context to which he/she belongs. This is particularly true with regard to minorities and especially to indigenous peoples, who proudly retain a strong link with their cultural roots, in a context where the individual identity of any member inextricably merges with the collective mystical condition of being part of a community that is indissoluble in its anthropological, social and spiritual (in a word, cultural) identity. In light of this, certain international legal instruments explicitly emphasize the need for safeguarding and preserving such identities. Article 1 of the 1992 UN Declaration on Minorities,[37] for example, solemnly declares as follows:

> 1. States shall protect the existence and the national or ethnic, cultural, religious and linguistic identity of minorities within their respective territories and shall encourage conditions for the promotion of that identity.
> 2. States shall adopt appropriate legislative and other measures to achieve those ends.

With specific regard to indigenous peoples, Article 2 of the 1989 ILO Convention on Indigenous and Tribal Peoples in Independent Countries (CITPIC)[38] states that:

> 1. Governments shall have the responsibility for developing, with the participation of the peoples concerned, co-ordinated and systematic action to protect the rights of these peoples and to guarantee respect for their integrity. 2. Such action shall include measures for: … (b) Promoting the full realisation of the social, economic and *cultural rights* of these peoples

---

35 See <www.ohchr.org/english/countries/ratification/11.htm> (last visited on 4 October 2005).

36 See <www.ohchr.org/english/countries/ratification/11.htm#reservations> (last visited on 4 October 2005; emphasis added).

37 See *Declaration on the Rights of Persons Belonging to National or Ethnic, Religious and Linguistic Minorities*, G.A. Res. 47/135 of 18 December 1992, available at: <www.unhchr.ch/html/menu3/b/d_minori.htm> (last visited on 4 October 2005).

38 See *Convention (No. 169) concerning Indigenous and Tribal Peoples in Independent Countries*, 1989, available at: <www.ilo.org/ilolex/english/convdisp1.htm> (last visited on 5 September 2006).

> *with respect for their social and cultural identity, their customs and traditions and their institutions.*[39]

This principle permeates the whole Convention and is reiterated in several provisions. In particular, article 5(a) affirms that, in applying the provisions of the Convention, '[t]he social, cultural, religious and spiritual values and practices of [the] peoples [concerned] shall be recognised and protected'.

The United Nations Declaration on the Rights of Indigenous Peoples (DRIP),[40] although non-binding, represents a real 'gold mine' with respect to the recognition of indigenous peoples' cultural rights. Article 1 recognizes their right to fully enjoy, also *as collective entities*, all human rights and fundamental freedoms recognized by international human rights law. Article 3 expressly recognizes their right to self-determination (the extent of which is elaborated on in the following provisions).[41] Their rights, *inter alia*, 'not to be subjected to forced assimilation or destruction of their culture' (both as peoples and as individuals), 'to practise and revitalize their cultural traditions and customs' (including the right to 'maintain, protect and develop the past, present and future manifestations of their cultures'), as well as to 'the dignity and diversity of their cultures, traditions, histories and aspirations' are also expressly contemplated, by Articles 8, 11 paras 1 and 15 respectively.[42] Furthermore, the right of indigenous peoples to 'their traditional medicines and to maintain their health practices, including the conservation of their vital medicinal

---

39 Emphasis added.

40 See U.N. doc. A/HRC/1/L.10 of 30 June 2006, p. 58 ff. The Declaration was adopted in 2006 by the new Human Rights Council and, at the time of writing, was due to be definitively approved by the General Assembly within a short time.

41 Article 4 affirms that '[i]ndigenous peoples, in exercising their right to self-determination, have the right to autonomy or self-government in matters relating to their internal and local affairs, as well as ways and means for financing their autonomous functions', while Article 5 states that they 'have the right to maintain and strengthen their distinct political, legal, economic, social and cultural institutions, while retaining their rights to participate fully, if they so choose, in the political, economic, social and cultural life of the State'.

42 The provisions of Articles 12 para. 1 ('[i]ndigenous peoples have the right to manifest, practice, develop and teach their spiritual and religious traditions, customs and ceremonies; the right to maintain, protect, and have access in privacy to their religious and cultural sites; the right to the use and control of their ceremonial objects; and the right to the repatriation of their human remains'), 13 para. 1 ('[i]ndigenous peoples have the right to revitalize, use, develop and transmit to future generations their histories, languages, oral traditions, philosophies, writing systems and literatures, and to designate and retain their own names for communities, places and persons') and 14 para. 1 ('[i]ndigenous peoples have the right to establish and control their educational systems and institutions providing education in their own languages, in a manner appropriate to their cultural methods of teaching and learning') are also of particular relevance for the purposes of this chapter.

plants, animals and minerals' (Article 24) is also provided. Last but not least, article 31 specifically affirms the right of indigenous peoples:

> to maintain, control, protect and develop their cultural heritage, traditional knowledge and traditional cultural expressions, as well as the manifestations of their sciences, technologies and cultures, including human and genetic resources, seeds, medicines, knowledge of the properties of fauna and flora, oral traditions, literatures, designs, sports and traditional games and visual and performing arts. They also have the right to maintain, control, protect and develop their intellectual property over such cultural heritage, traditional knowledge, and traditional cultural expressions.

The recently adopted UNESCO Convention for the Safeguarding of the Intangible Cultural Heritage[43] is also pertinent to the subject matter at hand, although rather indirectly. It recognizes the especially significant role of indigenous peoples 'in the production, safeguarding, maintenance and re-creation of immaterial cultural heritage'[44] and establishes that, in the context of access to intangible heritage (which includes indigenous 'knowledge and practices concerning nature and the universe'),[45] respect for 'customary practices governing access to specific aspects of [it]' is to be ensured.[46]

Also at UNESCO, the recent international attention paid to safeguarding the many different expressions of culture has of late resulted in the adoption of two standard-setting instruments concerning cultural diversity, which is finally perceived as the priceless heritage of humankind as a whole. This new legal conscience was first epitomized in the 2001 UNESCO Universal Declaration on Cultural Diversity through recognition of such diversity as:

> embodied in the uniqueness and plurality of the identities of the groups and societies making up humankind. As a source of exchange, innovation and creativity, cultural diversity is as necessary for humankind as biodiversity is for nature. In this sense, it is the common heritage of humanity and should be recognized and affirmed for the benefit of present and future generations.[47]

---

43 The Convention was adopted by the UNESCO General Conference on 17 October 2003. The full text of the Convention is available at: <www.unesco.org> (last visited on 5 September 2006).

44 See Preamble, sixth sentence.

45 See the definition of 'intangible cultural heritage' provided for by Article 2, particularly para. 2(d).

46 See Article 13(d)(ii).

47 Adopted by the UNESCO General Conference on 2 November 2001. The full text is available at: <www.unesco.org/confgen/press_rel/021101_clt_diversity.shtml> (last visited on 5 September 2006). See Article 1.

The evolution that started with the proclamation of the 2001 Declaration eventually led to the adoption by the UNESCO General Conference of the Convention on the Protection and Promotion of the Diversity of Cultural Expressions[48] on 20 October 2005. Its Preamble recognizes that 'cultural diversity forms a common heritage of humanity and should be cherished and preserved for the benefit of all'.[49] The essential significance of culture is seen in the 'diverse forms [it takes] across time and space[, a] diversity [that] is embodied in the uniqueness and plurality of the identities and cultural expressions of the peoples and societies making up humanity'.[50] Safeguarding the enjoyment of cultural rights is perceived as an essential means to ensure the preservation of the diversity of cultural expressions. This should be realized through defending the right of all persons,

> including [those] belonging to minorities and indigenous peoples, [to manifest] their freedom to create, disseminate and distribute their traditional cultural expressions and to have access thereto, so as to benefit them for their own development.[51]

Unfortunately, outside the statements of principle the preoccupation that inspired the drafters of the Convention was rather the preservation of certain national cultural industries and expressions (i.e. audiovisual products) than the need to safeguard the cultural identity of the peoples of the world in a 'holistic' perspective (through 'serious' and effective obligations for state parties, which are virtually lacking in the adopted text). Under the aegis of the noble concept of cultural diversity, then, the main intention was to use the resulting Convention to counter the detrimental effects of ongoing liberalization in trade on domestic industries and expressions. Still, the final text includes certain provisions proclaiming the equal dignity of all cultures[52] and expressing the need for preserving and encouraging the development of different cultural expressions.[53] It thus confirms the current trend within the international community of fostering the preservation of the idiosyncratic identity of

48 The full text of the Convention is available at: <www.unesco.org> (last visited on 5 September 2006).

49 See Second sentence.

50 See Preamble, Seventh sentence.

51 See Preamble, Fifteenth Sentece.

52 See, in particular, Article 2, which includes, among the 'Guiding Principles' of the Convention, the 'Principle of equal dignity and respect for all cultures' (No. 3), expressed as follows: '[t]he protection and promotion of the diversity of cultural expressions presuppose the recognition of equal dignity of and respect for all cultures, including the cultures of persons belonging to minorities and indigenous peoples'.

53 See Article 7, para. 1, according to which '[p]arties shall endeavour to create in their territory an environment that encourages individuals and social groups: (a) to create, produce, disseminate, distribute and have access to their own cultural expressions, paying due attention

all the peoples of the world (including indigenous ones) as irreplaceable components of the human family.

A number of international treaties, especially in the environmental field, include measures for the preservation of certain cultural rights, *inter alia* of indigenous peoples. These are generally prescribed as derogatory exceptions to the main principles contemplated by the treaties. Article III(1)(d) of the Polar Bears Agreement,[54] for example, allows hunting these bears when it is performed 'by local peoples using traditional methods in the exercise of their traditional rights …'. Similarly, Article III(5)(c) of the 1979 Convention on Migratory Species[55] affirms that the general prohibition on the taking of endangered migratory species may be derogated when, *inter alia*, it is carried out to 'accommodate the needs of traditional subsistence users of such species', thus protecting traditional hunting practices linked to the cultural heritage of the communities concerned. Article VII of the 1957 Convention on Conservation of North Pacific Fur Seals[56] carefully describes the aboriginal hunting practices that are exempted by the application of the Convention, linking the exemption to the cultural preservation of the identity of:

> Indians, Ainos, Aleuts or Eskimos dwelling on the coast … who carry on pelagic sealing in canoes not transported by or used in connection with other vessels, and propelled entirely by oars, paddles or sails, and manned by not more than five persons each, in the way hitherto practised and without the use of firearms; provided that such hunters are not in the employment of other persons or under contract to deliver the skins to any person.

In the context of the implementation of the 1946 International Convention for the Regulation of Whaling,[57] the above-mentioned International Whaling Commission renewed the scheme of aboriginal subsistence whaling for the years 2003-2007. This exemption from the general prohibition on whale hunting has, among its main objectives, the purpose of 'enabl[ing] harvests in perpetuity appropriate to *cultural* and nutritional requirements'.[58] The Commission decided to allow the catch of an

---

to the special circumstances and needs of women as well as various social groups, including persons belonging to minorities and indigenous peoples …'.

54 See 1973 *Agreement on Conservation of Polar Bears*, available at: <sedac.ciesin.org/entri/texts/polar.bears.1973.html> (last visited on 6 October 2005).

55 See 1979 *Convention on the Conservation of Migratory Species of Wild Animals*, available at: <www.cms.int/documents/convtxt/cms_convtxt.htm> (last visited on 6 October 2005).

56 See 1957 *Interim Convention on the Conservation of North Pacific Fur Seals*, *UNTS*, vol. 314, p. 105.

57 The full text of the Convention is available at: <www.iwcoffice.org/_documents/commission/convention.pdf> (last visited on 3 October 2005).

58 See <www.iwcoffice.org/conservation/aboriginal.htm#asw> (last visited on 3 October 2005).

adequate number of whales by some aboriginal populations living in Denmark (Greenland), the Russian Federation (Siberia), St. Vincent and the Grenadines (Bequia) and the USA (Alaska).[59]

Further evidence of the recognition of indigenous peoples' cultural rights within the framework of the international legal community is provided by the recent practice of the Inter-American Court of Human Rights. Specifically, in a judgment from 15 May 2005 the Court found the State of Suriname responsible for violating the right to physical, mental and moral integrity enshrined in Article 5.1 of the American Convention on Human Rights (ACHR),[60] to the prejudice of members of the Moiwana indigenous community, on account of the 'significant emotional, psychological, spiritual and economic hardship' suffered by these people due to state interference with their exercise of customary practices aimed at properly honouring their deceased, as well as to the separation of the individuals concerned from their traditional lands.[61] With respect to the first of these two reasons, the Court found a violation on account of the fact that:

> the N'djuka people have specific and complex rituals that must be precisely followed upon the death of a community member. Furthermore, it is extremely important to have possession of the physical remains of the deceased, as the corpse must be treated in a particular manner during the N'djuka death ceremonies and must be placed in the burial ground of the appropriate descent group. ... If the various death rituals are not performed according to N'djuka tradition, it is considered a profound moral transgression, which will not only anger the spirit of the individual who died, but also may offend other ancestors of the community ... This leads to a number of 'spiritually-caused illnesses' that become manifest as actual physical maladies and can potentially affect the entire natural lineage ... The N'djuka understand that such illnesses are not cured on their own, but rather must be resolved through cultural and ceremonial means; if not, the conditions will persist through generations ... Thus, one of the greatest sources of suffering for the Moiwana community members is that they do not know what has happened to the remains of their loved ones, and, as a result, they cannot honor and bury them in accordance with fundamental norms of N'djuka culture.[62]

---

59 See <www.iwcoffice.org/conservation/catches.htm#aborig> (last visited on 3 October 2005).

60 *OAS Treaty Series* n. 36. Article 5.1 affirms that '[e]very person has the right to have his physical, mental, and moral integrity respected'.

61 See *Case of Moiwana Village v. Suriname*, Series C No. 124, Judgment of 15 June 2005, available at: <www.corteidh.or.cr/pais.cfm?id_Pais=11> (last visited on 5 September 2006), para. 103.

62 *Ibid.* para. 98 ff.

The international practice just described corresponds to a trend followed rather uniformly at the domestic level, especially by the courts of a number of countries with large indigenous groups. To provide just one example, in 1999 the High Court of Australia confirmed the finding of a local magistrate dismissing a charge against a member of the aboriginal Gangalidda tribe who had caught two juvenile estuarine crocodiles in Queensland using a traditional harpoon. Although the appellant did not hold the hunting permit prescribed by the Fauna Conservation Act of 1974, the High Court agreed with the reasoning of the magistrate in concluding that the appellant was exempted from the obligation of obtaining the permit, since his act was based on a traditional aboriginal custom, according to which the catch of juvenile rather than adult crocodiles had 'tribal totemic significance and [was based on] spiritual belief'.[63]

Such domestic practice also strongly contributes to reinforcing the idea of the existence, within the context of the international community, of a general *opinio juris* recognizing the duty (*rectius*: the legal obligation) to preserve and protect cultural rights of an individual and collective nature, especially those resulting in the individual right to enjoy and practise one's own culture and the collective right to preserve the cultural identity of peoples.

This conclusion is further reinforced by analysis of recent international practice concerning indigenous peoples' land rights, which, on account of the special link between such peoples and their land (including its natural resources), represent the central element of their cultural identity. This special relationship was recently stressed by the World Bank, which emphasized how the lack of adequate protection of indigenous land rights may eventually lead to the disappearance of such peoples in their distinctive cultural identity:

> [f]or indigenous peoples, secure, effective, collective ownership rights over the lands, territories, and resources they have traditionally owned or otherwise occupied and used *are fundamental to economic and social development, to physical and cultural integrity*, to livelihoods and sustenance. Secure rights to own and control lands, territories, and resources are also essential for the maintenance of the worldviews and spirituality of indigenous peoples – in short, to their very survival as viable territorial communities. *Without secure and enforceable property rights, indigenous peoples' means of subsistence are permanently threatened.* Loss or degradation of land and resources results in deprivation of the basics required to sustain life and to maintain an adequate standard of living. Failure to recognize and respect

63 See *Yanner v. Eaton*, 166 *Australian Law Reports* (1999), p. 258 (High Court of Australia, 7 October 1999). For a more comprehensive assessment of relevant domestic practice, see F. Lenzerini, *cit. supra* note 25, p. 89 ff.

> these rights undermines efforts to alleviate indigenous peoples' poverty and to achieve sustainable development.[64]

The international community seems of late to have become conscious of this, as appears from the growing recognition of indigenous rights over ancestral lands. The rights in point have been deemed justiciable by the supreme courts of countries with some of the largest indigenous communities in the world (such as, *inter alia*, Australia,[65] Canada,[66] South Africa[67] and the United States[68]). These judgments recognize indigenous communities as titleholders of authentic sovereign powers over lands they have occupied with historic continuity since before the arrival of European colonizers.[69] Even at the supranational level, the assertion that states have the obligation to respect, at least to a certain extent, indigenous rights over traditional lands can be based on a relevant *corpus* of positive legal provisions and practice. For example, Article 13 of the CITPIC states that, in applying the provisions of the Convention, state parties must respect 'the special importance for the cultures and spiritual values of the peoples concerned of their relationship with [their] lands or territories, ... and in particular the *collective aspects* of this relationship'.[70] In a similar manner, Article 14 affirms that '[t]he rights of ownership and possession of the peoples concerned over the lands which they traditionally occupy shall be recognised'.[71]

Furthermore, the right to 'freely dispose of their natural wealth and resources' is part of the principle of self-determination of peoples (which today is contemplated by Article 3 DRIP with specific regard to indigenous peoples[72] and also crystallized

64 See *Striking a Better Balance*, Final Report of the World Bank Independent Extractive Industries Review, 15 January 2004, available at: <www.eireview.org/html/EIRFinalReport.html> (last visited on 30 September 2004), volume I, p. 40 (emphasis added).

65 See, *inter alia*, the landmark case of *Mabo v. Queensland* [No.2] (1992), 175 *Commonwealth Law Reports* 1.

66 See, ultimately, *Delgamuukw v. British Columbia* (1997), 3 *Supreme Court Reports* (1997), p. 1010, 37 *ILM* 261 (1998).

67 See *Alexkor Limited and the Government of the Republic of South Africa v. the Richtersveld Community and others*, 14 October 2004, available at: <www.concourt.gov.za/files/alexkor/alexkor.pdf> (last visited on 24 March 2005).

68 See, ultimately, *United States v. Lara*, 19 April 2004, 541 U.S. 193 (2004).

69 For a more comprehensive assessment of relevant national and international practice see, F. Lenzerini, 'Sovereignty Revisited: International Law and Parallel Sovereignty of Indigenous Peoples', *Texas International Law Journal*, Vol. 42 (forthcoming), section 4.1.

70 Emphasis added.

71 See also Article 26 of the DRIP (*cit. supra* note 40), according to which indigenous peoples have a right to 'the lands, territories and resources which they have traditionally owned, occupied or otherwise used or acquired'.

72 See *supra*, text following note 40.

in customary international law), as stated by ICCPR and ICESCR Common Article 1.2. Although only the internal dimension of the right in point can be considered applicable to indigenous peoples,[73] it nonetheless entails, *at a minimum*, their right to participate in the decision-making process and management of any kind of initiative taken by the territorial government concerning their traditional lands, as well as a certain degree of legal and administrative autonomy in the administration of such lands.

In its General Comment to Article 27 ICCPR,[74] previously cited, the HRC noted how, with regard to indigenous peoples, practices associated with their traditional lands constitute the primary component of the rights protected by the provision. According to the Committee, 'culture manifests itself in many forms, including a particular way of life associated with the use of land resources, especially in the case of indigenous peoples'.[75] Also,

> one or other aspect of the rights of individuals protected under that article – for example, to enjoy a particular culture – may consist in a way of life which is closely associated with territory and use of its resources. This may particularly be true of members of indigenous communities constituting a minority.[76]

---

73 The question of whether the term 'peoples' used in Article 1 common to the ICCPR and the ICESCR covers only national peoples or also other peoples, including minorities or racial communities living within a State, was widely debated during the *travaux préparatories* of the two covenants. No consensus was reached among State delegations on a solution to this debate. In particular, '[t]he word "peoples" was understood to mean peoples in all countries and territories, whether independent, trust or non-self-governing. Suggestions were made to the effect that "peoples" should apply to "large compact national groups", to "ethnic, religious or linguistic minorities", to "racial units inhabiting well-defined territories", etc. It was thought, however, that the term "peoples" should be understood in its most general sense and that no definition was necessary' (see A/2929, Chapt. IV, para. 10, reprinted in M.J. Bossuyt, *Guide to the* 'travaux préparatoires' *of the International Covenant on Civil and Political Rights* (Dordrecht/Boston/Lancaster, 1987), p. 32). In any event, in light of the evolution that has characterized international law from the 1960s to the present, it is today indubitable that, following an evolutionary interpretation pursuant to Article 31(3)(c) of the *Vienna Convention on the Law of Treaties* of 1969 (1155 *UNTS* 331), the term 'peoples' *also* encompasses non-national peoples, such as minorities and indigenous peoples.

74 See *supra* note 28.

75 See para. 7. The paragraph continues by affirming that this 'right may include such traditional activities as fishing or hunting and the right to live in reserves protected by law. The enjoyment of those rights may require positive legal measures of protection and measures to ensure the effective participation of members of minority communities in decisions which affect them'.

76 See para. 3.2.

In addition, with respect to Article 12 of the ICESCR (affirming 'the right of everyone to the enjoyment of the highest attainable standard of physical and mental health'), the Committee on Economic, Social and Cultural Rights considered that:

> indigenous peoples have the right to specific measures to improve their access to health services and care. These health services should be *culturally appropriate*, taking into account traditional preventive care, healing practices and medicines. States should provide resources for indigenous peoples to design, deliver and control such services so that they may enjoy the highest attainable standard of physical and mental health. The vital medicinal plants, animals and minerals necessary to the full enjoyment of health of indigenous peoples should also be protected. The Committee notes that, in indigenous communities, *the health of the individual is often linked to the health of the society as a whole and has a collective dimension*. In this respect, the Committee considers that *development-related activities that lead to the displacement of indigenous peoples against their will from their traditional territories and environment*, denying them their sources of nutrition and breaking their symbiotic relationship with their lands, *has a deleterious effect on their health.*[77]

Furthermore, according to the Committee on the Elimination of Racial Discrimination, the denial of the right of indigenous peoples 'to own, develop, control and use their communal lands, territories and resources and … to [be] return[ed] … [such] lands and territories [taken from them] without their free and informed consent'[78] entails a breach of the 1966 Convention on the Elimination of All Forms of Racial Discrimination.[79]

At the regional level, article 21 of the African Charter on Human and Peoples' Rights[80] is worth mentioning. This provision expressly states that '[a]ll peoples shall freely dispose of their wealth and natural resources. This right shall be exercised in the exclusive interest of the people. In no case shall a people be deprived of it.' In the landmark case of the *Ogoni* people, the African Commission on Human and Peoples' Rights found that the term 'peoples' in said provision includes a distinct

---

77 Cf. General Comment No. 14 (2000), 'The right to the highest attainable standard of health (Article 12 of the International Covenant on Economic, Social and Cultural Rights)', U.N. Doc. E/C.12/2000/4 of 11 August 2000, para. 27 (emphasis added).

78 See *General Recommendation XXIII (51) concerning Indigenous Peoples*, 18 August 1997, available at: <www.austlii.edu.au/au/journals/AILR/1998/6.html> (last visited on 30 September 2004), para. 5.

79 *UNTS*, vol. 660, p. 195.

80 21 *ILM*, 1982, p. 58.

indigenous people within a state and does not refer only to the national people as a whole.[81]

Similarly, in the famous case of the *Awas Tingni* indigenous community, the Inter-American Court of Human Rights held that the right to property affirmed by Article 21 of the ACHR[82] includes the collective rights of indigenous peoples over their ancestral lands and the natural resources they have traditionally used,[83] due to the fact that the right has a meaning in international law that transcends its significance in domestic law.[84] In its more recent judgment concerning the Moiwana indigenous community of Suriname, previously mentioned, the Court took a further step forward, emphasizing the need for indigenous peoples to retain possession of their ancestral lands as a decisive prerequisite for enjoyment of their basic right to safeguard their cultural identity and integrity. In particular, the judges found that:

> a N'djuka community's connection to its traditional land is of vital spiritual, cultural and material importance ... Indeed, ... *in order for the culture to preserve its very identity and integrity*, the Moiwana community members must maintain a fluid and multidimensional relationship with their ancestral lands.[85]

---

81 See *Communication 155/96, The Social and Economic Rights Action Center and the Center for Economic and Social Rights / Nigeria*, OAU doc. ACHPR/COMM/A044/1 of 27 May 2002, para. 55 ff.

82 See *infra* note 86.

83 See *Awas Tingni Mayagna (Sumo) Indigenous Community v. Nicaragua*, Judgement of 31 August 2001, available at: <www.indianlaw.org/IACHR_Judgement_Official_English.pdf> (last visited on 30 September 2004), para. 153.

84 *Ibid.*, para. 146. The Court also held that the indigenous right of ownership of lands and resources is founded on indigenous customary law rather than on the domestic law of the territorial State (see para. 146 ff.). See also, consistently, *Mary and Carrie Dann v. United States*, Report of 15 October 2001, available at: <heiwww.unige.ch/humanrts/cases/113-01.html> (last visited on 30 September 2004); *Maya Indigenous Communities of the Toledo District v. Belize*, Report of 24 October 2003, available at: <www.indianlaw.org/200310PrelimRpt.pdf> (last visited on 30 September 2004).

85 See *Case of Moiwana Village v. Suriname, cit. supra* note 61, para. 101 (emphasis added). In a separate opinion released in the context of a later Judgment of the Court concerning the 15 June 2005 Judgment (see *Case of Moiwana Village v. Suriname, Interpretation of the June 15, 2005 Judgment on the Preliminary Objections, Merits and Reparations (Article 67 of the American Convention of Human Rights)*, Series C No. 145, Judgment of 8 February 2006, available at: <www.corteidh.or.cr/pais.cfm?id_Pais=11>, last visited on 5 September 2006), Judge Conçado Trindade held that 'delimitation, demarcation, tilting and the return of [the N'djukas'] traditional territories [are] indeed essential. This is a matter of survival of the cultural identity of the N'djukas, so that they may conserve their memory, both personally and collectively. Only then will their fundamental right to life lato sensu be rightfully protected, including their right to cultural identity' (para. 20), on account of the fact that 'the universal

Two days later, in another judgment, the Court found that Paraguay had breached Articles 21 and 4.1 of the ACHR[86] for not having granted the Yakye Axa indigenous community the effective possession of its ancestral lands or the chance to exercise its own traditional activities (*i.e.* hunting, fishing and harvesting) therein – both of which are essential to ensure the effective enjoyment of the right to life of its members.[87] A number of passages in this judgment are highly significant for the purposes of this chapter. First, the Court recognized that in the instant case '*no se discute la existencia del derecho de los miembros de las comunidades indígenas … a sus territorios, en el entendido de lo que la tierra significa para sus miembros, ni se discute el hecho que la caza, pesca y recolección sea un elemento esencial de su cultura*'.[88] With respect, in particular, to the right to property of the indigenous community concerned, the Court noted that according to Article 21 of the ACHR the right may be restricted for reasons of public utility or social interest.[89] However, in applying such a restriction to indigenous peoples:

> *los Estados deben tener en cuenta que los derechos territoriales indígenas abarcan un concepto más amplio y diferente que está* relacionado con el derecho colectivo a la supervivencia como pueblo organizado, *con el control de su hábitat como una condición necesaria para la reproducción de su cultura, para su propio desarrollo y para llevar a cabo sus planes de vida.* La propiedad sobre la tierra garantiza que los miembros de las comunidades indígenas conserven su patrimonio cultural. *[Por lo tanto,] [a]l desconocerse el derecho ancestral de los miembros de las comunidades indígenas sobre sus territorios, se podría estar* afectando otros derechos básicos, como el

juridical conscience has evolved towards a clear recognition of the relevance of cultural diversity for the universality of human rights, and vice-versa' (para. 24).

86 Article 21 of the ACHR states that '1. Everyone has the right to the use and enjoyment of his property. The law may subordinate such use and enjoyment to the interest of society. 2. No one shall be deprived of his property except upon payment of just compensation, for reasons of public utility or social interest, and in the cases and according to the forms established by law'. Article 4(1) affirms that '[e]very person has the right to have his life respected. This right shall be protected by law and, in general, from the moment of conception. No one shall be arbitrarily deprived of his life'.

87 See *Caso Comunidad Indígena Yakye Axa vs. Paraguay*, Series C No. 125, Judgment of 17 June 2005, available at: <www.corteidh.or.cr/pais.cfm?id_Pais=5> (last visited on 5 September 2006), paragraphs 156 and 164 ff. At para. 167, in particular, the Court affirms that '[l]as afectaciones especiales del derecho a la salud, e íntimamente vinculadas con él, las del derecho a la alimentación y el acceso al agua limpia impactan de manera aguda el derecho a una existencia digna y las condiciones básicas para el ejercicio de otros derechos humanos, como el derecho a la educación o el derecho a la *identidad cultural*' (emphasis added).

88 *Ibid.*, para. 140.

89 *Ibid.*, para. 145.

derecho a la identidad cultural y la supervivencia misma de las comunidades indígenas y sus miembros.[90]

As a consequence, the right of indigenous peoples to their traditional lands is to be considered different from the 'ordinary' right to property owned by individuals, with respect to which '*la restricción … pudiera ser necesaria para lograr el objetivo colectivo de preservar las identidades culturales en una sociedad democrática y pluralista en el sentido de la Convención Americana*'.[91]

As can easily be noted, in the context of the practice just referred to, land rights are generally conceived as inclusive of the right to effectively control all natural resources on the lands concerned. Such resources are actually to be considered as indissolubly linked to the land, especially with regard to indigenous peoples, on account of their spiritual relationship to their traditional lands, which are conceived of as comprehending all associated living and inanimate entities. This principle is expressed, *inter alia*, by Article 15 CITPIC, which states that '[t]he rights of the peoples concerned to the natural resources pertaining to their lands shall be specially safeguarded[,] includ[ing] the[ir] right to participate in the use, management and conservation of these resources'.[92] This has also been confirmed, as previously noted, by the recent judgment of the Inter-American Court of Human Rights affirming that the activity of harvesting natural resources constitutes the expression of a

---

90 *Ibid.*, para. 146 ff. (emphasis added). See also para. 154, according to which '[l]a garantía del derecho a la propiedad comunitaria de los pueblos indígenas debe tomar en cuenta que la tierra *está estrechamente relacionada* con sus tradiciones y expresiones orales, sus costumbres y lenguas, sus artes y rituales, sus conocimientos y usos relacionados con la naturaleza, sus artes culinarias, el derecho consuetudinario, su vestimenta, filosofía y valores. En función de su entorno, su integración con la naturaleza y su historia, los miembros de las comunidades indígenas transmiten de generación en generación este patrimonio cultural inmaterial, que es recreado constantemente por los miembros de las comunidades y grupos indígenas' (emphasis added).

91 *Ibid.*, para. 148. However, in the view of the Court this conclusion is not to be interpreted as *necessarily* meaning 'que siempre que estén en conflicto los intereses territoriales particulares o estatales y los intereses territoriales de los miembros de las comunidades indígenas, prevalezcan los últimos por sobre los primeros. Cuando los Estados se vean imposibilitados, por razones concretas y justificadas, de adoptar medidas para devolver el territorio tradicional y los recursos comunales de las poblaciones indígenas, la compensación que se otorgue debe tener como orientación principal el significado que tiene la tierra para éstas' (*ibid.*, para. 149).

92 See para. 1. Para. 2 continues by stating that '[i]n cases in which the State retains the ownership of mineral or sub-surface resources or rights to other resources pertaining to lands, governments shall establish or maintain procedures through which they shall consult these peoples, with a view to ascertaining whether and to what degree their interests would be prejudiced, before undertaking or permitting any programmes for the exploration or exploitation of such resources pertaining to their lands. The peoples concerned shall wherever possible participate in the benefits of such activities, and shall receive fair compensation for any damages which they may sustain as a result of such activities'.

prerogative attached to land rights, as well as an essential element of the culture of the peoples concerned.[93]

Of course, the reference to 'natural resources' clearly encompasses all kinds of resources; and no reason exists for claiming that a distinction should be drawn between subsurface resources (to which Article 15 of the CITPIC mainly refers)[94] and surface resources (including plant genetic ones).[95]

Having said this, it is now to be emphasized that in the case of indigenous peoples the protection of plant resources requires a step forward. As seen in section 1, the significance of these resources for the peoples concerned is not limited to possible practical uses. Indigenous peoples see the world as a 'circle of life', which surrounds the earth, air, waters and land. All elements, particularly the living (including humans), but even inanimate ones, are integrated in a spiritual unity and act in deep connection with each other as part of a holistic harmony. This implies, *inter alia*, that:

> [n]o person 'owns' or holds as 'property' living things. Our Mother Earth and our plant and animal relatives are respected sovereign living beings with rights of their own in addition to playing an essential role in our survival.[96]

Traditional practices and knowledge concerning plant resources developed by indigenous peoples through the centuries are thus to be considered as inextricably linked to the resources as such, in a symbiosis that attains its own distinct significance. In other words, plant genetic resources and the traditional knowledge related to them represent two inseparable elements of a unique social (and legal) concept that expresses the spiritual relationship of indigenous groups to their natural resources. This relationship is essential to the survival of the groups' distinctive identity, as the example of the significance of *ayahuasca* for certain Amazon communities, described in section 1, illustrates.

This self-dependency between natural resources and related traditional knowledge is, for instance, implied in Article 8(j) of the 1992 Convention on Biological Diversity

---

93 See *supra*, text corresponding to note 87.

94 See para. 2, *supra*, note 92.

95 See, consistently, U.N. Sub-Commission on the Promotion and Protection of Human Rights, 'Indigenous peoples' permanent sovereignty over natural resources'. Final Report of the Special Rapporteur, Erica-Irene A. Daes, Addendum, doc. E/CN.4/Sub.2/2004/30/Add.1 of 12 July 2004, para. 11.

96 See International Indian Treaty Council (IITC), IITC Discussion Paper on Biological Diversity and Biological Ethics, 30 August 1996, p. 5, cited by A. Xanthaki, 'Indigenous Cultural Rights in International Law', *European Journal of Law Reform* (2000), p. 343, at p. 351.

(CBD),[97] according to which, in the context of *in situ* conservation of biodiversity, state parties must:

> respect, preserve and maintain knowledge, innovations and practices of indigenous and local communities embodying traditional lifestyles relevant for the conservation and sustainable use of biological diversity and promote their wider application with the approval and involvement of the holders of such knowledge, innovations and practices and encourage the equitable sharing of the benefits arising from the utilization of such knowledge, innovations and practices.

Generally speaking, the main practical consequence of this interconnection in legal terms is the following: having established that the right to retain control of their natural resources is, for indigenous peoples, an essential condition for the enjoyment of their internationally recognized cultural rights, this right is also to be extended to any form of traditional knowledge about the resources in question. Such knowledge is, after all, an essential part of the relationship of the peoples concerned to their natural resources. In light of this, the unlawful appropriation of indigenous traditional knowledge represents the intolerable breach of internationally protected cultural rights.

## 3. The controversy over the commercial exploitation of indigenous peoples' traditional knowledge

Debate concerning the commercial use of indigenous peoples' traditional knowledge is at present particularly vibrant. This debate originated in international preoccupation with a growing number of cases of misappropriation of indigenous traditional knowledge followed by the patenting of certain applications of this knowledge as new inventions. Sometimes, once misappropriated traditional knowledge has been patented, the resulting IPRs have even been used to try and suppress any form of traditional utilization of this knowledge by its traditional holders, considered 'unwanted competition'.[98] In a minority of these cases the competent patent offices have revoked the patents based on traditional knowledge for lack of novelty, ascertained *ex post facto*.[99] However, in most circumstances, due to the objective difficulty of recognizing and even knowing the existence of such knowledge, biopirates have successfully exploited traditional knowledge as their own creation, thereby obtaining immense

---

97 The full text of the Convention is available at <www.biodiv.org/doc/legal/cbd-en.pdf> (last visited on 5 September 2006).

98 See 'An Affront to Indigenous People of the Amazon', available at <www.biopark.org/peru/biopiracy1.html> (last visited on 6 October 2005).

99 See the examples described in F. Lenzerini, *cit. supra* note 18, para. III.3.

economic income without recognizing any role for the traditional holders of the knowledge concerned. At present this is 'legally' possible under international law, in particular on account of the lack of appropriate normative instruments addressing the issue of commercial exploitation of traditional knowledge. This phenomenon, especially with regard to indigenous peoples, is liable not only to create unjust economic income through unfair profit from knowledge developed by others but, for the reasons explained above, even to jeopardize the very cultural survival of the communities concerned.

This problem is currently under discussion in several international organizations and bodies, particularly WIPO (through the *ad hoc* Intergovernmental Committee on Intellectual Property and Genetic Resources, Traditional Knowledge and Folklore, established in October 2000),[100] the CBD Conference of Parties,[101] and the WTO. In the context of this last organization the debate is focused on revision of Article 27.3(b) of the TRIPS Agreement[102] by the Council for TRIPS. The provision in question allows state parties to exclude patentability of 'plants and animals other than micro-organisms, and essentially biological processes for the production of plants and animals other than micro-organisms', specifying that 'Members shall provide for the protection of plant varieties either by patents or by an effective *sui generis* system or by any combination thereof'. Finally, the provision establishes that its text should be revised four years after the WTO Agreement has entered into force. In 2001, six years after entry into force of the Agreement, paragraph 19 of the Doha Declaration instructed the Council for TRIPS, 'in pursuing its work programme including under the review of Article 27.3(b) ... to examine, inter alia, the relationship between the TRIPS Agreement and the Convention on Biological Diversity [and] the protection of traditional knowledge and folklore'.[103] It thus

100 See WIPO doc. WO/GA/26/6 of 25 August 2000. For further information see the homepage of the Committee, at: <www.wipo.int/tk/en/igc> (last visited on 6 October 2006).

101 Among the initiatives taken by the CBD Conference of Parties (COP) for addressing this issue, the establishment of an *ad hoc* Working Group with the competence to address the implementation of Article 8(j) is worth mentioning; the Working Group had its first meeting in March 2000 (see <www.biodiv.org/programmes/socio-eco/traditional/default.asp> (last visited on 6 October 2005). See also C.R. McManis, 'Intellectual Property, Genetic Resources and Traditional Knowledge Protection: Thinking Globally, Acting Locally', *Cardozo Journal of International and Comparative Law* (2003), p. 547, at p. 556 ff. Also, with Decision VI/24 of 2002, the COP adopted the *Bonn Guidelines on Access to Genetic Resources and Fair and Equitable Sharing of the Benefits Arising out of their Utilization* (Bonn Guidelines). The text of the decision VI/24 (including the Bonn Guidelines) is available at: <www.biodiv.org/decisions/default.aspx?m=COP-06&id=7198&lg=0> (last visited on 6 October 2006).

102 The text of the TRIPS Agreement is available at: <www.wto.org> (last visited on 5 October 2006).

103 See *Doha Ministerial Declaration*, WTO doc. WT/MIN(01)/DEC/1 of 20 November 2001, para. 19.

expressly recognized the relevance of traditional knowledge in the context of the patentability of plant genetic resources.

*In abstracto*, different solutions could be adopted for trying to put to an end the 'haemorrhagic' misappropriation of indigenous traditional knowledge. Of course, none of these solutions could work adequately without the establishment of specific and efficient systems for allowing patent offices and other competent bodies to have effective awareness of the existence of existing forms of traditional knowledge. (It is clear that no body or institution can ascertain whether or not a claimed invention is based on pre-existing traditional knowledge without being aware of the existence of such knowledge.) This is a problem endemic to the very nature of traditional knowledge and, unfortunately, seems unlikely to be resolvable in its entirety. Despite the positive impact of globalization, which, especially through the development of the Internet, has enormously reduced distances, a great portion of indigenous traditional knowledge continues to be hidden at the farthest corners of the planet. It is generally conserved by a few shamans and transmitted from generation to generation in oral form, without written documents testifying to its existence. Furthermore, patent applications based on traditional knowledge are generally submitted to offices in countries far from where such knowledge has been taken; and it is not easy for patent officers working, for example, in the United States to know all the (innumerable) forms of traditional knowledge in, e.g., Papua New Guinea, Micronesia or Equatorial Africa.

A number of solutions have been proposed to resolve this problem. One of the most interesting consists of the development of databases on traditional knowledge (e.g. a Digital TK Library),[104] although the same states that suggested this solution have admitted that, 'given the vast breadth and depth of such knowledge', these databases would be 'inherently' limited and non-comprehensive.[105]

As for possible legal schemes to regulate the problem of commercial or industrial exploitation of indigenous traditional knowledge, the most drastic solution would consist of prohibiting, *tout court*, any form of such exploitation. This solution may, *prima facie*, appear the most efficient, since it would prevent any kind of misappropriation. Nonetheless, it would also prevent traditional knowledge holders who wish to make commercial use of their knowledge from having the opportunity to exercise that option (either by directly applying for a patent or by selling the relevant knowledge to external individuals, corporations or firms in exchange for an equitable share of the benefits from its commercial and/or industrial exploitation). It would thus

104 See, *e.g.*, WTO docs. IP/C/W/356 of 24 June 2002 (Brazil, China, Cuba, Dominican Republic, Ecuador, India, Pakistan, Thailand, Venezuela, Zambia and Zimbabwe), para. 16, and IP/C/W/403 of 24 June 2003 (Brazil, China, Cuba, Dominican Republic, Ecuador, India, Pakistan, Peru, Thailand, Venezuela, Zambia and Zimbabwe), para. 16.

105 See doc. IP/C/W/403, para. 16.

prevent a potentially formidable opportunity for economic and social development in indigenous communities that presently live in a state of deep indigence.

A second possible option would consist of regulating traditional knowledge through existing patent law. However, even this solution appears inadequate to address the problem at issue, due to certain inherent limits in patent law. Among these limits are the fact that patents are only available to inventions that 'involve an innovative step',[106] while traditional knowledge is usually very old, since it results from knowledge developed and transmitted through the centuries from generation to generation. Also, patents, by their nature, are granted to individual entities (persons, firms or corporations), while traditional knowledge is usually owned by communities, and is thus inherently collective in nature.[107] Finally, a third insurmountable obstacle is presented by the fact that patents are limited in time, while traditional knowledge, considering its significance for the cultural identity of the community that owns it, should be safeguarded permanently – otherwise the very *rationale* of its protection would vanish.

As a consequence, the most appropriate solution for adequately protecting traditional knowledge and the cultural values (and rights) attached to it would consist of the adoption of *sui generis* systems for the protection of plant varieties and related knowledge. In recent years this solution has been advocated by the majority of states;[108] and it has been applied by a number of countries.[109] The detailed provisions

---

106 See Article 27(1) of the TRIPS Agreement (*cit. supra*, note 102).

107 However, this obstacle may be overcome through the establishment of associations, corporations or similar legal bodies acting individually, but representing the communities owning the relevant traditional knowledge.

108 See, *e.g.*, WTO docs. IP/C/W/356 of 24 June 2002 (Brazil, China, Cuba, Dominican Republic, Ecuador, India, Pakistan, Thailand, Venezuela, Zambia and Zimbabwe), para. 16; IP/C/W/383 of 17 October 2002, para. 67 ff. (EC); IP/C/W/369 of 8 August 2002, para. 55 (Switzerland); IP/C/W/404 of 26 June 2003, para. II (the African Group). See also the comment of Turkey to the WIPO draft provisions, available at: <www.wipo.int/tk/en/consultations/draft_provisions/pdf-tk/turkey.pdf> (last visited on 6 October 2006). The position expressed in the text is also shared by a number of scholars; see, *inter alia*, T. Cottier and M. Panizzon, 'Legal Perspectives on Traditional Knowledge: The Case for Intellectual Property Protection', *JIEL* (2004), p. 371, at p. 381 ff.; A.K. Gupta, 'Conserving Biodiversity and Rewarding Associated Knowledge and Innovation Systems: Honey Bee Perspective', in T. Cottier and P. C. Mavroidis (eds.), *Intellectual Property. Trade, Competition and Sustainable Development* (Ann Arbor, 2003), p. 373, p. 382 ff.

109 Among the various examples of *sui generis* systems adopted at the national level, the Indian one (see the Indian *Model Biodiversity Related Community Intellectual Rights Act*, available at: <www.prodiversitas.bioetica.org/draftindia.htm> (last visited on 6 October 2006)) is particularly renowned. See also Portugal, Decree-Law 118/2002 of 20 April 2002, available online at: <www.sipo.gov.cn/sipo/ztxx/yczyhctzsbh/zlk/gglf/P020050324_43281.htm> (last visited on 6 October 2006). At the international level, the *African Model Legislation for the Protection of the Rights of Local Communities, Farmers and Breeders, and for the Regulation of*

of such systems should be developed at the domestic level (shaped by the particular characteristics of specific forms of traditional knowledge in each state), but should be based on an international framework of protection establishing the fundamental criteria to be respected for granting adequate and homogeneous safeguarding of traditional knowledge. The preparation of an international instrument regulating this matter is, in fact, essential to ensure uniformity of protection at the international level and to grant effective defence in cases of exploitation of indigenous traditional knowledge with a transboundary character. In particular, any regulatory framework should comply with the following requirements: a) it should establish the basic rules to be followed in the context of the deliberative process leading to adoption of national *sui generis* schemes for the protection of traditional knowledge, including the requirement that traditional knowledge holders be fully involved; b) it should regulate the conditions of access to traditional knowledge when such knowledge is sold to external operators, as well as the terms and clauses to be respected to ensure that the prior consent given by traditional knowledge holders is *really* conscious and informed, based on information fully comprehensible to the peoples concerned from both the linguistic and philosophical point of view; c) it should include the requirement that an adequate share of the benefits deriving from the commercial/industrial exploitation of traditional knowledge by non-indigenous individuals, firms or corporations be granted to its traditional holders; d) in any case, it should grant traditional knowledge holders the right to refuse access to their knowledge if they wish to do so, as well as the right to establish the terms and limitations of such access, and the right to revoke their consent at any time (respecting the contractual terms agreed upon when access to their knowledge was given); e) last but not least, it should regulate the issue concerning identification and protection of all traditional knowledge holders that share the same kind of knowledge. This could be done by developing a scheme of 'denomination of cultural origin', which would allow all manifestations of the same kind of traditional knowledge to be associated on the basis of their 'cultural likeness' (also in the event that there is no geographical proximity among populations with the same kind of knowledge).

## 4. Conclusion. Rights of traditional knowledge holders *vs.* general interest of humanity

The use of *sui generis* schemes for the protection of traditional knowledge appears as the only possible solution with sufficient flexibility for adaptation to different manifestations of such knowledge, to the particular values and interests

---

*Access to Biological Resources*, developed by the Organization of African Unity (OAU Model Law), available at: <www.grain.org/brl_files/oau-model-law-en.pdf> (last visited on 6 October 2006), is worth mentioning.

they incorporate, as well as to the specific problems raised by their commercial exploitation. It would certainly permit the commercial exploitation of traditional knowledge and, at the same time, allow the adoption of special forms of protection not available under existing patent law – like, e.g., the possibility of recognizing IPRs of a collective character and without time restrictions (in light of the fact that the fulfilment of these conditions is usually indispensable for properly safeguarding traditional knowledge).

Another important aspect of *sui generis* protection systems consists in the suitability of allowing traditional knowledge holders to exclude the commercial exploitation of their knowledge *tout court*. The right to make this choice appears totally reasonable in light of the fact that traditional knowledge may have spiritual and philosophical significance, so that its sale or commercial exploitation may result in an intolerable offence to the spiritual and cultural roots, as well as the identity of the peoples concerned. Having said this, it is to be noted that this right may, in certain cases, (at least to a certain extent) conflict with other internationally recognized human rights. In particular, a conflict may arise in the event that certain populations develop knowledge that could bring significant benefits to humanity as a whole (especially in healthcare or nutrition) but are unwilling to disclose it. This situation would exist, for instance, in the event that an indigenous community, through the combination of certain endemic plants, developed a really efficient treatment for terrible diseases, like AIDS or certain forms of cancer. In a case like this, would the community retain the right to maintain the secret of such treatment (since it is considered an essential part of its spiritual identity) or would the common interest prevail, thus allowing the 'international community' to 'force' the population concerned to disclose its secret and give its consent to the use of the treatment for medical experimentation and eventually for treatment? We would have, on one side, the right of the traditional knowledge holders concerned to preserve their cultural identity and, on the other, the chance to appreciably improve certain fundamental human rights, like the right to life and to health, to the benefit of all humanity. *Quid juris* when such a conflict arises?

At the international level this problem was recently dealt with by WIPO, in Article 8 of its 2005 revised objectives and principles concerning the protection of traditional knowledge.[110] The provision, under the title of 'exceptions and limitations', states that:

> 1. The application and implementation of protection of traditional knowledge should not adversely affect: … (ii) the use of traditional medicine for household purposes; use in government hospitals, especially by traditional

[110] See WIPO Intergovernmental Committee on Intellectual Property and Genetic Resources, Traditional Knowledge and Folklore, 'The Protection of Traditional Knowledge. Revised Objectives and Principles', Geneva, 6-10 June 2005, doc. WIPO/GRTKF/IC/8/5 of 8 April 2005, Annex.

> knowledge holders attached to such hospitals; or use for other public health purposes …

The *ratio* of the provision in point, as explained in the 'Commentary on Article 8', is 'to avoid unreasonable prejudice to the interests of society as a whole', by ensuring that 'TK protection does not restrain and hamper the public health benefits which derive from the use of traditional medicine in non-profit government hospitals'. Thus, the solution adopted by WIPO is that the general interest should prevail over the specific interests of traditional knowledge holders, although this is conditioned on respect for a very important and strict condition, i.e. that the use of traditional knowledge for public health interests produce no economic profit. Legally speaking, this solution is not unreasonable. In particular, it can be based on the assumption that sacrificing the cultural rights of traditional knowledge holders would be necessary to safeguard certain legal values, particularly the individual right to life and health, which are of fundamental importance in the context of international law (so that they, particularly the right to life, have probably reached the status of *jus cogens*).

On the other hand, important legal arguments also support the opposite view, according to which the aprioristic assumption that the general interest linked to protection of human health should prevail over the cultural rights of traditional knowledge holders cannot be maintained. These arguments can be better understood by the analogical application of principles used for the regulation of similar subjects, at least from the point of view of the legal values safeguarded by pertinent provisions. So, for example, the same kind of conflict as may exist between protection of the cultural rights of traditional knowledge holders and the safeguarding of a general interest in the improvement of human health may also come into existence in the context of the research, use and exploitation of the human genome. As is well known, scientific research on the genome has opened new and potentially revolutionary perspectives on the treatment of certain terrible diseases, particularly of a genetic character, that at the moment are virtually incurable. At the present time, however, most possible applications remain at the level of expectation, and the only means for turning such expectations into concrete curative tools is continued research and experimentation on the genome. Research offers the concrete possibility that efficient results will be achieved to the benefit of all humanity. Notwithstanding this, virtually all international instruments dealing with the legal regime of research on the human genome express, in peremptory terms, the principle that in all cases of research, treatment or diagnosis affecting an individual's genome 'the prior, free and informed consent of the person concerned' is necessary,[111] and that no such

[111] See, *inter alia*, Article 5(b) of the *Universal Declaration on the Human Genome and Human Rights*, 11 November 1997, available in the UNESCO Web site, at <www.unesco.org> (last visited on 5 September 2006); Article 8 of the *International Declaration on Human Genetic Data*, 16 October 2003, *ibid.* (last visited on 5 September 2006); Article 6 of the *Universal Declaration on Bioethics and Human Rights*, 19 October 2005, *ibid.* (last visited on 5 September

activity may be performed without consent. In the absence of exceptions in relevant instruments, this requirement clearly implies that in the event that the person concerned does not consent to the use of his/her own genome any activity involving that genome is precluded, even if it would serve the general interest of improving the quality of healthcare. So, the question that now arises concerns the identification of a legal basis that would allow one to consider the right of the individual to retain full control of his/her own genome as more important than the right of indigenous peoples to safeguard their cultural identity by keeping their knowledge undisclosed. In other words, providing that traditional knowledge may actually be as significant for indigenous peoples (as collective entities) as the genome is for the individual, why should traditional knowledge holders be forced to consent to the use of their knowledge for the general interest of humanity, when an individual may not be forced to consent to the use of his/her genome for the same interest?

A similar argument can be taken from the international regime concerning the protection of IPRs on medicines. In principle it is rather fair, as well as essential for the development of scientific research, that pharmaceutical firms and corporations retain such rights over the medicines they have discovered and developed. Having said this, are the rights in point to be considered absolute? Are these rights to be protected even in the event that their recognition has the concrete consequence of denying access to healthcare for persons that, living in the poorest countries of the world, cannot afford the price of medicine for certain pandemics due to their high cost, which mostly derives from the amount of IPRs? For example, in the case of anti-AIDS medicines, the cost of a complete annual therapy may rise up to 15,000 USD per patient in some African countries; in Zimbabwe it corresponds to an amount 24 times the average annual income of the country,[112] making it virtually unaffordable for most citizens. If these medicines could be produced without paying the cost of the IPRs attached to them, the total price of a complete annual therapy would fall dramatically to 350 USD per patient.[113] In most developing countries, the difference between 15,000 USD and 350 USD thus corresponds to the difference between death and life; and the continued protection of IPRs on anti-pandemic medicines actually leads millions of people to death. With this in mind, if the international community insists on the protection of such IPRs despite a contrary general interest, as a matter of coherency the right of traditional knowledge holders not to consent

---

2006); Article 3 of the Charter of Fundamental Rights of the European Union, *O.J.* C 364 of 18 December 2000, p. 1; Articles 5 and 16 of the *Convention for the Protection of Human Rights and Dignity of the Human Being with regard to the Application of Biology and Medicine: Convention on Human Rights and Biomedicine* (Oviedo Convention), Oviedo, 4 April 1997, *CETS* n. 164.

112 See F. Lenzerini and M. Montini, 'The Activity of the World Trade Organization (2001)', *IYIL* (2001), p. 191, at p. 207.

113 *Ibid.*, p. 208.

to the use of their knowledge should, *mutatis mutandis*, also be protected – even if that use should prove necessary to fulfil the general interest of the international community. Otherwise, we would be forced to conclude that, legally speaking, indigenous peoples' cultural rights are less important than the economic interests of pharmaceutical corporations.

In reality, in light of recent practice, it is not properly correct to assert that IPRs on anti-endemic medicines always prevail over the right to health of people living in developing countries. In particular, the WTO General Council adopted a Decision in 2003 authorizing a waiver from the obligations set out in Article 31 paragraphs (f) and (h) of the TRIPS Agreement (which place strict conditions on possible use of the subject matter of a patent without the authorization of the right holder), to the extent necessary for allowing developing countries to face pandemic diseases.[114] This decision was later transformed, on 6 December 2005, into a permanent amendment to the TRIPS Agreement.[115] In practice, the amendment allows said countries to obtain anti-pandemic medicines at an affordable price, without being forced to comply with the IPR rules concerning such medicines.

On the one hand, this solution demonstrates that the right to health is considered paramount by the international community, so as to supersede even the gigantic economic interests attached to the pharmaceutical industry. On the other hand, it is also true that the 2005 amendment is only applicable in 'the case of a national emergency or other circumstances of extreme urgency or in cases of public non-commercial uses', on the condition that strict prerequisites are satisfied. The amendment in point thus tries to draw a balance between the interests at stake. In this writer's opinion, the solution adopted by the Decision in point could probably be extended, *mutatis mutandis*, to possible cases of incompatibility between traditional knowledge holders' cultural rights and the general interest in fulfilment of the right to health. As a consequence, holders of traditional knowldge should be obliged to disclose their knowledge, with no financial profit for 'external' users, only in the event that it may actually provide efficient treatment for particularly serious and widespread diseases, on account of the fact that the development and use of such knowledge would then be in the fundamental interest of all humankind.

---

114 See 'Implementation of paragraph 6 of the Doha Declaration on the TRIPS Agreement and public health', Decision of 30 August 2003, WTO doc. WT/L/540 of 1 September 2003. On this issue see F. Lenzerini and M. Montini, 'The Activity of the World Trade Organization (2003)', *IYIL* (2003), p. 189, at p. 199 ff.

115 See 'Amendment of the TRIPS Agreement', Decision of 6 December 2005, WTO doc. WT/L/641 of 8 December 2005.

# 7
# The Right of a People to Enjoy Its Culture: Towards a Nordic Saami Rights Convention

*Martin Scheinin*

## 1. Introduction

In mid-November of 2005, an expert commission established jointly by the three governments of Finland, Norway and Sweden and by the three national Saami Parliaments in the same countries, concluded its work of three years and delivered a public proposal for a Nordic Saami Rights Convention. The object and purpose of the proposed treaty is to affirm and strengthen such rights of the Saami people that are necessary to secure its language, culture, livelihoods and society, with the smallest possible interference caused by national borders.[1] The treaty would recognize the Saami people as the only indigenous people in the three Nordic countries in question. The treaty would regulate through a legally binding international treaty the rights of the Saami people and its individual members in a way that conforms to the evolving understanding in international law on the rights of indigenous peoples.[2]

The proposed Saami Rights Convention reflects a trend within international law and some national legal systems to give more serious attention than before to the interplay between collective and individual rights. Instead of reducing all individuals to equal and atomistic citizens of the nation state with equal but at the same time state-focused rights, it reflects the challenges of multiculturality and the multitude

---

1 *Nordisk samekonvensjon: Utkast fra finsk-norsk-svensk-samisk ekspertgruppe.* Oslo, Kopi og distribusjonsservice, 2005. An unofficial English translation of the draft treaty is available at: <odin.dep.no/filarkiv/280873/>. For the object and purpose of the treaty, see Article 1. Due to the unofficial nature of the translation, the present author has not followed the exact wording of the existing translation in referring to various provisions of the treaty.

2 See, Convention No. 169 concerning Indigenous and Tribal Peoples in Independent Countries by the International Labour Organisation (72 ILO Official Bulletin, 59), and the proposed United Nations Declaration on the Rights of Indigenous Peoples (as adopted by the Human Rights Council and included in its report to the General Assembly, UN document A/61/53).

Francioni and Scheinin (eds), *Cultural Human Rights*, 151–168

of identities that individuals may possess, and also the need for carving out space for collective rights in order to do justice to existing differences between individuals. Members of a particular group, in this case an indigenous people, demand respect for their right to enjoy their own culture in community with other members of the group. Failing to respond to such demands may amount not only to the denial of collective rights of the group but also to ignoring the identity of members of the group and sacrificing their individual rights on the altar of the presumed unity of a nation state.

Rights of indigenous peoples figure as an important theme in the international discourse on human rights. Nevertheless, indigenous peoples' rights are not an easy issue conceptually or juridically. Firstly, they do constitute a theme in the international discourse on human rights. This presumes their formulation and justification in a way that is in conformity with universal human rights which for the most part have been formulated as individual rights. In the context of the human rights discourse, indigenous peoples' rights are not particular privileges or separate rights but, rather, a functional device to ensure the enjoyment of universal human rights also for members of indigenous peoples. Without the additional device provided by indigenous peoples' rights, these individuals might fall short of effective protection for their universally recognized human rights.[3]

It is the point of departure for the category of indigenous peoples' rights that there is a need for special measures in respect of indigenous peoples. Because indigenous peoples in fact are subject to subordination, marginalization or exclusion, states have the right and even an obligation to take such measures that result in *de facto* equality.[4] Such positive or special measures are seen as permissible in respect of the prohibition against discrimination.

Secondly, indigenous peoples' rights carry the message of not only individual but also collective rights, or at least certain collective rights, being human rights.[5] For

---

3 For an elaboration of this position, see M. Scheinin, 'Minority Rights: Additional Rights or Added Protection?', in M. Bergsmo (ed.), *Human Rights and Criminal Justice for the Downtrodded: Essays in Honour of Asbjørn Eide* (Leiden, Martinus Nijhoff Publishers, 2003), pp. 487-504.

4 The Convention for the Elimination of All Forms of Racial Discrimination and the Convention for the Elimination of Discrimination Against Women articulate the position that special measures aiming at *de facto* equality are permissible. The Human Rights Committee responsible for the international monitoring of the International Covenant on Civil and Political Rights (ICCPR), in turn, takes the view that special measures amount to a state obligation that flows from the non-discrimination clause in Article 26 of the Covenant. See, General Comment No. 18 (1989) by the Human Rights Committee, para. 10. The same approach has been articulated by the European Court of Human Rights in the case of *Thlimmenos v. Greece* (Judgment of 6 April 2000, para. 44).

5 ILO Convention No. 169 and the UN Declaration on the Rights of Indigenous Peoples (see *supra* note 2) deal fairly extensively with collective rights, although they also include provisions

some human rights lawyers, educated in the tradition of human rights pertaining to the vertical relationship between the state and the individual, the whole thought of collective rights as human rights may appear as strange or even dangerous. If all human rights are about is to protect the individual against infringements by the state, i.e. guarantees for individual liberty, is there not a real risk that explaining some human rights as collective rights of a group or a people will turn on its head the whole setting about human rights? Will the result be that collective rights will in fact become a tool for the subordination of an individual by a community that will possess powers in relation to him or her?[6]

A third challenge relates to the recognition of indigenous peoples as peoples among peoples, putting into question the role of the nation state as a cornerstone of modern constitutions. If one does not refer to the people merely as a synonym for the whole population of a country, how will our perception of democracy and popular sovereignty need to be rethought?

The expert commission that was to draft a Nordic Saami Rights Convention was established in the fall of 2002 by constituting it to comprise experts nominated by the governments of Finland, Norway and Sweden, and by the national Saami Parliaments of the same countries.[7] Through the same procedure, an alternate was nominated and appointed for each expert. The author of this chapter had the honour of serving on the expert commission as a member nominated by the Finnish Saami Parliament and appointed jointly by the three governments and three Sami Parliaments. Among the experts, there were some heavyweight Nordic lawyers, such as Professor *Carsten Smith*, former Chief Justice of Norway and Justice *Hans*

---

on the rights of individual members of indigenous peoples. Article 27 of the ICCPR on the rights of persons belonging to ethnic, religious or linguistic minorities is written in the form of individual rights but taking into account their collective dimension ('... in community with the other members of their group ...'). Article 1 of the same treaty, proclaiming the right of all peoples to self-determination, in turn, is a clearly collective right that according to the Human Rights Committee cannot even on its own be invoked by individuals despite its inclusion in a human rights treaty. See, for instance, the Committee's Views in the case of *Apirana Mahuika et al. v. New Zealand* (Communication No. 547/1993), affirming the Committee's position that Article 1 cannot be invoked in the procedure for individual complaints under the Optional Protocol to the ICCPR.

6 For various approaches to the tension between individual and collective rights, see, W. Kymlicka (ed.), *The Rights of Minority Cultures* (Oxford, Clarendon Press, 1995), A. Shachar, *Multicultural Jurisdictions: Cultural Differences and Women's Rights* (Cambridge, Cambridge University Press, 2001), M. Scheinin, 'How to Resolve Conflicts Between Individual and Collective Rights?', in M. Scheinin and R. Toivanen (eds.), *Rethinking Nondiscrimination and Minority Rights* (Turku/Åbo, Åbo Akademi University Institute for Human Rights and German Institute for Human Rights, 2004), pp. 219-238.

7 The mandate of the expert commission (7 November 2001, as amended 13 November 2002) is reproduced in *Nordisk samekonvensjon* (see *supra* note 1), pp. 85-86.

*Danelius*, former Swedish Supreme Court judge and former member of the European Commission of Human Rights.

The proposal for a Nordic Saami Rights Convention is the result of three years of intensive work by the expert commission. The proposed underlying principles and individual treaty provisions were not chosen arbitrarily or easily but represent careful and systematic consideration of the treaty as a whole. Of course, some of the provisions are at the same time compromises between competing views within the expert commission. As such, the commission was unanimous in its proposal as a whole. Nevertheless, the cover letter transmitting the proposal to the three governments and the three national Saami Parliaments explains that the expert nominated by the Finnish government, and his alternate, had had 'difficulties' in accepting some specific treaty provisions. The wording chosen in the cover letter indicates that the difficulties referred to were a matter pertaining to the past and had not prevented reaching unanimity through compromises.[8]

## 2. About the notion of indigenous peoples

The United Nations has for a long time been struggling with a difficult drafting process for a declaration on the rights of indigenous peoples.[9] At the time our volume goes to press, that project is closer than ever before to becoming a reality. The newly established Human Rights Council adopted in June 2006 the text of a United Nations Declaration on the Rights of Indigenous Peoples,[10] and the final adoption of the resolution is on the agenda of the ongoing 61st session of the General Assembly. The Declaration does not, however, define the notion of indigenous peoples.[11] In contrast, ILO Convention No. 169 does include a definition, or at least it lists characteristics of groups that qualify as indigenous peoples under the Convention in question. Article 1, paragraph 1(b), of the Convention reads as follows:

> Peoples in independent countries who are regarded as indigenous on account of their descent from the populations which inhabited the country, or a

8 *Ibid.*, p. 2.

9 For a long time the discussions were based on a draft proposed by the Sub-commission on the Promotion and Protection of Human Rights, UN document E/CN.4/Sub.2/1994/2/Add.1 (1994).

10 Human Rights Council Resolution 1/2, adopted by a recorded vote of 30 votes to 2, with 12 abstentions. UN document A/61/53. The Declaration, as contained in UN Document A/61/L.67 was adopted by the General Assembly on 13 September 2007, with 143 votes against 4, and 11 abstentions.

11 For a discussion by the present author on the notion of indigenous peoples, see M. Scheinin, 'What Are Indigenous Peoples?', in N. Ghanea and A. Xanthaki (eds.), *Minorities, Peoples and Self-Determination* (Leiden, Martinus Nijhoff Publishers, 2005), pp. 3-13.

> geographical region to which the country belongs, at the time of conquest or colonisation or the establishment of present State boundaries and who, irrespective of their legal status, retain some or all of their own social, economic, cultural and political institutions.[12]

Despite the quoted specific provision on the characteristics of indigenous peoples covered by ILO Convention No. 169, also in the framework of that Convention the notion of indigenous peoples is more multi-layered than what one treaty provision seems to indicate. The quoted provision itself expresses directly or indirectly four central characteristics of indigenous peoples:

(1) *Being first*, 'indigenousness' in the meaning of the natural language usage of the term, i.e., the presence of a group in a particular geographic area prior to other human communities and in particular prior to the currently dominant population.[13] It needs to be stressed that neither this provision nor any other part of ILO Convention No. 169 reduces the notion of indigenous peoples to the first known owners of certain parcels of land, or their currently living biological successors. What 'being first' means here relates to the presence of a *culture* in a particular territory prior to other cultures, and to the continuity of the legacy of this culture down to the human beings that live and constitute cultural communities today.

(2) *Subordination* in respect of the current dominant population, whose power is built on colonization, or more broadly on the demarcation of the borders of nation states on other grounds than based on the presence of distinctive cultural communities. Inherent in the usage of the term of indigenous peoples as a legal concept is the idea of a *relation* between the historically original group of people and the population that today is in a dominant

---

12 72 ILO Official Bulletin 59. The Convention entered into force in 1991. Of the three countries relevant in the context of the Nordic Saami Rights Convention, Norway is a party to ILO Convention No. 169, in contrast to Finland and Sweden who still hesitate to ratify the Convention because of the unsettled stage of Saami land and resource rights.

13 The requirement of inhabiting a certain territory prior to others distinguishes the notion of indigenous peoples from the parallel concept of *tribal peoples* in ILO Convention No. 169. See, Article 1, para. 1(a) of the Convention. In relation to a broader international discussion on indigenous peoples' rights the reference to tribal peoples in ILO Convention No. 169 represents an extensive application of the principles related to indigenous peoples' rights, affording them to certain groups that do not match the criterion of 'being first'. The broad scope of application chosen in ILO Convention No. 169 is one explanation for the existence of Article 1, para. 3, according to which the treatment of a particular group as an indigenous or tribal people in the meaning of the Convention does not on its own mean that the group in question would always be 'a people' generally under public international law.

position.[14] This criterion is apparent when one looks at ILO Convention No. 169 as a whole: the treaty is about the obligations of the state in respect of an indigenous people, all the time presuming that the state is governed by someone else than the indigenous people itself. If the original population of a certain country is at the same time the only cultural or ethnic community in the territory, or the dominant one, it is not an indigenous people in the legal meaning of the term.

(3) *Distinctiveness* in respect of other communities or groups. The distinctive nature of an indigenous people and its culture is based on the conditions that prevailed prior to the entry of the currently dominant population and the drawing of the borders between nation states. This distinctiveness may manifest itself in social, economic, cultural or political special characteristics. One must not reduce the notion of indigenous peoples to the protection of 'acquired rights' or to remedying past injustices to the original owners or inhabitants of a particular territory. At least to an equal degree, the protection of the rights of indigenous peoples is about seeing the cultural diversity of humankind as an end in itself, resulting in a determination to secure the continuity and transmission to future generations of existing distinctive forms of culture.

(4) *Cultural continuity* between the historical situation of 'being first' and the present, and the future. The justification of the rights of indigenous peoples is largely conditioned by the preservation of a distinctive culture up until today and the wish of the community concerned to transmit this culture also to future generations. Cultures that have undergone a collapse and have perished are of historical and ethnological interest,[15] but without the continuity of some distinctive social, economic, cultural or political features they do not give rise to present-day rights of indigenous peoples.

In addition to these four characteristics derived from Article 1, paragraph 1(b), of ILO Convention No. 169, the same Convention as a whole gives rise to two further characteristics for determining what communities constitute indigenous peoples:

(5) *Self-identification* is, according to Article 1, paragraph 2 of ILO Convention No. 169, a fundamental criterion for determining the groups to which the provisions of the Convention apply. More precisely, the provision refers to the self-identification of the group as indigenous or tribal, and not for instance

---

[14] For a discussion on the relational approach to the notions of minorities and indigenous peoples, see T. Makkonen, *Identity, Difference and Otherness: The Concepts of People, Indigenous People and Minority in International Law* (Eric Castrén Institute Research Reports 7/2000, Helsinki University Press, 2000).

[15] See J. Diamond, *Collapse: How Societies Choose to Fall or Succeed* (Viking, 2005).

to the self-identification of an individual who proclaims himself or herself as a member of a community. The negative dimension of the provision is clear: if a group does not consider itself to be indigenous or tribal, it must not be classified or treated as such. As to the positive dimension, the outcome is that the wish of a community to be regarded as an indigenous or tribal one should be given legal significance. The treaty provision in question does not address the issue of how to resolve a claim by an individual to be accepted as a member of an indigenous or tribal community.

(6) *Special relationship with the lands and natural resources* of a specific territory.[16]

Three of the defining elements presented above, related to being first, to distinctiveness, and to continuity, are closely related to one more characteristic of indigenous peoples, namely the fact that their distinctive culture, that through continuity bridges the present with the time prior to colonization, did not develop by way of coincidence. Instead, the natural environment of a particular territory shaped the way of life of the people concerned into what became their distinctive culture. Through centuries or even millennia the climate and the available natural resources provided a platform for a way of life that was adjusted to the natural environment and quite often also provided for sustainable harmony with it. Certainly there were also in the past communities that exploited their natural resources and perished together with them. But those groups that managed to develop a way of life that was in harmony with the natural environment brought about cultures that were transmitted from generation to generation. Fishing, hunting, gathering, nomadic herding of animals and certain forms of agriculture are in global comparison typical forms of livelihood of indigenous peoples and at the same time the starting point for the evolution of social organization, material and immaterial culture and political institutions. The social life of indigenous communities would often be conditioned by the available natural resources and the accumulated ways of utilizing them. The same historical evolution also has contributed to the development of language, the production of cultural artefacts and artistic expression. The special relationship between indigenous peoples and the natural resources of their traditional territory is also a key to the understanding of their vulnerable or subordinated situation. The displacement of communities and the introduction of new forms of economic life may improve the GNP per capita among an indigenous group but at the same time may be incompatible with the rights of the indigenous people. Such measures

[16] In ILO Convention No. 169 the criterion in question is expressed, *inter alia*, in a reference to ecological harmony in the preamble, and in Article 13 that opens Part II on land rights and recognizes the special importance for the cultures and spiritual values of the peoples concerned of their relationship with the lands or territories which they occupy or otherwise use, and in particular the collective aspects of this relationship.

detach the indigenous people from its natural resources and the historical continuity that is based on them. As a result, also the distinctiveness of the culture concerned may be lost forever.

Although Finland, Norway and Sweden have on various occasions recognized that the Saami people constitutes an indigenous people within their territories, and although Finland does this explicitly in its Constitution,[17] these acknowledgments have not necessarily been made on the basis of a juridically articulate understanding of the notion of indigenous peoples or with full awareness of the legal consequences that the notion carries with it. In the context of the Nordic Saami Rights Convention the three countries will finally need to be much more articulate than so far; when the Saami people are officially recognized as the only indigenous people in all three countries, this will necessarily entail juridical consequences.

## 3. The articulation of indigenous peoples' rights: The right to the past, the right to the present and the right to the future

In an earlier article the author of this chapter addressed the various ways in which indigenous peoples' claims can be articulated within the framework provided by different international and regional human rights treaties. Although the specific human right invoked may differ from system to system, the claims tend to have the same aim, the protected possession and utilization of the lands and natural resources within a particular territory, as the material basis for the distinctive culture of the indigenous group in question.[18] Where ILO Convention No. 169 on indigenous and tribal peoples primarily speaks about *land*,[19] the Covenant on Civil and Political Rights turns the focus on *culture*.[20] And where the American Convention on Human Rights extends the right to *property*[21] to cover indigenous peoples' land rights, the

17 Section 17, subsection 3, of the Finnish Constitution of 1999.

18 M. Scheinin, 'The Right to Enjoy a Distinct Culture: Indigenous and Competing Uses of Land', in T.S. Orlin, A. Rosas and M. Scheinin (eds.), *The Jurisprudence of Human Rights Law: A Comparative Interpretive Approach* (Turku, Åbo Akademi University Institute for Human Rights, 2000), pp. 159-222.

19 ILO Convention No. 169, Part II (Articles 13-19).

20 See, ICCPR Article 27 and as central interpretive material emanating from the Human Rights Committee, General Comment No. 23 (1994) and the Views in the cases of *Ivan Kitok v. Sweden* (Communication No. 197/1985), *Bernard Ominayak (Lubicon Lake Band) v. Canada* (Communication No. 167/1984), *Ilmari Länsman et al. v. Finland* (Communication No. 511/1992), *Jouni E. Länsman et al. v. Finland* (Communication No. 671/1995) and *Apirana Mahuika et al. v. New Zealand* (Communication No. 547/1993).

21 See, American Convention on Human Rights (1144 U.N.T.S. 123), Article 21 and the judgment by the Inter-American Court of Human Rights in the case of *Awas Tingni v. Nicaragua* (31 August 2001). The radical dimension of this ruling is the Court's interpretation that the notion

European Convention on Human Rights appears most promising under the notion of the right to *private and family life*.[22] The varying articulation of the claims can usually be explained by the fact that the texts of the treaties vary, providing for different 'windows' through which indigenous peoples' rights can be addressed within each respective treaty and through the monitoring mechanisms it creates. This kind of setting demonstrates also the interdependent nature of different human rights, as very similar claims can be articulated in several alternative ways.[23]

The proposed Nordic Saami Rights Convention offers several alternative windows for presenting legal claims to support the existence and well-being of the distinctive Saami culture that developed over centuries and continues to exist on the basis of the utilization of Arctic natural resources. Following the Saami legal scholar Ánde Somby, these legal strategies can be analysed by using as a framework the notions of the right to the past, the right to the present and the right to the future.[24] Here those notions are used as a tool for presentation, without claiming that the three categories would represent an analytical legal classification.

### *1. The right to the past*

It is fully possible to claim, address and determine indigenous peoples' rights, including the rights of the Saami people and of its individual members, on the basis of arguments and sources that pertain to the past. The justification for such an approach lies in the criterion of being first as a dimension of the notion of indigenous peoples. As the indigenous people inhabited a specific territory prior to the arrival of the now dominant population, it often has claims to the restitution of its lands, based on its historical possession of those lands in the past. The emphasis given in ILO Convention No. 169 to land rights, including the importance of historical continuity for rights of ownership and possession in Article 14, provides support for choosing this approach and arguments for pursuing it. Also in the Nordic countries arguments based on the historical possession of lands have had a prominent role in discussions on the recognition of the rights of the Saami as an indigenous people.

---

of property in the Convention is an autonomous concept that refers not only to property rights as recognized by national law but also to customary law systems of indigenous peoples.

22 See, the inadmissibility decision by the (then) European Commission of Human Rights in the case of *G. and E. v. Noway (the Alta River Dam Case)*, European Commission of Human Rights, *Decisions and Reports*, vol. 35 (1984) s. 30-45.

23 This interdependence is in a graphic way illustrated by the Views of the Human Rights Committee in the case of *Hopu and Bessert v. France* (Communication No. 549/1993). When a declaration by France was treated as a permissible reservation and precluded the application of Article 27, the Committee resorted to the ICCPR provisions on the right to privacy and family in Articles 17 and 23, deriving from them consequences largely similar to those attributed in earlier cases to Article 27.

24 Á. Somby, *Juss som retorikk* (Oslo, Tano Aschehoug, 1999).

This can be explained partly by the existence of highly qualified work by legal historians,[25] partly by the prominent role that ILO Convention No. 169 has received in public discussion and the drafting of new legislation.

However, it needs to be emphasized that the status and rights of the Saami as an indigenous people will not be settled through historical analysis of the ownership and possession of lands in the past. Such studies are valuable as the factual basis for decisions to be taken through legislative or judicial avenues. In particular, caution is needed in respect of efforts to trivialize the issue of indigenous peoples' rights into the question of whose title to specific parcels of land was first recognized by the state. That type of research is inherently based on the concept of *terra nullius*, as all ownership to land is presumed to depend on title afforded or denied by the state.

The proposed Saami Rights Convention does not define the areas that in Finland, Norway or Sweden belong to the Saami, to the state, or to someone else. In line with the provisions of ILO Convention No. 169, the three states would commit themselves to investigating in good faith what are the areas in respect of which the long-term traditional possession of lands and waters by the Saami today constitutes a basis for the individual or collective ownership by the Saami. Where the Saami traditionally have used certain areas jointly with other population groups, for purposes such as reindeer herding, hunting or fishing, they shall have the right to the continued control and usage of these areas. Furthermore, the special characteristics of Saami usage shall be recognized by taking into account when assessing the evidence that Saami land and water usage often does not leave permanent traces in the environment. The Nordic Saami Rights Convention would not put any obstacles for presenting more far reaching collective or individual claims to land. Therefore the proposal includes a clause according to which the treaty shall not be construed as implying any limitation in the right to restitution that the Saami might have under national or international law.[26]

Through the treaty the three states would commit themselves to taking measures that effectively protect Saami land rights. Appropriate procedures for settling issues concerning Saami rights to land and waters shall be available under national law. In particular the Saami shall, in court proceedings concerning rights to land and waters, have access to such legal aid that is necessary for them to have their case tried.[27]

---

25 See, K. Korpijaakko, *Saamelaisten oikeusasemasta Ruotsi-Suomessa. Oikeushistoriallinen tutkimus Länsi-Pohjan Lapin maankäyttöoloista ja – oikeuksista ennen 1700-luvun puoliväliä* (Helsinki 1989); Lakimiesliiton kustannus.

26 Proposal for a Nordic Saami Rights Convention, Article 34.

27 Article 35.

## 2. *The right to the present*

In the international discourse on indigenous peoples' rights, these rights can be claimed, as well as on the basis of facts and arguments related to their historical possession of lands and their unjust dispossession, also on the present. In the context of indigenous peoples, the right to the present primarily relates to the fact that today's indigenous peoples represent distinct cultures, the preservation and transmission of which to future generations is an end in itself – irrespective of the juridical construction of ownership to the lands and territories that constitute the material basis for those cultures. Legal claims that are based on the aspiration to protect the survival and sustainability of indigenous cultures build upon the distinctiveness of these cultures, but also on the historical continuity they represent in respect of the past and the special relationship formed through centuries or even millenia between each culture and the specific natural resources of a particular territory that form the material basis of those cultures. In the human rights discourse 'the right to the present' can be articulated through the right of a group and its individual members to enjoy their own culture. The notion of 'culture' has a central place in Article 27 of the International Covenant on Civil and Political Rights and the institutionalized practices of interpretation that have evolved under that provision. It is an established line of interpretation under the treaty provision just mentioned that particularly in the case of indigenous peoples the notion of culture encompasses the traditional or otherwise distinctive forms of livelihood based on lands and natural resources.[28] Using this wide understanding of the notion of culture as its point of departure, the Human Rights Committee has developed a test in its interpretation of Article 27 according to which it will treat as prohibited 'denial' of the right to enjoy one's culture such competing usage of lands and natural resources that is authorized or tolerated by the state and results in the indigenous people's forms of livelihood losing their economic or cultural sustainability. For instance, oil and gas extraction, mining or quarrying of stone, or the cutting of forests, may amount to a violation of Article 27 if it results in destroying or risking the sustainability of the indigenous people's way of life.[29]

Although largely underdeveloped, also Article 8 of the European Convention on Human Rights, on the right to respect for private and family life, provides a legal basis for such human rights claims of indigenous peoples that build upon their present-day way of life and its material basis.

The proposal for a Nordic Saami Rights Convention affirms a broad understanding of the notion of culture, in line with Article 27 of the ICCPR. The treaty would

28 See, General Comment No. 23 (see *supra* note 20), in particular para. 7, and the case law mentioned in the same footnote.

29 See, in particular, the *Ominayak (Lubicon) v. Canada* case where a violation of Article 27 was established and the case of *Ilmari Länsman et al. v. Finland*, see *supra* note 20.

explicitly require that the obligations of the contracting states in respect of the Saami culture will extend to the material basis for that culture so that the Saami will enjoy the necessary economic preconditions for preserving and developing their culture through the sustainability of their distinctive forms of economic livelihood.[30] In accordance with the case law by the Human Rights Committee[31] the treaty would also require that the Saami have effective means of participation in respect of decision-making about the conditions of their life. Public authorities would always have to consult with the Saami Parliament of the country concerned before making any decision in a matter that is of significant importance for the Saami. These consultations must take place early enough so that the Saami Parliament will be able to influence the consideration of the matter and its outcome. A specific provision would prescribe that the three states shall neither take nor allow any measure that could considerably damage the basis for the Saami culture, livelihood or society, unless the Saami Parliament concerned gives its consent.[32]

### *3. The right to the future*

In the international discourse on human rights, the right of indigenous peoples to their future partly flows from their right to the present: much of the securing of the sustainability of a distinctive culture is in its successful transmission to future generations. But the right to the future can also be based on the latter part of the notion 'indigenous peoples', the fact that the communities in question are *peoples* among peoples and hence entitled to the right of self-determination. The Human Rights Committee has on several occasions, including in its consideration of periodic reports by Finland, Sweden and Norway, emphasized that the right of all peoples to self-determination, as enshrined in Article 1 of the ICCPR, is applicable not only in respect of the whole population of nation states but also in respect of many indigenous peoples including the Saami in the three Nordic countries.[33] The Committee has expressed the same position in respect of several other indigenous peoples as well.[34]

---

30 Proposal for a Nordic Saami Rights Convention, Article 33: 'The contracting states' obligation with regard to the Saami culture also includes protection for the material basis for the Saami culture in that the Saami shall be secured the livelihoods and economic possibilities that are necessary to preserve and develop the Saami culture'.

31 See, e.g., the cases of *Ilmari Länsman et al. v. Finland*, para. 9.6, and *Jouni E. Länsman et al. v. Finland*, para. 10.7. See *supra* note 20.

32 Proposal for a Nordic Saami Rights Convention, Article 16.

33 See the latest concluding observations issued by the Human Rights Committee in the consideration of periodic reports by Norway (CCPR/C/79/Add.112; 1999 and CCPR/C/NOR/CO/5; 2006), Sweden (CCPR/CO/74/SWE; 2002) and Finland (CCPR/CO/82/FIN; 2004).

34 The Human Rights Committee has made similar pronouncements on indigenous peoples as beneficiaries of the right of self-determination in respect of, *inter alia*, Canada (CCPR/C/79/

The right of all peoples to self-determination as a norm of international law does not entail that every group that constitutes a people would have the right to establish its own state and unilaterally secede from an existing, possibly multi-ethnic, state. Such a right to secession can be sustained only under particular conditions such as military occupation, colonial domination and other forms of oppression that result in the denial of effective participation and other human rights.[35] When addressing the right of indigenous peoples to self-determination, the Human Rights Committee has repeatedly emphasized the importance of paragraph 2 of ICCPR Article 1, i.e. the so-called economic or resource dimension of the right of self-determination. For most indigenous peoples in the world, self-determination does not primarily mean an aspiration to establish a state of their own but, rather, a right to control their traditional lands and natural resources.

In the international discussion the Nordic governments have been active in defending formulations through which indigenous peoples can also be recognized as beneficiaries of the right of self-determination. Their role has been important in solving the stalemate which for a long time appeared to block progress in the elaboration of a United Nations Declaration on the Rights of Indigenous Peoples. When defending the right of indigenous peoples to self-determination, the Nordic countries have nevertheless emphasized that the recognition of this right does not entail an automatic right to unilateral secession.[36]

---

Add.105; 1999 and CCPR/C/CAN/CO/5; 2006), Mexico (CCPR/C/79/Add.109; 1999), Australia (CCPR/CO/69/AUS; 2000) and the United States (CCPR/C/USA/CO/3; 2006).

35 For a discussion on the relationship between the right of self-determination and the right to unilateral secession, see the opinion by the Supreme Court of Canada in *Reference re Secession of Quebec*, [1998] 2 S.C.R. 217; J.B. Henriksen, M. Scheinin, and M. Åhrén, 'Det samiska folkets rätt till självbestämmande', Annex 3 in *Nordisk samekonvensjon* (see *supra* note 1), pp. 299-357; J. Crawford, *The Creation of States in International Law* (Second edition, Oxford, Clarendon Press, 2006), in particular pp. 383-418. See, also, C. Tomuschat, 'Secession and Self-determination', pp. 23-45 (in particular, p. 37), and P. Dumberry, 'Lessons Learned from the Quebec Secession Reference before the Supreme Court of Canada', pp. 416-452 (in particular, pp. 431-435), both in M.G. Kohen (ed.), *Secession: International Law Perspectives* (Cambridge, Cambridge University Press, 2006). According to Tomuschat 'indigenous peoples, who undoubtedly are peoples in the ethnic and cultural sense, have never been recognized as holders of a right to self-determination involving secession' (p. 37). Dumberry, in turn, concludes that 'the ten Amerindian nations as well as the Inuit nation living in Quebec are also, without doubt, peoples under international law' (p. 436). A third view is presented by the editor of the same volume, Kohen, who in his 'Introduction' (pp. 1-20) categorically states 'that a clear distinction among three different categories of human communities is made in international law, each having their corresponding rights: peoples, minorities and indigenous populations' (p. 9).

36 The joint Nordic proposals have been published as annexes to the report by the expert commission that drafted the proposal for a Nordic Saami Rights Convention, see *Nordisk samekonvensjon* (see *supra* note 1), pp. 358-373.

The proposed Nordic Saami Rights Convention is up-to-date in relation to the international discussion on the right of indigenous peoples to self-determination. According to the expert commission's draft the Saami, 'as a people, enjoy the right to self-determination pursuant to the rules of international law and this treaty'. Furthermore, the provision would continue with emphasis on the resource dimension of the right of self-determination, affirming that the Saami enjoy the right to determine their economic, social and cultural development and to dispose, to their own benefit, of their natural resources.[37]

## 4. References to the Saami culture in the proposed Saami Rights Convention

The draft treaty contains many references to the existence of a Saami culture and to the right to its continued enjoyment. Already in the preamble of the treaty, the three states would affirm that the Saami people 'has its own culture', that lands and waters constitute the foundation for the Saami culture, that this culture enriches to the countries' collected cultures and societies, and that the states themselves have a national and international responsibility to provide adequate conditions for the Saami culture. Of the 43 treaty articles that deal with substantive rights, no less than 17 include references to the Saami culture. To mention just some of these provisions, reference can be made to:

- Article 1, on the object and purpose of the treaty;
- Article 3, proclaiming cultural development as a dimension of the Saami peoples' right to self-determination;
- Article 16, providing the national Saami Parliaments with a power to *veto* measures taken or allowed by the states that may significantly damage the basic conditions for Saami culture;[38]
- The provisions of Chapter III on Saami language and Saami culture (Articles 23-33), ending up with a provision on the material basis for the Saami culture; and
- Article 41 on Saami forms of livelihood and Article 42 specifically about reindeer herding as a form of Saami culture.

---

37 Proposal for a Nordic Saami Rights Convention, Article 3.

38 See, also, Article 36, para. 2.

### *A. A difficult challenge: Reindeer herding as 'culture' in Finland*

Through the case law of the Human Rights Committee it has been affirmed that in the case of the Saami, reindeer herding as a traditional, nature-based and still today typical form of Saami livelihood constitutes a dimension of 'culture' in the meaning of ICCPR Article 27.[39] Against this background it is only natural that the proposal for a Nordic Saami Rights Convention should include a specific provision according to which reindeer herding, 'as a particular and traditional livelihood and a form of culture' shall enjoy special legal protection.[40] However, it is also important that the treaty would not reduce Saami culture or the material basis thereof to reindeer herding as the best-known and most visible form of Saami livelihoods. Instead, the quoted provision would be preceded by a general clause according to which Saami livelihoods and Saami usage of natural resources shall, to the extent they constitute the basis for the Saami culture, enjoy specific protection through legal or economic measures. In this context, Saami livelihoods and Saami use of natural resources are defined through an open-ended reference to 'such activities that are important to the maintenance and development of the Saami local communities'.[41] For instance hunting, fishing and gathering would clearly be covered by the provision, in addition to reindeer herding.

A difficult challenge to the status of reindeer herding as a dimension of Saami culture is posed by the fact that in Finland, unlike the situation in Norway and Sweden, reindeer herding has never been recognized by law as a specific Saami right. Instead, the Finnish Reindeer Herding Act proclaims the right to herd reindeer in the northern part of the country as a general right of all permanent residents who are European Union citizens or nationals of other countries that belong to the European Economic Area.[42] In the Accession Treaty on the membership of Finland and Sweden in the European Union, both countries already obtained a permission to regulate reindeer herding as an exclusive right of the Saami.[43] As this is already the situation under Norwegian and Swedish law and even Finland has obtained in EU law a permission to follow suit, a Nordic Saami Rights Convention cannot ignore the issue of whether reindeer herding in Finland will continue as everyone's right or whether it will become a distinctive right of the Saami. At present, however, the majority of all reindeer in Finland are owned by non-Saami Finns who usually do

---

39 See, the cases of *Ivan Kitok, Ilmari Länsman et al.* and *Jouni E. Länsman et al.* (see *supra* note 20).

40 Proposal for a Nordic Saami Rights Convention, Article 42, para. 1.

41 Article 41.

42 Reindeer Herding Act of 14 September 1990/848, as amended, Section 4.

43 Treaty Concerning the Accession of Republic of Austria, the Republic of Finland and the Kingdom of Sweden to the European Union, Protocol No 3 on the Sami People, OJ C241 of 29 August 1994.

not practise semi-nomadic herding in the nature but keep their reindeer in fences like cattle.

The expert commission spent a lot of time discussing transitory arrangements through which Finland could follow the model of Norway and Sweden and transform reindeer herding into an exclusive right of the indigenous Saami. This kind of change would certainly strengthen the identity and culture of the Saami in Finland where their number is smaller than in Norway or Sweden and where the wide involvement of non-Saami in reindeer herding tends to cause confusion about the distinctiveness of the Saami way of life. The Saami in Finland are threatened by assimilation into the mainstream population, and the Reindeer Herding Act is a piece of legislation enacted by the state that contributes to that threat.

Due to the sensitivity of the issue in Finland, the proposed Nordic Saami Rights Convention is a very modest compromise on this particular point. According to the proposal, Norway and Sweden would commit themselves to maintaining and developing reindeer herding as an exclusive right of the Saami in the Saami reindeer grazing areas, whereas Finland would, acknowledging Protocol No. 3 to its EU accession treaty, undertake to strengthen the position of Saami reindeer herding.[44]

The Saami way of life and the Saami culture is not based on reindeer herding alone. Also in Finland there are Saami communities, including along the river Tana (Teno), whose social life and Saami identity is constituted around salmon fishing practised since time immemorial. Despite this, strengthening the sustainability of the Saami culture in Finland will require measures to support reindeer herding as a distinctive Saami livelihood. The social life of the remaining Saami communities, the Saami language, the relationship of the Saami to their natural environment, the artistic expression of the Saami and the transmission of Saami culture to future generations all depend on the fate of nature-based Saami reindeer herding in Finland. The continued cutting of old forests in the winter herding lands of the Saami reindeer herders and the treatment in Finnish agricultural policy of reindeer as just one source of meat among others constitute risks to the sustainability and existence of Saami reindeer herding in Finland. In the last resort, this risks threaten also the Saami language, the Saami culture and the existence of a Saami people in Finland.

Article 8 of the UN Declaration of the Rights of Indigenous Peoples, as adopted by the Human Rights Council, protects indigenous peoples against forced assimilation or destruction of their culture.[45] The current legislation and other measures by public authorities in Finland appear to match three out of five forms of assimilation or destruction, as specified in that provision:

---

44 Proposal for a Nordic Saami Rights Convention, Article 42.

45 See *supra* note 2.

(a) Any action which has the aim or effect of depriving them of their integrity as distinct peoples, or of their cultural values or ethnic identities;

(b) Any action which has the aim or effect of dispossessing them of their lands, territories or resources; and

(d) Any form of forced assimilation or integration by other cultures or ways of life imposed on them by legislative, administrative or other measures.

## 5. The prospects for a Nordic Saami Rights Convention

The establishment and work of the expert commission that drafted the proposal for a Nordic Saami Rights Convention represent a fundamental change in the attitudes of Nordic governments in respect of the indigenous Saami people. The expert commission was composed with respect for the equality of the governments and the national Saami Parliament as participants in a process towards a treaty. This was in conformity with the character of the envisaged Nordic Saami Rights Convention as a social contract between the Saami people and the three nation states involved. During the work of the expert commission the principle of equality between the involved parties was respected in the sense that no government or other party had a greater say than the others in formulating the commonly agreed proposal.

In November 2005 the expert commission delivered its proposal in a public event in Helsinki, Finland, jointly to the three cabinet members of the respective governments and the three Presidents of the national Saami Parliaments. Subsequently, the continued preparation of the treaty for parliamentary adoption proceedings is under the common responsibility of the involved parties. Without breaching the nature of the whole project, further negotiations on the substance of the treaty cannot be made subject to a mere intergovernmental process. While it is important to consult other interested and affected entities, such as municipalities, state agencies and non-governmental organizations active in issues pertaining to the Saami culture, it will be out of the question to reduce the national Saami Parliaments to the position of one interested party among others. Consulting interested parties must be seen as a joint enterprise by the three governments and the three national Saami Parliaments to evaluate and improve the proposal by the expert commission.

If and when consensus will be achieved between the three governments and the three Saami Parliaments on the text of the final treaty, what will follow is the signing of the treaty by the three Nordic governments,[46] subjecting the signed treaty to approval by the three national Saami Parliaments,[47] and parliamentary proceedings

[46] Proposal for a Nordic Saami Rights Convention, Article 48.

[47] Article 48.

as required by the constitutions of the three countries involved.[48] It is one of the particular characteristics of the draft treaty proposed by the expert commission that although the treaty will become a legally binding international treaty between states under public international law, the entry into force of that treaty will, in addition to constitutionally regulated parliamentary proceedings, also require the consent by the three national Saami Parliaments.[49]

Furthermore, the requirement of consent by the three national Saami Parliaments as a condition for the entry into force of the treaty reflects the nature of the Saami Rights Convention as a social contract between the Saami people and the governments of the three Nordic countries.

48 Article 49.

49 Article 51.

# 8
# Cultural Identity and Legal Status: Or, the Return of the Right to Have (Particular) Rights

*Enikő Horváth*

Despite increasing recognition that 'without affording full guarantees for ... cultural rights ... the protection offered ... by other rights can become practically meaningless',[1] the substance and possibly even the idea of such rights remain problematic. There is no general agreement on what they constitute or who – individuals, groups or perhaps individuals as members of particular groups – are to be their beneficiaries. There does seem to be some consensus on the fact that states remain uniquely placed in affecting (and effecting) their protection, however. The recent UNESCO Convention on the Protection and Promotion of the Diversity of Cultural Expressions (CPDCE), for example, underlined the 'sovereign right of States to maintain, adopt and implement policies and measures that they deem appropriate for the protection and promotion of cultural expressions on their territory'.[2] The clearest affirmation of a state role came in 2002, however, in a resolution by the UN Commission on Human Rights, where it was recognized that '[s]tates have the primary responsibility for the promotion of the full enjoyment of cultural rights by everyone and for the enhancement of respect for different cultural identities'.[3]

The nature of this responsibility and respect in the context of individuals claiming a special status on the basis of cultural identity – or, rather, its dubious certainty – is the topic of this chapter. In short, culture is an increasingly conflictual matter for

1 D. Türk, Final Report of the Special Rapporteur of the Sub-Commission on Prevention of Discrimination and Protection of Minorities on the Realization of Economic, Social and Cultural Rights. UN Doc. E/CN.4/Sub.2/1992/16, para. 198 (1992).

2 Art. 1(h), Convention on the Protection and Promotion of the Diversity of Cultural Expressions (2005). See also Arts. 2 and 5(1).

3 Art. 5, UN Commission on Human Rights Resolution 2002/26, Promotion of the enjoyment of the cultural rights of everyone and respect for different cultural identities.

Francioni and Scheinin (eds), *Cultural Human Rights*, 169–191

the state.[4] On the one hand, no state is culture-neutral; nor does it wish to be, given that some shared collective identity is believed to be necessary for the creation and maintenance of the state-focused community, as circumscribed by national citizenship. (Whether a state claims to be multicultural, integrationist or assimilationist is of little importance in this regard.[5]) On the other, calls for culturally differentiated rights on the basis of a distinction between equality in law and effective equality have placed states on the defensive.[6] Should certain groups of nationals – officially recognized minorities – have special rights? In a further question, is legal membership to be a prerequisite for such rights or may permanent residents also claim particularized treatment? Finally, should membership in the form of nationality encompass some culture-specific requirements, such as linguistic ability? Can cultural identity even serve as the basis for special legal statuses?

At the heart of all of these questions lies that of recognition: To what extent will the given state recognize cultural differences? Will any public recognition be mirrored in law? If so, how? Will special rights flow from recognition? And how will the beneficiaries of these rights be identified? On the basis of such underlying considerations, legal recognition of special status – for a group or as a member of a national, indigenous, religious or other accepted group – within the state and, increasingly, also beyond it, has in certain cases become the first battle to win.[7] But

---

[4] As discussed by a number of authors, 'culture' is a contested concept. See, e.g. C. Jenks, *Culture* (1993) for a survey of views from the perspectives of sociology, anthropology and cultural studies; and R. Stavenhagen, 'Cultural Rights: A Social Science Perspective', in A. Eide, C. Krause and A. Rosas (eds.), *Economic, Social and Cultural Rights* (2001), pp. 85, 86-91, for a look at understandings of culture in legal and social science discourse. For an early approach to culture as a repertoire of capacities, the role of which changes in different periods, see A. Swidler, 'Culture in Action: Symbols and Strategies', *American Sociological Review* (1986), p. 273. For a call to approach culture in less essentialist terms in legal and political discussion, see R. Dhamoon, 'Shifting From "Culture" to "Cultural": Critical Theorizing of Identity/ Difference Politics', *Constellations* (2006), p. 354.

We define culture here as shared customary beliefs, symbols, attitudes, values and social forms passed on from one generation to the next. Accordingly, in line with sociological and psychological approaches, we consider it a learning process, a dynamic. It thus makes little sense to speak of 'protecting a culture', for example – only elements of an individual's attempt to live her culture can be defended.

[5] In fact, policies of assimilation and multiculturalism both view culture as a self-sustained container of values, traditions and habits. As a general matter, policy instruments and legal instruments, both domestic and international, rarely spell out their conception or underlying assumption of culture. See also R. Stavenhagen, *cit. supra* note 4, at 87.

[6] See *Minority Schools in Albania* (Advisory Opinion), P.C.I.J. (1935) and *Case of the German Settlers in Poland* (Advisory Opinion), P.C.I.J. (1923).

[7] See, for example, discussion of a 2005 German Administrative Court decision on an attempt by Muslim associations to be recognized as a 'religious community', to allow them to provide religious instruction in public schools, in 58 *Neue Juristische Wochenschrift* 2101 (2005); and D. Zacharias, 'Access of Muslim Organizations to Religious Instruction in Public Schools:

law is, by its very (categorical) nature, ill-equipped to adjudicate questions of culture and identity – how can one possibly pin down a process, after all?[8]

As state attempts to do just this, described below, will show, it is in part through public discourse on and legal oversight of such state recognition – as well as by constant re-evaluation of the content of religious and other freedoms – that the content of cultural rights plays out at state level. Thus, at least in Europe, it is domestic laws on minorities and nationality, and their indirect assessment by the European Court of Human Rights (ECtHR), that are determinative of the kind of rights to be protected, not to mention of the groups and individuals to whom such protection will be extended.

## 1. A right to cultural identity in the international framework

The central role of national laws becomes all the more apparent when we consider that there seems to be no one internationally accepted enumeration of what cultural rights are. The recent UNESCO Universal Declaration on Cultural Diversity (2001) (UDCD) does attempt to specify a bundle of rights to which this tag can be attached, but does so on the basis of an existing, rather scattered framework. Article 5, in particular, is worth quoting at full length:

> Cultural rights are an integral part of human rights, which are universal, indivisible and interdependent. The flourishing of creative diversity requires the full implementation of cultural rights as defined in Article 27 of the Universal Declaration of Human Rights and in Articles 13 and 15 of the International Covenant on Economic, Social and Cultural Rights. All persons have therefore the right to express themselves and to create and disseminate their work in the language of their choice, and particularly in their mother tongue; all persons are entitled to quality education and training that fully respect their cultural identity; and all persons have the right to participate in the cultural life of their choice and conduct their own cultural practices, subject to respect for human rights and fundamental freedoms.

---

Comment on the Decision of the Federal Administrative Court of 23 February 2005', 6(10) *German Law Journal* (2005).

[8] As social identity has shown, individual identity – however complex – is in all cases constructed and maintained, at least in part, through and in response to 'meanings imparted by a structured society'. J.E. Stets and P.J. Burke, 'Identity Theory and Social Identity Theory', *Social Psychology Quarterly* (2000), pp. 224, 226. See also discussion in M.A. Hogg, 'Social Identity' in M.R. Leary and J.P. Tangney (eds.), *Handbook of Self and Identity* (2003), p. 462. It is, accordingly, in constant flux; and hence better viewed as a dynamic process (of action and reaction) than a fixed quality.

The basic definition of 'cultural rights' thus seems to be that enunciated in the foundational international human rights instruments; and centres on two central concerns, participation and distinctness.

The first reference to 'culture' in an international human rights instrument was, in fact, in the American Declaration (rec. 5 and art. 13), which referred to the right of every person to 'take part in the cultural life of the community'. The declaration of the UDHR, in the form of an individual right 'freely to participate in the cultural life of the community, to enjoy the arts and to share in scientific advancement and its benefits'[9] came approximately six months later. The ICESCR echoes this formulation and adds an obligation for states to 'achieve the full realization' of this right.[10] Cultural rights are thus understood here as a right of participation in a general culture; in light of similar provisions in state constitutions of the time,[11] the reference is closely linked to the right to education.[12] The right to culture is thus understood here in terms of the availability of culture to all. To the extent that the ICESCR leaves the implementation of cultural rights in the hands of a particular state, however, the '[s]tate's cultural monopoly has been consolidated'.[13] This should not be surprising, in light of the manner in which states have generally seen cultural assimilation or at least integration as an element of full national citizenship.

The general, participatory approach has continued to play an important role,[14] but has been complemented by one focused on specific cultures, or distinctness. The UNESCO Declaration of Principles of International Cultural Co-Operation (1966), in particular, declared in Article 1(2) that 'every people has the right and the duty to develop its culture'.[15] This more particularistic approach to 'cultural

---

9 UDHR Art. 27(1). See also UDHR Art. 22. As Art. 27(2) of the UDHR shows, cultural rights in the widest sense include intellectual property rights; but will not be touched on here. A broader approach would also include rights that contribute to the maintenance of culture, such as a right to education, a right to free expression (including the use of a chosen language), a right to religion and a right to equal treatment, as well as the right to political participation and self-determination. For a discussion of all aspects of cultural rights, see A. Eide, 'Cultural Rights as Individual Human Rights' in A. Eide, C. Krause and A. Rosas, (eds), *cit. supra* note 4, p. 289.

10 See ICESCR Art. 15, paras. (1)(a) and (2) respectively.

11 See rec. 13 of the *Préambule* of the French Constitution of 1946; Art. 70/F of the Hungarian Constitution of 1949.

12 See UDHR Art. 26(1).

13 I. Szabó, Cultural Rights 48 (1974) (Emphasis in the original). Compare also note 2, *supra*.

14 See Article 14 of the Additional Protocol to the American Convention on Human Rights in the Area of Economic, Social and Cultural Rights (1988). But see Art. 17(2) of the African Charter of Human and Peoples' Rights (1981) (where the reference is to 'his' culture, i.e. a particular one).

15 See also Arts. 2(1) and 4(2) of the UN Declaration on the Rights of Persons Belonging to National or Ethnic, Religious and Linguistic Minorities (1992) [hereinafter UNDRM]; See also

rights' has developed rapidly since that time, taking two principal directions: one, a focus on the protection of the objective elements (or output) of culture – cultural expression and heritage[16] – has emerged;[17] two, cultural diversity has become a matter of concern, most clearly in the right to (a specific) cultural identity – as can be seen in UDCD Article 5, above.[18]

This latter concept is difficult to grasp, at least if we try to understand it as a right, but has nonetheless become influential.[19] A right to cultural identity has been included in Articles 1(3) and 5(1) of the UNESCO Declaration on Race and Racial Prejudice (1978), Article 1 of the UN Declaration on the Rights of Persons Belonging to National or Ethnic, Religious or Linguistic Minorities (1992) and Articles 4, 8 and 12 of the UN Draft Declaration on the Rights of Indigenous Peoples (1994).[20] However, none of these instruments are legally binding. Moreover, their treatment of cultural identity is somewhat sloppy: sometimes groups, at other times individuals are referred to, while there is not always a clear addressee. The attempt to move from a general focus on culture to a consideration of its most socially intangible realm – identity – is thus fraught with obstacles.[21]

---

Art. 4 of the UNESCO Recommendation on Participation by the People at Large in Cultural Life and their Contribution to it (1976).

16 The determination of what constitutes cultural heritage is still a matter of debate. The definition found in Art. 1 of the UNESCO Convention Concerning the Protection of the World Cultural and Natural Heritage (1972) [hereinafter CCPCH] or the ever-evolving explanation provided in its Guidelines are no longer exhaustive. See Art. 2(1) and (2) of the UNESCO Convention for the Safeguarding of the Intangible Cultural Heritage (2003). The concept of 'cultural expression', as introduced by CPDCE Art. 4(3), must now also be considered in discussion.

17 See the UDCD *supra*, as well as the CCPCH; see also, in the context of Europe, Arts. 1 and 5 of the Council of Europe European Cultural Convention (1954); Arts. 1 and 2 of the Council of Europe European Declaration on Cultural Objectives (1984).

18 See also, *inter alia*, Council of Europe Declaration of the Committee of Ministers on Cultural Diversity (2000).

19 Y. Donders, 'The Right to Cultural Identity in International Human Rights Law' in Y. Donders et al. (eds.), *Law and Cultural Diversity* (1999), pp. 65, 69. See also *ibid.*, *Towards a Right to Cultural Identity?* (2002) for a comprehensive look at the right to cultural identity in international law.

20 ILO Convention No. 169 concerning Indigenous and Tribal Peoples in Independent Countries (1991) also includes references to culture in a number of provisions, most clearly in Art. 2(2) (respect for cultural identity) and Art. 5(a) (recognition and protection of cultural values). The Convention, with 17 signatories (as of 2006) is the only binding legal instrument in the realm of cultural rights, but is limited to a very distinct type of group. See Art. 1(a) and (b).

21 The attempted legal definition of cultural identity developed by the UNESCO Project Concerning a Declaration of Cultural Rights highlights the absurdity of the approach. Cultural identity was defined there as 'all the cultural references through which individuals or groups define and express themselves and by which they wish to be recognized; cultural identity

The Council of Europe, in its Framework Convention for the Protection of National Minorities (1995) (CEFCM) – the first regional instrument to deal seriously with a right to cultural identity – does not even attempt a definition. Instead, the 'essential elements' of this identity are mentioned, and are named as 'religion, language, traditions and cultural heritage'.[22] Given the difficulty of definition, a list of fundamental elements is not a bad approach; its exhaustive nature is, however, unfortunate.[23] In fact, even the language of the relevant sections of the Convention[24] is not formulated in terms of a specific right to a cultural identity; on the other hand, it is formulated in the language of obligations. Thus, CEFCM Article 5(1) requires that states 'undertake to promote the conditions necessary' for members of national minorities to preserve their culture and identity. Thus, we again find an addressee in the state, as well as, for once, a subject in the 'person belonging to a national minority'.[25] But the programmatic language of the article masks a certain vagueness: the general formulation leaves states with a wide degree of latitude in determining what is 'necessary' in a given circumstance, albeit checked by the reports of the CEFCM Advisory Committee.[26] In certain articles,[27] moreover, the state obligated to act is not named – a fact not left unnoticed by the kin-states of particular minorities.

---

embraces the liberties inherent to human dignity and brings together, in a permanent process, cultural diversity, the particular and the universal, memory and aspiration'. (Art. 1(b) of Draft Declaration on Cultural Rights prepared by the UNESCO Project Concerning a Declaration of Cultural Rights (11th Version) (1996)). The drafters of this definition seem to have gotten lost in prose – as a legal definition it is simply useless.

22 CEFCM Art. 5(1).

23 A working group discussed the possible addition of a protocol to the ECHR on the right to cultural identity, but eventually decided against its drafting, due to concerns about the vagueness of the concept and the uncertain consequences. See Council of Europe Committee for the Protection of National Minorities, Draft Articles and Alternative Versions for Possible Inclusion in a Protocol Complementing the ECHR in the Cultural Field, CAHMIN(95)17 (1995).

24 CEFCM, Preamble and Art. 5.

25 But see Arts. 1 and 12(1), where the 'minority' is recognized as the bearer of distinctive traits. Despite such references, the rights extended in the Convention are not collective, as Art. 1 makes clear. Moreover, the rights of the Convention extend only to members of national minorities, not other cultural groups. See Council of Europe, Explanatory Report on the Framework Convention for the Protection of National Minorities, paras. 11 and 29, 20(2) NJCM Bulletin 199 (1995).

26 That said, the Advisory Committee has focused mainly on the importance of consultation, participation and financial support, rather than specific measures. See discussion in G. Gilbert, 'Article 5', in M. Weller (ed.), *The Rights of Minorities in Europe: Commentary on the European Framework Convention for the Protection of National Minorities* (2005), p. 153.

27 See CEFCM Art. 4, as compared with Art. 12.

In the entirety of the Convention then, we do not find either a specific object of protection, since the conditions the state must promote are left undefined, or (in some cases) one specific addressee. Such flexibility can be both a burden and a blessing, depending on the situation. In any case, the Convention at least presents a way forward for the idea of cultural identity in (regional) international law. It should be noted, however, that a number of Council of Europe member states with minority issues have refused to (sign and) ratify the treaty;[28] moreover, the CEFCM system does not provide for judicial remedies, despite extensive monitoring.[29]

## 2. Cultural identity in the context of the exercise of fundamental rights

Given its inherent limitations, perhaps it comes as no surprise that the Framework Convention has played no role in recent case law at the ECtHR dealing with questions of cultural identity. Rather, the Court has used existing provisions to manage submissions that touch on identity matters and has gone out of its way to 'abstain … from formulating any opinion on the issue of identity itself'.[30] It has instead tried to ensure that 'individuals are free to define themselves in the way they wish, to express attachment to a certain community, and to associate in order to promote a culture or defend a group they consider to belong to, even if their views do not fit with the dominant conception of national culture and history'.[31]

In one case, however, the Court determined, in line with the generally accepted approach, that objective substantiation may be required by a state when individuals – as opposed to groups – claim a particular minority cultural identity as the basis for a special right. Thus, '[w]hile the notion of the State sitting in judgment on the state of a citizen's inner and personal beliefs is abhorrent and may smack unhappily of past infamous persecutions', when a 'claim to a privilege or exemption to which [an individual is] not entitled unless he [is] a member of the faith [or other community] concerned and in circumstances which arguably give rise to doubts as his entitlement … it [is] not unreasonable or disproportionate to require [that individual] to show some level of substantiation of his claim'.[32] Thus, while state

---

28 As of October 2006, these states include Belgium, France, Greece and Turkey (Latvia and the Netherlands, as well as Georgia ratified in the course of 2005).

29 See the contributions in M. Weller, *cit. supra* note 26, for discussions of the role of the Advisory Committee.

30 J. Ringelheim, 'Identity Controversies Before the European Court of Human Rights: How to Avoid the Essentialist Trap?', 3(7) *German Law Journal* (2002).

31 *Ibid.*

32 *Kosteski v. (FYRO) Macedonia*, ECtHR Application No. 55170/00 (2006), paras. 39 and 46, respectively. Applicant had argued that requirement of proof of his Muslim faith (incidentally

courts may take decisions on identity matters, the Court continues to refrain from doing so.

Even in the context of groups, there are limits to accepted legal definitions, however, as a series of submissions – in which groups claimed a cultural (and minority) identity their states refuse to acknowledge the existence (or legal recognition) of – has shown. In essence, these cases force the question of the relationship between a cultural identity and (domestic) legal status. In the first of the cases, *Ahmet Sadik v. Greece*[33] – centring on the use of the designation 'Turk' (i.e. a cultural/ ethnic category) in an electoral campaign by a minority politician, when the government considers the group a religious minority only – the Court refused to examine the merits of the case; however, the partly dissenting opinion of Judge Martens[34] pointed the way toward the Court's later judgments. Specifically, in the *Sidiropoulos* case,[35] arising from the refusal of Greek authorities to allow the registration of an association aiming to promote Macedonian culture and identity – the existence of which Greece viewed as a threat to 'the maintenance of national security, the prevention of disorder and the upholding of Greece's cultural traditions and historical and cultural symbols'[36] – the Court found a violation under ECHR Article 11. It argued that '[t]erritorial integrity, national security and public order were not threatened by the activities of an association whose aim was to promote a region's culture, even supposing that it also aimed partly to promote the culture of a minority; the existence of minorities and different cultures in a country was a historical fact that a "democratic society" had to tolerate and even protect and support according to the principles of international law'.[37]

The *Stankov* case,[38] decided three years later, confirms the right of groups to claim a publicly recognized minority identity – in fact, the Court extends protection to the political views of that minority, as long as these are not to be reached through violent

found to be lacking by all domestic courts), by organs of the state, amounted to violation of ECHR Arts. 9 and 14.

33 *Ahmet Sadik v. Greece*, ECtHR Application No. 18877/91 (1996).

34 See para. 19 ('When criminal provisions purporting to prevent disturbance of public peace are relied on against a politician who is not only an opponent and a critic of the Government but also a member of a minority, the European Court of Human Rights should apply its highest standards of scrutiny in order to ascertain whether these provisions have been abused, as they easily may be and often are. There is all the more reason for extreme vigilance because the criticism concerned the Government's attitude towards the minority in question and more especially their policy of denying that the minority is not only a religious but also an ethnic one').

35 *Sidiropoulos and Others v. Greece*, ECtHR Application No. 26695/95 (1998).

36 *Ibid.*, para. 37.

37 *Ibid.*, para. 41.

38 *Stankov and the United Macedonian Organisation Ilinden v. Bulgaria*, ECtHR Applications No. 29221/95 and 29225/95 (2001).

means.[39] Thus, the refusal by Bulgarian authorities, of registration, and later ban of an association claiming the recognition and unity of the Macedonian minority was found to be in violation of ECHR Article 11. Moreover, '[t]he fact that what was at issue touched on national symbols and national identity cannot be seen in itself… as calling for a wider margin of appreciation to be left to the authorities'.[40]

In a series of cases dealing with the Turkish Constitutional Court's dissolution of certain political parties – owing to a refusal to recognize the existence of a Kurdish nation[41] – the Court even upheld the right of a cultural group to claim a legal status (even if this was prohibited by the Constitution).[42] Thus, Turkey's view that 'the proposals… covering support for non-Turkish languages and cultures were intended to create minorities, to the detriment of the unity of the Turkish nation' – although 'national unity was achieved through the integration of communities and individuals who, irrespective of their ethnic origin and on an equal footing, formed the nation and founded the State' – was essentially rejected.[43] The Court has also found in a number of cases that questioning the current principles and structures of the state could not be grounds for the dissolution of political parties, so long as the means used are legal and democratic, and the change proposed is itself compatible with fundamental democratic principles.[44]

Thus, the Court has developed a line of case law establishing the right to claim legal recognition of a particular cultural or political identity on the basis of freedom of association. The most recent opinion in this line of case law, in which the refusal of authorities in Moscow to (re-) register the Salvation Army was found to violate the ECHR, noted that 'citizens should be able to form a legal entity in order to

39 *Ibid.*, para. 97.

40 *Ibid.*, para. 107. The Court has also denied state claims of necessity on national security and territorial integrity grounds in cases of religious minorities. See *Metropolitan Church of Bessarabia and Others v. Moldova*, ECtHR Application No. 45701/99 (2001), especially para. 123.

41 *Inter alia*, *Unified Communist Party of Turkey and Others (TBKP) v. Turkey*, ECtHR Application No. 19392/92 (1998); *Socialist Party of Turkey and Others v. Turkey*, ECtHR Application No. 21237/93 (1998); *Party of Freedom and Democracy (ÖZDEP) v. Turkey*, ECtHR Application No. 23885/94 (1999); *Affaire Dicle pour le Partie de la Democratie (DEP) c. Turquie*, ECtHR Application No. 25141/94 (2002); *Affaire Parti Socialiste de Turquie (STP) et Autres c. Turquie*, ECtHR Application No. 26482/95 (2003).

42 See *ibid.*, *TBKP*, paras. 56-57.

43 *Ibid.*, para. 10 (paraphrasing the Turkish Constitutional Court). See also *Socialist Party*, para. 15 and *ÖZDEP*, para. 14.

44 See *Tsonev v. Bulgaria*, ECtHR Application No. 45963/99 (2006); and paras. 97 and 98 of *Ždanoka v. Latvia* (First Section), ECtHR Application No. 58278/00 (2004). See also, *inter alia*, *Socialist Party*, para. 47 and *ÖZDEP*, para. 41; and the discussion in *Selim Sadak and Others v. Turkey*, ECtHR Applications No. 25144/94, 26149/95 to 26154/95, 27100/95 and 27101/95 (2002).

act collectively in a field of mutual interest [since it] is one of the most important aspects of the right to freedom of association, without which that right would be deprived of any meaning.'[45]

In fact, there has only been one case dealing with the issue of cultural (minority) identity in which the Court has not found a violation – *Gorzelik*, where applicants' claims were twice rejected by the Court.[46] The issue raised in the case was whether the refusal by Polish authorities to register an association of the 'Silesian national minority' – since the state considered the group an ethnic minority only – constituted an infringement of ECHR Article 11. While the Fourth Chamber judgment focused on the applicants' refusal to make certain changes to their association's name and its memorandum's provisions that the Court considered were reasonable – and touched on the question of what a national minority is only in passing[47] – the second judgment devotes considerable space to this question.

The Grand Chamber approaches this issue by stating that '[i]t is not for the Court to express a view on the appropriateness of methods chosen by the legislature of a respondent State to regulate a given field' and that, accordingly 'practice regarding official recognition by States of national, ethnic or other minorities within their population ... must, by the nature of things, be left largely to the State concerned, as it will depend on particular national circumstances'.[48] Legal recognition, as such, thus generally remains a domestic matter. In fact, the Court made much of the lack of agreement for the term 'national minority' in international law, as well as the various meanings given to the term in domestic systems,[49] as if to underline that a decision by the Court on this matter would be incongruous. In line with this view, the Court eventually found that the lack of an express definition in Polish law did not constitute a lack of legal precision infringing ECHR Article 11(2).

The Court's general reference to 'official recognition' is misleading, however. A distinction needs to be made between legal recognition for the purposes of minority protection, in which recognition comes with particular benefits, and legal recognition for the purposes of freedom of association. Thus, the line of cases presented above falls into the second camp, since no particular benefits accrue to the cultural minority legally recognized as such. The Polish law, with its linkage of 'official recognition' as a national minority to special benefits would rather be an instance of the former. Granted, the difference may be minor in many instances. More importantly, however, the consequences of legal recognition should not determine whether recognition

---

45 *Case of the Moscow Branch of the Salvation Army v. Russia*, ECtHR Application No. 72881/01 (2006), para. 59. See also para. 71.

46 *Gorzelik and Others v. Poland* (Fourth Section), ECtHR Application No. 44158/98 (2001) and *Gorzelik and Others v. Poland* (Grand Chamber), ECtHR Application No. 44158/98 (2004).

47 *Gorzelik* (Fourth Section), para. 62.

48 *Gorzelik* (Grand Chamber), para. 67.

49 *Ibid.*, paras. 67-68.

takes place. To the extent that the Court's conflation of recognition and its consequences seems to leave Poland with near-unfettered discretion in determining which groups can legally constitute a national minority – with all rights that may attach to such a status – we enter dangerous waters, however. Even if a definition is 'difficult to formulate',[50] the lack of practically all real oversight – despite a reference to conformity with the Convention – is hard to explain. Specifically, it is difficult to reconcile the outcome of this case with those in *Stankov* or *Sidiropoulos* – as even the Joint Concurring Opinion acknowledges. Though the Grand Chamber agrees with the Fourth that the particular facts of this case – specifically appellants' refusal to make the modifications requested by the state – make the difference, the underlying reason for the outcome seems to be another.

While in the former cases, the states refused registration on the basis of dubious public security arguments (and defended non-recognition on this basis), Poland relied on the existing legal category of 'national minority' as the basis for its refusal. Thus, Polish courts repeatedly stated that Silesians were not a national minority, because there was no such thing as a Silesian nation;[51] a Silesian nation, in turn, did not exist because it was missing 'national awareness established on the basis of the existing culture by a society residing on a specific territory'.[52] The Grand Chamber does not really examine the reasoning behind these opinions (though it discusses them, in paragraph 71), since it believes its task is confined to examining whether the methods used and their effects are in conformity with the Convention.[53] In other words, given the existence of law considered precise enough, its content is not for the Court to judge. Reliance on a domestic legal category – however vague – thus seems like a good strategy for a defending state, especially given the inability of the Court to interpret domestic law; while reliance on terms in the Convention – which may be interpreted by the Court – is riskier. Though the group in this particular case was not claiming the special rights and benefits attached to national minority status explicitly, the Court, in effect, comes close to deciding the question of identity here.[54]

It is with the Court's reasoning on the question of what constitutes a 'pressing social need' for refusing recognition to the association that there are real difficulties, however. First, the Court acknowledges the importance of political parties and associations to democracy, generally speaking, and even recognizes that 'freedom of association is particularly important for persons belonging to minorities, including national and ethnic minorities, and that ... [i]ndeed, forming an association in order

---

50 *Ibid.*, para. 67.

51 See, *inter alia*, *ibid.*, para. 36 (quoting the Polish Constitutional Court).

52 *Ibid.*, para. 32 (quoting the Katowice Court of Appeal).

53 *Ibid.*, para. 67.

54 This, despite its claim that such a finding is not for the Court to make. See *Gorzelik* (Fourth Section) para. 55.

to express and promote its identity may be instrumental in helping a minority to preserve and uphold its rights'.[55] However, it then finds that 'the appropriate time for countering the risk of the perceived mischief, ensuring that the rights of other persons or entities participating in parliamentary elections would not be actually infringed, was at the moment of registration of the association and not later'.[56] Considering that the refusal to register constituted a de facto ban on the association's activities, as well as the lack of any stated intention by the association to run in elections, the finding of a pressing social need, in the name of the protection of the rights of others – or a seeming balance of interests – seems a dubious approach, at best.

As if assuring itself that it was the minority's refusal of flexibility that led to the difficulties, the Court then states:

> [i]n the instant case the refusal was not a comprehensive, unconditional one, directed against the cultural and practical objectives that the association wished to pursue, but was based solely on the mention, in the memorandum of association, of a specific appellation for the association. … It by no means amounted to a denial of the distinctive ethnic and cultural identity of Silesians or to disregard for the association's primary aim, which was to "awaken and strengthen the national consciousness of Silesians" … On the contrary, in all their decisions the authorities consistently recognised the existence of a Silesian ethnic minority and their right to associate with one another to pursue common objectives.[57]

To the extent, however, that the group considers itself a national minority and not an ethnic one, as repeatedly declared in its programme – in contravention of the definition of national minority in Polish law – the Court (purposefully?) misconstrues the problem. The ECHR does not include any right to a cultural identity – except for religious – so that any question of group belonging is likely to be funnelled through Article 11, whether such recognition comes with particular benefits or not. In other words, questions of the social and legal existence of minorities – and of the possible risk they pose to the majority – will arrive in the guise of freedom of association. The Court even seems to recognize this, when it notes that '[t]he disputed restriction on the establishment of the association was essentially concerned with the label which the association could use in law – with whether it could call itself a "national minority" … As such, it did not go to the core or essence of freedom of association'.[58] True. That is why it is so easy for the Court to focus on the supposed

55 *Gorzelik* (Grand Chamber), para. 93.

56 *Ibid.*, para. 103 (emphasis added).

57 *Ibid.*, para. 105.

58 *Ibid.*

intentions of the minority to contravene electoral laws, and gloss over 'labels'. But are questions of designation so unimportant?

## 3. Cultural identity in nationality and immigration law

If the nationals of given states sometimes have difficulties in being recognized as members of particular groups, with special rights, the situation of resident foreigners is incomparably harder. In effect, though nationality is no guarantee of legal recognition of cultural identity in the territory of a given state, it remains, in fact if not in theory, a prerequisite. The principle of territorial sovereignty, combined with the generally recognized monopoly of the state in regulating education, language use and other culture-linked policies[59] often results – in practice – in the impossibility of, for example, education fully respecting the cultural identity of many permanent residents. In fact, to the extent that integration requirements have made a strong comeback in the nationality regulations and increasingly also the residence requirements of European states,[60] there is an expectation that individuals will adapt (at least to a minimal degree) to the culture of the society in which they reside. The clearest expression of this expectation in legislation can be found in a recently approved French law which, in addition to introducing a citizenship ceremony,[61] also requires (rather than, as in the past, offers) that future immigrants sign a 'reception and integration contract' with the French state, in which they promise to attend civic courses (comprised of a presentation of French institutions,

---

59 Neither the development of an EU cultural policy since 1992 (see Art. 151(1) of the Maastricht Treaty) nor existing language policies have, thus far, proven as threatening to member-state competence in cultural (including educational) matters than the evolving nature of European citizenship. Decisions like those in Case C-274/96 *Criminal Proceedings against Bickel and Franz* [1998] ECR I-7637, or Case C-147/03 *Commission v. Austria* [2005] ECR I-5969, which touched on minority language use and education policy respectively, have potentially wide-ranging effects. Through such decisions, the ECJ is increasingly drawing the outlines of the areas in which national identity may continue to matter.

60 Hungary, for example, requires a test of basic constitutional principles, in Hungarian, of all applicants for naturalization since 1993. Germany, as part of a major reform of its nationality regulation, introduced a language test in 2000, as well as an oath to uphold the principles of the Basic Law; the United Kingdom introduced a requirement of 'sufficient knowledge' of life in the UK in 2002 and added a language test as of July 2004, as well as an oath or affirmation of allegiance to the Queen and citizenship pledge to the state.

61 Art. 86 of *Loi No. 2006-911 du 24 juillet 2006 relative à l'immigration et à l'intégration* (JO no. 170 du 25 juillet 2006, at 11047). The law touches on a number of other elements of immigration, including family reunification and special residence permits, as well as transposition of European Council and Parliament Directive 2004/58/EC of 29April 2004 on the right of citizens of the Union and their family members to move and reside freely within the territory of the Member States (OJ 2004 L 229/35).

as well as the 'values of the Republic, notably equality between men and women and laicity') and, if necessary also language instruction.[62] Though a future decree is to set out the exact form (duration, renewal, content) and role of this contract, the law notes that 'disregard, manifested by blatant will, for the stipulations of the welcome and integration contract by the foreigner'[63] will be taken into account when decisions on the renewal of residence permits are made. Thus, immigrants will now be expected to 'integrate' linguistically and, to some extent, culturally, to the given society before they may even be considered for membership.[64] In fact, the future membership of immigrants hinges, at least in part, on their conduct being deemed 'French' enough – as judged by whom, one wonders?[65] – so that questions of identity are here linked to legal status in a more conspicuous manner than is usually done in the context of immigration. Thus, individuals will be expected to behave in a manner demonstrating a conscious choice 'for' the state.[66]

One could raise a number of questions with regard to this law, but we will limit ourselves to its (questionable) compatibility with the jurisprudence of the European Court of Human Rights, which, while tentative on matters relating to the recognition of particular groups, seems to have little difficulty examining individual identity claims in the context of immigration matters; specifically expulsion or deportation measures examined in light of ECHR Article 8 on respect for 'private and family life'. One theorist has gone so far as to claim that the wide scope of interpretation utilized by the Court has led to the creation of a '*quasi-nationalité*' on the basis of social and cultural ties.[67] The beginnings of the approach reach back to 1985, when the Court announced that 'although some aspects of the right to enter a country are governed by Protocol No. 4 … it is not to be excluded that measures taken in the

---

62 '*Contrat d'accueil et d'intégration*' and '*valeurs de la République, notamment l'égalité entre les hommes et les femmes et la laïcité*'. *Ibid.*, Art. 5(1). (All translations by the author, unless otherwise noted.)

63 '*non-respect, manifesté par une volonté caractérisée, par l'étranger, des stipulations du contrat d'accueil et d'intégration*'. *Ibid.*

64 The integration and Dutch language courses now required of potential immigrants to the Netherlands – even before they have left their state of origin – is a more radical implementation of the same principle.

65 Art. 7(1) of the *Loi relative à l'immigration et à l'intégration* stipulates that the mayor of the town in which the immigrant is resident give her opinion on the integration of the person in question.

66 The draft of the law presented to the National Assembly in May 2006 used the words 'will to integrate' ('*volonté d'intégration*'). See Art. 5(1) of the *Projet de Loi relatif à l'immigration et à l'intégration* (No. 576) (2006).

67 M. Verwilghen, 'Conflits de nationalités: Plurinationalité et apatridie', 277, *Recueil des Cours* (1999), pp. 9, at p. 112. See also the dissenting opinion of Judge Pettitti in *Beldjoudi v. France*, ECtHR Application No. 12083/86 (1992), where he states that the Court has considered applicant 'a quasi-Frenchman, a concept which is unknown in international law'.

field of immigration may affect the right to respect for family life.'[68] Thus, although immigration questions – specifically the decision as to entry and exit rights – remain, for the most part, for states to regulate, the latter are no longer fully sovereign in this capacity.[69] (The increasing coordination of such matters at EU level is also a development with significant effects on domestic policies; but is obviously of a different quality than monitoring out of human rights concerns.) Since that decision, the ECtHR has developed a wide-ranging balancing test, with consideration of all elements of the individual's personal situation (from integration to life history), as well as state interests.[70] In *Boughanemi*, for example, the Court conducted a veritable sociological inquiry, before finding no violation of Article 8:

> applicant had failed to show either that he had particularly close ties with his family living in France or that he was in any way integrated in the society of that country, where he had never really worked. Furthermore, on attaining his majority he had not sought French nationality. At the same time he had retained ties with Tunisia that went beyond mere nationality. His parents were Tunisian; he had spent his infancy there and in France he moved in Tunisian circles. Mr Boughanemi could speak Arabic or at least had an adequate command of everyday language. Moreover, having lived in Tunisia up to the age of 8, the two years of schooling that he had received there had laid the foundations of his education. In addition, the applicant did not claim that he had never returned there or that he had cut all ties with that country. Finally, he maintained active relations with the Tunisian community so that his life was not confined to the French dimension.[71]

On the basis of such determinations, individuals have gained the right to remain in states of which they are not nationals, but to which they have social and cultural ties.[72] In fact, one judge has gone so far as to state that 'mere nationality does not constitute an objective and reasonable justification for the existence of a difference as regards the admissibility of expelling someone from what, in both cases, may

---

[68] *Abdulaziz, Cabales and Balkandali v. the United Kingdom*, ECtHR Applications No. 9214/80, 9473/81, 9474/81 (1985), para. 60.

[69] See also the string of cases brought under ECHR Art. 3. E.g. *Hilal v. the United Kingdom*, ECtHR Application No. 45276/99 (2001); *Venkadajalasarma v. the Netherlands*, ECtHR Application No. 58150/00 (2004). (See also ECHR Art. 5(1)(f) and Protocol Nos. 4 and 7.)

[70] See *Gül v. Switzerland*, ECtHR Application No. 23218/94 (1996), esp. para. 38. See also, *inter alia*, *Berrehab v. the Netherlands*, ECtHR Application No. 10730/84 (1988).

[71] *Boughanemi v. France*, ECtHR Application No. 22070/93 (1996), para. 39 (Emphasis added).

[72] *Moustaquim v. Belgium*, ECtHR Application No. 12313/86 (1991); *Beldjoudi v. France*, ECtHR Application No. 12083/86 (1992).

be called his "own country".[73] This is a rather radical view, given that only the nationals of a given state have the right to freely enter and remain in that state under international and constitutional law[74] – it remains, in any case, a minority one as the existence of complete integration without nationality has been denied by states;[75] and, incidentally also by the UN Human Rights Committee.[76]

---

[73] Concurring opinion of Judge Martens in *Beldjoudi, ibid.* See also the determination of the European Commission of Human Rights that '[a]ltough legally an alien, applicant has his family and social ties in France, and the nationality which links him to Algeria, though a legal reality, does not reflect his actual position in human terms'. *Djeroud v. France*, E.Comm.H.R. 13446/87 (1991), see *EHRR* (1992), p. 68, at pp. 78-79.

[74] See UDHR Art. 13(2), as well as ICCPR Art. 12(4) and Art. 3(2) of Protocol No. 4 to the ECHR; see also Art. 69(2) of the Constitution of the Republic of Hungary (1949, as amended); Art. 16 of the Constitution of the Republic of Italy (1948); Art. 23 of the Constitution of the Republic of Turkey (1982); Art. 51 of the Arab Republic of Egypt (1980); sec. 14 of the Constitution of the Republic of Argentina. See also *In re Martonelli*, 63 F. 437 (C.C.S.D.N.Y. 1894) where the court held that a national has the constitutional right to enter his own country.

[75] States generally attribute functions far beyond just the legal to naturalization. As the French Commission on Nationality, constituted in 1987 to examine all aspects of nationality before a major overhaul of the country's laws noted, 'the Code of Nationality is simultaneously conceived as *a tool of ... integration* and a *reference point for national identity*. It should organize, together, the right to integration of the foreigners concerned, acknowledging their individual choice, and, if the need arises, a capacity to verify the degree of this integration. National identity effectively expresses itself through nationality'. ('*le Code de la Nationalité est conçu à la fois comme* un instrument d['] intégration ... *et* un point de référence pour l'identité nationale. *Il doit organiser, ensemble, le droit à l'intégration des étrangers concernés, la prise en compte de leur choix individuel et une capacité à verifier, le cas échéant, le degré de cette intégration. L'identité nationale trouve en effet à s'exprimer à travers la nationalité*.') *Être français aujourd'hui et demain: Rapport de la Commission de la nationalité* (Long Rapport), Tome I, at 87 (1988) (emphasis in original). See also at pp. 25-26 and p. 28. See also *Fünftes Bericht über die Lage der Ausländer in der Bundesrepublik Deutschland* 53 (2002); and the remarks of United Kingdom Home Secretary David Blunkett on the occasion of the first citizenship ceremony performed in February 2004, in accordance with the requirements of the Nationality, Immigration and Asylum Act (2002). For the views of some of the participants, see: <www.indymedia.org.uk/en/regions/london/2004/02/285998.html> (last visited September 16, 2006).

On the flip side, the assumption of a link between nationality and cultural identity is (still) firmly maintained in private international law, resulting in the application of domestic law to individuals who are not resident in a given state. See E. Jayme, 'Identité culturelle et intégration: Le droit international privé postmoderne', 251, *Recueil des Cours* (1995), p. 9, at p. 253. See also H. Gaudemet-Tallon, 'La désunion du couple en droit international privé', 226, *Recueil des Cours* (1991), p. 9, at pp. 219-220. See also the *Convention entre le Gouvernement de la République française et le Gouvernement du Royaume du Maroc relative au statut des personnes et de la famille et à la coopération judiciaire* (1981, in force since 1983), which notes, in its Preamble, 'the necessity of preserving, for individuals, the principles of their national identity' ('*la nécessité de conserver aux personnes les principes de leur identité nationale*').

[76] The Committee found that an individual who lawfully entered a country that facilitated the acquisition of nationality, but who refrained from getting such nationality cannot consider

(Unsurprisingly), state courts also seem more reluctant to break down the distinction between national and non-national. In a 2004 case, for example, the German Constitutional Court refused an applicant's request to be treated as a '*faktischer Inländer*'[77] (factual non-alien) – given that he had been born and had grown up in Germany and was in possession of an unlimited residence permit – in order to prevent expulsion to Turkey, his state of nationality. After having determined that reliance on a claimed '*Verwurzelung in den Lebensverhältnissen in Deutschland*'[78] (rootedness in living conditions in Germany) was not enough, in balance, to save him from expulsion under the Basic Law, the Court proceeded to a lengthy examination of the case at issue from the point of view of the ECHR; the result, in light of the crimes committed and of the applicant's knowledge of the Turkish language, as well as lack of children or a wife in Germany, was unchanged.[79]

On the other hand, claimed cultural identity serves, openly, as a basis for states to grant a growing array of legal statuses with international effects. Accordingly, a number of states in Europe grant members of kin-minorities a special status with attendant rights in their territory (and sometimes even in their homes states), while other states (in Europe, Latin America and Asia) have granted former nationals and even individuals whose ancestors once emigrated special entry, property and participation rights, as well as the possibility of plural nationality.[80] These kinds of laws, in turn, may raise the problem of pinning down identity already referred to above.

Germany's legislation on *Spätaussiedler*,[81] for example, though based on a premise of discrimination against members of those with '*deutsche Volkszugehörigkeit*' after the Second World War – and accordingly, due to finally expire in 2010 – involves a presumption of German cultural identity (in addition to descent) that must be proved before public authorities before the individual may immigrate to Germany

---

the state her 'own country' as per Art. 12(4) of the ICCPR, even though he had never lived elsewhere. *Stewart v. Canada*, UN Human Rights Committee Communication No. 538/1993 (1996).

77 BVerfG, 2 BvR 1570/03 (March 1, 2004) para. 6.

78 *Ibid.*, para. 10.

79 *Ibid.*, paras. 20 *et seq.*

80 For examples of both kinds of legislation, see E. Horváth, 'Mandating Identity: Citizenship, Kinship Laws and Plural Nationality in the European Union', unpublished Ph.D. Thesis,European University Institute (2006). In the context of emigrants, see the contributions in 'Symposium, A Tribute to the Work of Kim Barry: The Construction of Citizenship in an Emigration Context', 81(1) *New York University Law Review* (2006).

81 See Art. 6 of the *Bundesvertriebenen und Flüchtlingsgesetz* (BVFG, 1953, as amended) are '*deutscher Volkszugehöriger*' (members of the German nation) and Art. 116(1) of the *Grundgesetz.* The regulation still in force applies only to nationals of the member states of the former USSR and (since 1996 and 2000, respectively) requires language exams and integration courses once in Germany.

(and get German nationality). The very idea that the individuals in question are German in a manner recognizable as such in Germany relies on the existence not of a living culture (which changes by definition), but of the remains of a traditional 'Germanness' supposedly handed down through generations. Because in many instances the imagined pattern of elements no longer exists, we are essentially dealing with an ethnic category, realistically leached of all concerns beyond that of descent.[82] However, the fact that this category is also a legal one leads to highly questionable court (or administration)-made determinations of identity. Thus, after determination of descent, *Statusdeutsche* are required to pass further hurdles: they most prove their Germanness, in essence 'imitating' a German as sketched by law. In a case from 1995, for example, the Federal Administrative Court looked at the applicant's family history, social practices (including holidays celebrated), language skills and '*Gruppenbewußtsein*' (group-consciousness) to determine whether her claim to be German – rejected by authorities – was true.[83] Thus, even as people are expected to 'live' a specific identity, its contents are legally predetermined. In a comparable manner, the post-1991 encouragement of Jewish immigration from Eastern Europe[84] – newly regulated as of 1 January 2005 – was infused with an understanding of culture as object.

It is exactly this approach that Hungary attempted to avoid, in its 2001 kinship law. The law (amended in 2003 after international protest) granted members of kin-minorities in neighbouring states a special status in Hungary, with a number of attendant (social, cultural and entry) rights, as well as funds in their home-states. To gain access to the benefits of the law in Hungary, individuals were required to show so-called Hungarian certificates; these were originally granted to anyone 'declaring themselves to be of Hungarian [kinship]',[85] as verified by a minority

---

82 As Roll argues, for many *Aussiedler* 'while being German is a part of their social identity, it is largely constructed through descent and fragmentary knowledge of German language and culture. Russian language and culture were the background of their socialization'. H. Roll, 'Young Ethnic German Immigrants from the Former Soviet Union: German Language Proficiency and its Impact on Integration', in P.H. Schuck and R. Münz (eds).*Paths to Inclusion: The Integration of Migrants in the United States and Germany* ( 1998), p. 272, at p. 286.

83 BVerwG 9 C 392.94 (1995). See also BVerwG 9 C 8.96 (1996) (discussing the meaning of the 'mediation of German culture' required under BVFG Art. 6(2)(1)).

84 Strangely enough, the practice of a liberal immigration policy for Jews from Eastern Europe was inherited from East-Germany and, through a quiet re-interpretation by *Land* Prime Ministers of an existing law (the *Kontingentflüchtlingsgesetz* of 1980) in 1991, allowed for a continuation of the policy. Since 1991, over 200,000 individuals have immigrated to Germany under the provisions. See 'Bund will Zuzug von osteuropäischen Juden begrenzen', Der Spiegel (18 December 2004); and 'Tuerer Exodus', Der Spiegel (21 February 2005).

85 Art. 1(1) of *2001. évi LXII. törvény a szomszédos államokban élő magyarokról* (Act LXII of 2001 Concerning the Hungarians Living in Neighbouring States). In the English version of the text, 'nationality' is used here, in the sense of membership in an ethno-cultural community;

'evaluating authority', including a Hungarian church or political party (in line with Articles 19 and 20). The Act's requirement of self-declaration only was consistent with domestic minority legislation and also assumed to be in line with international approaches.[86] The relaying of such a declaration through a recommendation from a Hungarian minority organization and the absence of objective criteria raised all kinds of uncomfortable possibilities, however. How would such a Hungarianness-examining panel function? What if one was an atheist and ignored politics – who would vouch for her Hungarian identity? Who had the right to even judge identity? One possibility with echoes of the past:

> The president of the tribunal glances glumly at her assessors – the decision is difficult. The written exam has proven successful, but the environmental-survey reveals that the ratio of those representing the majority nation in the social circle of the candidate is higher than expected. Moreover, he does not intend to send his kindergarden-age child to a Hungarian school in three years time. The tribunal finally determines that it cannot grant the recommendation necessary for the candidate to obtain the special license.[87]

In a related question, what if the individual – found Hungarian enough – is more interested in moving to Hungary than in receiving support for staying in her home-state? The granting of the Hungarian certificate was (and is) closely linked to showing that the individual does not wish to settle in Hungary (or, presumably, elsewhere than their home-state), since one of the stated aims of the law was (and continues to be) to help the minorities to stay 'within their home country.' Thus, the special status was seen as necessary to a form of kin-state minority protection – itself a controversial idea.

---

in the English text after the 2003 revision 'ethnic origin' is utilized. In the Hungarian original, the word used in both versions is '*nemzetiség*'.

86 See Art. 1(1) of the *1993. évi LXXVII. törvény a nemzeti és etnikai kisebbségek jogairól* (Act LXXVII of 1993 on the rights of national and ethnic minorities); the 2005 amendment of the law did not affect this basic principle, although participation in minority elections now requires registration. For provisions in international law, see Art. 3(1) of the Framework Convention, Art. 32 of the Copenhagen Declaration, and Art. 2(1) of the Protocol proposed in Recommendation 1201.

87 Ottó Neumann, Magyarságot igazoló hivatal, Magyar Hírlap (11 July 2000). ('*Komoran tekint ülnökeire az ítélőszéki elnök – nehéz a döntés. Az írásbeli nyelvvizsga sikeresnek bizonyult, ám a környezettanulmányból kiderül, hogy a jelölt baráti körében a többségi nemzetet képviselők aránya az elvártnál magasabb mértékű. Sőt, óvodás gyermekét három év múlva nem magyar iskolába készül beíratni. Az ítélőszék végül úgy határoz, hogy nem adhatja meg az ajánlást, amely a különleges igazolvány megszerzéséhez kellene a jelöltnek*').

The 2003 amendment of the Act added a number of objective criteria[88] – as requested by the Venice Commission of the Council of Europe – but, due to perceived watering down, has led to demands of dual nationality on the part of minority organizations; these have, in turn, led to a number of political crises in Hungary.[89]

## 4. The interaction of law and cultural identity

As the examples discussed above show, legal determinations of cultural identity, specifically ones that are prerequisites to special rights, are problematic on a number of levels. In the most obvious sense, they are a return to a time when a given status served as a 'right to have rights'.[90] If a minority is not recognized as a 'national' one by a state, for example, when this status is a prerequisite for certain rights, the group's room for action in a number of areas may be curtailed; the refusal of a number of Western European states to recognize immigrant minorities as 'national' ones relies on exactly this logic. Indirect state limitation is obviously even clearer when the very existence of a particular group, by any name, is refused acknowledgement. In turn, individuals who are found, for some reason, not to fulfil the specific culture-linked criteria set out in legislation (in some cases very consciously to limit the possibilities of success) are left without the rights that go with the status in question, whether 'French national' in the context of naturalization or 'kin-Hungarian' in the context of (claimed) minority rights.

The concept of 'mimesis' is an apt one to utilize here, as individuals attempt to conform to a particular idea of who to be. While such questions are not generally for states to care about in so familiar a manner, the linkage of legal status with cultural identities results in an unusual interaction. In effect, the functions of socialization are legalized, so that the question is finally not whether someone is 'French' or 'Hungarian', but the manner in which she is.

A comparison from a different discipline is perhaps useful here. There is ongoing discussion in literary theory of the extent to which literary works can (and should) represent reality. Some authors have recognized that our very manner of viewing the world is limited by socialization, however. In other words, even our perception of reality is culturally-bounded. Any attempt to represent 'reality' thus relies on

---

88 According to Art. 19(2)(a) of the amended law, any individual declaring herself to be Hungarian must also be either proficient in Hungarian, or registered in their state of residence as a person declaring herself as such, or registered by a Hungarian church as Hungarian, or a member of a Hungarian organization in her state of residence.

89 See discussion in M.M. Kovács, 'The Politics of Dual Citizenship in Hungary', *Citizenship Studies* (2006), p. 431.

90 United States Supreme Court Chief Justice Warren (himself echoing Hannah Arendt), in referring to nationality. *Perez v. Brownell*, 356 U.S. 44, 64 (1958) (Warren J., dissenting).

the existence of the very social reality it attempts to describe. For this reason, any attempt at mimesis is itself a form of control, a 'matter for the police'.[91] In applying this principle to our topic, we must note that any community will attempt to create an image for itself (and re-create it) on the basis of perceived resemblance of its members. As a first step in this process, members must be identified. Mimesis for legal purposes thus serves to affirm and re-affirm the image of the collectivity that the given membership hopes to express.

To the extent that matters of cultural rights and identity remain firmly in state hands, however, unrecognized claims to recognition are channelled through claims to other rights, such as freedom of association or respect for private and family life in the context of the ECtHR, discussed above. In this manner, identity issues are not only legalized and adjudicated, but are, as a matter of rights, reframed in guises that are only indirectly related to the underlying question. In the process, national and international courts are rendered arbiters of something they know nothing about. In the context of the ECtHR, in particular, the channelling of questions of cultural identity through other human rights – thereby prompting an inability to call them by their name – results in inconsistencies.

To the extent that courts are merely reacting to social processes, as identity claims are made by groups and individuals on an ever-growing number of grounds, such re-channelling is an understandable attempt at dealing with matters states cannot (or will not) deal with directly. As a general matter, however, the use of cultural (and social) ties as a basis for special statuses for individuals and groups is an instance of playing with fire. The boundary approach sketched by Barth[92] or clear categorical thinking, whereby categories are 'assumed to be abstract containers, with things either inside or outside',[93] simply does not apply to collective identities. The characteristic fluidity of belonging (*qua* sociological process) does not allow for membership by fixed criteria. Accordingly, legal classification that attempts to create groups identifiable (by insiders and outsiders) only by the given criteria is bound to fail. Hence, the 'Germanness' of *Spätaussiedler* has increasingly been (administratively and legally) questioned; their integration seems no easier than that of other immigrants. This fact is increasingly reflected in legislation and practice, as they are treated more and more like other immigrants.[94]

---

91 J. Derrida, 'La dissemination', in *La dissemination* (*Ibid.* 1972), p. 319. See also *ibid.*, 'Du droit à la justice', in *Force de loi* 11 (*Ibid.* 1994), at pp. 26-27.

92 F. Barth, 'Introduction', in F. Barth (ed.), *Ethnic Groups and Boundaries: The Social Organization of Culture Difference* (1994), at p. 14 [1969]. Clear boundaries are considered a means of 'continuing dichotomization between members and outsiders'.

93 G. Lakoff, *Women, Fire and Dangerous Things: What Categories Reveal About the Mind* (1987), p. 6.

94 See D. Levy, 'Coming Home? Ethnic Germans and the Transformation of National Identity in the Federal Republic of Germany' in A. Geddes and A. Favell (eds.), *The Politics of Belonging:*

On the other hand, legal categorization can create social reality: the introduction of European citizenship, for example, has created the category of 'third-country national' in legal discourse and has had an equivalent social effect, as the concept of 'us' in national discourse is increasingly, if sometimes reluctantly, extended to include the nationals of other member states. This phenomenon was, ironically, also important in the maintenance of a German-consciousness among individuals in the former Soviet Union, as 'ethnic identity was transformed from a self-inscribed, predominantly cultural frame of reference to a more politically and administratively defined category, partly ascribed to the group from outside.'[95]

In this context, some final remarks about the interaction of law and identity are necessary. As Bourdieu noted, 'we create the categories by which we construct the social world; and these categories produce the world, within the limits of their correspondence with pre-existing structures'.[96] Legal categorization, in particular, can create social reality, due to the prescriptive role of law in modern societies. Thus, 'a new order of legal classification results in a new mode of organizing what is real'.[97] For this reason, legal authority is a unique (and privileged) form of power, especially when it is used to establish categories that are essential to the (maintenance of) public order.

Increased court involvement in determinations pertaining to identity, as discussed in the context of kinship laws (for national courts) and national identity or immigration matters (for the ECtHR) is a new dimension of such classification. In essence, 'law, after having proceeded for its own needs to simplify the concrete person, in turn influences the sense of the concrete person of remaining the same through time and [changing] situation[s]'.[98] The problem is one of process and classification, however. It is in the context of immigration that this dichotomy is

---

*Migrants and Minorities in Contemporary Europe* (1999), p. 93, at pp. 102-103.

95 R. Münz and R. Ohlinger, 'Long-Distance Citizens: Ethnic Germans and Their Immigration to Germany' in P.H. Schuck and R. Münz (eds.), *Paths to Inclusion: The Integration of Migrants in the United States and Germany* (1998), p. 155, at pp. 163.

96 ('[N]*ous produisons les catégories selon lesquelles nous construisons le monde sociale et … ces catégories produisent le monde*'). P. Bourdieu, 'La force du droit: éléments pour une sociologie du champ juridique', 64, *Actes de la recherche en sciences sociales* (1986), p. 3, at p. 13.

97 ('[D]*u nouvel ordre de classement juridique résultera un autre mode d'organisation du réel*'). J. Caillosse and P. Bourdieu, 'Juris lector: anti-juridisme et science du droit', 56-57, *Droit et Société* (2004), p. 17, at p. 33. See also V. Roussel, 'Le droit et ses formes', 56-57, *Droit et Societé* (2004), p. 41, at pp. 50-51.

98 ('[L]*e droit, après avoir procédé pour ses besoins propres à und réduction de la personne concrète, influe en retour sur le* sentiment *de la personne concrète de demeurer la même au travers du temps et des situations*'.) D. Gutmann, *Le Sentiment d'Identité: Étude de Droit des Personnes et de la Famille* (2000), p. 13 (emphasis in the original). A parallel process is also present in the law itself. In the realm of human rights, for example, individuals are considered abstract and universal 'persons' for the purposes of the applicability of general principles, while their

most easily glimpsed, not only when a court plays a role in judging an individual's degree of integration, per se, but also in a wider context, such as when the life histories of asylum seekers are judged for authenticity and subsumed into existing legal categories. Only when a life story – as *Statusdeutsche* or as asylum seeker – has been confirmed and placed in a given context does it exist for the purposes of the law.[99]

Any link of law and identity thus assumes 'a veritable philosophy of personal identity, centred on the idea that, at least from the legal point of view, an immutability of the essential characteristics of the person exists'.[100] No identity remains unchanged, however. The assumption that preservation or protection of a cultural identity circumscribed by legislation is a means of protecting cultural rights is accordingly problematic at best. To the extent that respect for (freedom of) cultural identity is a constitutive element of respect for human dignity, it certainly gives rise to negative obligations (like non-interference). In particular, it requires that states allow individuals and groups to claim the cultural identities they choose. But legal recognition of a particular (individual or group) cultural identity is rarely just a matter of public acknowledgement. Rather, specific measures are requested as an expression of respect. As shown above, attempts at formulating positive obligations on identity matters – as a consequence of which courts are required to adjudicate particular identity claims – raise a whole new set of problems. As multicultural claims spread across borders and cultural rights gain prominence in both practice and theory, the inadequacy of law in dealing with identity matters will certainly need to be addressed – but preferably through public discussion rather than in courts. As things stand, it is unclear whether the adjudication of legal statuses based on cultural identity solves more problems than it creates.

---

distinctiveness (race, culture, religion, language, nationality, etc.) is recognized in practical application.

99 Hence attempts at coding reality in a very specific manner. In the experience of this author when dealing with asylum cases in the United States, admittedly horrific but very diverse events were often framed in the exact same way in order to maximize the chances of success.

100 ('[U]*ne véritable philosophie de l'identité personelle, centré sur cette idée qu'il existe, au moins du point de vue juridique, une immutabilité des caractéristiques essentielles de la personne*'). *Ibid.*, at p. 376.

# 9
# Minorities' Right to Maintain and Develop Their Cultures: Legal Implications of Social Science Research

*Timo Makkonen*

## 1. Minority rights

Nation state ideology, characterized by the principle of 'one nation, one state', was in the historical perspective most closely implemented in 19th-century Europe. According to that line of thinking, the boundaries of the state, as a political and geopolitical entity, should coincide with the boundaries of the nation, as a cultural and/or ethnic entity. Moreover, the state should actively seek to enhance social cohesion through promotion of common language, culture and values. The nation state ideology is axiomatically antithetical to recognition of internal ethno-cultural diversity.

European countries have, in recent decades, increasingly started to acknowledge the inherent – and due to international migration, growing – ethno-cultural diversity of their populations, and have tried to come to grips with it. This is also reflected in the regional European instruments that set out minority rights. While most of these instruments are non-binding,[1] the Framework Convention for the Protection of National Minorities, drawn up within the Council of Europe, was the first legally binding international instrument devoted entirely to minority rights. The Framework Convention, which entered into force in February 1998, is often taken to be the leading standard in the international law of minority rights.[2] As such, the instrument

---

1 Most important non-binding instruments in Europe have been drawn up within the confines of the Organization for Security and Co-operation in Europe. These include the Helsinki Final Act (1975) and the Document of the Copenhagen Meeting of the Conference on the Human Dimension of the Conference on Security and Co-operation in Europe (1990).

2 M. Weller (ed.), *The Rights of Minorities: A Commentary on the European Framework Convention for the Protection of National Minorities* (Oxford, Oxford University Press, 2006).

Francioni and Scheinin (eds), *Cultural Human Rights*, 193–206

has been – and continues to be – subject to great expectations, particularly on the part of the minorities themselves, as well as the people who advocate their cause.

Yet not all stakeholders, particularly scholars and minority organizations, have hailed the Framework Convention as a major achievement. The Convention has been accused of being 'vague' and 'weak', and of providing for rights formulated in such general terms and in such highly qualified language as to be almost empty of legal consequence in practice.[3] Indeed, the Convention is notorious for its cautious language, which leaves a lot of room for interpretation and even policy considerations. These structural properties are, in part, undoubtedly a consequence of Europe's nation-statist legacy and the lack of solid legal and political traditions in securing the rights of minorities.

It should, however, be noted that laws are almost always drafted in general terms and that it is the task of legal science to explain, clarify and elaborate upon the *practical implications* of law. Further elaboration of minority rights is particularly challenging, since the subject area involves complex questions that revolve around such issues as 'identity', 'culture' and 'group membership'. For instance culture is – at once – something that surrounds us and of which we have an intuitive sense, and an abstract, complex and vague phenomenon that far exceeds the bounds of our practical ability to reason and observe, perhaps even to imagine. And that which is difficult to observe, rationalize or imagine is difficult to explain. Lawyers often appear to feel that they don't have the theoretical and empirical knowledge, or even competence, to engage in a discussion that involves these subject areas. However, this has the unfortunate consequence that minority rights, as laid down for instance in the Framework Convention, remain abstract, general and largely undefined. All of this reinforces the relative weaknesses of the Convention and contributes to the risk that its provisions will not lead to tangible improvements in the status of minorities.[4]

This need not be the case. Ethnicity and cultural diversity are key themes for contemporary social sciences and therefore also subject to an impressive amount of research and theorizing. Lawyers, and especially those writing legal commentaries, can only benefit from tapping into the findings of other disciplines, as this can significantly enhance their understanding of the practical implications of legal obligations. Some may disagree with this point of view and claim that lawyers need

---

3 For some of the debates on these issues, see Council of Europe, *Filling the Frame: Five years of monitoring the Framework Convention for the Protection of National Minorities* (Strasbourg, Council of Europe Publishing, 2004).

4 It should perhaps be made clear that the aim here is not to downplay the importance of the Advisory Committee to the Framework Convention, an expert body that has been entrusted with the task of assisting the Contracting States in implementing the Convention. The nature of the work of the Advisory Committee does not, however, allow it to issue comprehensive and in-depth analyses of specific articles of the Convention, as its 'jurisprudence' accumulates in piecemeal fashion through dialogue with governments.

not, or indeed should not, cross the boundary between law and social sciences. Yet everyone, even lawyers, hold presumptions and views about the 'real world' – and these presumptions inevitably affect their thinking when they set out to clarify the implications of law for social reality. These presumptions – or premises, as they are called in scientific parlance- necessarily affect their analyses and conclusions, and can only be more or less elaborate.

The following discussion looks at the right of persons belonging to minorities to maintain and develop their culture in the light of some contemporary social science research.

## 2. 'To maintain and to develop'

Under Article 5(1) of the Framework Convention for the Protection of National Minorities, states parties have undertaken to promote the conditions necessary for persons belonging to national minorities to 'maintain and develop their culture' and to 'preserve the essential elements of their identity, namely their religion, language, traditions and cultural heritage'. Article 3(2) of the Convention makes it clear that this right can be enjoyed both individually and in community with others.

Article 5(1) explicitly recognizes three important things. First, it recognizes that people can set out not just to *maintain* but also to *develop* their culture. Most legal literature on the subject, generally on cultural and religious accommodation, focuses on what is required for minority groups to be able to preserve and express their identity and culture, while the issue of the conditions under which cultural change can take place or be promoted is seldom brought up. Second, Article 5(1) recognizes the role of human agency, and sees members of minorities as having an active role in sustaining and changing their culture. This is reflected by the fact that all the verbs involved – 'maintain', 'develop' and 'preserve' – imply an active role. Third, Article 5(1) recognizes that the ability of members of minority groups to maintain and develop their culture may in practice be circumscribed by external factors. Hence, the obligation is on the states concerned to create favourable conditions for the maintenance and development of culture.

That said, Article 5(1) is formulated in general and abstract terms that provide little, if any, guidance on how it should be implemented in practice. The key question is: What exactly are the conditions under which minorities can maintain and develop their cultures? To determine these conditions – to determine what the Article is all about – we need to address three questions:

- What is 'culture'? Which matters belong to the domain of culture?
- How are cultures maintained? How do they change?
- What is the relationship between individuals and culture? How do individuals relate to their culture and how can they aspire to maintain or change them?

## 3. Culture

Culture is a phenomenon that can be approached from many different perspectives and be given different definitions. A classic, and broad, definition of culture was given by Herskovits, who defined it as the human-made part of the environment.[5] This definition of culture can be broken down into objective aspects (tools, roads, radio stations) and subjective aspects (categories, norms, roles, values).[6] Many contemporary understandings of culture focus on the latter part, and define culture for instance as 'a set of cognitive and evaluative beliefs that are shared by the members of a social system and transmitted to the new members'.[7] Culture is thus, content-wise, about interpretations and understandings regarding how things are and how they should be, subtle indications about what should be important for us and how we should orient ourselves. As Triandis put it, one way to think of culture is to think of unstated assumptions, ways of doing things that have been internalized to such an extent that people do not argue about them.[8]

Culture can be, and should be, approached not only in terms of content and substance, but as a process. Cultural understandings are transmitted via socialization; the primary sites of socialization and value transmission being schools, workplaces and family.[9] Formerly, socialization was envisioned as a process whereby children and adolescents passively and individually received knowledge and skills from adults. More recently, scholars have largely come to agree that socialization is an active, collective process in which children and adolescents both affect and are affected by adults, society and culture, and thus partake in producing their own worlds and peer cultures.[10]

From the process perspective, culture may be characterized as *meaning-making* and *meaning-maintaining* activity. This activity takes place in a social setting, and is thus interactive in nature. It is not only the interaction among members of a national or ethnic group that creates culture. It is commonly accepted that occupational groups, social classes, genders, clubs and social movements may become the basis of specific

5 Cited in P.B. Smith and M.H. Bond, *Social Psychology Across Cultures* (Essex, Pearson Education Limited, 1998), p. 38.

6 H.C. Triandis, *Culture and Social Behaviour* (New York, McGraw-Hill, 1994), pp. 2, 16.

7 See e.g. K. Miller-Loessi J. Parker, 'Cross-Cultural Social Psychology', in J. Delamater (ed.), *Handbook of Social Psychology* (New York, Kluwer, 2003), p. 529.

8 H.C. Triandis, *cit. supra* note 6, p. 16.

9 J.D. McLeod and K.J. Lively, 'Social Structure and Personality', in J. Delamater, *cit. supra* note 7, p. 83.

10 W.A. Corsaro and L. Fingerson, 'Development and Socialization in Childhood', in J. Delamater, *cit. supra* note 7, p. 125; D. Eder and S. Kawecka Nenga, 'Socialization in Adolescence', in J. Delamater, *cit. supra* note, p. 157.

subcultures.[11] For instance, most occupations have some aspects of distinct cultures, such as special vocabulary and a shared set of assumptions.[12] Cultural diversity is therefore not born just out of ethnic diversity, since each and every ethnic group is also characterized by internal cultural diversity.

## 4. Ecology, biology, religion and culture

There are a number of external, profoundly important factors that shape cultures and human behaviour. Three of them will be addressed here: ecology, biology and religion.

Ecology refers to where people live. It consists of the objects, the resources and the geography of an environment, and the ways one can make a living and survive.[13] Ecology shapes the cultures that emerge in it, and culture in turn shapes particular kinds of behaviours.[14] Triandis provides an account of how particular types of ecology have an impact on culture:

> In hunting and fishing societies, people must be able to move around, to follow their prey. These cultures then acquire elements that encourage physical mobility. People who are resourceful, self-reliant, and independent do well in such environments. Thus, child-rearing practices emphasise these qualities. As a result, parents socialize their children by giving them much freedom and by encouraging independence.
>
> In agricultural cultures, cooperation is often required. A person who is not dependable or does not conform would not be a good coworker. As a result, socialization in such cultures emphasises dependability, responsibility, and conformity.[15]

Information society, for its part, is characterized by increasing complexity, occupational specialization and greater gender equality.[16]

Data from the World Values Survey provides further evidence on the relationship between ecology and culture, and has demonstrated that the level of general affluence is linked in a significant way to a wide range of things, including levels of religiosity and birth rates. The data systematically show that, whereas poorer nations experience rapid population growth, virtually all industrial societies today have fertility rates

---

11 H.C. Triandis, *cit. supra* note 6, p. 19.

12 *Ibid.*

13 *Ibid.*, p. 14.

14 *Ibid.*, p. 15.

15 *Ibid.*, p. 23.

16 *Ibid.*, p. 132.

far below the population replacement level.[17] In just as systematic a way, people in poorer nations engage in social forms of religious activity (attendance at religious services) and private forms of religious activity (prayer) significantly more often than do people in affluent countries. Given these facts, it should come as no surprise that some scholars see cultures primarily as responses to ecological circumstances, and characterize them either as 'survival strategies for a society'[18] or as sources of traditions that tell people 'what has worked in the past'.[19]

The fact that there are many universals in human behaviour has led some scholars to argue that cultures are canalized expressions of our instincts.[20] All humans have language, food habits, art, myths, religious practices, family structures, economic systems, 'truth', government, war, kinship, shelter, training systems, hygiene and incest taboos.[21] The above-mentioned examples of course represent broad categories and hide many differences, but nonetheless constitute important pieces of evidence.[22] Furthermore, there are many other, perhaps less obvious examples of universals in human behaviour: all societies have status hierarchies and make divisions between in-groups and out-groups; most humans understand the difference between intimacy (e.g. self-disclosure) and formality (e.g. doing what etiquette requires); in all societies adult males are more likely to kill one another than are adult females; and in all cultures people recognize facial signals, for example for anger, in quite the same way.[23] Many modern evolutionary theorists assume that these and other common features related to human cognition, motivation and behaviour were designed through natural selection.[24] Some, particularly those who espouse theories about 'selfish genes', believe that they are genetically dictated. While we have good reason to believe that at least the latter assumption is somewhat of an overstatement,[25] various aspects of human behaviour likely do have some type of biological basis.[26]

Religion is another major culture-shaping force, especially in social settings where there is or has been only one predominant religion. The influence of religion

---

17 P. Norris and R. Inglehart, *Sacred and Secular: Religion and Politics Worldwide* (Cambridge University Press, 2004), pp. 24, 216.

18 *Ibid.*, p. 18.

19 H.C. Triandis, *cit. supra* note 6, p. 15.

20 See D. Kenrick et al., 'Evolutionary Social Psychology: Adaptive Predispositions and Human Culture', in J. Delamater, *cit. supra* note 7, p. 103.

21 H.C. Triandis, *cit. supra* note 6.

22 P.B. Smith and M.H. Bond, *cit. supra* note 5, pp. 73-74.

23 D. Kenrick et al., *cit. supra* note 20, p. 113; H.C. Triandis, *cit. supra* note 6; P.B. Smith and M.H. Bond, *ibid.*, p. 74.

24 D. Kenrick et al., *ibid.*, p. 105.

25 M.E. Clark, *In search of human nature* (London, Routledge, 2002).

26 *Ibid.*; P.B. Smith and M.H. Bond, *cit. supra* note 5, p. 93.

can be overwhelming and long-lasting. Norris and Inglehart conclude on the basis of their analysis of data from the World Values Survey that:

> the historically predominant religious tradition of a given society tends to leave a lasting impact on religious beliefs and other social norms, ranging from approval of divorce, to gender roles, tolerance of homosexuality, and work orientations. Where a society started continues to influence where it is at later points of time, so that the citizens of historically Protestant societies continue to show values that are distinct from those prevailing in historically Catholic or Hindu or Orthodox or Confucian societies. These cross-national differences do not reflect the influence of the religious authorities today – they persist even in societies where the vast majority no longer attends the church.[27]

Interestingly, nationally predominant religion also seems to have an impact on the values of those who are not religious at all or who adhere to a minority religion.[28] This is because the predominant religion has influenced national culture over a long period of time, rendering the originally religious influences indistinguishable from other cultural influences, and because such influences thereby become part of the content of socialization and transmission of values that takes place through the general educational system and mass media.[29]

In addition to ecology, biology and religion, there are many more 'external' or contextual factors that shape cultures. Cultures change, for instance, because of wars and other major historical events, because of rapidly increasing contacts between cultures through commerce, tourism and migration, and because of technological, medical and other scientific advances. The factors that prompt cultural change are therefore often beyond direct human control.

## 5. Cultural stability and change

That cultures change is evident even for the casual observer. Our contemporary cultures are changing rapidly, as can be seen for instance in the increasing acceptance of gender, sexual and religious equality. In a longer and more global perspective one can observe the extinction of many cultural practices, such as headhunting and slavery, and the near extinction of many more, such as widow-burning and blood

---

27 P. Norris and R. Inglehart, *cit. supra* note 17, p. 220.

28 *Ibid.*

29 *Ibid.*, p. 17.

feuds. As Clifford Geertz has put it, what we are witnessing is the process of the softening of cultural contrast.[30]

All cultures are in a permanent state of ferment. Part of that continuous reworking of cultural meanings is due to the fact that cultural meanings usually mutate somewhat during transmission: noone understands and tells a (cultural) story quite in the same way, since personal beliefs, values and motives tend to get involved. As all of us interact with a huge number of people, we create a multitude of variations on a cultural theme – even within a 'single culture'. Thus, as Verkuyten has pointed out, all cultures have numerous rules, convictions and values permitting divergent and conflicting interpretations.[31] And not just that, but, as the traditions of any group are rich and diverse, there is always a considerable degree of selectivity involved when particular traditions are emphasized and cherished.

As is clear by now, cultures are not giant cloning systems producing like-minded people: heterogeneity is an inevitable quality of any culture. To put it in another way, the cultural framework of an individual does not predict her behaviour in a particular situation with any significant degree of accuracy. It is only when we look at the behaviours of larger groups of people that certain patterns and tendencies become visible.

While cultures are in a permanent state of ferment, it is safe to say that some aspects of a culture are less likely to change than others. The more fundamental an aspect is to a culture, the more embedded it is in various deeply held beliefs, the more functional it is in the current ecology, the deeper it is ingrained in the memory and consciousness of a group (e.g. a memory of war), the more resistant it is to change. The most fundamental of these aspects can be called cultural syndromes.

A cultural syndrome is a pattern of beliefs, attitudes, self-definitions, norms and values that are organized around some identifiable theme in a society.[32] The following four are examples of cultural syndromes:

- *Individualism*. Some cultures structure social experience around autonomous individuals. These cultures tend to value independence and individual achievement.[33] Most of the English-speaking countries, as well as most European countries, belong to this category.
- *Collectivism*. Some cultures organize their subjective cultures around one or more collectives, such as the family, the tribe, the religious group or the country. These cultures tend to place value on interdependence and group

[30] C. Geertz, *Available Light: Anthropological Reflections on Philosophical Topics* (Princeton University Press, 2001), p. 68.

[31] M. Verkuyten, *The Social Psychology of Ethnic Identity* (Hove, Psychology Press, 2005), p. 230.

[32] H.C. Triandis, *cit. supra* note 6, p. 4.

[33] J.A. Howard and D.G. Renfrow, 'Social Cognition', in J. Delamater, *cit. supra* note 7, p. 294.

harmony. There are two types of collectivism. One emphasizes oneness and might be called horizontal (e.g. some Southern European nations); the other emphasizes serving the group and might be called vertical (e.g. Pacific Asian nations).[34] Collectivist cultures are often, but not always, organized hierarchically.[35]

- *Tightness*. Some cultures impose many norms, rules and constraints on social behaviour, while others are rather loose in imposing such constraints.[36] The maintenance of a tight culture is usually possible only in a homogeneous setting. Looseness is prototypical to heterogeneous and pluralist cultures, and to social settings that are located at the intersection of major distinct cultures.[37]
- *Complexity*. Some cultures are more complex than others. An information society is more complex – e.g. in terms of occupational specialization – than an industrial one; an industrial society is respectively more complex than an agrarian one.[38]

Some of these syndromes are to a certain extent inter-related. Tightness tends to go with collectivism, looseness and complexity with individualism.

What is particularly important to note from this discussion is, firstly, that there are aspects in every culture that change only slowly; and secondly, that rules internal to a culture can regulate how cultural change may take place.

## 6. Culture and the individual

While it is true that cultures do not necessarily dictate our understandings and values, but rather 'influence' or 'shape' them, we should be aware of the fact that cultural influences go very deep, even to the heart of our sense of ourselves and others. To the people living in highly individualist societies it may come as a surprise that people from collectivist contexts simply may not share a conception of the individual as in some way autonomous or separate from the social context, with a largely stable inner self that is the final explanation for her/his behaviour.[39] In the words of Clifford Geertz:

---

34 H.C. Triandis, *cit. supra* note 6, p. 164; P.B. Smith and M.H. Bond, *cit. supra* note 5, p. 64.

35 H.C. Triandis, *ibid.*, p. 165.

36 *Ibid.*, p. 159 ff.

37 *Ibid.*

38 *Ibid.*

39 See, e.g., P.B. Smith and M.H. Bond, *cit. supra* note 5, p. 97.

> The Western conception of the person as a bounded, unique, more or less integrated motivational and cognitive universe, a dynamic centre of awareness, emotion, judgment and action organized into a distinctive whole and set contrastively both against other such wholes and against its social and natural background is, however incorrigible it may seem to us, a rather peculiar idea within the context of the world's cultures.[40]

To illustrate the way culture influences how we understand ourselves, we can outline a basic typology of prototypical independent and interdependent self-construals.[41] In looking at the typology it should be kept in mind that cultural collectivism can be hypothesized to press for generally high levels of interdependent self-construals, but for lower levels of independent self-construals.[42]

| *Prototypical independent self-construal: Independent items* | *Prototypical interdependent self-construal: Interdependent items* |
|---|---|
| I am a unique person separate from others;<br>My personal identity is very important to me;<br>I should be judged on my own merit;<br>I try not to depend on others;<br>If there is a conflict between my values and the values of groups of which I am a member, I follow my values;<br>I don't support a group decision when it is wrong. | I am a member of my family, my religious community, nation, etc;<br>My relationships with others are more important than my accomplishments;<br>I maintain harmony in groups of which I am a member;<br>I will sacrifice my self-interest for the benefit of my group;<br>I respect the majority's wishes in groups of which I am member. |

People with a particular type of self-construal tend to perceive and also describe their peers in similar terms. To take an example from one study, three out of four US respondents described their peers in a context-free (independent) way – such as 'he is selfish' – while less than half of the Indian respondents (India being a more collectivist culture) did so, choosing instead to describe them in more contextualized terms – such as 'he is hesitant to give money away to his family'.[43]

Two important points may be made now. First, most cultures include a mixture of individualistic and collectivist elements.[44] Second, even in the most extremely

---

40 C. Geertz, *The Interpretation of Cultures* (New York, Basic Books, 1974), p. 225.

41 Self-construals are understandings we develop about ourselves – our traits, beliefs, motivations, values and behavioural style. The items in the table below are based on P.B. Smith and M.H. Bond, *cit. supra* note 5, p. 110; H.C. Triandis, *cit. supra* note 6, p. 165 ff.

42 P.B. Smith and M.H. Bond, *cit. supra* note 5, p. 111.

43 *Ibid.*, p. 113.

44 H.C. Triandis, *cit. supra* note 6, p. 172.

individualist cultures a portion of the population has interdependent self-construals, just like there are individualists in collectivist cultures. So, while there are significant differences between cultures, the differences are simply differences in the *frequency* with which people using different types of construals can be found in particular settings. Consequently, it cannot be plausibly argued that the processes of social cognition are fundamentally different in different cultures.[45] A more probable explanation is that people in individualist/collectivist cultures have gradually internalized different rules that lay out the *priorities* as to what one should attend to in any situation.[46] 'Collectivism' and 'individualism' are socially produced and reproduced.

Finally, we need to take a look at how ethnic identity is linked to culture. While the concepts of self and identity are closely linked to each other, and are often confused, they are nevertheless distinct.[47] According to Owens, what distinguishes self from identity is that self is a *process and organization born of self-reflection*, whereas identity is a *tool* by which individuals or groups categorize themselves and present themselves to the world.[48] Verkuyten, drawing on the work of Phinney, has identified four dimensions or aspects of ethnic identity. These dimensions are the following:

- *Being*. This refers to the ethnic label people use for themselves on the basis of their descent or e.g. visible characteristics.
- *Feeling*. Whether a person accepts her/his ethnic identity and feels positively about it.
- *Doing*. This concerns involvement in the social life and cultural practices of the ethnic in-group. Various aspects may include: language use, friendship patterns, cultural traditions and symbols (such as celebrations, dress, music, food and newspapers), and participation in religious practices.
- *Knowing*. To what extent a person is interested in and knowledgeable about the culture and history of his/her group.[49]

The different aspects of ethnic identity can combine in different ways and create unique profiles.[50] The four aspects are not only dimensions by which people's ethnic identities may be described, but also provide the accounts or repertoires that people use when they 'negotiate' what their group is all about and who exactly should be

45 P.B. Smith and M.H. Bond, *cit. supra* note 5, p. 112 ff.

46 *Ibid.*, p. 114.

47 T. Owens, 'Self and Identity', in J. Delamater, *Handbook of Social Psychology* (New York, Kluwer, 2003), p. 206.

48 *Ibid.*

49 M. Verkuyten, *cit. supra* note 31, pp. 198-200.

50 *Ibid.*, p. 200.

considered a 'real' member.[51] Typically, 'being' and 'doing' are contrasted, since the aspects of 'feeling' and 'knowing' provide less practical (or less accessible) bases for determining group identity. To give an example, in a group of people who identify themselves as Roma some may be of the view that to be a Roma it is enough to have parents who are Roma, whereas another part of the group may consider that in addition to having Roma parents one must also follow Roma traditions (and/or speak a Roma language) to be considered a 'real' Roma.

There are thus many different ways in which individuals may identify with a group. Whether others recognize one as a member of that group is another matter. Sometimes a group is able to agree on a visible cultural marker, such as a particular type of dress or headgear, the wearing of which is then taken as a presumptive sign of committed membership.

A certain tendency has been visible among many immigrants in Europe lately. While an overwhelming majority of immigrants continue to identify themselves in ethnic terms, and feel strongly about it, this ethnic identification is often only weakly correlated with personal participation in distinctive cultural practices, such as language, religion and dress. As Verkuyten, for instance, has observed, ethnic identification can persist while increasingly becoming drained of cultural content.[52] This should not be surprising, as we have observed a similar process in relation to secularization and religious identity: in the Nordic countries many people have retained formal adherence to their religious identities, even though the substantive meaning of these identities has largely faded away.[53]

Yet, at the same time, there are people who seek to revive and maintain their ethnic culture. People from collectivist contexts and those with interdependent self-construals tend to see the maintenance of the group and its culture as a moral obligation.[54] In addition, present and aspiring community leaders often espouse essentialist and highly conservative conceptions of the culture of the group.[55] Essentialist arguments are powerful, since they portray the group and its culture as natural and non-negotiable. This is why these arguments are used by groups that seek public recognition and accommodation of their cultural and religious needs. Such arguments provide a very limiting account of the group and its internal diversity, however.

51 *Ibid.*, p. 201.

52 M. Verkuyten, *cit. supra* note 31, p. 104.

53 See also P. Norris and R. Inglehart, *cit. supra* note 17, p. 18.

54 M. Verkuyten, *cit. supra* note 31, p. 104.

55 *Ibid.*, pp.104, 124.

## 7. Wrapping it all up: implications for minority rights

What are the implications of all this for minority rights? Does any of it shed light on the conditions under which persons belonging to minorities are able to maintain and/or develop their culture? What does the legal obligation, incumbent upon states, to promote such conditions imply in practice? I would like to present three very broad conclusions.

First, if anything, it has been demonstrated that a minority faces tremendous challenges in aspiring to *maintain* its culture. Available evidence suggests that the influence and pressure of the majority culture is penetrating, even if that pressure is not always exerted on purpose. In addition, there are many external factors – factors that are beyond direct human control – that affect cultures and their continuity. This means that state parties have to take seriously their obligation to promote the conditions necessary for cultural maintenance. Given the challenges, it is clear that abstaining from assimilationist policies is not sufficient, but that positive measures need to be taken to support minority cultures. It has also been established that cultures are maintained and developed in *interaction*. Uninhibited interaction requires – in addition to respect for all other human rights – particular reverence for freedom of assembly, speech and association, the right to use one's own language and the right to publish newspapers and to broadcast radio and television programmes, as these constitute important mediums for socialization and interaction. The more challenged a group is in terms of economic resources, the clearer the state obligation to provide financial support for the above-mentioned purposes.

Second, people are neither masters nor slaves of their cultures. Cultures are not giant cloning systems producing like-minded individuals, but they do have a profound impact on all of us, affecting even the way we understand ourselves and others. The fact that our cultures do not have a permanent grip on us means that it is possible to *challenge* and attempt to *change* those aspects of our culture that we feel are dysfunctional or oppressive. It is fair to assert that all cultures – majority and minority cultures alike – have dysfunctional and oppressive elements, for instance in the form of socially shared views about the 'appropriate' (restrictive) roles of women. All cultures are rich in content, especially in traditions, allowing for different and even conflicting interpretations and manifestations, and thus change.[56] The mechanisms and measures that states adopt to support minority cultures should therefore always allow internal discourse and evaluation of the various elements of their culture by members of the minority concerned.

Third, all minority groups are likely to include at least these three kinds of people: (i) those who see their ethnic identity as very important, but who are in

56 It should be noted that some cultural elements are more fundamental and uncontroversial than others; and reinterpretations that build upon less controversial elements are more likely to succeed.

practice rather indifferent toward partaking in cultural practices and traditions; (ii) those that see it as their moral duty to uphold group values and to ensure the maintenance of group cohesion and harmony; and (iii) chosen or self-proclaimed community leaders who often espouse essentialist, absolutist and conservative forms of culture. The latter may seek to use their authority to impose a particular vision of the 'right' culture upon other members of the group. However, since the right to maintain and develop their culture belongs to *every* member of a minority, states should steer clear of supporting or encouraging particularist viewpoints. When consulting members of minority communities or when appointing representatives of minorities to consultative bodies, states should be cognizant of, and recognize, the internal diversity of all groups.

At the end of the day, the ability of members of minorities to develop their culture is critical to the very continuity of the culture. A culture that is overly conservative and essentialized as unchangeable risks becoming dysfunctional over time. And a culture that is experienced as dysfunctional, possibly even oppressive, by those that share in it can, in the end, only be maintained by some form of coercion. Coercion on its behalf is likely to lead to an increase in the number of individuals who feel indifferent towards the culture and the traditions of the group, putting the continuity of the culture at risk. The pressures and risks faced by minority groups are thus not just external, but internal as well.

# 10
# The Role of the State in Balancing Religious Freedom with Other Human Rights in a Multicultural European Context

*Stéphanie Lagoutte and Eva Maria Lassen**

## 1. Introduction

An underlying tenet in this volume is that there are tensions within the human rights discourse because of the dual dimension of cultural rights. Cultural rights are human rights but at the same time they may come into conflict with individual human rights or individual perceptions of human rights. As much of these tensions relate to the role of the state, the participants in the discourse tend to revisit the following questions: To what extent should the state remain tolerant of cultural – in our case, religious – practices that appear to restrict the enjoyment of some individual members of a community? To what extent should the state enforce individual rights even in relation to religious, ethnic and cultural communities?

In a manner similar to cultural rights, religious rights (freedom of religion and freedom to manifest one's religion) are caught in a dilemma. Religious pluralism, which is a logical consequence of the protection of freedom of religion in European democracies, is also a challenge to the very idea of universal human rights, as it seems to create a multiplicity of sets of norms, not all of which appear at first sight to be reconcilable with human rights.

In European democracies, two movements can be registered. On the one hand, there is a more or less generalized establishment of some form of separation between the state and religious communities, caused among others by 'the irreducible plurality of competing religious groups and the diversity of their beliefs that pushes the state

* A related paper by the same authors was published in March 2006: S. Lagoutte and E.M. Lassen, 'Meeting the Challenge: Redefining Europe's Classical Model for State Intervention in Religious Practices', *Netherlands Quarterly of Human Rights* (2006), pp. 33-59.

Francioni and Scheinin (eds), *Cultural Human Rights*, 207–222

toward neutrality'.[1] On the other hand, when several religions coexist within one and the same population, the public authorities have to deal *actively* with this religious diversity by both protecting it in the name of freedom of religion and placing some restrictions on some of its expressions. The aim of such endeavours is to reconcile the interests of the various religious and non-religious groups and to ensure that everyone's beliefs are respected.[2]

Religious traditions are also part of culture and in many cases the frontier between religious and cultural practices is very thin. Yet historically religious traditions have been dealt with as a case apart, first in the 'free' European constitutions of the 19th century, then in international human rights law, where religious freedom stood out as one of the most central human rights, allowing religious communities a very substantial freedom in continuing the practice of their traditions. Western Europe has traditionally pursued what we have called the Classical model for state intervention in religious matters. In this model, religious communities and individuals enjoy extended freedom to have their own rules for personal behaviour and internal organization.

Recently, we have seen another tendency in European debates, according to which religious traditions should no longer experience this privileged absence of state interference. In fact, the human rights community is caught in heated debates on state intervention in such religious practices which are incompatible with the norms of society at large. In many cases, the incompatibility between religious practices and legal norms is being presented as a human rights issue. Among potential discrepancies between religious practices and human rights are issues concerning gender, family and children, as for example headscarves and other religious signs, female and male circumcision, ritual slaughter, religious divorce, and homosexuality. These examples or areas have often been perceived as a reflection of a conflict between religious freedom and other human rights.

Today, a human rights culture suffuses European states and societies.[3] Europeans have become increasingly aware of their human rights, and personal claims tend to be perceived as legal human rights claims. Accompanying this greater awareness is a new discourse, according to which human rights norms should be transferred to religious communities with a view to bringing religious practices in compliance with human rights. The idea suggests itself that it is up to the State to ensure such

---

1 P. Hirst and J.N. Figgis, 'Churches and the State', in D. Marquand & L. Ronald Nettler, *Religion and Democracy* (Oxford, Blackwell, 2000), pp. 104-120.

2 See the position of the European Court of Human Rights in some of its prominent case-law on freedom of religion: *Leyla Sahin v. Turkey*, 29 June 2004; *Serif v. Greece*, 14 December 1999; *Kokkinakis v. Greece*, 25 May 1993.

3 K. Hastrup, 'Accommodating Diversity in a Global Culture of Rights: An Introduction', in K. Hastrup (ed.), *Legal Cultures and Human Rights* (The Hague/London/New York, Kluwer Law International, 2001), p. 7 ff.

compliance, eliminating discrepancies between religious practices and human rights. Transposing this radical vision into the legal sphere, it is argued that the State even has a positive obligation to ensure such compliance. This view is reinforced by the expansion of the *Drittwirkung* doctrine according to which human rights may also apply between private parties, that is – in our case – in the relation between a religious community and an individual.[4]

The present article addresses this new focus put on the positive obligation of the state to protect these personal claims. Accordingly, our central question is whether the State has a human rights obligation to interfere in certain religious practices in order to establish harmony between human rights and religious practices. It seems to us that, largely based on the view that harmony between religious practices and human rights is mandatory from a human rights perspective, the answer to this question is gradually becoming more and more affirmative: the State must intervene and put an end to those religious practices that are incompatible with human rights. Our article challenges this affirmation, and points at a further extension of legal claims as a problematic aspect in the new discourse. We suggest instead the adoption of a more complex version of the Classical European model for state intervention in religious affairs.

After analysing the human rights framework in which European states are operating when dealing with religious matters, this article attempts at offering a redefinition of the European model for state intervention in religious practices.

## 2. The European human rights framework

The purpose of evoking European human rights law here is to attempt to bring clarity into a debate that is blurred by a variety of discourses and meanings in the multi-religious and multi-cultural context that has become a reality in Europe. Therefore, it is indispensable to identify where human rights are already playing a role – and to which extent – in the relationship between state and religion.

---

4 In international and European human rights law a state party can be held responsible for the violation of the human rights of an individual by a third – private – party, if the state did not take all the relevant and necessary measures to prevent this violation, see: P. Van Dijk and G.J.H. Van Hoof, *Theory and Practice of the European Convention of Human Rights* (The Hague, Kluwer, 3rd ed., 1998), p. 22 ff. See also on this phenomenon called *Drittwirkung*, horizontal effect or privatisation of human rights: A. Clapham, 'The Drittwirkung of the Convention', in R.St.J. Macdonalds, F. Matscher and H. Petzold (eds.), *The European System for the Protection of Human Rights* (The Hague/Boston/London, Martinus Nijhoft Publishers, 1993), p. 163. Often only an *indirect Drittwirkung* is recognized in the sense that the only party which can be held responsible for a human rights violation is the State, see: P. Van Dijk and G.J.H. Van Hoof, *cit. infra*, p. 23 ff.

Over the past decades the European Court of Human Rights has established a number of general principles which play an essential role in its case law related to freedom of religion.[5] However, the circumstances of the various cases play a decisive role in the formation of the Court's solution to a specific problem and hence it is difficult to give a general picture of the view of the Court.

Freedom of thought, conscience and religion is considered by the European Court of Human Rights as one of the foundations of a democratic society.[6] The Court has stated very clearly that religious pluralism is an inherent feature of European democracy;[7] indeed, the Court has had to operate with this diversity and to try to protect it throughout its judgments. Under Article 9 of the Convention, the state finds itself in a complicated position: it has, simultaneously, an obligation of neutrality in religious matters, an obligation to abstain from interfering in freedom of religion, and an obligation to interfere to protect religious freedom as well as more generally human rights.[8]

### A. Neutrality and impartiality of the state

The European Court of Human Rights has frequently emphasized the role of the state as the neutral and impartial organizer of the exercise of various religions, faiths and beliefs. This principle relates to the role of the state as the *organizer* of the exercise of various religions. Accordingly, the role of the authorities in such circumstances is not to remove the cause of tension by eliminating pluralism, but to ensure that the competing groups tolerate each other.[9]

The principle of the neutrality and impartiality of the state implies a number a consequences.

First, the autonomous existence of religious communities, which is indispensable for pluralism in a democratic society, is an issue at the very heart of the protection

5 See the principles that are stated at the beginning of the ruling of the European Court of Human Rights in, for example: *Leyla Sahin v. Turkey*, Judgment of 29 June 2004, paras. 97-102; *Refah Party v. Turkey* [GC], Judgment of 13 February 2003, paras. 90-95; *Metropolitan Church of Bessarabia v. Moldova*, Judgment of 13 December 2001, paras. 114-119.

6 *Kokkinakis v. Greece*, Judgment of 25 May 1993, A. 260-A, para. 31.

7 *Manoussakis and Others v. Greece*, Judgment of 26 September 1996, para. 44.

8 ECHR, Article 9, paragraph 1: 'everyone has the right to freedom of thought, conscience and religion; this right includes freedom to change his religion or belief and freedom, either alone or in community with others and in public or private, to manifest his religion or belief, in worship, teaching, practice and observance'. Paragraph 2: 'Freedom to manifest one's religion or belief shall be subject only to such limitations as are prescribed by law and are necessary in a democratic society in the interests of public safety, for the protection of public order, health or morals, or for the protection of the rights and freedoms of others'.

9 *Metropolitan Church of Bessarabia v. Moldova*, Judgment of 13 December 2001, para. 116; *Serif v. Greece*, 14 December 1999, Application No. 38178/97, ECHR 1999-IX para. 53.

which Article 9 affords. It directly concerns not only the organization of the community as such but also the effective enjoyment of the right to freedom of religion by all its active members.[10] In this respect, where the organization of the religious community is an issue, Article 9 of the Convention must be interpreted in the light of Article 11, which safeguards associative life against unjustified state interference.[11]

Second, the state can play no part in assessing the legitimacy of religious beliefs[12] or the legitimacy of the ways in which those beliefs are expressed.[13] In addition, in a country where the exercise of the right to freedom of religion – or of one of its aspects – is subject under domestic law to a system of prior authorization, recognized ecclesiastical authority may not be involved in the procedure for granting authorization.[14]

Finally, positive obligations are also imposed on the state, which may have to take action to reconcile the interests of the various religious groups that coexist in a democratic society. Accordingly, the state shall ensure mutual tolerance between opposing groups.[15]

The principle of neutrality and impartiality has to accommodate the institutional or constitutional framework existing for the relations between the state and the churches in a specific state.

In general, the European Court of Human Rights has been quite indifferent to the organization of the relationship between state and church in a specific country as long as the public authorities generally remain neutral and impartial. More recently, the case law concerning Turkey shows that a state which has chosen the principle of secularism as a fundament for its constitutional order will benefit from a large margin of appreciation in order to keep religious manifestations out of its public sphere. Nevertheless, the extent of the intervention of the state in religious matters

---

10 *Hasan and Chaush v. Bulgaria* [GC], 26 October 2000, para. 62.

11 *Hasan and Chaush v. Bulgaria* [GC], 26 October 2000, para. 62.

12 *Cha'are Shalom Ve Tsedek v. France* [GC], no. 27417/95, para. 84, ECHR 2000-VII.

13 *Metropolitan Church of Bessarabia v. Moldova*, Judgment of 13 December 2001, para. 117.

14 *Metropolitan Church of Bessarabia and Others v. Moldova*, No. 45701/99, para. 117, ECHR 2001-XII; *Pentidis and Others v. Greece*, 9 June 1997, para. 46.

15 *Metropolitan Church of Bessarabia and Others v. Moldova*, No. 45701/99, para. 123, ECHR 2001-XII. See also, for instance, in a case concerning the conviction of the applicants (Jehovah's witnesses) for having operated a place of worship without first obtaining the authorisations required by Greek law, the Court stated that the right to freedom of religion excludes any discretion on the part of the state to determine whether religious beliefs or the means used to express such beliefs are legitimate. (*Manoussakis v. Greece*, 26 September 1996, para. 47). Recently confirmed in *Hasan and Chaush v. Bulgaria* [GC], 26 October 2000, para. 78. More generally, in democratic societies, the state does not need to take measures to ensure that religious communities are brought under a unified leadership (*Serif v. Greece*, 14 December 1999, Application No. 38178/97, ECHR 1999-IX para. 53).

will vary according to the circumstances of each case and thereby according to more concrete parameters.[16]

### *B. Legal intervention is possible*

There is no doubt that legal intervention in religious matters is possible. According to Article 9 of the European Convention on Human Rights, the right to *manifest* one's religion can be restricted by the state. The legitimacy and the extent of these restrictions remain under the control of the domestic courts and – in the last instance – of the European Court of Human Rights. In order to be compatible with Article 9, state interferences have to be prescribed by law, pursue a legitimate aim and be proportionate to the aim that they pursue as, for example, the protection of the interests of society or of the rights and interests of others.

A central element here is to find out what type of practices or manifestations can be qualified as 'religious' and therefore be afforded the – relative – protection of Article 9. Indeed, what is considered a religious matter by individuals or by the public opinion sometimes has little to do with religion or religious practices: in this case, the specified behaviour or action is not protected by freedom of religion because it cannot be defined as a religious manifestation. Still, determining whether a given behaviour or action is linked to the religion of an individual is a very hard task for the European Court of Human rights – or any court – as it does not necessarily possess any insight into the religion in question and – in addition – clearly does not own the legitimacy to do so.

---

[16] Traditionally, the organs of the European Convention of Human Rights have not regarded state-church systems as incompatible *per se* with the principle of neutrality and impartiality of the state in religious affairs (see concerning the – former – Lutheran Church of Sweden: Application No. 11581/85, *Darby v. Sweden*, Comm. Rep 9 May 1989, para. 45). Today, the principle of secularism, understood as a rather strict separation of state and church, seems to have become the cornerstone of the case-law of the Court (*Refah Party v. Turkey* [GC], Judgment of 13 February 2003, para. 92; See also judgment in *Kalaç v. Turkey*, 1 July 1997). However, it should be underlined that this position has only been expressed by the Court in cases concerning Turkey, where secularism is one of the foundations of the state. For instance, the *Sahin* judgment is built around the principle of secularism, as understood in the Turkish legal order. In its judgment, the Court accepts the reasoning of the Turkish Constitutional Court, according to which secularism in Turkey is the guarantor of democratic values, the principle of the inviolability of freedom of religion, and the principle of equality of all citizens before the law.

Traditionally, the approach followed by the former European Commission of Human Rights[17] – and more occasionally by the Court[18] – was based on the point of finding out whether the activity in question was necessary for the fulfilment of the obligations incumbent upon those maintaining a particular religion. This approach is very problematic as it forces the Court, and consequently the national authorities, to assess the necessity of a particular religious activity or expression. Indeed, some of the old findings from the Commission are probably very disputable from a religious point of view. In this respect, the latest judgment from the Court concerning the Islamic headscarf has at least the merit of taking as its starting point the individual's personal religious motivation for choosing a specific outfit.[19]

A margin of appreciation is left to the state in order to establish the necessity and the proportionality of the interference, but its extent as well as the intensity of the proportionality control operated by the Court seem to vary from quite strict[20] to very indulgent.[21] Two intertwined factors, responsible for this huge variation, are important for our study. First, the organization in a specific country of the relationship between the state and the religions plays nowadays a larger role than previously in the outcome of a concrete case. Second, the position in society of the religion concerned appears to play a role as to the extent of the margin of appreciation left to the state. Hence, the margin of appreciation is rather narrow in cases concerning the freedom of religion of individuals belonging to a religious minority (for instance Jehovah's Witnesses in Greece or the Muslim community in Bulgaria); it becomes much larger when the Court deals with individuals belonging to the majority religion (for instance Muslims in Turkey). Indeed, the European Convention on Human Rights acknowledges that religion is part of the public sphere and therefore can be interfered with or influenced by the state: 'To insist that religion belongs in the private sphere is meaningless to and indeed induces alienation in, the vast majority of religious believers in the world.'[22] In practice, the implications will be very different for majority and minority religions. The various European

---

17 See Application No. 8160/78, *X. v. UK*, *DR* (1981) 27, p. 36, or Application No. 1753/63, *X. v. Austria*, *Yearbook of the European Commission* (1965), p. 184. See also references to decisions and reports of the European Commission of Human Rights in M.D. Evans, *Religious Liberty and International Law in Europe* (Cambridge, Cambridge University Press, 1997), p. 307.

18 *Cha'are Shalom Ve Tsedek v. France* [GC], Judgment of 27 June 2000, paras. 73-74.

19 *Leyla Sahin v. Turkey*, Judgment of 29 June 2004, para. 71. In a previous decision concerning a teacher, the Court moved directly to examining whether the disputed measure was prescribed by the law. Application No. 42393/98 *Dahlab v. Swiss*, 15 February 2001, p. 12.

20 *Manoussakis and Others v. Greece*, Judgment of 26 September 1996, para. 44.

21 See *Leyla Sahin v. Turkey*, Judgment of 29 June 2004, para. 71.

22 K. Boyle, 'Human Rights, Religion and Democracy: the *Refah Party* Case', *Essex Human Rights Review* (2004), p. 16.

states do not operate in a religious vacuum and in most states one religion, directly or implicitly, officially or in practice, dominates the public sphere.

### *C. Legal intervention is an obligation only in few cases*

The state has the positive obligation to take action in order to ensure the effective protection of human rights by, for example, prosecuting and punishing crimes as prescribed by criminal law. In this respect, it is important to recall that not every act prescribed, influenced or inspired by religion is protected by freedom of religion.[23] Therefore, it is possible for the state to limit the freedom to manifest a religion, if it clashes with the aim of protecting public order, public safety or the rights and freedom of others. The existence of an actual positive obligation to interfere will therefore depend on the interests at stake.

Until now, the European Court of Human Rights has avoided a direct pronouncement on the existence of such a positive obligation for the state. Still, in 1999, the Court stated that 'it could be argued that it is in the public interest for the state to take special measures to protect from deceit those whose legal relationships can be affected by the acts of religious ministers'.[24] However, the concrete case concerned a situation where the acts of religious ministers had *legal* value.[25] In addition, it is worth underlining that the Court states, in this judgment, that Article 9 of the

[23] For instance, female genital mutilation is a criminal offence in most European countries. It is criminalised in the United Kingdom under the Prohibition of Female Circumcision Act 1985. In Sweden the 1982 Act Prohibiting the Genital Mutilation ('Circumcision') of Women stipulates that 'an operation may not be carried out on the outer female sexual organs with a view to mutilating them or bringing about some other permanent change in them ('circumcision'), regardless of whether consent has been given for the operation or not (Section 1); anyone committing a breach of Section 1 is to be sentenced to a term of imprisonment of not more than four years (Section 2). The situation is different in France: in 1983, the Court of Cassation judged that removing the girl's clitoris was a mutilation within the meaning of Article 312 of the Penal Code; since then, the domestic courts have used the Penal Code's general provisions on violence and mutilation (Article 222-7, 222-8, 222-9 and 222-10) to sentence the perpetrator of different forms of female genital mutilation to imprisonment and fine.

[24] *Serif v. Greece*, 1999, para. 50.

[25] 'The Court notes ... that although Article 9 of the Convention does not require States to give legal effect to religious weddings and religious courts' decisions, under Greek law weddings celebrated by ministers of 'known religions' are assimilated to civil ones and the muftis have competence to adjudicate on certain family and inheritance disputes between Muslims. In such circumstances, it could be argued that it is in the public interest for the State to take special measures to protect from deceit those whose legal relationships can be affected by the acts of religious ministers. However, the Court does not consider it necessary to decide this issue, which does not arise in the applicant's case' *Serif v. Greece*, 1999, para. 50.

Convention does not require the state to give legal effect to religious weddings and religious courts' decisions.[26]

### D. The impossibility of legal pluralism in a European context

To make the picture complete, we need to briefly deal with the temptation to contemplate legal pluralism as another radical answer to our question. Here, the position of the European Court of Human Rights on the feasibility – in a European context – of legal pluralism based on religious law is very clear. In the *Refah Party* case, the Court has explicitly stressed the incompatibility with the Convention of a 'plurality of legal systems [that] would introduce into all legal relationships a distinction between individuals grounded on religion [and] would categorise everyone according to his religious beliefs and would allow him rights and freedoms not as an individual but according to his allegiance to a religious movement.'[27]

In this judgment, the reasoning of the European Court of Human Rights concerning Shari'a has been heavily criticised for lacking the refinement one could expect from such a prominent institution.[28] Indeed, the *Refah Party* case shows how the absence of dialogue between a secular institution (the Court) and a religious community has been prejudicial to the legitimacy and the authority of the judgment. However, the principle set down by the Court remains clear and undisputable: the European Convention on Human Rights prohibits a plurality of legal systems that would be *fundamentally* discriminatory.

* * *

The case law of the European Court of Human Rights is very naturally under the influence of both the Classical model for state intervention in religious practices (neutrality of the state) and the new discourse (increasing intervention of the state). We will now turn to a more general discussion of the Classical model as observed in Europe.

---

26 See *supra* (note 81).

27 *Refah Party*, 2003, para. 119; in this Grand Chamber Judgment, the Court reproduces the findings from the 2001 Chamber Judgment (3rd section), 31 July 2001.

28 Legal experts and researchers from all over Europe have been extremely critical of the approach followed by the Court. One of the more weighty criticisms is that the Court on several occasions in its judgment expresses rigid views and simplified misgivings concerning Islam and Shari´a. See, for instance: K. Boyle, *cit. supra* note 22 and references in footnote 13, p. 3, as well as C. Moe, *Strasbourg's Construction of Islam: A Critique of the Refah Judgment*, Paper presented at the Conference of Experts on 'The Turkish Welfare Party Case: Implications for Human Rights in Europe', Central European University, Budapest, Hungary, 2-3 June 2002.

## 3. Redefining the European model for state intervention in religious practices

In this second main part of our article, we want to argue in favour of a continuation of the Classical model, according to which freedom of religion allows an individual or a community to endorse such norms that do not constitute criminal offences as prescribed by the law of the state. However, we will also show that a redefinition of the model is necessary. Thus we argue in favour of a combination of the traditional limited state intervention with increased information offered by the state about human rights as well as intensification of the dialogue between the state and the religious sphere.

### *A. Defence of the Classical model*

Developing at a different pace over the past two centuries the Western European states have adopted what may be called *the Classical model* for state intervention in religious matters. Within the framework of this model, freedom of religion is interpreted so as to allow religious communities to have their own rules for personal behaviour and internal organization. Based on the idea that a large number of religious practices are – and should be – out of the realm of state intervention, the underlying assumption is that it is not *per se* a human rights concern if religious practices are not in harmony with human rights. The reason why religious communities are able to carry out practices that do not conform to human rights is that these practices have no direct effect on the law of the state and no effect on the legally established rights of the individual. The intervention of the state in religious practices is limited to what is absolutely necessary. The identification of what is 'absolutely necessary' is not seen as static; the state may criminalize previously lawful practices, for instance if medical research proves them to be harmful to the individual.

In other words, if the principle of limited state intervention is implicit in the Classical model, the interpretation and implementation of the model have never been inflexible. The tolerance shown by the state towards discrepancies between state laws and religious practices varies over time, and therefore also the catalogue of discrepancies which are legitimate and those which are not. Moreover, the model is practised differently by European states, partly depending on the degree of separation between the state and the religious communities which exists in a given country. Thus there is much variation as far as religious practices are concerned, as shown by the reaction to the use of headscarves.[29] Indeed, today the ways in which

29 Contrary to most other European countries, France has chosen to ban 'religious signs' from public schools, in practice mainly headscarves worn by Muslim girls. According to Article 1 of Law (2004-228) of 15 March 2004, the wearing of any signs or clothing by which students visibly display a religious affiliation is forbidden in public schools (new article L.141-5-1 of the Code of Education).

religious freedom has typically been practised are being disputed more than ever before, creating confusion and challenging the Classical model.

### B. Undesirability of increased legal intervention

As mentioned in the introduction to this chapter, there is a new discourse in Europe today, according to which human rights norms should be *transferred* to religious communities with a view to ensuring that religious practices are in compliance with human rights. This claim is played out at different levels: in the media, among politicians, in legislation, and within the scholarly community. Advocates of increased state intervention tend to present certain religious practices as posing *proper human rights violations*, also in cases where these practices have no legal consequences.[30]

The new discourse in Europe focuses to a very large extent on Muslims, whose practices in a number of ways (headscarves, male circumcision, ritual slaughter, and religious divorce) make a strong contrast to Christian practices and symbols and hence stand out with marked visibility. But many attempts at targeting, by means of increased state intervention, certain Muslim practices have consequences for other religious minorities; this applies in particular to the Jews (especially Orthodox Jews), whose traditions in many areas resemble Muslim traditions, notably with regard to gender. And not only members of minority religions are affected. Attempts at expanding human rights and state obligations into the religious sphere have consequences for the majority – the Christian Churches which have traditionally thrived on the classical relationship between state and religion which accepts a certain discrepancy between the two norm systems. It follows that the impact of increased state intervention in religious life in Europe is potentially momentous.

In our view, increased legal intervention is not desirable for a number of reasons.

First, state intervention is largely *pointless* because the collision between religious practices and human rights practices does not per se constitute a human rights violation in so far as religious practices have no legally binding consequences. This fact is often overlooked, creating a discourse not infrequently marred with confusion.

Second, in a European secular model, the legal intervention of the state in religious matters related to individual rights will often be *fruitless*: the state cannot change religious law and other religious rules, and hence cannot change the foundation from which the problems arise and from which they are fed.

---

30 See, e.g., Raday, who argues that in the case 'where there is a clash between cultural practices or religious norms and the right to gender equality, it is the right to gender equality that must have normative hegemony'. F. Raday, 'Culture, Religion, and Gender', *International Journal of Constitutional Law* (2003), p. 710.

Third, increased state intervention may in some cases *endanger* the very existence of a particular theology. The harmonization strategy, calling for increased state intervention, carries the risk of putting pressure on all religious movements to become *reform* movements; this is a limitation or even serious violation of religious freedom. Thus state intervention may well prove highly counterproductive in relation to the very religions the state set out to protect.

### C. Overlapping consensus?

However, continuing only on the road of the Classical model as traditionally practised may not meet the challenges and needs of modern European societies. First of all, it is not in society's interest that the divide between religious norms and the norms of the state progressively widen. It may therefore be useful if the state assists in creating a bridge between the two spheres. Secondly, although an individual's human rights may not be violated *per se* because a religious practice is not in compliance with human rights, such discrepancy might nevertheless put the individual in a very difficult situation, and the state may wish to assist in improving this situation. We therefore suggest a modified and more open-ended form of the Classical model. In this model, the principle of legally limited state intervention blends with the state's primarily non-legal support of religious communities and individuals in their attempts to decrease discrepancies between, on the one hand, norms deriving from human rights and, on the other hand, religious laws and practices.

We suggest a modern version of the dialogue between state and religious communities as a key element in the modified version of the Classical model, viewing this dialogue as a central part of the solution to clashes between religious practices and individual human rights. The reason why dialogue seems particularly useful is to be found with the religious communities themselves. Over the last 30 years, representatives of the majority as well as the minority religions have been consistently active participants in public debates about the relationship between human rights and religion. Adherents as well as representatives of the religious communities offer widespread – although far from undisputed – support to basic ideas underlying human rights (for instance, dignity) as well as to specific human rights.[31] At a theological level, hermeneutic reinterpretations of sacred texts have made this support possible.[32]

---

31 Evidence of the work of religious communities on human rights is vast. For an introduction see, e.g., A. Tergel, *Human Rights in Cultural and Religious Traditions* (Uppsala, Acta Universitatis Upsaliensis, 1998).

32 See, e.g., J. Witte, 'Introduction', in J. Witte and J.D. Van der Vyer (eds.), *Religious Human Rights in Global Perspective. Religious Perspectives*, Vol. 1 (The Hague/Boston/London, Martinus Nijhoff Publishers, 1996), XXI.

This normative harmony may be entitled 'overlapping consensus', a notion which, articulated by John Rawls[33] has been applied with success to the area of human rights. Heiner Bielefeldt, to give an example, has positioned the concept in the context of human rights in multicultural societies with regard to three aspects: first, 'the genuinely normative and critical claims of political justice'. Second, 'the limited scope of political justice as compared to "comprehensive" world views'. Third, 'the possibility of appreciating political justice from different religious or philosophical perspective'.[34] In the context of the present chapter, the third aspect – the appreciation of human rights from religious perspectives – is particularly valuable, together with another of Rawls' notions, namely the idea of a *comprehensive doctrine*.[35] Thus, it may, for instance, be argued that 'the unalienable dignity of every human being constitutes both the basic ethical principle of human rights and a central element of the teachings of various religions and philosophies'.[36]

A *fourth dimension* of the notion of overlapping consensus has to be strongly emphasized, namely the recognition of areas where such consensus *does not* exist.[37] This fourth dimension is exceptionally important to keep in mind when discussing the normative relationship between state and religion, because this relationship is characterized by unavoidable and substantial clashes, caused amongst other things by the following factors.

First, state norms and religious norms develop to different music. Over the last several decades, European states and societies have developed to the tunes of human rights, whereas religious norms have developed partly to the internal tune of religious traditions, and only partly to the sounds of the music of society and state. Gender equality, to take an example, is in a religious context examined against, amongst other things, the ecclesiology of the religion and the model of leadership (typically patriarchal models of leadership competing with visions of the more horizontal covenant model of leadership). The state has no such concerns. Religious reformist movements naturally experience fewer difficulties in creating the overlapping consensus in specific areas than conservative and orthodox movements.

---

33 This notion is seen developed throughout J. Rawls, *Political Liberalism* (New York, Columbia University Press, 1996); see in particular pp. 150-154 and 385-95.

34 H. Bielefeldt, '"Western" versus "Islamic" Human Rights Conceptions? A Critique of Cultural Essentialism in the Discussion on Human Rights', *Political Theory* (2000), p. 114.

35 See in particular J. Rawls, *cit. supra* note 33, pp. 13, 175, and 374.

36 H. Bielefeldt, *cit. supra* note 34, p. 116.

37 In Rawls' terminology, this means that a doctrine is 'partially comprehensive'. See, e.g., J. Rawls, *cit. supra* note 33, p. 175: 'A doctrine is fully comprehensive when it covers all recognized values and virtues within one rather precisely articulated scheme of thought; whereas a doctrine is only partially comprehensive when it comprises certain (but not all) non-political values and virtues and is rather loosely articulated'.

Second, the normative development of state/society and religious traditions respectively takes place at an often very different pace. Religious norms are, generally speaking, more slow to evolve than the norms of society. It follows that in the endeavour to accept and implement change, religious communities typically lag behind society and state. Again, this tendency is particularly characteristic of conservative and orthodox movements.

As a result of these characteristics, it is a complicated and slow process to reinvent religious norms and practices in order to bring about such changes which in a number of areas would be necessary if a consensus between religious practices and human rights should be reached. In other words, the discourse calling for increased harmony between the two spheres – a harmony resting on the acceptance of human rights norms by the religious communities – has created a problem that is very difficult to solve. However, the overlapping consensus which exists between human rights and the religious sphere as far as some basic notions as well as some specific rights are concerned may have a positive effect on areas of discrepancies.

### *D. Sustainable solutions*

The sense of substantial overlapping consensus makes religious communities and individuals belonging to these communities ready for dialogue with the state and at the same time legitimizes such endeavours. Indeed, very extensive discussions about the most problematic issues in relation to human rights already take place within most of the religious communities, among theologians and other scholars, as well as lay people.[38]

With the aim of finding sustainable solutions which respect human rights norms as well as religious norms, we recommend in particular the following two avenues for future interaction between, on the one hand, state and society and, on the other hand, religious communities and individuals:

First, the state must inform individuals about their legal rights and obligations, thus reaffirming the rights of the individual. For example, with regard to family matters, where religious traditions might play an important albeit non-legal role in many individuals' situation, it is important that the individuals concerned may be informed about their actual rights and legal remedies regarding, for instance, marriage, divorce or the acquisition or inheritance of property; in such cases, information can take the form of a document distributed by the competent authorities amongst both members and leaders of religious communities, and which makes clear that only civil law is legally binding and that religious rules have no legal effect in the country.

---

[38] An example of inter-religious dialogues dedicated to find shared ways to promote universal human rights – specific human rights and the human rights catalogue as a whole – is the International Council for Christians and Jews, an umbrella organisation of 38 national Jewish-Christian dialogue organisations worldwide. See: <www.ICCJ.org>.

Second, the state should engage in systematic dialogues with the religious communities, making use of the overlapping consensus on central human rights notions and principles. Such dialogues will benefit from the in-depth debate and discussion about human rights issues which takes place within most of the religious communities, among theologians and other scholars as well as lay people, for instance about gender equality and roles, circumcision, marriage and divorce, and homosexuality. These non-legal debates should be acknowledged as an essential part of the solution to clashes between religious norms and individual human rights.

The dialogue could, for instance, take the following forms: first, the state could facilitate an ongoing dialogue between the authorities and the religious communities in order for the legislative and administrative authorities to comprehend the actual existence, nature and extent of a particular problem. In addition, it would ensure that the authorities have the means to make a qualified proportionality assessment in their attempt to find solutions to the problem. Second, as a support of initiatives of the religious communities to solve a problem, the state could, at the request of religious communities or individuals, attempt to offer legal assistance in some specific cases. Although such legal assistance may not offer a complete solution to the problem, it will serve as a signal, supporting the religious communities in their efforts to comply with human rights norms.

## 4. Conclusion

A current and future challenge facing Europe in the field of religious freedom is the problem of identifying the legitimacy and usefulness of state intervention in cases where religious norms clash with the human rights legal system. Central to this identification is an assessment of whether normative harmonization is in fact necessary. We have argued that the state must acknowledge the existence of inevitable discrepancies between religious and human rights norms as well as the desirability of reducing them.

In our suggested redefined version of the Classical model, we have combined traditional limited state intervention with increased information offered by the state about human rights as well as with increased dialogue between the state and the religious sphere.

Concluding this argument, two preconditions for a meaningful dialogue should be underlined.

First, trust between the state and the religious sphere is a decisive factor in the implementation of human rights norms in the space occupied by the religious communities, its leaders and members. Trust facilitates the acceptance of religious authorities of state assistance as legitimate and sometimes necessary, and encourages the state to have faith in the religious communities' capacity and willingness to endorse human rights.

Second, the willingness and ability of religious communities to endorse human rights are decisive. A great number of religious leaders and lay people in Europe constantly struggle to make sense of their religious traditions in order to make them more than mere museum pieces or prisons for the modern individual. Even very conservative communities have shown that they have the capacity to adapt to the demands of modern society, sometimes demonstrating an immense creativity to accommodate yet circumvent very strict rules.[39] Thus many would subscribe to the words of the Israeli author Amos Oz, who, challenged on his sometimes controversial use of Judaic texts, replied defiantly: 'I don't see myself as a museum keeper. I do not belong to tradition, tradition belongs to me.'[40]

---

39 An example is the creation of the *eruv* of the North West London's Orthodox Jewish Community, which permits Jews to follow the Sabbath rules also outside of their home. This *eruv* has a boundary 11 miles long and encloses an area of 6.5 square miles. In this area, observant Jews can carry or push objects on the Sabbath, without violating a Jewish law that prohibits carrying anything except within the home.

40 *The Independent*, 24 February 2001.

# 11
# Accessing Culture at the EU Level: An Indirect Contribution to Cultural Rights Protection?

*Evangelia Psychogiopoulou*

## 1. Introduction

It is generally acknowledged that culture may represent different things in different contexts, an element which complicates the formulation, understanding and scope of cultural rights. As suggested, culture may be regarded as the accumulated material heritage of humankind, it may be identified with the process of artistic creation or it may be viewed as the sum total of the material and spiritual activities of a given social group which distinguishes it from other similar communities.[1] Under the first conception of culture, cultural rights centre on access aspects with respect to this accumulated cultural capital, and are closely related to cultural development in terms of quantitative and qualitative growth in the cultural goods and services available to a given society. When culture is identified as a creative process, cultural rights focus on rights of access to cultural activity and free cultural expression with subsequent guarantees of free cultural enjoyment. In the case of culture regarded as a system of values and practices of a specific cultural group, cultural rights encompass rights to preserve, develop and have access to the culture of one's choice. They are primarily connected with protection and promotion of one's cultural identity.

Whatever definition of culture one may embrace to perceive cultural rights, cultural rights are hedged with access qualifications, viewed in terms of the concrete opportunities available for individuals or community groups to gain access to the culture that best matches their cultural profile. This access dimension of cultural

---

1 R. Stavenhagen, 'Cultural Rights: A Social Science Perspective', in A. Eide, C. Krause and A. Rosas (eds.), *Economic, Social and Cultural Rights* (2001), p. 85, at pp. 87-91.

Francioni and Scheinin (eds), *Cultural Human Rights*, 223–245
 ISBN 978 90 04 16294 5. Printed in the Netherlands.

rights incorporates both active and passive elements,[2] ranging from the freedom to engage in creative activity, innovate and further develop culture to the freedom to acquire cultural information, enjoy cultural goods and services or endorse cultural values. Embodied in the notion of *freedom of access to and participation in cultural life*, the access facet of cultural rights relies upon the promotion of socio-economic conditions, which enable individuals and groups to both produce and appreciate culture.

From a cultural rights perspective, the European Union (EU) represents a rather unique case study. Given the establishment of the common market, where persons, goods and services may circulate unhindered, respecting and promoting cultural rights evokes three different trajectories: ensuring access to one's culture in the state of origin, guaranteeing access to one's culture in a Member State other than the state of origin, and securing access to the cultural life of a Member State other than the state of origin. This three-pronged approach blurs the distinction commonly drawn between majorities and minorities in terms of cultural rights protection. Although attention is occasionally afforded to the cultural demands of particular vulnerable groups,[3] in an EU context, cultural rights are of relevance and importance for both majorities and minorities.

In an attempt to provide some insight into the way the EU is confronted with cultural rights, the analysis proceeds as follows. Section 2 identifies the EU's normative commitment to the protection of cultural rights, and highlights those provisions which allow for the development of policies with cultural impact. Given the absence of a precise legal basis for the formulation of genuine cultural rights action, as will be shown, sections 3 and 4 delve into the tools employed to stimulate access to cultural activity and cultural enjoyment, exploring whether the EU indirectly contributes to the realisation of cultural rights at Member States' level. Section 5 concludes by clarifying whether the EU has blazed a trail to expand cultural protection for Member States' nationals, and examines whether there is a real need for a proper EU cultural rights policy.

## 2. Cultural rights in the EU legal system

The EU constitutional texts do not contain any cultural rights as such. Though revised on several occasions since the 1957 Treaty of Rome – each enactment heralding

2 J. Symonides, 'Cultural Rights', in J. Symonides (ed.), *Human Rights: Concepts and Standards* (2000), p. 175, at pp. 189-190.

3 See, for instance, Act Concerning the Conditions of Fccession of the Kingdom of Norway, the Republic of Austria, the Republic of Finland and the Kingdom of Sweden and the Adjustments to the Treaties on which the European Union is founded, Protocol No. 3 on the Sami people, *OJ* C 241, 29/08/1994, p. 352.

a major step in advancing fundamental rights in the EU legal order[4] – there is no provision that binds the EU to actively pursue a cultural rights policy. Notwithstanding, various clauses contained in the Treaties and the Charter of Fundamental Rights of the European Union may have a role to play in the protection and promotion of cultural rights.

As a general statement, Article 6(1) TEU proclaims that '[t]he Union is founded on the principles of liberty, democracy, respect for human rights and fundamental freedoms, and the rule of law, principles which are common to the Member States'. The reference made to human rights potentially covers all categories of human rights, thus also cultural rights. Article 6(2) TEU further provides that '[t]he Union shall respect fundamental rights, as guaranteed by the European Convention for the Protection of Human Rights and Fundamental Freedoms [ECHR] signed in Rome on 4 November 1950 and as they result from the constitutional traditions common to the Member States, as general principles of Community law'. Although the ECHR accords priority to political and civil rights, many of its provisions can be read as incorporating cultural rights in the broader sense. Article 8 on respect for private and family life, Article 9 on freedom of thought, conscience and religion, Article 10 on freedom of expression, Article 11 on freedom of assembly and association and Article 14 which prohibits discrimination *inter alia* on the grounds of race, colour, language, religion, national or social origin and association with a national minority are crucial for the preservation of one's cultural features.[5] Their proclamation to general principles of Community law entails important consequences. On the one hand, such rights function as a limitation to the discretion of the European

---

4 Notwithstanding a preliminary mention of the promotion of fundamental rights in the preamble of the 1986 Single European Act, it was the Treaty of Maastricht which affirmed the EU's obligation to respect fundamental rights as guaranteed by the European Convention for the Protection of Human Rights and Fundamental Freedoms and as resulting from the constitutional traditions common to the Member States (ex-Article F(2), now Article 6(2) TEU). The Treaty of Amsterdam proudly pronounced in Article 6(1) TEU, applicable to all three pillars, that '[t]he Union is founded on the principles of liberty, democracy, respect for fundamental rights and fundamental freedoms, and the rule of law, principles which are common to the Member States'. It also established, by means of Article 7 TEU, a sanctioning mechanism against serious and persistent breaches of fundamental rights by the Member States (subsequently reinforced by the Treaty of Nice). Respect for fundamental rights was singled out as one of the admission conditions for any European state willing to join the EU club (Article 49 TEU), and the powers of the European Court of Justice were extended to cover a fundamental rights observance test with regard to the functioning of the European institutional apparatus (Article 46 TEU).

5 On the contribution of the ECHR to the protection of cultural rights, see Y. Donders, 'The Protection of Cultural Rights in Europe: None of the EU's Business?', *Maastricht Journal of European and Comparative Law* (2003), p. 117.

institutions.[6] Their protection must be ensured, and forms part of the European Court of Justice (ECJ)'s *acquis judiciaire*. On the other, Member States have a duty to respect relevant provisions when they act within the scope of EU law, that is, when they implement EU legislation or enact restrictions on the EC free movement principles. In this context, the ECJ can monitor their compliance performance.

Interestingly, the ECJ has broadened the scope of Article 6(2) TEU by including fundamental rights set out in other international treaties amongst the Union's principles.[7] One could argue therefore that Article 27 of the Universal Declaration of Human Rights and Article 15 of the International Covenant on Economic, Social and Cultural Rights (ICESCR), concerning the right to take part in cultural life, the right to benefit from the protection of the moral and material interests resulting from any literary or artistic production of which the beneficiary is the author, and the freedom indispensable for creative activity, amount to general principles of Community law. Plainly, the ECJ has so far shown little interest in drawing on the Universal Declaration of Human Rights and the ICESCR for inspiration in elucidating the content of the general principles of Community law.[8] At the time of writing, there has been no judgment specifically referring to their cultural rights safeguards.[9]

That being so, the Treaty establishing the European Community (EC) contains several provisions which generate rights for individuals closely linked to cultural protection. The common market freedoms merit attention in this respect. The ECJ has stated in several instances that cultural goods, in so far as they can be valued in money and form the object of a commercial transaction, are within the scope of the common market rules.[10] Articles 28 and 29 EC prohibiting quantitative restrictions and all measures having equivalent effect for intra-Community trade apply

6 See in this respect A. Von Bogdandy, 'The European Union as a Human Rights Organization? Human Rights and the Core of the European Union', *CML Rev*, (2000), p. 1307, at p. 1335.

7 See Case 4/73, *Nold v. Commission*, [1974] ECR 49, at para. 13.

8 See T. Ahmed and I. de J.Butler, 'The European Union and Human Rights: An International Law Perspective', *EJIL* (2006), p. 771, at pp. 772-775.

9 Note however that various formulations of cultural rights find their place in Member States' Constitutions, and could thus be construed as *common constitutional traditions*. Artistic freedom is protected in Germany, Italy, Greece and Portugal, and is implicitly covered by freedom of expression in many Member States. A state duty to protect, promote and develop domestic culture may be found in the Italian, Dutch, Spanish, Portuguese, Greek and some of the German Länder Constitutions. Authors' rights, protected by the right of property in most Member States, are explicitly recognised in Portugal. For detailed analysis, see B. De Witte and H.G. Post, 'Educational and Cultural Rights', in A. Cassese, A. Clapham and J. Weiler (eds.), *Human Rights and the European Community: The Substantive Law* (1991), p. 123, at pp. 130-133.

10 See, in particular, Case 7/68, *Commission v. Italy*, [1968] ECR 423.

to trade in cultural goods, and can be construed as ensuring individuals' freedom to unrestricted imports and exports of cultural goods.

Pursuant to Article 30 EC, discriminatory barriers to trade may be justified on grounds of 'public morality, public policy or public security; the protection of health and life of humans, animals or plants; *the protection of national treasures possessing artistic, historic or archaeological value*; or the protection of industrial and commercial property', provided they do not constitute a means of arbitrary discrimination or a disguised restriction of trade. Although the justification regarding national treasures has never been raised in litigation before the ECJ, it reflects a formal recognition of the special place that cultural goods of remarkable cultural significance occupy in the Community system.[11]

It is worthwhile noting that recourse to Article 30 EC to justify protectionist measures on general cultural policy grounds is not permitted. According to the Court, Article 30 EC, derogating from a fundamental rule of the Treaty, must be interpreted strictly and cannot be extended to cover objectives not expressly enumerated therein. To give an example, in *Leclerc*, the Court ruled that national legislation on book-price-fixing, enacted to protect creativity and cultural diversity at national level, could not escape the prohibition of Article 28 EC, since protecting cultural creation and diversity was not expressly mentioned in Article 30 EC.[12] Contrariwise, the Court did not oppose broad interpretation of derogations that are explicitly recognized. Protection of literary and artistic property by copyright was found to be covered by the protection of industrial and commercial property, which may justify restrictions to free movement of goods under Article 30 EC.[13]

Turning to free circulation of workers, the Court held that cultural professionals are within the scope of the EC Treaty as any other operators exercising an economic activity in a Member State other than the state of origin.[14] Taking the view that the exception of Article 39(4) EC with regard to employment in the public sector has to be narrowly interpreted,[15] and may not justify restrictions to the admission of non-nationals to certain functions in the public cultural sector, the Court affirmed

11 See generally P. Pescatore, 'Le commerce de l'art et le marché commun', 21 *Revue Trimestrielle de Droit Européen* (1985), p. 451, and A. Mattera, 'La libre circulation des oeuvres d'art à l'intérieur de la Communauté et la protection des trésors nationaux ayant une valeur artistique, historique ou archéologique', *RMUE* (1993), p. 9.

12 Case 229/83, *Leclerc v Au blé vert*, [1985] ECR 1.

13 See Joined Cases 55/80 and 57/80, *Musik-Vertrieb membrane GmbH et K-tel International v. GEMA – Gesellschaft für musikalische Aufführungs – und mechanische Vervielfältigungsrechte*, [1981] ECR 147, and Case 341/87, *EMI Electrola GmbH v. Patricia Im – und Export and Others*, [1989] ECR 79.

14 See Case C-290/94, *Commission v. Greece*, [1996] ECR I-3285.

15 The Court held in *Commission v. Belgium* that the notion of 'employment within the meaning of Article 48(4) (now Article 39(4)) of the Treaty must be connected with the specific activities of the public service in so far as it is entrusted with the exercise of powers conferred by public

that Greece, by imposing a Greek nationality condition as regards access to musicians' posts at the Athens opera and in municipal and local orchestras, failed to fulfil its obligations under Article 39 EC.[16]

With respect to freedom to provide services and freedom of establishment, the ECJ similarly asserted that the principle of free movement applies to both operators providing cross-border cultural services and self-employed cultural actors.[17] As to derogations, the Court excluded the possibility of bringing cultural justifications within any of the permitted grounds for exemption under Article 46 EC (public policy, public security and public health), which relates to the right of establishment, but also applies to services by means of Article 55 EC.[18] Cultural considerations do not ground any authorized exemption.

Certainly, following the seminal *Cassis de Dijon* ruling,[19] it was acknowledged that impediments to cross-border mobility and trade, arising from generally applicable national rules (i.e. rules which do not distinguish on grounds of origin), can be justified by imperative reasons relating to the public interest, a notion defined widely, to incorporate national cultural policy goals pertaining to fulfilment of cultural rights. To illustrate, protecting national historical and artistic heritage,[20] facilitating the widest possible dissemination of knowledge of a country's patrimony,[21] and safeguarding freedom of expression of the various (in particular, social, cultural, religious and philosophical) components of a Member State[22] have been accepted as grounds on which indistinctly applicable restrictions to free movement could be justified. Of course, the balance between market integration and the protective function of national legislative or administrative practice has been carefully circumscribed. For a Member State successfully to plead a mandatory requirement in its defence, the

law and with responsibility for safeguarding the general interests of the State'. See Case 149/79, *Commission v. Belgium*, [1982] ECR 1845, at para. 7.

16 *Supra* note 14.

17 See, in particular, Cases 155/73, *Sacchi*, [1974] ECR 409, and 197/84, *P. Steinhauser v. City of Biarritz*, [1985] ECR 1819.

18 See, for instance, Case C-17/92, *Federación de Distribuidores Cinematográficos v. Estado Español et Union de Productores de Cine y Televisión*, [1993] ECR 2239. On whether there is scope for the Member States to bring cultural policy justifications on grounds of public policy under Article 46 EC, see G. Karydis, 'Le juge communautaire et la préservation de l'identité culturelle nationale', *Revue Trimestrielle de Droit Européen* (1994), p. 551, at pp. 557-558.

19 Case 120/78, *Rewe-Zentral AG v. Bundesmonopolverwaltung für Branntwein (Cassis de Dijon)*, [1979] ECR 649.

20 Case C-180/89, *Commission v. Italy*, [1991] ECR 709.

21 Case C-154/89, *Commission v. France*, [1991] ECR I-659. See also Case C-198/89, *Commission v. Greece*, [1991] ECR 727.

22 Cases C-353/89, *Commission v. Netherlands*, [1991] ECR 4069, and C-288/89, *Stichting Collectieve Antennevoorziening Gouda and others v. Commissariaat voor de Media*, [1991] ECR 4007.

schemes under review have been required not only to apply without distinction on the basis of origin, but also to be necessary, appropriate and proportionate to the cultural goals pursued.

Apart from the Community's freedom rights, the principle of equal treatment can also be seen from a cultural standpoint. The prohibition of any discrimination on grounds of nationality, prescribed by Article 12 EC, applies to the cultural domain, and hence guarantees access to cultural activity irrespective of nationality conditions. In addition, Article 13 EC, by empowering the Council to combat discrimination based, amongst others, on racial or ethnic origin and religion or belief, contributes to the preservation of the cultural characteristics of individuals residing in the EU, precisely because race, ethnic background and religion are important elements of one's cultural identity.[23]

That said, it should be stressed that the EU and EC Treaties strongly abide by cultural diversity precepts. Whilst Article 6(3) TEU stipulates that '[t]he Union shall respect the national identities of its Member States', preservation and promotion of cultural diversity forms the mainspring of Article 151 EC, dedicated to culture.[24] The tactics employed to avoid any arrangements which might jeopardize cultural plurality are based on a set of both explicit and implicit powers. Paragraph 1 of Article 151 EC stipulates that '[t]he Community shall contribute to the flowering of the cultures of the Member States, while respecting their *national* and *regional* diversity, and at the same time bringing the common cultural heritage to the fore'. According to paragraph 2, internal Community cultural activity must be aimed at encouraging cooperation between the Member States and, if necessary, supporting and supplementing their action, so as to improve the knowledge and dissemination of the culture and history of European peoples, safeguard the cultural heritage of European significance, promote non-commercial cultural exchanges and facilitate literary and artistic creation, including in the audio-visual sector. Further, on the international scene, the EC is invited, under Article 151(3) EC, together with the Member States, to foster cooperation with third countries and international organizations active in the cultural sphere, in particular with the Council of Europe.

---

23 See, for instance, Article 3(g) of Council Directive 2000/43/EC implementing the principle of equal treatment between persons irrespective of racial or ethnic origin, OJ L 180, 19/7/2000, p. 22, which might encourage the emergence of a favourable environment for multicultural education.

24 For detailed analysis see B.F. Lévy, *Les compétences culturelles de la Communauté Européenne* (2004), at pp. 275-352, R. Craufurd Smith, 'Community Intervention in the Cultural Field: Continuity or Change?', in R. Craufurd Smith (ed.), *Culture and European Union Law* (2004), p. 19, at pp. 49-53, N.N. Shuibhne, *EC Law and Minority Language Policy: Culture, Citizenship and Fundamental Rights* (2002), at pp. 107-114, and B. De Witte, 'The Cultural Dimension of Community Law', *Collected Courses of the Academy of European Law* (1993), *IV-1*, p. 229, at p. 291-299.

The implicit cultural powers of the Community are unfolded in paragraph 4 of Article 151 EC, the so-called 'cross-sectional' or 'policy-linking' cultural clause, according to which '[t]he Community shall take cultural aspects into account in its action under other provisions of this Treaty, in particular in order to respect and to promote the diversity of its cultures'. By requiring the integration of cultural reasoning in the elaboration of the various EC Treaty provisions, Article 151(4) EC coins the protection and promotion of cultural diversity as a transversal, horizontal EC policy principle, which has to underpin overall Community action. Evidently, cultural diversity is seen in both a negative (to respect) and a positive (to promote) sense, which means that the EC is not simply bound to refrain from interfering with its enjoyment but also under a duty to take appropriate measures to further encourage it.

A more moderate approach is followed by the Charter which in Article 22 states that '[t]he Union shall respect cultural, religious and linguistic diversity'. While it may be inferred from Article 151(1) EC that the provision covers both diversity *between* and *within* the Member States, it does not require a proactive role on the part of the European institutions, or the Member States when they implement EU law, to confer positive rights on individuals and groups. Instead, the clause is tied to the concept of non-interference, giving concrete expression to the task entrusted primarily to the EU institutions of avoiding jeopardizing cultural differentiation when exercising their competences.[25] The same 'negative obligation' pattern is discernible in Article 13 on freedom of the arts, as well as in relation to the right of the elderly 'to participate in social and cultural life', enshrined in Article 25.[26]

Similarly to the ECHR, which incorporates no rights explicitly referring to culture, the Charter does not safeguard a general right to participate in cultural life, as prescribed by the ICESCR, or a right to protect, promote and enjoy culture. Concerns pertaining to cultural rights occupied a marginal place in its drafting; they were left to be addressed in a much broader sense by other provisions that might acquire a cultural dimension: Article 7 on respect for private and family life, Article 10 on freedom of religion, Article 11 on freedom of expression and pluralism of the media, Article 12 on freedom of assembly, Article 14 on the right to education and Article 21 on equal treatment.[27]

---

25 Taking note of the fact that Article 22 forms part of Chapter III on Equality, and that affirmative action is often required to achieve substantive equality in addition to formal equality, the provision might be read as extending beyond mere negative obligations. See supra note 5, at p. 142.

26 Note that, in other instances, the Charter explicitly calls for the adoption of positive measures designed to fulfil the rights incorporated in it. See, for example, Article 23 on equality between men and women and Article 26 on the integration of persons with disabilities.

27 The latter, building on Article 13 EC, has added, amongst others, colour, language, opinion and membership of a national minority amongst the prohibited grounds for discrimination.

The legal effect of the Charter is for the time being that of a declaration,[28] which, moreover, is not intended to provide a catalogue of substantive human rights but rather to codify the existing rights recognized at the EU level, so as to render them more visible to the European citizen and exemplify their relevance in the minds of policy-makers and legislators.[29] It is difficult therefore to imagine individuals and communities enforcing their rights before European or national courts. Should the Charter become legally binding, it will inevitably bear the mark of similar concerns, as the majority of its provisions, formulated in general terms, are unlikely to acquire direct effect, the final decision lying, of course, with the ECJ.

On the basis of the preceding analysis, the balance sheet offers a mixed picture. First, cultural rights may be perceived as general principles of Community law, despite the ECJ's reluctance to openly rely on the cultural liberties of the Universal Declaration of Human Rights and the ICESCR. Secondly, the EU constitutional texts contain a series of provisions, which either confer on Member State nationals rights that can be exercised in the cultural field or allow for the development of policies, responsive to the need to preserve Member States' national and regional cultural diversity. Yet, no legal basis exists that enables the design and implementation of a genuine EU cultural rights policy.

Arguably, ensuring strict respect for free movement rights and the principle of non-discrimination, and launching initiatives to preserve the Union's cultural richness indirectly contribute to protection and enhancement of cultural rights by the Member States. This is highly likely when the action taken has as its object or effect the stimulation of those factors apt to improve access to, and participation in, cultural life, the common denominator of all possible manifestations of cultural rights. The following sections serve to verify whether the European institutions have proved innovative in providing an implicit route for the encouragement of a cultural rights ethos within the Member States.

## 3. Free movement rights and equal treatment: tracing multi-cultural standards in judicial review

In the course of the years, the ECJ has been called upon, on numerous occasions, to determine the legality of Member States' restrictive legislative and administrative

[28] Given extensive use of the Charter's provisions by Advocates General and the Court of First Instance, it has been suggested that the Charter, though not formally binding, already has much legal bite. See, in particular, A.J. Menéndez, 'Chartering Europe: Legal Status and Policy Implications of the Charter of Fundamental Rights of the European Union', *Journal of Common Market Studies* (2002), p. 471.

[29] Lord Goldsmith Q.C., 'A Charter of Rights, Freedoms and Principles', *CML Rev.* (2001), p. 1201, at pp. 1204.

schemes in the field of culture. In adjudicating the compatibility of domestic laws and regulations with Community law, it has dealt with various types of cases. Next to rulings indirectly improving access to local cultural activity for nationals of the Member States exercising their free movement rights, it is possible to identify disputes which raised fundamental questions about protection and promotion of one's cultural identity.

Regarding the first category of judgments, *Steinhauser* and *Commission v. Spain* are illuminating.[30] *Steinhauser* arose from the refusal of French administrative authorities to allow a German professional artist to participate in a tendering procedure for allocation of public property used for the exhibition and sale of craft products on grounds of nationality. The Court held that the discrimination suffered by the cultural operator fell within the scope of Article 43 EC. In *Commission v. Spain*, discriminatory rules on admission to state museums based on nationality were found to breach Article 49 EC on free provision of services. In both cases, by demanding compliance with free movement principles, the Court simultaneously supported increased access to, and participation in, the cultural life of a Member State other than the state of origin. Whereas *Steinhauser* encouraged performance of cultural activities in the host country, in *Commission v. Spain* equal access to culture for all Community nationals, irrespective of nationality considerations, was ensured.

More prominently, in *Gerritse* the Court sought to reform Member States' tax withholding income systems, likely to discourage provision of cultural services in a Member State other than the state of residence.[31] The proceedings originated in a dispute between a Dutch musician who performed as a drummer at a radio station in Berlin, and the German tax authorities, who taxed him at source for his performance at a flat rate of 25 per cent, without deduction of business expenses. The Court held that domestic legislation, by requiring non-residents to be taxed on their gross income without deduction of business expenses, whilst residents were taxed on their net income after deduction of expenses, operated to the detriment of other Member State nationals and therefore constituted indirect discrimination on grounds of nationality, in violation of Article 49 EC. No less importantly, the Court observed that the distinction drawn between non-residents (subject to a definitive tax at the uniform rate of 25 per cent) and residents (subject to taxation on the basis of a progressive table including a tax-free allowance) could not be justified on objective differences in situation between Gerritse and residents in Germany. Since advantages comparable to those claimed by Gerritse were similarly granted in the Netherlands, for the Court, Gerritse was placed in a situation comparable to residents in Germany. Application to him of a higher rate of income tax than

30 See Cases 197/84, *supra* note 17, and 45/93, *Commission v. Spain*, [1994] ECR I-911.

31 ECJ, Case C-234/01, *Arnoud Gerritse v. Finanzamt Neukölln-Nord*, [2003] ECR I-5933.

applicable to residents – an issue for the national court to verify – would constitute indirect discrimination.

The facts of the case and the reasoning employed by the Court may seem technical and unrelated to cultural considerations. Nonetheless, non-deductibility of business expenses and high withholding tax rates can limit artists' mobility by strongly influencing the choice of a place of performance.[32] The Court's readiness to align Member States' withholding income systems with free movement enhances participation in the cultural life of a Member State other than the state of residence, and supports an increase in the range of cultural services available.

In other instances, by ensuring respect for free movement and the principle of non-discrimination, the Court has ultimately sustained preservation of the cultural identity of Member State nationals exercising free movement rights. In *Mutsch*, for example, relating to a Luxembourg national, residing and pursuing an activity as an employed person in Belgium,[33] the Court ruled that the principle of free movement of workers as laid down in Article 39 EC (and Council Regulation 1612/68) allowed a national of a Member State residing in another Member State for the purpose of employment to require that criminal proceedings against him take place in German under the same conditions applying to Belgian citizens. In the same vein, in *Bickel and Franz*, the Court ascertained that the right of Italian nationals, residents in the Province of Bolzano, to have criminal proceedings conducted in German should be granted, pursuant to Article 12 EC, to German-speaking nationals of other Member States, occasionally or temporally present in the region.[34] Whilst in *Mutsch* domestic legislation was found to be discriminatory on the basis of nationality, in *Bickel and Franz*, it was the criterion of residence imposed by national legislation for acknowledgement of the right to have proceedings in German that proved decisive in the Court's assessment. Notably, by mandating extension of domestic linguistic benefits to nationals of other Member States, the ECJ hinted at the need to protect language, one of the most sensitive aspects of one's cultural identity.

*Konstantinidis* addressed similar concerns. The case related to the entry of the name of a Greek national, settled in Germany as a self-employed person, in civil status registers, and using a form of spelling to which he objected.[35] The Court took the position that adoption of legislative or administrative rules for transcription of names in Roman characters was incompatible with freedom of establishment, in

---

32 In Germany, following the 1996 tax increase for foreign artists, the number of performances is reported to have fallen by 33%. See in this respect D. Molenaar, 'International Obstacles for International Performing Artists', *European Taxation* (2002), p. 149, at pp. 149.

33 Case 137/84, *Criminal proceedings against Rober Heinrich Maria Mutsch*, [1985] ECR 2681.

34 ECJ, Case C-274/96, *Criminal proceedings against Horst Otto Bickel and Ulrich Franz*, [1998] ECR I-7637.

35 ECJ, Case C-168/91, *Christos Konstantinidis v. Stadt Altensteig – Standesamt and Landratsamt Calw – Ordnungsamt*, [1993] ECR 1191.

so far as their application caused Member State nationals such a degree of inconvenience as to interfere with the exercise of establishment rights. Unsurprisingly, the Court clarified that such interference occurs when Member State nationals are obliged by the legislation of the state in which they are established to use a spelling that modifies the pronunciation of their name, and thus 'exposes [them] to the risk that potential clients may confuse [them] with other persons'.[36] Nevertheless, the statement made by Advocate General Jacobs that 'it is our name that gives us a sense of identity, dignity and self-esteem', reveals that considerations pertaining to cultural protection influenced the outcome of the case.[37]

In *Garcia Avello*, the Court itself acknowledged this point, building upon Article 12 on non-discrimination and Articles 17 and 18 EC on Union citizenship.[38] Proceedings concerned the refusal of the Belgian administration to change the surname of the children of a married couple residing in Belgium, Carlos Garcia Avello, a Spanish national, and Isabelle Weber, a Belgian national, from 'Garcia Avello' to 'Garcia Weber'. The children, both having dual Spanish and Belgian nationality, were born in Belgium, and registered by domestic authorities, in accordance with Belgian law, under the patronymic surname of their father, i.e. 'Garcia Avello'. In line with Spanish custom, however, the children were also registered with the consular section of the Spanish Embassy in Belgium under the family name 'Garcia Weber', namely the first surname of the father followed by that of the mother. Claiming that the children should bear the name to which they are entitled according to Spanish law and tradition, Garcia Avello challenged the refusal of the Minister of Justice to modify the children's name before the *Conseil d'Etat*. The domestic court stayed proceedings, and asked the ECJ for a preliminary ruling.

Contrary to the views expressed by the Belgian state and the Danish and Netherlands governments, the Court stated that the case under review came within the scope of Community law and, in particular, the EC Treaty provisions on EU citizenship. Recalling that Article 17 EC confers the status of EU citizen on every person holding the nationality of a Member State, the Court held that Garcia Avello's children, possessing the nationality of two Member States, enjoyed such status. Consequently, they should enjoy equal treatment when exercising the fundamental freedoms guaranteed by the Treaty, especially those involving freedom to move and reside freely within the territory of the Member States, conferred by Article 18 EC. Being nationals of one Member State (Spain) lawfully resident in the territory of another Member State (Belgium), the children could rely on the right set out in

---

36 *Ibid.*, at para. 16.

37 See Opinion of Advocate General Jacobs delivered on 9 December 1992, Case C-168/91, *supra* note 35, at para. 40.

38 ECJ, Case C-148/02, *Garcia Avello*, [2003] ECR I-11613.

Article 12 EC not to suffer discrimination on grounds of nationality with regard to the rules governing their surname.[39]

Stressing that Article 12 EC does not only prohibit Member States to treat comparable situations differently, but also to treat different situations in the same way, the Court found that Garcia Avello's children were subjected to discriminatory treatment. Given their dual Spanish and Belgian nationality, their situation was different from that of persons possessing only Belgian nationality and identified by one surname alone; they had divergent surnames under Belgian and Spanish legislation. According to the Court, such a discrepancy was 'liable to cause serious inconvenience … at both professional and private levels resulting from, *inter alia*, difficulties in benefiting, in one Member State of which they [were] nationals, from the legal effects of diplomas or documents drawn up in the surname recognised in another Member State of which they [were] also nationals'.[40]

Rejection of the argument, adduced by the Danish government, that a common regime on attribution of names would encourage integration of Spanish nationals into Belgium made clear that freedom to move and reside within the territory of the Member States must not lead to cultural assimilation. Again, the opinion of Advocate General Jacobs is instructive: the concept 'of moving and residing freely in the territory of the Member States is not based on the hypothesis of a single move from one Member State to another, to be followed by integration into the latter. The intention is rather to allow free, and possibly repeated or even continuous, movement within a single area of freedom security and justice, in which both cultural diversity and freedom from discrimination are ensured'.[41]

The Court's rigour in demanding compliance with EC free movement provisions and the principle of non-discrimination reflects market integration precepts, widely espoused in the EC legal order. But, beyond this, it indicates the creation of a free market space where multicultural standards prevail. On the one hand, an open, borderless, cultural market of goods, services and operators significantly increases prospects of cultural interaction. By widening the range of cultural choices available to Member State nationals, the opportunities for access to, and participation in, cultural life are inevitably multiplied. On the other, protection of the cultural identity of Member State nationals exercising free movement rights is highly valued. Establishment of the common market must not cause loss of cultural diversity but rather prompt diffusion of various cultural practices.

---

39 The mere fact that the children had also Belgian nationality and that the state of residence only recognised that nationality could not rule out application of Article 12 EC.

40 *Supra* note 38, at para. 36.

41 See Opinion of Advocate General Jacobs delivered on 22 May 2003, Case C-148/02, *cit. supra* note 38, at para. 72.

## 4. EC action to protect Member States' cultural diversity

The EC strives, in its internal cultural conduct, to create a common area founded on the acceptance and recognition of Member States' diverse cultural patterns. Preservation of national and regional cultural identities forms the starting point of EC initiatives to sustain the production and distribution of cultural content, and conserve cultural heritage. The mechanisms used to that purpose are primarily based on financial assistance. Funding opportunities come under the EC cultural policy *stricto sensu* and other Community policies that indirectly contribute to the maintenance of Member States' cultural diversity.

### *A. EC cultural action under Article 151 EC*

The legal basis for the launch of culture-related initiatives may be found in paragraph 5 of Article 151 EC which restricts the instruments that may be used for the attainment of EC cultural policy objectives to mere incentive measures and recommendations. Unanimity is imposed for their adoption, and harmonization of the laws and regulations of the Member States is excluded. The soft law approach prescribed has translated into a number of support measures, designed to give vent to creativity and rejuvenate the distribution of cultural goods and services. Between 1996 and 1999 three sectoral framework programmes were launched, providing financial assistance to cooperation projects carried out by operators from various Member States: Kaleidoscope focusing on performing, visual and applied arts; Ariane supporting books and reading, including translations; and Raphael which engaged the theme of heritage protection.[42]

With a view to increasing the effectiveness and consistency of Community cultural action, a single guidance and programming framework for cultural cooperation was introduced in 2000, *Culture 2000*.[43] The programme operated from 1 January 2000 until 31 December 2004, with a total budget of €167 million. Its duration was subsequently extended to December 2006, with a financial allocation of up to €236.5

---

[42] Decision 719/96/EC of the European Parliament and of the Council of 29 March 1996 establishing a programme to support artistic and cultural activities having a European dimension (Kaleidoscope), *OJ* L 99, 20/4/1996, p. 20, Decision 2085/97/EC of the European Parliament and of the Council of 6 October 1997 establishing a programme of support, including translation, in the field of books and reading (Ariane), *OJ* L 291, 24/10/1997, p. 26, and Decision 2228/97/EC of the European Parliament and of the Council of 13 October 1997 establishing a Community action programme in the field of cultural heritage (Raphael), *OJ* L 305, 8/11/1997, p. 31.

[43] Decision 508/2000/EC of the European Parliament and of the Council of 14 February 2000 establishing the Culture 2000 programme, *OJ* L 63, 10/3/2000, p. 1.

million.[44] Aimed to establish 'a cultural area common to the European people',[45] *Culture 2000* sought to intensify cooperation between cultural operators in all artistic and cultural disciplines. Amongst its key objectives were the 'promotion of cultural dialogue and of mutual knowledge of the culture and history of European peoples', stimulating 'creativity and the transnational dissemination of culture', 'highlighting cultural diversity and the development of new forms of cultural expression' and 'improved access to and participation in culture in the European Union for as many citizens as possible'.[46] Complementary to initiatives launched at the national level, the programme supported three distinct types of cultural action: specific innovative and/or experimental actions; integrated actions covered by structured, multi-annual cultural cooperation agreements; and special cultural events with a European and/or international dimension.

The first category related to projects carried out in partnership or in the form of networks for a period of one year by operators from at least three different states participating in the programme. Considerable attention was afforded to 'facilitating access to culture and wider cultural participation by the people in Europe, in all their social, regional and cultural diversity'.[47] Community support, not exceeding 60 per cent of the total project budget, ranged from €50,000 to €150,000 per year.

The second action group covered projects possessing a European dimension, of up to three years' duration, involving operators from at least five states participating in the programme. Intended to create sustainable cultural networks, Community assistance was fixed at 60 per cent of total project costs, implemented through cultural cooperation agreements, with a ceiling of €300,000 per year in Community finance. Endowments sought to facilitate circulation of cultural goods and mobility of artists, cultural training and heritage protection, multilingualism, dissemination of cultural information and use of new technologies in the cultural domain.[48]

'Special cultural events' referred to projects of substantial scale and scope, devised to strike 'a significant chord with the people of Europe', and increase 'their sense of belonging to the same community' while 'making them aware of the cultural diversity of the Member States'.[49] Support here was limited to 60 per cent of total project costs, with different funding ceilings applicable according to the nature of

---

44 Decision 626/2004/EC of the European Parliament and of the Council of 31 March 2004 amending Decision 508/2000/EC establishing the Culture 2000 programme, *OJ* L 99, 3/4/2004, p. 3.

45 *Supra* note 43, recital 7.

46 *Ibid.*, Art. 1.

47 *Ibid.*, Annex I, point I.1.(i).

48 *Ibid.*, Annex I., point I.2.

49 *Ibid.*, Annex I, point I.3.

activities financed, and covered initiatives, such as the 'European capitals of culture',[50] the award of European prizes in the fields of architecture and heritage conservation, and the 'European heritage laboratories' which encourage development and dissemination of innovative methods for the preservation of cultural sites accessible to the general public.

Alongside *Culture 2000*, from 2002 to 2004, budget lines A-3042, A-3015 and A-3035 directed financial assistance to preserve memorial sites of historical significance, and cover the management and operational costs of cultural organizations active at the European level. Within this framework, the European Bureau for Lesser-Used Languages and Mercator, both active in promoting regional and minority languages in Europe, were supported. In 2004, Decision 792/2004/EC codified these special actions into a specific action programme, operational until December 2006 with a total budget of €19 million.[51]

A wide-ranging evaluation exercise, carried out in 2001 with the aim of examining the effectiveness of EC cultural action, documented a dispersal of efforts and financial resources. Despite *Culture 2000*'s contribution to the recovery, valorization and documentation of heritage assets, the production and distribution of cultural content, and cultural training, the great variety of the objectives pursued was found to undermine overall coherence. Lengthy selection procedures, programme administration difficulties and inability to create or exploit synergies with actions providing support for European cultural organizations and 'cultural capitals' were further identified as impeding fruitful cultural collaboration.

An attempt to correct inconsistencies in EC cultural action, the Education, Audiovisual and Culture Executive Agency (EACEA) was established on 1 January 2005,[52] and a single financing and programming cultural instrument, operational

---

50 See Decision 1419/1999/EC of the European Parliament and of the Council of 25 May 1999 establishing a Community action for the European Capital of Culture event for the years 2005-2019, *OJ* L 166, 1/7/1999, p. 1. Decision No. 1622/2006 of the European Parliament and of the Council of 24 October 2006 establishing a Community action for the European Capital of Culture event for the years 2007 to 2019, *OJ* L 304, 3/11/2006, p. 1, amended the selection process laid down in Decision 1419/1999/EC and improved monitoring procedures.

51 Decision 792/2004/EC of the European Parliament and of the Council of 21 April 2004 establishing a Community action programme to promote bodies active at European level in the field of culture, *OJ* L 138, 30/4/2004, p. 40.

52 See Commission Decision of 14 January 2005 setting up the Education, Audiovisual and Culture Executive Agency for the management of Community action in the fields of education, audiovisual and culture in application of Council Regulation (EC) No. 58/2003, *OJ* L 24, 27/1/2005, p. 35. The Education, Audiovisual and Culture Executive Agency became operational on 1 January 2006. The Agency manages Community funded programmes and actions in the fields of education and training, active citizenship, youth, audiovisual and culture. Its activities include drawing up calls for proposals, selecting projects, signing project agreements, project monitoring, etc. It reports to the Directorates General Education and Culture (EAC) and Information Society and the Media (INFSO) of the European Commission.

for seven years, was adopted on 12 December 2006.[53] Whereas the EACEA seeks to improve programme management through the provision of technical and financial expertise, *Culture (2007-2013)*, building on *Culture 2000*'s experience, substitutes a more coordinated approach to cultural cooperation. With a total budget of €400 million, it concentrates on three objectives considered to offer maximum added value at the European level: enhanced transnational mobility of cultural players; increased circulation of works and cultural and artistic products; and reinforced intercultural dialogue.[54]

The programme allows for three levels of intervention. The first strand consists of direct financial support for cultural cooperation projects of variable length and scale. Community assistance may cover up to 50 per cent of total project costs for 'multi-annual cooperation projects', ranging from three to five years and implicating operators from at least six different participating countries.[55] It may also finance 'cooperation measures' for a maximum of 24 months, involving operators from three states participating in the programme.[56] Special actions can benefit from Community funding that does not exceed 60 per cent of the project budget.[57]

The second strand targets interventions of a more structural nature, providing for the grant of operating subsidies to highly specialized European organizations active in the field of culture. Relevant institutions must carry out their activities at European level – alone or in the form of coordinated associations – and cover at least seven European countries. Funds are distributed on the basis of annual calls for proposals, and may not cover more than 80 per cent of the bodies' admissible yearly expenditure.[58]

The final strand focuses on research and information sharing, to promote the exchange of experience and best practice. Grants can be awarded to develop comparative data that increase knowledge on cultural cooperation in Europe or maximize the impact of funded projects.[59] The role of cultural contact points, set up voluntarily at the national level to foster targeted, grass-roots dissemination of practical information on the programme, is particularly highlighted.[60] Community support seeks to facilitate access to *Culture* by as many operators as possible, create

---

53 Decision No. 1855/2006/EC of the European Parliament and of the Council of 12 December 2006 establishing the Culture Programme (2007-2013), *OJ* L 372, 27//12/2006, p. 1.

54 *Ibid.*, Article 3.

55 *Ibid.*, Annex, point 1.1.

56 *Ibid.*, Annex, point 1.2.

57 *Ibid.*, Annex, point 1.3.

58 *Ibid.*, Annex, point 2.

59 *Ibid.*, Annex, point 3.2 and 3.3.

60 *Ibid.*, Annex, point 3.1.

links with various national/regional institutions sustaining the cultural sector and disseminate information on other EC programmes open for cultural projects.

The laudable objective of broadening access to, and participation in, cultural life, directly linked to the very essence of cultural rights, requires the launch of measures which help improve the socio-economic conditions required to obtain cultural information and knowledge, engage in cultural activities or enjoy cultural assets. Embarking upon initiatives at EU level which stimulate mobility of cultural practitioners, reinforce the cross-border circulation of cultural goods and services and strengthen intercultural dialogue improves prospects of cultural creation and diffusion. Does a cultural policy, conceptualized in such terms, sustain Member States in their efforts to fulfil cultural rights? The answer should be in the affirmative. Creating an open space where cultures may freely interact automatically increases the chances that individuals and groups may access the culture of their choice. Provided with a vast variety of opportunities to participate in cultural life either via the establishment of cultural cooperation platforms or via an increase in the cultural goods and services available, individuals and the various communities residing within the EU may opt for those cultural activities and products which best fit their cultural characteristics.

### *B. Community policies and endowment to culture: the case of structural funds*

The EC's contribution to the preservation of Member States' cultural diversity does not manifest itself solely in the context of funding measures adopted within its cultural policy properly speaking. It is equally discernible in the action undertaken under other EC policy headings that may have an impact on cultural affairs. The generous application of the EC cultural state aid derogation regarding Member States' culture-orientated support schemes is clearly a case in point. On the basis of Article 87(3)(d) EC, the Commission has sanctioned a series of funding mechanisms, devised by national or regional authorities to increase participation in cultural creation, diversify the production of cultural output and promote enjoyment of heritage assets. Whilst relevant decisions have been discussed elsewhere and therefore will not be repeated here,[61] EC cohesion policy will form the core subject of analysis, as it represents an optimum platform for accommodation of cultural diversity considerations. Though maintenance of cultural distinctiveness, and stimulation of cultural life, in particular, do not amount to clear-cut objectives of EC activities in the field, cultural initiatives have been regularly used as an extra means to reduce

61 E. Psychogiopoulou, 'EC State Aid Control and Cultural Justifications', *Legal Issues of Economic Integration* (2006), p. 3.

development gaps among EC regions,[62] prompting the launch of domestic strategies favourably disposed to fulfilment of cultural rights.

From 2000 to 2006, the Structural Funds (SF), the Community's primary tool to redress regional development disparities,[63] grouped together the European Regional Development Fund (ERDF), the European Social Fund (ESF), the European Agricultural Guidance and Guarantee Fund (EAGGF) and the Financial Instrument for Fisheries Guidance (FIFG).[64] Reformed in 1999, with a view to increased effectiveness and simplified operation, the SF sustained attainment of three priority goals: promoting the development and structural adjustment of regions whose development was lagging behind (objective 1); encouraging economic and social conversion of areas facing structural difficulties (objective 2); and modernization of policies and systems of education, training and employment (objective 3). By channelling resources to cultural infrastructure, cultural activities and heritage conservation, the SF sought to develop the endogenous cultural potential of EC declining urban and rural areas, bringing issues of culture into the mainstream of regional development agendas.

The cultural dimension of funded programmes and projects varied widely. Some projects focused on conservation and better management of heritage assets, such as the unification of archaeological sites surrounding the Acropolis hill in Athens[65] and the creation of a folklore museum, presenting an impressive testimony of Saami culture in Sweden.[66] Attempts were also made to create spaces for cultural enjoyment. In Sheffield (UK), for instance, an underused urban wasteland was transformed into a cultural industries quarter, attracting more than a hundred cultural and media

---

62 See in this respect European Commission, Communication to the Council, the European Parliament, the Economic and Social Committee and the Committee of the Regions, Cohesion policy and culture, COM(1996) 512.

63 See Art. 159 EC, read in conjunction with Art. 158 EC.

64 See Council Regulation (EC) No. 1260/99 laying down general provisions on the Structural Funds, *OJ* L 161, 26/6/1999, p. 1, Regulation (EC) No. 1783/1999 of the European Parliament and of the Council of 12 July 1999 on the European Regional Development Fund, *OJ* L 213, 13/8/1999, p. 1, Regulation (EC) No. 1784/1999 of the European Parliament and of the Council of 12 July 1999 on the European Social Fund, *OJ* L 213, 13/8/1999, p. 5, Council Regulation (EC) No. 1257/1999 of 17 May 1999 on support for rural development from the European Agricultural Guidance and Guarantee Fund (EAGGF) and amending and repealing certain Regulations, *OJ* L 160, 26/6/1999, p. 80, and Council Regulation (EC) No. 1263/1999 of 21 June 1999 on the Financial Instrument for Fisheries Guidance, *OJ* L 161, 26/6/1999, p. 54.

65 From total project costs amounting to €3,85 million, the EC contributed €2,887,500. See project description, available at: < ec.europa.eu/comm/regional_policy/projects/stories/details.cfm?pay=GR&the=9&sto=875&la n=5>.

66 From total project costs amounting to €3.3 million, the EC contributed €1.254 million. See project description, available at: <ec.europa.eu/comm/regional_policy/projects/stories/details.cfm?pay=SE&the=9&sto=208&lan =5>.

businesses, ranging from art studios and exhibition galleries to film production and music recording firms.[67] Steps to bolster local economies through rational exploitation of cultural resources and an increase in the cultural goods and services available were frequent,[68] likewise measures to facilitate entry and integration into the cultural labour market of less advantaged, socially excluded, groups.[69] Although not directly associated with cultural rights, via endowments to culture, the action taken served to alleviate some of the main deterrents to participation in cultural life of underdeveloped EC regions. By directing financial assistance to the promotion of cultural activities and the modernization of cultural facilities and institutions, the SF sought to strengthen the cultural image of regions, transforming them into spaces where culture(s) may be widely accessed.

Minority cultures formed an integral part of the process. Indeed, by contrast to the EC cultural policy *stricto sensu*, which has so far refrained from embracing protection of minority cultures in a comprehensive manner, EC cohesion policy has triggered the launch of initiatives that enhance access to minority cultural activity. The basic conceptual approach followed for cohesion builds on the notion of partnership, which requires close involvement of sub-national bodies in the planning and implementation of development programmes. Bearing in mind that many of the regions benefiting from Community support are minority-inhabited areas, participation of regional actors in development structures creates fertile ground for minority cultural concerns to be taken on board.[70] EC cohesion policy, representing not just a policy *for* the regions but also a policy *by* the regions,[71] induces domestic authorities – some extremely keenly, others less enthusiastically – to incorporate minority cultural needs in their action.

In July 2006, the Council and the European Parliament adopted a new package of regulations to support regional growth for the period 2007-2013, structured on

---

67 The EC contributed ECU1.44 million. See project description, available at: <ec.europa.eu/comm/regional_ policy/projects/stories/details.cfm?pay=UK&the=9&sto=143&lan=5>.

68 See, in particular, the programmes financed for the development of the Öarna region in Sweden, East Flanders in Belgium, the Niedersachsen region in Germany, the eastern part of the Netherlands and the Alsace region in France, available at: <ec.europa.eu/comm/regional_policy/country/prordn/ index_en.cfm>.

69 See the Gabreta, Ancient crafting builds a future, Creative jobs for young people in Madeira and Promoting local commerce and craftsmen projects, available at: <ec.europa.eu/employment_social/esf2000/docs/d-20-en.pdf>, <ec.europa.eu/employment_social/esf/en/member/examples/youexamp/german2.htm>, <ec.europa. eu/comm/employment_social/esf2000/docs/pt2_en.pdf>, <ec.europa.eu/comm/employment_social/esf200 0/docs/fr5_en.pdf>.

70 For a detailed overview of the effects of EC cohesion policy on territorially concentrated minorities and their cultural politics, see the special issue 'Regions, Minorities and European Integration', *Romanian Journal of Political Science* (2007).

71 D. Allen, 'Cohesion and the Structural Funds: Transfers and Trade-Offs', in H. Wallace and W. Wallace (eds.), *Policy-Making in the European Union* (2000), p. 243, at p. 259.

the basis of three priority objectives: convergence; regional competitiveness and employment; and European territorial cooperation.[72] Intended to mobilize and reinforce regions' development capacity through economic diversification and job creation, the instruments established place renewed emphasis on structural interventions and adjustments likely to improve access to local cultural life. Under the convergence objective, the ERDF is explicitly required to encourage 'investments in culture, including protection, promotion and preservation of cultural heritage; development of cultural infrastructure in support of socio-economic development, sustainable tourism and improved regional attractiveness; and aid to improve the supply of cultural services through new higher added-value services'.[73] In seeking to enhance the adaptability of workers and industries to labour needs, access to employment and social inclusion, the ESF, in turn, traces the way for increased engagement in cultural creation. Due attention must be afforded, in particular, to 'pathways to integration and re-entry into employment for disadvantaged people', including 'minorities'.[74]

---

72 Council Regulation (EC) No. 1083/2006 of 11 July 2006 laying down general provisions on the European Regional Development Fund, the European Social Fund and the Cohesion Fund and repealing Regulation (EC) No. 1260/1999, *OJ* L 210, 31/7/2006, p. 25, Regulation (EC) No. 1080/2006 of the European Parliament and of the Council of 5 July 2006 on the European Regional Development Fund and repealing Regulation (EC) No. 1783/1999, *OJ* L 210, 31/7/2006, p. 1, Regulation (EC) No. 1081/2006 of the European Parliament and of the Council of 5 July 2006 on the European Social Fund and repealing Regulation (EC) No. 1784/1999, *OJ* L 210, 31/7/2006, p. 12, Council Regulation (EC) No. 1084/2006 of 11 July 2006 establishing a Cohesion Fund and repealing Regulation (EC) No. 1164/94, *OJ* L 210, 31/7/2006 p. 79, and Regulation (EC) No. 1082/2006 of the European Parliament and of the Council of 5 July 2006 on a European grouping of territorial cooperation (EGTC), *OJ* L 210, 31/7/2006, p. 19. To increase the added value of EC cohesion policy, aid for rural development and the fisheries sector has been integrated into the instruments of the common agricultural policy and the common fisheries policy (Council Regulation (EC) No. 1698/2005 of 20 September 2005 on support for rural development by the European Agricultural Fund for Rural Development (EAFRD), *OJ* L 277, 21/10/2005, p. 1, and Council Regulation (EC) No. 1198/2006 of 27 July 2006 on the European Fisheries Fund, *OJ* L 223, 15/8/2006).

73 See Regulation (EC) No. 1080/2006, cited above, Art. 4(7). Note that under the regional competitiveness and employment objective, action to protect and enhance natural and cultural heritage, and exploit natural and cultural assets in order to encourage sustainable tourism may also be supported (Art. 5(2)(f). The European territorial cooperation theme encourages cross-border economic, social and environmental activities that improve cultural capacity building and promote joint use of cultural infrastructure (Art. 6(1)(b) and (e)). Initiatives specifically intended to promote sustainable urban development on a transnational basis incorporate a cultural heritage protection concern as well (Art. 6(2)(d)).

74 See Regulation (EC) No. 1081/2006, *supra* note 72, Art. 3(1)(i).

## 5. Conclusion

The EU's active involvement in the preservation of Member States' diverse cultural systems, although not couched in terms of a 'cultural rights policy', significantly supports the emergence of an environment conducive to increased access to, and participation in, cultural life, vital for any regime of cultural rights protection. The main thrust of the initiatives launched, complementing domestic action, resides in the promotion of socio-economic factors that encourage cultural interaction and diffusion, providing an increased variety of cultural options for the European citizen both insofar as cultural creation and cultural enjoyment are concerned. The funding mechanisms elaborated by the EU, combined with an assortment of ECJ judgments that abide by multicultural standards, set the stage for reinforced participation in cultural activities and appreciation of cultural assets at national and regional level.

Admittedly, in view of the absence of a comprehensive and coherent EU human rights policy,[75] EU action is not specifically aimed to ensure respect for cultural rights. One could only speak of an indirect EU contribution to cultural rights protection. The influence exerted on Member States' cultural policies may have a positive impact on the realization of cultural rights by domestic, national or regional authorities, but this is not the primary objective that guides European institutions.

On the basis of such considerations it may be queried whether EU culture-driven endeavours obfuscate the need for a genuine EU cultural rights policy. The issue is highly contentious. This is not only because Member States are, in principle, free to devise and implement their domestic cultural policies as they consider most appropriate in accordance with national priorities and available resources,[76] but also because they, undoubtedly, remain the principal guardians of human rights in their own territories.[77] Internal cultural policy dynamics, coupled with general reticence to accept binding positive cultural rights obligations at supranational level, lie at the very heart of the parameters that mark the contours of EU action.

In the near future prospects for a concrete, fully-fledged EU cultural rights policy seem bleak. This should not, however, be used as a pretext for failing to further reflect upon the place cultural rights should occupy in the European integration process. Widespread demands for access to, and participation in, cultural life by Member State nationals who exercise their rights of movement caution the need for measures to preserve their cultural identity, assisting at the same time the discovery

---

75 P. Alston and J.H.H. Weiler, 'An "Ever Closer Union" in Need of a Human Rights Policy', in P. Alston (ed.), *The EU and Human Rights* (1999), p. 3, at p. 6.

76 Note that the Council in a Resolution of 25 July 1996 on access to culture for all emphasised that, 'in accordance with the principle of subsidiarity, promotion of wider access to culture within the Member States is the principal responsibility of the Member States' (*OJ* C 242, 21/8/1996, p. 1).

77 *Supra* note 75, at p. 7.

of new cultural frames. The time appears ripe to critically examine the cultural implications of the European project, inquiring into the role the Union can play in the emergence of all-inclusive, culturally diverse societies, founded on protection and enhancement of cultural liberties.

# 12
# Language Rights as Cultural Rights: A European Perspective

*Susanna Mancini and Bruno de Witte*

## 1. Introduction

For the purpose of this chapter, we will define language rights as fundamental rights protecting language-related acts and values. The term 'fundamental' denotes the fact that these rights are entrenched in the constitution of a country, or in an international treaty binding on that country. In this sense, language rights constitute limits to the ordinary operation of the politics of language within a state (or within a region or a supranational entity such as the European Union) which is expressed in statutes and administrative acts regulating the use of languages. A new development of recent decades is that these fundamental rights for individuals are no longer only to be found in (some) national constitutions, but that European law (comprising both Council of Europe and European Union norms) increasingly sets limits to national language policies in order to protect the linguistic rights of individuals.

The title of our chapter assumes that linguistic rights are part of the broader category of cultural rights, which in turn assumes that the category of cultural rights is not limited to the very few rights that are labelled as such (even if only implicitly) in the UN Covenant on Economic, Social and Cultural Rights. It is generally accepted that the use of a particular language not only serves as a means of functional communication, but also expresses that person's cultural identity as well as the cultural heritage developed by all previous speakers of that language. This point concerning cultural identity and cultural heritage is made in many international instruments. For example, Article 5(1) of the Framework Convention on National Minorities affirms that, for persons belonging to a minority, language forms one of the essential elements of their identity; the preamble of the European Charter of Regional and Minority Languages provides that 'the protection of the historical regional or minority languages of Europe, some of which are in danger of eventual extinction, contributes to the maintenance and development of Europe's

Francioni and Scheinin (eds), *Cultural Human Rights*, 247–284

cultural wealth and traditions'; the UNESCO Convention on the Intangible Cultural Heritage, in its Article 2, protects language as 'a vehicle of the intangible cultural heritage'. Restricting the use of a language is, then, not only a practical inconvenience for those who speak it, but also a potential threat to a person's cultural identity. Therefore, there is no doubt that linguistic rights are part – indeed, a very prominent part – of the broader category of cultural rights.

The core linguistic right is the right to speak one's language, or, more precisely, the language of one's choice. The core right is, or can be, accompanied by a series of ancillary rights without which the right to speak a language becomes less valuable for its beneficiaries, such as: the right to be understood by others (for example, by public authorities), the right to a translation or an interpretation from other languages (for example, in the course of a meeting or trial at which those other languages are spoken), the right to compel others to speak one's language, and the right to learn the language.

In terms of the legal recognition of these rights, a crucial distinction is that between the *private* and *official* use of the language. It is traditionally considered that states are free to decide whether, and to what extent, they allow the use of a plurality of languages for official purposes, in public administration and the courts, in the public service media and in public educational institutions. States can either opt for a system of rather strict linguistic uniformity (as do France and Germany) or give wide official recognition to regional and minority languages (as do Spain, Italy and the United Kingdom). However, the private use of language is not within the control of the State; as the UN Human Rights Committee held in its *Ballantyne* opinion of 5 May 1993, 'a State may choose one or more official languages, but it may not exclude, outside the spheres of public life, the freedom to express oneself in a language of one's choice'.[1]

This statement of the HR Committee points to another important legal feature of linguistic rights, namely the fact that they can be either directly and expressly protected as such, or indirectly or implicitly protected by general fundamental rights. Examples of *express protection* are Article 18 of the Swiss Constitution stating tersely: 'La liberté de la langue est garantie', and Article 27 of the UN Covenant of Civil and Political Rights according to which persons belonging to linguistic minorities 'shall not be denied the right, in community with the other members of their group, … to use their own language'. An illustration of *implicit protection* is provided precisely by the *Ballantyne* case: the Human Rights Committee held, quite rightly, that the *freedom of expression* naturally includes 'the freedom to express oneself in a language of one's choice', for example, in the case at hand, when advertising by means of commercial signs posted outside business premises. Although most

1 Human Rights Committee, 47th session, Communications Nos. 359/1989 and 385/1989, *John Ballantyne and Elizabeth Davidson, and Gordon McIntyre v. Canada*, views adopted on 31 March 1993, para. 11.4.

constitutional and international fundamental rights documents protect freedom of expression without highlighting the linguistic component of this freedom, that component is inherently part of freedom of expression.[2] The same is true with *equality and non-discrimination*. Although language is, in some constitutions and in some international human rights treaties, singled out as one of a series of 'suspect' grounds of discrimination, the principle of equality logically protects the right not to be discriminated on account of one's language even when this ground of discrimination is not spelled out in so many words. A third major instance of this implicit protection is the fundamental *right of education*. The freedom to establish private schools arguably includes the freedom to use the language of instruction for those schools, whereas the right to education might be considered to include a right to receive at least part of that education in one's mother tongue.[3]

None of the rights mentioned so far is absolute or unqualified, but the general introductory point which we wish to make is that arguments based on *general* fundamental rights can offer *prima facie* protection for language-related claims of persons (often belonging to a linguistic minority) and require the government to give good arguments why the language-related claim cannot be honoured in a given case.[4] The underlying consideration is that 'language should not be a liability in the enjoyment of one's general status of civil, social, and political rights and opportunities in society'.[5] However uncertain their precise substantive content may be, and however defective their enforcement, those general fundamental rights serve as a 'platform' on which weaker groups and individuals can stand in order to make their voices better heard.

The protection of linguistic *rights*, which is the primary focus of this chapter, stands in close relationship to the protection of linguistic *diversity*. Indeed, this relationship is so close that the EU Charter of Fundamental Rights and Freedoms, which is logically supposed to contain *rights*, also includes an Article 22 which does not use rights to language but rather states: 'The Union shall respect cultural, religious and linguistic diversity'. In other words, the authors of the Charter considered that the protection of the value of linguistic diversity is somehow part of the agenda of

---

2 For an elaboration of the argument that freedom of expression includes the freedom to express oneself in the language of one's choice, see F. de Varennes, 'Language and Freedom of Expression in International Law', *Human Rights Quarterly* (1994) 163.

3 On the linguistic dimension of educational rights, see the comparative law study by A. Milian i Massana, *Derechos linguisticos y derecho fundamental a la educación* (1994).

4 Generally, on the contribution of general fundamental rights to minority protection, see K. Henrard, *Devising an Adequate System of Minority Protection. Individual Human Rights, Minority Rights and the Right to Self-Determination* (2000), chapter II.

5 R. Rubio Marín, 'Language Rights: Exploring the Competing Rationales', in W. Kymlicka and A. Patten, *Language Rights and Political Theory* (2003) 52, at 63. This author proposes the term 'instrumental language rights' to describe this category, as opposed to non-instrumental language rights which protect the use of languages for its own sake.

fundamental rights protection in the European Union.[6] While recognizing this close link between the recognition of the value of linguistic diversity and the recognition of particular linguistic rights, we have preferred, in this chapter, to deal mainly with the latter, namely legal norms that protect specific linguistic entitlements which may be claimed by individual persons.

This emphasis on individual persons may sound surprising if one considers, as many scholars do, that linguistic rights are essentially group rights, or collective rights, rather than individual rights. However, the constitutional, European and international instruments that we will explore below do not attribute rights to a group but always to individual persons, and therefore to use the expression 'collective rights' might be misleading.[7] Often, these individual beneficiaries are identified by their membership of a group (for example, the Framework Convention on National Minorities contains linguistic rights that are reserved for persons belonging to a national minority), but in other cases there is no such group identification (as for example with the freedom from discrimination on grounds of language, which does not presuppose membership of any particular language group). Thus, linguistic rights may well protect collective *goods* (namely, the cultural value of a language and the collective identity of a language community), but that does not make them collective *rights* – not more so than, say, freedom of expression which also presupposes the existence of a collective audience to be truly meaningful.

In the following pages, we will start with an exploration of the national constitutional law of European countries, in recognition of the fact that linguistic rights are still primarily defined and regulated within the national context. This exploration will be structured on the basis of a typology of distinct constitutional models (section 2). After that, we will turn to the analysis of the common standards that have been developed at a transnational European level, in the context of the Council of Europe (section 3) and also in the context of the European Union (section 4). Although these common European standards have limited the previously complete discretion that states had in regulating language use, their relevance is limited and uneven. There is, arguably, not yet a 'comprehensive and coherent package'[8] of European (or international) linguistic rights, but it may be in the making.

---

6 On some of the interpretative puzzles raised by this Article 22, see Y. Donders, 'The Protection of Cultural Rights in Europe: None of the EU's Business?', *Maastricht Journal of European and Comparative Law* (2003) 117, at pp. 142-144.

7 We thus adopt a rather restrictive, but legally operational, view of the distinction between individual and collective rights, which is based on who is the formal beneficiary of the right. This corresponds, for example, to the view exposed in J. Ringelheim, 'Droits individuels et droits collectifs: avenir d'une équivoque', in E. Bribosia et L. Hennebel (dir.), *Classer les droits de l'homme* (2004) 231, at p. 231.

8 R. Dunbar, 'Minority Language Rights in International Law', *International and Comparative Law Quarterly* (2001) 90, at p.119.

## 1. National constitutional models

### A. *The constitutional irrelevance of minority languages*

Western political theories have traditionally neglected the claims of linguistic minorities. During the whole 19th century and the first part of the 20th century, the 'great nations' were seen as the carriers of historical development, while smaller, less developed nations could only progress by abandoning their national character and assimilating with one of the 'great nations'.[9] This concept of historical development, according to which progress and civilization require assimilation of smaller groups, was common both to the liberal tradition, as well as the Marxist-Leninist theory. Their different theoretical basis did not prevent both political theories from being basically hostile to minorities, on the common ground of ethnocentric nationalism.[10]

Traditional liberalism, which postulates the supremacy of individual rights and equal treatment of all, constitutes the premises of the French model of cultural indifference, based on the notion of popular sovereignty as a normative principle for democratic state organization, on the one hand, and the liberal notion of individual equality before the law regardless of race, language, sex, etc. on the other. In such 'a rigorously neutral state, that is, a state without cultural or religious projects or, indeed any sort of collective goals beyond the personal freedom ... of its citizens'[11] the *ethnos* is supposed to converge on the political community, irrespective of the existence of different groups, which are left to a merely 'existential' status.[12] Cultural-blindness does not obviously correspond to ideological neutrality. But when it comes to the specific field of language, state-blindness is actually impossible, as all states must function at least in one language. Therefore, the inclusion or exclusion of the official use of minority languages always represents a political and an ideological choice. In other words, it is undeniable that minority languages *de facto* exist, but from a strictly legal point of view, their relevance depends only on a state choice, as the French experience clearly shows.

Despite the image that arises from Article 2 of the Constitution, France can in fact be described as a true '*mosaique des cultures*'. Nevertheless, linguistic pluralism was never reflected in the French legal system: since the edict of Villers-Cotterets (1539) by King Francis I, the only official state language has been French. This official character became increasingly aggressive towards regional languages and cultures with the 1789 Revolution and the victory of the Jacobins. Various regulations of the Convention imposed the exclusive use of French in education and tribunals

---

9 E. Hobsbawm *Nation and Nationalism since 1780: Programme, Myth and Reality* (1990).

10 W. Kymlicka. (ed.), *The Rights of Minorities Cultures* (1995).

11 M. Walzer (1994), quoted by S. Tierney, *Constitutional Law and National Pluralism* (2004).

12 G. Koubi, *Droit et minorités dans la République française*, in A. Fenet (ed), *Le droit et les minorités. Analyses et textes* (1995) at. 200.

and prohibited the use of other languages such as 'the dialect called *bas Breton* and Basques and the Italian and German languages', guilty of having 'perpetuated the power of fanaticism and superstition, served the dominion of priests and aristocrats' and, finally, 'favoured the enemies of France'.[13] From the Abbé Grégoire to the Pedagogists of the Third Republic, there has been a constant application of the Jacobin centralist conception of French culture and society, unified at the expense of minority cultures and languages; in other words, the indivisibility of the state had to produce as a consequence the cultural and linguistic uniformity of its citizens[14] and, therefore, the monopoly of *Sa Majesté, la langue française.*[15]

Having said all this, it would be unfair not to recognize that minority languages do enjoy a certain degree of protection in France, although not as the expression of cultural diversity, but rather as part of the cultural richness of the country. The relationship between French and the regional languages is therefore asymmetrical, as they all coexist but the latter may not substitute the former. This principle of 'linguistic coexistence' is developed on the basis of two territorial criteria: the first concerns the protection of regional languages everywhere in the national territory, the second the use of regional languages at local level, where specific regimes may be applied for particular geographical, social, ethnic or cultural reasons.

The basis of the regime of regional languages at national levels was fixed by the *Loi Deixonne* of 1951 (now repealed), that recognized for the first time a (albeit instrumental) *droit à l'existence des langues régionales,*[16] which could be taught for no more than two hours per week and never on a compulsory basis. Moreover, teachers were authorized '*à recourir aux parlers locaux dans les écoles primaires et maternelles chaque fois qu'ils pourront en tirer profit pour leur enseignement,* notamment pour l'étude de la langue française' (Article 2) (emphasis added).

---

13 i B. Barère de Vieuzac (1755-1841), rapport du Comité de Salut public sur les idomes, 8 pluviose an II, 27 January 1794.

14 A. D. Smith, *The Ethnic Origins of Nations* (1986).

15 V. Delaporte, 'La loi relative à l'emploi de la langue française', in *Revue critique de droit international privé,* (1976). 448. For a critical reconstruction of the myth according to which French Republicanism has always been hostile to minority languages see J. Ziller, *Le droit français de la langue,* entre *les mythes d'une tradition interventionniste et la réalité de nouvelles angoisses,* EUI Working Paper Law No. 2006/10.

16 Article 1: « Le Conseil supérieur de l'Éducation nationale sera chargé dans le cadre et dès la promulgation de la présente loi, de rechercher les meilleurs moyens de favoriser l'étude des langues et dialectes locaux dans les régions où ils sont en usage ». A less limited space was recognised to regional languages by art. 12 of the loi Haby of 1975 , which constitutes the basic text on education in France ("Un enseignement des langues et des cultures régionales peut être dispensé tout au long de la scolarité"). The loi *Toubon* of 1994 (which repealed the loi *Bas-Lauriol* of 1975) on the use of French deals with regional languages only at art. 21: « Les dispositions de la présente loi s'appliquent sans préjudice de la législation et de la réglementation relatives aux langues régionales de France et ne s'opposent pas à leur usage»

But the French constitutional attitude toward minorities and their languages emerges clearly in the *circulaire* 95-086 of 7 April 1995 (that contains the only detailed disciplines of the teaching of regional languages in France), which affirms '*le souci de veiller à la préservation d'un élément essentiel du patrimoine national*' and '*l'engagement de l'État en faveur de cet enseignement*'. According to it, 'Each teacher … must help pupils to discover cultural and linguistic richness and teach them regional issues *not as opposing local particularisms, but as a component of the national culture*' (emphasis added). It was therefore not surprising that the Constitutional Council ruled that Article 7 of the Preamble of the European Charter of Regional Languages is not consistent with the French Constitution because it confers 'specific rights to those speaking regional or minority languages within the territories in which such languages are spoken'.[17]

### *B. The legal recognition of linguistic diversity*

Contemporary constitutionalism postulates a close connection between civil and social rights (i.e. between freedom and equality) as well as a necessary link between human rights and the Constitution. The crisis of national states and the phenomenon of ethnic revival leave no space to the illusion of a society in which linguistic specificities remain a private matter and contemporary democracies can no longer rely upon a high level of consensus on matters such as identity, religion and language as a prerequisite for their functioning. France constitutes, from this point of view, an exception. Most European constitutions provide for the protection of linguistic or national minorities and/or minority or national languages,[18] postulating a synthesis between traditional liberalism and communitarism. Without denying the primarily individual dimension of human rights, such constitutional systems do recognize the role that groups play in the formation and recognition of individual identity.[19] In other words, the constitutional protection of (albeit individual) linguistic rights of minorities produces a legal differentiation within the *people* of the state, as it postulates the existence of a plurality of communities of citizens, which can be granted different *status* on the grounds of their linguistic diversity.

---

17 Conseil Constitutionnel, Décision no 99-412 DC of 15 Juin 1999.

18 Art. 6 of the Constitution of Italy; Art. 3, para. 2 and 3 of the Constitution of Spain; Art. 4 and 70 of the Constitution of Switzerland; Art. 2 and 30 of the Constitution of Belgium; Art. 8 of the Constitution of Ireland; Art. 17 of the Constitution of Finland; Art. 2, para. 4 and Art. 15 of the Constitution of Sweden; Art. 8 of the Constitution of Austria; Art. 6 and 33 of the Constitution of Slovakia; Art. 27 and 35 of the Constitution of Poland; -Art. 12 and 15 of the Constitution of Croatia; Art. 20, para. 1 of the Constitution of Albania; Art. 6, 32, para. 2, 59, para. 2, 127, para. 2 of the Constitution of Rumania; Art. 11 and 64 of the Constitution of Slovenia; and, Art. 45 of the Constitution of Lithuania; Art. 37 of the Constitution of Estonia.

19 See for example C. Taylor, *The Politics of Recognition* (1992).

Italy constitutes a good example of this synthesis: according to Article 2 of the Constitution ('Human Rights') 'The republic recognizes and guarantees the inviolable human rights, *be it as an individual or in social groups expressing their personality*' (our emphasis), 'importing', so to say, pluralism from the theoretical into the constitutional dimension.[20] Therefore, minority protection, which, according to Article 6 should take place 'by special laws' does not derogate from the prohibition to discriminate on the grounds of language (Article 3). Affirmative action policies that favour linguistic minorities should not be conceived as an exception to the principle of equal treatment, but, on the contrary, have to be regarded as a concrete projection of the principle of equality – one that emphasizes the latter's central core, understood as its vocation to bring about substantive equality.

Minority membership is defined on the basis of a twofold criterion: a subjective one (the voluntary identification of a person with a minority) and an objective one, i.e. the *existence* of that given minority. Since there is no universally agreed definition of minority in international (and European) law, constitutional systems are free to determine what features a group must include to be defined as a minority. Legally speaking, even in constitutional systems which do provide for minority protection, minorities do not exist as such. Their legal existence (and the extent to which they are protected) depends on a state choice: special protection may be granted in much broader and effective terms to some groups, while other groups may rely only on the principle of non-discrimination. Numerical, historical, political and economic differences may be the reasons for choosing different models and degrees of protection, as well as for denying certain groups any kind of positive tools.

### *C. The protection of linguistic minorities through special clauses*

The protection of linguistic rights (and minorities) is shaped according to two constitutional models. The first is that of the states which recognize the existence of a linguistic majority/minority relationship and provide for the protection of minority linguistic rights through special clauses, which are enshrined in the Constitution and are part of the latter's hard core. The second can be defined as a 'multinational' model.

Within this first model, minority languages are protected through a number of legal tools that can be summarized as follows: special linguistic and cultural rights, advisory and decision-making bodies in which minorities are represented, in particular with regard to education, culture and religion; elected bodies and assemblies of national minority affairs; local and autonomous administration, as well as autonomy on a territorial basis, including the existence of consultative, legislative and executive bodies chosen through free and periodic elections; self-administration by a national minority of aspects concerning its identity in situations

[20] M. Stipo, 'Minoranze etnico-linguistiche', *Enciclopedia giuridica* XX, (1990) p. 1.

where autonomy on a territorial basis does not apply; and decentralized or local forms of government.

Uniform minority protection is not the rule in most European constitutional systems. In some cases, the Constitution draws an explicit differentiation among minority languages and groups: according to Article 11 of the Slovene Constitution, for example: 'The official language in Slovenia is Slovene. In those municipalities where Italian or Hungarian national communities reside, Italian or Hungarian shall also be official languages', while Article 64 contains a detailed discipline of the 'Special Rights of the Autochthonous Italian and Hungarian National Communities in Slovenia', which ought to be guaranteed irrespective of the number of members of these communities. Such rights include the right to freely use their national symbols, to establish organizations and develop economic, cultural, scientific and research activities, as well as activities in the field of public media and publishing. Moreover, these two national communities and their members have the right to education and schooling in their own languages, as well as the right to foster relations with their nations of origin and their respective countries. In order to exercise their rights, the members of these communities shall establish their own self-governing communities in the geographic areas where they live. Italians and Hungarians in Slovenia shall also be directly represented in bodies of local self-government and in the National Assembly. Finally, laws, regulations and other general acts that concern the exercise of the constitutionally provided rights and the position of the national communities exclusively may not be adopted without the consent of representatives of these national communities.

Some of the special rights asymmetrically accorded to the two autochthonous minorities have been challenged before the Constitutional Court. One case concerned the 'double voting rights', according to which Italians and Hungarians elect their special representatives to the national assembly and local councils and are also granted general voting rights, which the Court considered legitimate and not violating voting equality, because this exception is set down 'in the Constitution itself as a form of so-called positive discrimination'.[21] Another thorny issue was whether the representatives of the two minorities could vote in the election of the Prime Minister. The matter was referred to the Constitutional Court after the two MPs affected the outcome of the election of the Prime Minister, arguing that their mandates and voting rights should be limited to issues related to national minorities. But, according to the Court, the mandates of the Italian and Hungarian representatives are equal to that of all other MPs.[22]

---

[21] Quoted by C. Ribičič, *Constitutional Protection of National Minorities in Slovenia*, paper presented at the World VI Congress of Constitutional Law, Santiago de Chile, 12-16 January 2004.

[22] *Ibid.*

The *rationale* of the constitutional privilege accorded to Italians and Hungarians is their autochthonous character, certainly not their numerical consistence. According to the 2002 census, Italians represented 0.11 per cent and Hungarians 0.31 per cent of the population, while Serbs and Croatians amounted (each group) to almost 2 per cent.

The current definition of autochthonous minorities as groups which have traditionally lived in clustered areas and who do not perceive themselves as foreigners, but as part of the native population, contains a certain degree of ambiguity and in certain cases it is almost impossible to draw a convincing dichotomy between 'native' and 'new' minorities. Finland and Russia are mutually obligated by two bilateral treaties of 1992[23] to support the preservation of identity and distinctiveness of Russians (in Finland) and of Finns and Finno-Ugrics (in Russia), which include the protection of languages.[24] But, although Finland recognized that the 'Old Russians' (but not the 'new' ones) actually constitute a minority in its 1999 periodical report to the Secretary General of the Council of Europe on the application of the Framework Convention, it later applied to them only the general principles of Article 7 of the 1992 Charter. Moreover, the Report of the Committee of Experts on the Application of the 1992 Charter (20 September 2002) expressed dissatisfaction with the limited possibilities for Russian-speaking schoolchildren to learn their mother tongue, encouraging Finland to 'explore further possibilities of resolute action to promote the use of the Russian language'.

Moreover, autochthony, which plays a significant role in justifying arbitrariness in most constitutional contexts, constitutes the grounds on which the Roma are often denied positive tools of protection or granted very limited ones. The Slovenian Constitution provides for their protection in Article 65, by simply stating that: 'The status and special rights of the Romany community living in Slovenia shall be regulated by law'. The difference between this provision and that protecting Hungarians and Italians is striking, especially if one considers that Roma communities have been traditionally living in Slovenia for centuries. Here autochthony is interpreted strictly as synonymous with territoriality, so only groups that are traditionally settled within clustered areas are entitled to linguistic protection. This close relationship between language and territory emerges also in the Italian law of 15 December 1999, which lists the languages and cultures that can be granted protection: Albanian, Catalan, German, Greek, Slovene Croatian, French, Franco-Provençal, Friulian, Ladin, Occitan, Sardinian (Articles 1 and 2). Reference to the Roma communities, which was contained in earlier drafts of this law, 'disappeared' in the final version, which

23 Treaty on the Foundations of Bilateral Relations, Helsinki 20 January 1992, in force 11 July 1992, *Finnish Treaty Series 63/1992* and Finno-Russian Cultural Treaty, Helsinki, 11 July 1992, in force 12 November 1992, *Finnish Treaty Series 100/1992.*

24 Russian is recognized as a minority language in Finland by the European Bureau of Lesser-Used Languages.

emphasizes (and even celebrates) the territorial dimension of linguistic rights. Provincial Councils have to delimit the territory where this law will be applied, if requested by a third of the members of the Council, by at least 15 per cent of the resident population, or by means of a referendum (Article 3).The emphasis of the law is placed on education: in elementary schools, as well as in primary and secondary schools; the protected languages may be taught upon parents' request.

The emphasis on the territorial dimension of minority protection is also clearly perceivable in the Italian Law n. 38/2001, which 'recognizes and protects the rights of the Italian citizens belonging to the Slovene minority'. As with the national Law of 1999, communes can decide to become a 'minority territory' on the basis of a proposal by at least 15 per cent of the citizens or one third of the municipal councillors. Moreover, this law provides for the establishment of a joint committee to be consulted in every step of the implementation of the law.[25]

### *D. Protection through asymmetrical autonomy*

Autochthony is one, but not the sole foundation staking a claim for justifying arbitrariness in minority language protection. Special (derogatory) territorial autonomy is likely to produce discrimination among numerically or economically 'stronger' groups, or groups which can count on a stronger 'kin state' (and in some cases on the international anchoring of their status as in the case of German speakers in South Tyrol and the Åland Islands in Finland) and groups which do not share such advantages. Think of the Italian case. Notwithstanding the neutral wording of Article 6 of the Constitution, which refers to (presumably all) 'linguistic minorities', only German, French and (to a much lesser extent) Slavic speaking minorities have traditionally been protected, thanks to the system of 'Special Regional Statutes' (which are formally constitutional laws, i.e. special autonomy is entrenched in the Constitution). Even after the enactment of the aforementioned Law of 1999, such 'strong' minorities enjoy a wider degree of autonomy in comparison to other equally autochtonous groups, which are now granted a number of linguistic and cultural rights, but not the kind of control over 'their' territory that special autonomy entails. The same can be said about Spain, where the *Comunidades Autonomas* inhabited by the strongest ('historical') nationalities are granted a higher degree of autonomy. It is true that the differenciation between 'ordinary' and 'special' *Comunidades* (based on the different procedure by which they were formed) is diminished by the possibility guaranteed to the latter to widen their range of competences. Still, 'special' regions enjoy a higher degree of autonomy and the tendency towards the

25 F. Palermo, *Asymmetric, 'Quasi-Federal' Regionalism and theProtection of Minorities: The Case of Italy*, in G. A. Tarr, R. F. Williams, J. Marko (eds.), *Federalism, Subnational Constitutions, and Minority Rights*, Praeger, Westport, Connecticut, London, (2004), p. 121.

strenghthening of a quasi-federalist model within them seems to suggest that the differentiation is likely to remain.[26]

Inequality among languages, however, should not always be regarded as an expression of injustice.[27] German speaking minorities in South Tyrol and Trentino and Slovene and Croat speaking minorities in Friuli-Venezia-Giulia were annexed to Italy as a result of the new frontiers that the latter was granted by the post WWI peace treaty, while smaller minorities (the so-called 'linguistic islands') never experienced annexation and have traditionally integrated well with the surrounding population. However, it is clearly irrational when the same linguistic group is treated differently depending on its geographical collocation within the same state. This is the situation of Ladin speakers, who in the province of Trento are granted only basic linguistic rights, while in the province of Bolzano they enjoy a very high degree of protection, including the mandate of minority representatives in the provincial council[28] and the application of the quota system known as 'ethnic proportionality representation'. The explanation for this different treatment is the territorial contiguity of the Ladins with the (super protected) German speaking population, which clearly played an osmotic role in expanding the principle of special protection from one group to another. The same can be said about Aranés, a linguistic *enclave* within the larger Catalan community: regional law n. 16/1990 provided for trilinguism within the territory where this community is settled.

Asymmetrical regionalism proves effective (probably the most effective means) in protecting minority languages; nevertheless, the derogatory character of autonomy carries the risk of an 'ethnocentric' rather than 'multicultural' understanding of minority protection, as the product of a conflict between different nationalisms. Moreover, special autonomy can result in a challenge to the uniform application of human rights. This challenge is twofold. On one side, subnational entities can claim to develop their own bills of rights in order to better reflect local needs and aspirations.[29] Catalonian nationalists 'have argued for such an instrument which would allow a stronger focus upon issues of specific concern to Catalans, such as language rights';[30] in Scotland it has been suggested that the ECHR could have been given effect by the Scottish Parliament in a manner which promoted specific Scottish needs.[31] On the other side, the state becomes 'less and less a direct source of

---

26 G. Poggeschi, *Le nazioni linguistiche della Spagna autonomia* (2002), p. 56 *et seq.*

27 R. Rubio-Marin, 'Exploring the Boundaries of Language Rights: Insiders, Newcomers and Natives', in S. Macedo, A. Buchanan (eds), *Secession and Self-Determination* (2003) p. 152.

28 The Constitutional Court has declared the consistency of this rule with the Constitution, arguing that German and Ladin speaking minorities have the constitutional right to be represented 'in condition of effective equality' (judgement n. 438/1993).

29 S. Tierney, *Constitutional Law and National Pluralism* (2004), p. 329.

30 *Ibid.*

31 *Ibid.*

concrete rights and more and more the source of rules for determining the matter in which rights can be exercised'. In other words, the role of the state is increasingly confined to setting basic principles and controlling their application, while other levels of governance set the operational rules for specific rights. In the specific fields of linguistic rights, the basic principles are formal and substantive equality, but within this framework it is up to the sub-national levels to choose the relevant legal and political means to achieve the goal of minority protection.[32] This tendency is clearly perceivable in the Italian system, but also in Spain, where policies for the protection of regional languages and culture have been widely developed by the *Comunidades Autonomas*, and certainly not by the central state.[33]

In the Province of Bolzano, where German speakers are a majority, the whole system is based on the separation of the two main linguistic groups. Public jobs 'are reserved for citizens belonging to each of the three language groups in proportion to the size of the groups themselves, as they appear in the declaration of the official census' (Article 89) and preference is given to citizens who have resided in South Tyrol for at least two years. This quota system is based on the results of the official census, which is carried out every decade and contains a linguistic section which all inhabitants must fill in, declaring which linguistic group they belong to. This mechanism, also known as 'ethnic proportional representation', has been challenged on various occasions before the Constitutional Court, which has declared it legitimate and a direct expression of the constitutional principle of linguistic minority protection (Article 6) (*Corte Costituzionale*, 289/87).

In South Tyrol, 'the German language has parity with the Italian language which is the official language of the state'. Citizens can therefore use either of the two in their dealing with judiciary offices and the public administration. Public employers must be bilingual (and trilingual in Ladin valleys), which must be proved by state examination; judicial trials can also be carried out in German, toponyms must be bi (or tri) lingual, and a provincial media board must broadcast on radio and TV programmes in German.

The Spanish Constitution does not guarantee linguistic rights as such, but their respect constitutes a structural state principle. According to Article 3 of the Constitution, Castilian is the official state language, but 'the other Spanish languages shall be official in the respective Autonomous Communities'. These two principles – linguistic pluralism and the co-official character of 'the other Spanish languages' – constitute the basis of the whole linguistic matter, in which the principle of territoriality plays a key role, as regional languages are co-official only within the borders of the Autonomous Communities in which they are spoken.

---

32 F. Palermo, *supra* n. 25, p.121.

33 E. J. Ruiz Vieytez, 'Federalism, Subnational Constitutional Arrangements, and the Protection of Minorities in Spain', in G. A. Tarr R. F. Williams J. Marko (eds.), *Federalism, Subnational Constitutions, and Minority Rights*, (2004) p.150.

Both the state and the regions are competent in regulating the linguistic matter. In general terms, the state is competent as far as the official character of Castilian across the whole national territory is concerned, but cannot regulate regional linguistic matters. So, within each region, linguistic rights may be exclusively regulated by regional sources

As far as education is concerned, the various Statutes provide for different models. In the Basque country, there are two strictly separated and parallel schooling systems, and the right to be educated implies the right to receive education either in Euskera or Castilian.[34] In Catalunya, the system is closer to bilingualism: while proficiency in the two languages is mandatory for teachers, only children between the age of five and seven have the right to be educated in their mother tongue (Catalan or Castilian). Then it is up to the Catalan executive to state in which language the single subjects must be taught. So, in the Spanish system, the right to be educated implies the guarantee to receive education in a language which the pupil understands or which is made comprehensible to him/her, but not the right to be taught in one's mother tongue. The latter may obviously be granted, but does not constitute part of the hard core of the right to be educated and might therefore be limited according to the principle of proportionality, if the protection of a linguistic minority so requires.[35]

In Finland, the Swedish character of the Åland Islands also constitutes the basis for a deeply asymmetrical regional solution. The Ålanders are granted special autonomy 'in accordance with what is specifically stipulated in the Act on Autonomy' (Section 120 of the Finnish Constitution). This Act can be amended or repealed only by consistent decisions of both the Finnish and the Åland Parliaments. In the Parliament of Finland the decision shall be made as provided for by the amendment and repeal of the Constitution (i.e. according to Section 73 of the Finnish Constitution) and in the Åland Parliament by at least a two thirds' majority of votes cast (Section 69 of the Act on Autonomy). In other words, the amending procedure for the Act of Autonomy is more rigid than that which is required to amend the Finnish Constitution. This is likely to suggest the federal nature of Åland autonomy. In federal states, such as the USA and Australia, the consent of single Member States in the amending procedure is not required in principle, but it is mandatory when the amendment entails a state's vital interest (e.g. territorial borders and parliamentary representation). Moreover, the Islands are granted what could be defined as a right of 'interposition': according to sections 28 and 59 of the Act on Autonomy, state acts which relate to the principles governing real or business property in Åland and

---

[34] The Constitutional Tribunal declared this provision consistent with the Constitution, as long as it does not interfere with the freedom to teach Judgement. n. 137 of 6 November 1986, *fund. jur.* n.1.

[35] A. Milian Massana, 'Droits linguistiques et droits fondamentaux en Espagne', in *Revue générale de droit,* 23, p. 575.

international treaties in matters within the competence of Åland shall not enter into force in the Islands without the consent of the local assembly.

On the other hand, the Ålanders are granted legislative autonomy in limited matters which are mostly directly connected with the preservation of their linguistic and cultural specificity, such as education, culture and management of historical sites, radio and television, etc. Åland is a strictly monolingual province, the official language and the language of education is Swedish (Sections 36 and 40). A satisfactory proficiency in Swedish also constitutes one of the conditions that has to be fulfilled in order to be granted the 'right of domicile ("regional citizenship")',[36] together with Finnish citizenship and uninterrupted residency in Åland for at least five years –a condition which is interpreted very strictly by the Supreme Administrative Court as to exclude all but trips and short stays off Åland.[37]

The right of domicile in Åland, which was introduced to protect the local culture and, in particular, the Swedish language, constitutes a limit to the application of European Union law. *Protocol No 2*, annexed to the Act of accession, 'taking into account the special status that the Åland islands enjoy under international law', states that European law shall not preclude the application of the existing provisions *in force on 1 January 1994* concerning regional citizenship (emphasis added). In other words, the Protocol legitimized a regime which obviously derogates from some of the fundamental principles of EC law, but, 'freezing' it to 1 January 1994; European law introduced a limit to the possibility of further expanding Åland special autonomy, at least as far as the discipline of the (critical) right of domicile is concerned. The Protocol seems to suggest a certain European sensitiveness towards cultural (and specifically, linguistic) diversity within Member States and the favour for a model of integration which takes into account the specific cultural needs of sub-state entities.[38]

---

36 According to Section 6 of the Act of Autonomy, the right of domicile in Åland shall belong to 1) a person who at the time of the entry into force of this Act had the right of domicile under the Autonomy Act for Åland (28 December 1951/670); and 2) a child under 18 years of age who is a citizen of Finland and a resident of Åland, provided that his father or mother has the right of domicile. Only persons with the right of domicile are entitled to vote and stand as candidates in elections for the Åland Parliament. Anyone who has had his or her habitual residence in a municipality in Åland for the last three years has the rights to vote and stand as a candidate in municipal elections. There are also limitations on the right to acquire real property and the right to exercise a trade. The Act on the Acquisition of Real Property in Åland lays down the principles for such acquisitions. Anyone who has resided outside the province for more than five years forfeits his or her right of domicile.

37 M. Suksi, Ålands Konstitution (2005) at 38 *et seq.*

38 D. Perrot, F. Miatti, 'Les Lapons et les Åland dans le quatrième élargissement. Contribution à l'étude de la différenciation juridique au sein de la Communauté Européenne', in *Revue du Marché Commun et de l'Union européenne*, 413, dec. (1997) 681.

### *E. Corporative autonomy*

Autonomy does not necessarily have to be connected with the territorial dimension, and can in fact be defined in not exclusively spatial and geographical terms. C.J. Friedrich, on the basis of a proposal by Karl Renner aimed at solving the minority question within Austria-Hungary, theorized a federal model which he defined as 'corporative', with the purpose of protecting minority groups not concentrated in clustered areas.[39]

A corporative solution was successfully implemented in Estonia in the 1920s, where members of the German and Jewish communities could elect their Councils which were granted legislative power in culture-related matters.[40] In Cyprus, a corporative system was introduced by the 1960 Constitution. Greeks and Turks were granted a high degree of autonomy: each group elected its own representative assembly as well as separated municipal councils in the five main cities of the island. The Assemblies had exclusive legislative power in religious, education and cultural matters and in the sphere of personal status.[41]

In Finland, the Swedish speaking population is protected through a combined application of the personal and territorial criteria. Legally, Swedish speaking Finns do not constitute a linguistic minority, given that Swedish is, together with Finnish, one of the two national languages (Section 17 of the Constitution -*'Right to one's language and culture*'). So, linguistic rights are granted to both groups on an equal footing and they are not framed as minority clauses, as they both apply to the (numerical) majority and to the (numerical) minority within the bilingual nation'.[42]

Swedish-speaking Finns number almost 300,000 people (5.6 per cent of the total population), most of whom reside in the coastal areas of southern and western Finland, but they do not form a majority in any clustered area of the country, except Åland. The *Svenska-Finlands Folketing*, which represents (although it is not directly elected by) all Swedish speaking Finns, regardless of their geographical residence, is aimed at protecting the interests of Swedish speaking Finns and provides a forum for political discussion and cooperation, while also taking part in the law drafting process and issuing statements on topics involving the Swedish-speaking population.

At the territorial level, the basic unit of linguistic division of the country is the municipality, which can be either unilingual or bilingual, if the population includes

---

39 C. J. Friedrich, *Man and his Government. An Empirical Theory of Politics* (1963), p. 597, n. 29.

40 G. Von Rausch, *The Baltic States – Estonia, Latvia and Lithuania: The Years of Independence 1917-1940* (1974), p. 142.

41 On corporative federalism see E. McWhinney, *Corporative Federalism, States' Rights and National Powers* (1965).

42 M. Scheinin, *Constitutional Coexistence: Minority Rights and Non-Discrimination under the New Finnish Constitution of 2000*, in M. Scheinin, R. Toivanen (eds.), *Rethinking Non-Discrimination and Minority Rights* (2004), p. 8.

both Finnish and Swedish speakers and the minority comprises at least eight per cent of the population or at least 3,000 persons. Each individual has the right to use his or her own language in dealing with governmental authorities or local authorities of bilingual municipalities.

The Hungarian system is also based on a combined application of the personal and territorial criteria. According to Law 65/1990, counties are granted most competences in the field of culture. Both in urban and rural areas, historical communities can opt for personal autonomy at a municipal, local and national level, according to their territorial density and provided they share a sufficient degree of common identity which has to be manifested though a capacity of political aggregation.[43]

### *F. Multinational states*

In multinational states all main languages are co-official, despite the numeric consistence of linguistic groups. According to this model, the linguistic monopoly of each linguistic group roughly corresponds to the territorial dimension of the state sub-unit.[44] This is typically the case of asymmetrical federations[45] such as Belgium and Switzerland, where all languages are equally co-official at the federal level, while at the local level linguistic territoriality is strictly applied (whether or not the principle of territoriality is enshrined in the Constitution). The difference between this state model and the one in which protection takes place through special clauses, is that in a multinational state, minorities are not legally defined as such. Linguistic groups enjoy an equal status and are therefore protected through the territorial and institutional state organization itself, as well as through ordinary legislation, applicable to all groups, and not through special constitutional clauses and/or special autonomy.

In fact, this model shows a certain degree of similarity to the French system, in the sense that it results in a sum of strictly homogeneous sub-units, in which the elevation of collective linguistic goals over individual linguistic rights results in the weakening of the latter.

Linguistic rights are a key element in the Belgian federal structure, as Belgian federalism is not based on the equal position of its sub-units, but rather on that of its two main linguistic communities So, while Belgium is composed of three regions (Flemish, Walloon and Brussels-Capital) and of three communities (Flemish, French and German), the core of the Belgian state and the basis of its functioning at all levels are the two largest linguistic communities. The federal government (as well

---

43 See S. Pierré-Caps, 'Le principe de l'autonomie personnelle et l'aménagement constitutionnel du pluralisme national. L'exemple hongrois', in *Revue de Droit Public*, 1994, pp. 401 *et seq*.

44 F. Delpérée, *Droits des minorités, droits de l'homme*, in *Les droits de l'homme au seuil du troisième millénaire, Mélanges en hommage à Pierre Lambert* (2000), p. 312.

45 C. D. Tartlon, 'Symmetry and Asymmetry as Elements of Federalism: A Theoretical speculation', in *Journal of Politics*, 27, 1965, n. 4, pp. 868 ss.

as the Court of Arbitration) must have an equal number of Flemish and French speaking ministers (apart from the 'asexual' Prime Minister); a fixed number of civil servants are appointed according to their language in the federal administration. Linguistic groups, to which MPs belong, are critical in decision-making processes, as each linguistic group may block the legislative procedure in all 'sensitive' matters, according to the so-called procedure of the '*sonnette d'alarme*'.[46] Moreover, each linguistic group can in practice veto constitutional reforms, given that a majority within the two communities – and the two linguistic groups which represent them in Parliament – is not only necessary from a political standpoint, but also a numerical necessity for the amending procedure. Finally, for fundamental (quasi-constitutional) legislation, a double majority (i.e. an overall two thirds majority in each chamber and a majority in each linguistic group) is required by the Constitution.

The complexity of Belgian federalism is due also to the overlapping of the competences of regions and communities. Both are political sub-national entities with governments and elected assemblies. The regions are vested with powers in the fields of economic and employment policy, environment, local authorities, transport etc., while the communities have powers in the fields of education, culture, health and social policy, but the division is not as clear in reality, due to the deep asymmetry of the system. While there is a concurrence between the Flemish Community and the Flemish Region, the Walloon region covers two linguistic regions (French and German) and also the 'the sociological and political independence of the Brussels francophones with regards to Wallonia'.[47] The Community level was initially thought in 'corporative' terms, as a response to the hopes of the francophones to unify all French-speaking Belgians, though preserving the linguistic rights of those living in Flanders. The linguistic dimension was therefore a crucial issue in their creation: while there is a region of Brussels-Capital, there is no Brussels Community, just as there is no homogeneous linguistic culture in Brussels. The initial project, however, was not successful. According to the Court of Arbitration, the competences of both Communities and Regions can be exercised only within their territory.[48]

The region of Brussels-Capital represents an exception, because here both the French and the Flemish Communities exercise competences in fields such as education and culture. It has been pointed out that this overlapping of regional and community levels constitutes a good solution, because 'the region gives protection to the French-speaking Brussels population. With a built-in protection for the Dutch-speaking population', while the 'presence of the Communities … guarantees

---

46 If at least three quarters of the members of one group sign a motion the procedure is suspended and the motion is referred to the government which plays an arbitration role.

47 A. Alen, P. Peeters, 'The Competences of the Communities in the Belgian Federal State: the Principle of Exclusivity Revisited', in *European Public Law*, 2, 1997, pp. 165 et seq.

48 *Ibid.*, p. 165.

the cultural and social rights of each group' and that the positive aspect of the system is that it offers 'choice to the population'.[49]

This choice, however, is denied to the rest of the population by the strictly monolingual systems applied within the other two regions. In the latter, the situation is in fact similar to that of a typically monolingual state: there is only one official language and linguistic freedom of those who do not belong to the majority group is highly limited. This results in a high degree of protection of the linguistic rights of the individuals belonging to each majority group within the two main regions, but also in the discrimination of 'regional' minorities, which are not recognized as such, that are subject to a duty of linguistic assimilation. The definition of linguistic minorities in Belgium is a particularly thorny issue. The difficulties do not concern the federal level, where only German speakers can be viewed as a linguistic minority, but rather the status of trapped minorities within the two monolingual regions. According to Resolution 1301 (2002) of the Parliamentary Assembly of the Council of Europe on 'The Protection of Minorities in Belgium', such groups (Francophones in Flanders and in the German-language Region, as well as Flemish and German speakers in the French-language Region) could actually be regarded as linguistic minorities.[50] Such recognition, however, is likely to challenge the principle of territoriality, which 'remains the fragile and therefore static basis on which the actual Belgian state rests'.[51] It is not by chance that Belgium signed the Framework Convention in 2001, but made the reservation that 'the notion of national minority will be defined by the Belgian inter-ministerial conference on foreign policy'.

Moreover, the risk that the Belgian system embodies, which is clearly perceivable in the absence of a supremacy clause for federal sources of law in the Constitution, is a de-legitimization of the latter, which becomes more of a 'compact' between states rather than a 'Constitution over them' (Calhoun). In other words, the federal formula in its Belgian application does not attain its main objective, which is to conciliate unity with diversity, and rather has a disintegrating role[52] that is likely to bring about a deeper separation between the linguistic communities.

The Swiss case is slightly different. The federal system is based on equality among cantons and on the official status of German, French, Italian and (to a certain extent)

49 W. Pas, *A Dynamic Federalism Built on Static Principles: The Case of Belgium*, in G. A. Tarr, R.F. Williams, J. Marko (eds.), *Federalism, Subnational Constitutions, and Minority Rights*, (2004), p. 164.

50 This Resolution represents an important step forward with respect to the traditional view, expressed in the HRC decision in the *Ballantyne* case according to which 'the minorities referred to in article 27 (of the 1966 Covenant) are minorities within … a State, and not minorities within any province' (11.2).

51 W. Pas, at 173.

52 This tendency is not the monopoly of multilingual federations. Think for example of the 'new federalism' theorized at first by former President Ronald Reagan and then developed by Newt Gingrich in the U.S.A.

Ladin, which are also the national languages of the state. But unlike in Belgium, where the two main linguistic communities have a similar (albeit not identical) numerical consistence, in Switzerland German speakers constitute the overwhelming majority. Linguistic freedom was enshrined in the Swiss Constitution only in 1996. Until then, it was considered as part of the 'unwritten constitutional law', developed by the case law of the Federal Tribunal[53] which recognized linguistic freedom as an individual right with an active and a passive aspect, and also as a precondition to the exercise of other rights (in the first place free speech) and the concretization of various fundamental constitutional values, such as the full development of all human beings and the protection of minorities[54]. Despite such a wide initial recognition, linguistic freedom was in the later case law gradually eroded by another principle, also developed by the Federal Tribunal since 1932: linguistic territoriality.[55] The Tribunal never clarified to what extent territoriality could be applied by the cantons and ended by implicitly authorizing them to take all necessary measures in order to safeguard their linguistic homogeneity. It was also unclear whether the cantons had[56] or did not have[57] the duty to protect weaker languages. In practise, the Federal Tribunal case law ended up authorizing linguistic assimilation within monolingual Cantons (*Association de l'Ecole Française*,[58] *Derungs*,[59] *Brunner*[60]) thus leaving without effective protection the lesser spoken official and national languages of the federation. The lack of balance between the protection of linguistic freedom and the application of linguistic territoriality threatened one of the pillars of the Swiss Constitution, that is to say, the equality of all official languages.

In 1996, in order to prevent the Swiss Latin languages from becoming the victims of a phenomenon of 'linguistic Darwinism', an amendment of Article 116 of the (then) Constitution[61] enshrined linguistic freedom as an individual right that

53 On 'unwritten principles of constitutional law' as developed by the case law of the Federal Tribunal during the 1960s, see M. Rossinelli, *Le libertés non écrites. Contribution à l'étude du pouvoir créateur du juge constitutionnel* (1987).

54 DTF 911 480.

55 The text of this case has not been published. It was issued by the Federal Tribunal, section of public law, on 3 June 1932.

56 Morand, 'I diritti linguistici in Svizzera', in *Le Regioni*, (1987) p. 1362.

57 M. Rossinelli, 'La question linguistique en Suisse: bilan critique et nouvelles perspectives juridiques', in *Rivista di diritto svizzero*, (1989), p. 169.

58 DTF 911 480.

59 DTF 100 I a 462, del 30-10-1974.

60 Judgement of 25-4-1980, in *Arrêts du T. f.*, 106, Ia, 299 ss.

61 In the new Swiss Constitution of 1999, Article 18 protects linguistic freedom, while Articles 4 Art. 4 declares German, French, Italian, and Romans as National Languages and Article 70 refers to the role of the principle of territoriality, to 'indigenous linguistic minorities' and specifically to the Romansh and Italian: '1. The official languages of the Confederation are

must constitute the parameter for the interpretation of all provisions concerning linguistic matters. As for all fundamental rights, limitations to linguistic freedom must therefore have a legal basis, pursue a public interest and respect the principle of proportionality. Territoriality was also constitutionalized in 1996 as a general principle to be applied in the first place by the cantons, and, secondly, by the federal state. It does not follow that it should be applied to the same extent in all cantons and situations. Linguistic freedom can be legitimately limited by the application of the principle of territoriality only if a language is threatened, despite its status of majority or minority language within a canton. Federal authorities must therefore interfere in cantons' linguistic affairs only in order to protect weaker linguistic minorities. On the other hand, cantons may pursue the maintenance of their traditional linguistic homogeneity, but respecting such conditions, and especially the principle of proportionality. As a result of this amendment, and in clear contradiction to its past case law (*Association de l'Ecole Française*) the Federal Tribunal ruled that to oblige a French speaking child resident in the germanophone Canton of Berne to receive education in German constitutes a disproportionate limitation of the freedom of language.[62]

The Swiss case represents in fact a combination of the two constitutional models of protection: while it states equality among all autochthonous languages, it does not refuse to face *de facto* inequality among formally equal languages and it provides for the special tools of protection which are critical in safeguarding lesser spoken languages and cultures.

### G. Central and Eastern European countries

While it is impossible to draw a uniform 'Central-Eastern European' model of linguistic minority protection, it is true that certain features recur in many – albeit not in all – Central and Eastern European Constitutions. In fact, some scholars have suggested that in Central and Eastern Europe, minority-related issues need to be approached differently.[63] Certainly, the bottom-up dynamic of the construction of national identity 'from state to nation' emphasized a constitutional culture based on

---

German, French, and Italian. Romansh; shall be an official language for communicating with persons of Romansh language. 2. The cantons shall designate their official languages. In order to preserve harmony between linguistic communities, they shall respect the traditional territorial distribution of languages, and take into account the indigenous linguistic minorities. 3. The Confederation and the cantons shall encourage understanding and exchange between the linguistic communities. 4. The Confederation shall support the plurilingual Cantons in the fulfilment of their particular tasks. 5. The Confederation shall support the measures taken by the Cantons of Grisons and Ticino to maintain and to promote Romansh and Italian'.

62 DTF 122 I 236 of 15-7-1996.

63 Kymlicka-Opalski; in T.H. Malloy,(ed.) *National Minority Rights in Europe*, (2005) pp. 40-44.

ethnic affiliation and on the idea of one people in possession of its own state under the formula of self-determination, political function of which is not democratic state organization, but rather unification for state-formation. Nationalism-related values and the right of ethnic nations to statehood also constitute the basis for minority protection.

Typically, Central and Eastern European Constitutions affirm the unitary character of the state and the principle of non-discrimination on, among other grounds, language, race, nationality and ethnic origin. Moreover, most of them contain specific clauses of minority protection, which are not self-executing, but require an intervention by the legislator. Their implementation has, in many cases, been delayed by an ultra-nationalistic nation-building process, and the subsequent ethnification of the political process.[64] Many Constitutions (e.g. those of Albania, Croatia, Slovakia, Poland etc) use the term 'national minority', but in some cases, (e.g. Poland) both the term 'national minorities' and 'ethnic groups' are used. While a clear distinction lacks in international law (where the two terms are often treated as interchangeable), the Polish Supreme Court, when ruling on the inadmissibility of registration of the Union of People of Silesian Nationality, adopted the criterion based on statehood, 'according to which "national minority" is a group which form parts of a nation whose main seat is in another state, while an ethnic minority is a group distinguished from the given nation by the possession of certain specific cultural features'.[65]

The overlapping of the concepts of language and/or culture and 'ethnicity' is typical of Central and Eastern European constitutional cultures. The Preamble of the (very controversial) Slovakian Law of 1995 on the State language of the Republic of Slovakia[66] defines the 'Slovak language' as 'the most important feature of the individuality of the Slovak nation, the most precious value of its cultural heritage and the expression of sovereignty of the Slovak Republic'. Here the Slovak language becomes an articulation of the sovereign character of the Slovak republic, but the consequence seems to be that only those who belong to the Slovak speaking population are part of the Slovak nation, while members of linguistic minorities are excluded. The equality of all citizens, regardless of their nationality, is also affirmed

---

64 M. Rooker, *The Legal Situation of Slovakia's Minorities*, in S. Trifunovska (ed.), *Croatia, Estonia and Slovakia*, cit., p. 178 ff.

65 E. Gdulewicz, M. Curie-Sklodowska, E. Poplawska, *National Minorities in Poland*, paper presented at the World Congress of Constitutional Law, Santiago de Chile, 10-17 January 2004.

66 The subsequent Law 'on the use of minority languages' of 11 July 1999 overcomes must of the shortcomings indicated by the European observers See the Report of the European Commission on Slovakia of 1998: <europa.eu.int/comm/enlargement/report_11_98/pdf/en/slovakia_en.pdf>, and also the report of the FCNM of 2000, which pints out how numerous provisions of the law of 1995 could produce discriminations against members of national minorities in relation to free speech and freedom of association.

by the Preamble of the Croatian Constitution of 1990, but again, the majority nation is the only subject which, having the right to statehood, is entitled to legitimize the new-born state: 'Proceeding from ... the inalienable, indivisible, nontransferable and inexpendable right of the Croatian nation to self-determination and state sovereignty, the Republic of Croatia is ... established as the national state of the Croatian people and a state of members of other nations and minorities who are its citizens'. In other words, Croatia is the state of a collective subject (the Croatian people) entitled to statehood, and of some individuals that do not belong to it. Provisions conferring equal rights and special protection to such citizens cannot upgrade them to the status of the founding nation: they will always be excluded from the sole subject that legitimizes the very existence of the Croatian state. The same can be said with regard to other Constitutions, including the Serbian one, approved in the 28-29 October 2006 referendum, which in the first article defines Serbia as the 'state of the Serb people and all its citizens'.

Today, in Croatia, after the adoption of the three laws in the field of language and minority protection,[67] the (formal) standards of protection fulfil the Copenhagen criteria. According to Article 7 of the Constitutional Law on the Rights of National Minorities in the Republic of Croatia,[68] 'the Republic of Croatia shall ensure the exercise of special [derogatory?] rights and freedoms of members of national minorities which they enjoy individually or together with other persons belonging to the same national minority, and together with members of other national minorities when it is stipulated by this Constitutional Law or a special law'. Such rights include the use of their language and script, privately, publicly and officially; education in the language and script of use; the use of their signs and symbols; access to the media and the performance of activities of public information (receiving and forwarding information) in the language and script of use and a general right to 'cultural autonomy' ('by way of preservation, development and expression of one's own culture and the preservation and protection of one's cultural assets and tradition').[69] Still, the opinion of the European Commission of April 2004 on the

---

67 <dev.eurac.edu:8085/mugs2/do/browse>.

68 See comment by A. Petricusic, 'Constitutional Law on the Rights of National Minorities in the Republic of Croatia', in *European Yearbook on Minority Issues*, Vol. 2, 2002/2003, p. 607-629.

69 The other rights listed by Art. 7 are: the right to profess one's religion and to establish religious communities together with other members of that religion; self-organising and association for the purpose of exercising mutual interests; representation in the representative bodies at the state and local level and in administrative and judicial bodies; participation of members of national minorities in the public life and in management of local affairs through the councils and through representatives of national minorities; protection from any activity which endangers or may endanger their existence, the exercise of rights and freedoms.

application of Croatia for access to the EU, points out that Croatia must, *inter alia*, strengthen the level of minority protection.[70]

Another tool aimed at protecting minorities in Central and Eastern European constitutional systems is the mandatory representation of minorities in the national parliament and in the regional and local assemblies and in the administrative and jurisdictional bodies. The system is aimed at preventing the effects of the lack of interest – not to say explicit rejection – of minority claims by state-based political parties.[71] In some cases, minorities are also protected through the creation of 'Councils for National Minorities' that have the purpose of discussing, proposing, regulating and resolving issues related to the exercise and protection of rights and freedoms of national minorities and, specifically, the task of proposing issues of significance for the national minority to the bodies of state authorities.

Finally, while territorial autonomy is not typically implemented in Central and European states with the aim of protecting minorities, since the constitutional reform of 2001, Croatia is moving towards a regional model. So far, the only regional statute that deals explicitly with minority issues is the Istrian one. Some of its provisions were struck down by the Constitutional Court in 1995, during the aggressively nationalistic Tudjman era,[72] but were later re-adopted by the Istrian Assembly (although in more prudent terms) in the new Statute of 9 April 2001. According to its Preamble, 'Istria is a multiethnic, multicultural and multilingual community' and 'an area where every citizen or community enjoys the full right of expression, respect, insurance and development of social, ethnic, religious, cultural, political and *linguistic* freedoms and self-awareness.' In order to enable direct participation in public affairs to members of the most representative Istrian national minority – the Italians – Article 6 of the Statute of the Istrian County prescribes, 'In the Istrian County the Croatian language and the Italian language are equal.' Furthermore, Article 22 states that 'the Istrian County guards against every activity which may endanger the multicultural and multiethnic character of Istria', while Article 23 goes on to state that 'the Istrian County acknowledges "Istrian-ness" as an expression of regional affiliation to Istrian multi-ethnicity'.

---

70 <europa.eu.int/comm/enlargement/croatia/key_documents.htm>.

71 Thanks to Prof. Giovanni Poggeschi for clarifying this aspect.

72 The Statute of the Istrian County adopted on 30 October 1994 was the subject of a request by the Government of the Republic of Croatia to the Constitutional Court for an evaluation of the compatibility of 36 articles of the Statute with the Constitution. Passing its decision on 2 February 1995, the Constitutional Court repealed 18 articles of the Statute and rejected the request made by the Government for another 18 articles See comment by V. Piergigli, 'Lo statuto istriano e il bilinguismo al vaglio delle autorità croate', *Quaderni costituzionali*, n. 3, 2001, p. 630-632.

## 3. An emerging European minimum standard on language rights: the Council of Europe instruments

As was mentioned in the introduction of this chapter, the national constitutional models for dealing with linguistic diversity, and the national constitutional choices on the recognition of linguistic rights, are increasingly constrained by European-level legal standards. The main sources of language rights with a pan-European scope are the European Convention of Human Rights and the 'twin conventions' of the Council of Europe that entered into force in 1998: the European Charter for Regional or Minority Languages and the Framework Convention on National Minorities.[73]

The European Convention of Human Rights contains a provision prohibiting discrimination on grounds of language in the exercise of the rights of the Convention, and it also guarantees a right for the accused to use an interpreter if they cannot understand the language of criminal proceedings. However, it does not lay down general standards for the use of languages and does not contain any specific minority rights. Despite this absence of specific attention to languages and minorities, there has been, in recent years, a 'burgeoning' minority rights jurisprudence of the European Court of Human Rights.[74] General human rights listed in the Convention are being explored and tested by applicants from minority groups as to their implicit minority protection potential. These minority cases have only rarely addressed questions of language use. In fact, among the many minority-relevant European Court cases discussed in the survey by Geoff Gilbert,[75] only two (*Ekin* and *Cyprus v. Turkey*, both discussed below) involved the use of languages.

Notwithstanding this relative failure, so far, to test the language rights potential of the European Convention, there is no doubt that such a potential exists. For instance, following the *Ballantyne* doctrine of the UN Human Rights Committee,[76] restrictions on the use of a particular language (say, Kurdish in Turkey) in private domains, including in private broadcasting or print media, would certainly be considered by the Court as restrictions of freedom of expression, a right guaranteed in Article 10 of the Convention. Further support for this view can be found in the

---

73 It would lead too far to examine in this paper the impact on European countries of the corresponding *universal* human rights instruments. Of particular relevance is Article 27 of the UN Covenant on Civil and Political Rights, on the significance of which, see for example : K. Henrard, *Devising an Adequate* System, cit., at p. 158 ff.; F. de Varennes, *Language, Minorities and Human Rights* (1996), chapter 5; and S. Ramu, 'Le statut des minorités au regard du Pacte international relatif aux droits civils et politiques', *Revue trimestrielle des droits de l'homme* (2002) 587.

74 The terms are borrowed from the title of G. Gilbert, 'The Burgeoning Minority Rights Jurisprudence of the European Court of Human Rights', *Human Rights Quarterly* (2002) 736.

75 See reference in previous footnote.

76 For the *Ballantyne* case, see the introduction of this chapter.

*Association Ekin v. France* judgment of 2001, in which the Strasbourg Court held that French legislation allowing for the administrative seizure of foreign publications or publications in a foreign language (as opposed to 'Franco-French' publications) was a violation of Article 10.[77] The Court's most remarkable ruling on the implied linguistic dimension of general fundamental rights occurred in the case of *Cyprus v. Turkey*, in which the Grand Chamber held that the fact that the Northern Cyprus government provided Greek language primary schooling for the Greek minority living in Northern Cyprus, but did not provide any follow-up at the secondary school level, amounted to a breach of the right to education guaranteed by Article 2 of Protocol No. 1 to the Convention.[78]

What is missing, so far, in the Convention system, is a *general right to equal treatment* which could form the basis for various language rights claims, for example the claim that states that guarantee the official right to use a particular minority language should also recognize the right to use another minority language of comparable size.[79] At present, as is well known, Article 14 of the European Convention prohibits discrimination on the grounds of language (alongside many other grounds) only within the ambit of one of the substantive rights of the Convention. Since the right to use one's language in dealing with public authorities is not protected by one of the substantive provisions of the Convention, Article 14 cannot be used to challenge the unequal distribution of such a right to public language use.

Now, this is precisely the point where the other, more directly language-related Council of Europe instruments, namely the Framework Convention and the Charter on Languages, may offer added value compared to the ECHR. With regard to these instruments, the preliminary question arises – before examining their content – as to whether they can really be considered to form a 'European standard'. Both entered into force in 1998 and contain binding obligations for the states parties. Neither of the two is as yet so universally accepted as the European Convention of Human Rights, but the number of states parties is rising. At the latest count, 22 states had ratified the Charter on Regional and Minority Languages, including 14 out of the

---

[77] European Court of Human Rights, judgment of 17 July 2001, Appl. 39288/98, *Association Ekin v. France*. See the case comment by F. Julien-Laferrière, 'L'incompatibilité du régime des publications étrangères avec la Convention européenne des droits de l'homme', *Actualité Juridique Droit Administratif* (2002) 52.

[78] *Cyprus v. Turkey*, judgment (Grand Chamber) of 10 May 2001, no. 25781/94, para. 278. See further on this point, J. Ringelheim, *Diversité culturelle et droits de l'homme. La protection des minorités par la Convention européenne des droits de l'homme* (2006) at pp. 203-207.

[79] Protocol no. 12 to the European Convention, containing a general prohibition of discrimination, has entered into force only recently, in 2005, and has so far been ratified by only a dozen Member States of the Council of Europe, so that there is scope for interesting developments in this respect. See, for some reflections on the possible future impact of this Protocol, R. Wintemute, 'Filling the Article 14 "Gap": Government Ratification and Judicial Control of Protocol No.12 ECHR', *European Human Rights Law Review* (2004) 484.

27 Member States of the European Union. The Framework Convention is much closer to becoming a genuine pan-European standard. It has now been ratified by 39 states and the only ones missing, apart from some mini-states, are Turkey and four EU states: Belgium (which has only signed but not ratified), France, Greece and Luxembourg.

Apart from the question of the degree to which these Conventions have been accepted by the European states, there are also doubts about their legal value. It is true that the provisions of these two treaties do not seem easily capable of direct effect in the national legal orders of the states parties. Also, their international supervision mechanisms do not lead to binding judicial or quasi-judicial decisions. Instead, periodical state reports on the application of the Conventions must be submitted to the committees of experts that were set up under each of the two Conventions. However, the dynamic approach adopted by these committees in fulfilling their monitoring tasks is quite remarkable, perhaps even unprecedented in international monitoring practice. They have established a dialogue with the governments concerned, they visit the country and meet with spokesmen of minority groups, and they do not hesitate to make statements as to whether the states have adequately complied with their obligations, and to express detailed views on how to improve the situation. These statements then lead to recommendations adopted by the Committee of Ministers of the Council of Europe and, in fact, the ministers have so far largely followed the views of the experts.[80] Pressure is thus exerted on the states to adopt best practices as formulated by the expert bodies.[81]

In terms of their substance, the European Charter for Regional or Minority Languages is the more directly relevant of the two agreements, since it focuses directly and exclusively on the regulation of the use of languages. It applies to 'autochthonous' languages, excluding expressly the languages of migrants. In the Charter system, no distinction is made between regional and minority languages, but both categories are clearly defined in territorial terms, that is, with reference

80 These various reports and recommendations can be found on the web site of the Council of Europe.

81 For accounts of the incipient monitoring practice under the *Framework Convention*, see R. Hoffmann, 'Protecting the Rights of National Minorities in Europe. First Experiences with the Council of Europe Framework Convention for the Protection of National Minorities', *German Yearbook of International Law* (2001) 237; C. Pekari, 'Review of the Monitoring Process of the Council of Europe Framework Convention for the Protection of National Minorities', *European Yearbook of Minority Issues* (2003-2004) 347. See also the earlier study by G. Pentassuglia, 'Monitoring Minority Rights in Europe: The Implementation Machinery of the Framework Convention for the Protection of National Minorities – With Special Reference to the Role of the Advisory Committee', *International Journal on Minority and Group Rights* (1999) 417. The literature on the monitoring of the *Regional Languages Charter* is more limited; see A. Bultrini, 'Developments in the Field of the European Charter for Regional or Minority languages: June 2003-June 2004', *European Yearbook of Minority Issues* (2003-2004) 377.

to particular geographical areas in which those languages are spoken by a sizeable group of people.

The Charter's main characteristic is its *à la carte* approach. Not only are state parties free to indicate which regional and minority languages they choose to protect under the terms of the Charter, but they also have considerable discretion in picking and choosing from among the many, rather detailed, substantive provisions of the Charter. The Charter is therefore a very flexible instrument, requiring the contracting states to undertake only those obligations that they are positively willing to undertake, with the expectation that a process of emulation among states will get underway. As an illustration of this sliding scale approach, one may mention the position adopted by the United Kingdom. It decided to bring no less than seven languages within its domestic Charter regime: Irish, Scottish Gaelic, Welsh, Scots, Ulster Scots, Manx Gaelic and Cornish, including therefore, in the latter case, a virtually extinct language. However, the UK government was careful to specify that it would not accord the same status to each language or the same benefits to the speakers of each language, but would modulate those in relation to the number of speakers and their territorial pattern of settlement.[82] States are free to make these distinctions. However, once they have decided to undertake commitments for the promotion of a given language in a given field (be it education, the media or public administration), then the Committee of Experts will closely check their compliance with those commitments.[83] This is the reason why, despite the cautious formulation of this Charter which studiously avoids the use of the term 'rights', its content may nevertheless give rise to genuine individual rights in those countries in which it has been transposed into domestic laws that contain clear commitments for public authorities – and the states concerned may be called to task for their failure to respect those commitments.

The Framework Convention on National Minorities, for its part, includes some linguistic rights within the broader context of its minority protection provisions. Of particular importance is Article 10(2) which contains a very cautious and qualified *obligation* for states to allow the use of minority languages in relation to administrative authorities, and Article 12(1) which contains a much more straightforward *right* for every person belonging to a national minority to learn his or her minority language. These clauses, and some others of lesser importance, have formed the focus of intensive interpretative debates between the governments

---

82 See the United Kingdom's second periodical report on its application of the Charter, 1 July 2005, MIN-Lang/PR (2005) 5.

83 See for example the recent report of the Committee of Experts on Spain, of 21 September 2005, ECRML (2005) 4, which amounts to 170 pages of detailed analysis and recommendations addressed to the Spanish government. The impact of the Charter on Spanish law is examined by I. Agirreazkuenaga Zigorraga, 'La carta Europea de lenguas regionales o minoritarias del Consejo de Europa como derecho interno', in J.M. Pérez Fernández (coord.), *Estudios sobre el estatuto jurídico de las lenguas en España* (2006) 105.

and the Framework Convention's Advisory Committee over the past six years, with the experts pushing governments to give a more generous interpretation to their obligations under the Framework Convention. One small example, among many, may serve as an illustration of this dynamic monitoring mechanism. Article 9 of the Convention states, in very vague terms, that minorities should have adequate access to the media. The Italian Law 482/99 on the protection of linguistic minorities, which was partly conceived as an implementation of the Framework Convention, made a rather more robust commitment to increase transmission time for minority language programmes on public radio and television. The lack of effective implementation of this commitment was criticized by the Advisory Committee in its opinion on Italy of February 2005.[84] This criticism does not have any immediate domestic legal effects, but it 'shames' Italy into improving the situation in view of its next report to the Advisory Committee.

In sum, it can be said that both these Conventions form an important site for the gradual development of a minimum standard with regard to the legal position of regional and minority languages. In fact, the decision to ratify these two instruments prompted a number of European countries to adopt new laws on the protection of minority languages, so that one could witness a mini-wave of new minority protection legislation in the late 1990s.[85] They also played a distinctive role in the preparation of the recent enlargement of the European Union. They offered benchmarks for assessing whether the applicant countries offered adequate protection to their minorities, which is one of the political criteria for accession formulated in 1993 by the European Council meeting of Copenhagen. In certain cases, the role of the EU has been decisive. For instance, the 'carrot' of accession to the EU was instrumental in the adoption of the relatively liberal Slovak law on the use of minority languages in 1999.[86]

However, the conclusion that these two conventions form the basis of a genuinely common European standard of minority language rights is subject to one major reservation. Several countries have so far consciously refrained from

---

84 Advisory Committee on the Framework Convention for the Protection of National Minorities, Second Opinion on Italy adopted on 24 February 2005, para. 89-91 and para. 154 (first recommendation).

85 In addition to the already mentioned Italian law of 1999, one may add the Slovak language law of 1999, and the Swedish Law on national minorities of 1999, which was immediately followed by two specific Laws providing for the use of the Finnish and the Sami language.

86 There is a vast literature on this theme, including the following: G. Pentassuglia, 'The EU and the Protection of Minorities: The Case of Eastern Europe', *European Journal of International Law* (2001) 3; B. de Witte, 'Politics versus Law in the EU's Approach to Ethnic Minorities', in J. Zielonka (ed), *Europe Unbound. Enlarging and Reshaping the Boundaries of the European Union* (2002) 464; G. Sasse, 'Minority Rights and EU Enlargement: Normative Overstretch or Effective Conditionality?', in G.N. Toggenburg (ed), *Minority Protection and the Enlarged European Union: The Way Forward* (2004) 61.

ratifying one or both of these conventions, and, in the case of France, both have been rejected as incompatible with national constitutional principles. The French *Conseil Constitutionnel* declared in a decision of 1999, on rather spurious grounds, that the envisaged ratification of the Charter for Regional or Minority Languages would be contrary to the Constitution (and the same assessment would apply *a fortiori* for the Framework Convention on National Minorities).[87] France is thus among the few countries (with Belgium and Greece) that refuse to ratify either of these two conventions. This reluctance of some Member States of the EU has also prevented the Council of Europe conventions from directly shaping the European Union's own 'domestic' policy with regard to language minorities, a matter to which we now turn.

## 4. Language rights in the European Union

Until the recent adoption of its Charter of Fundamental Rights, in December 2000, the European Union was not involved in standard-setting regarding cultural rights. Nevertheless, some language related rights have developed over the years and have acquired a 'fundamental' legal status within the legal order of the European Communities and the European Union, even before the adoption of the Charter. Essentially, these are (a) the right to use any of the official languages of the European Union when dealing with its institutions and (b) the right of European Union citizens not to be discriminated on account of the language they speak. We will briefly describe the evolution and present scope of these two rights.[88]

### *A. The right to use the official languages*

The European Union institutions function in many languages. This institutional multilingualism embodies, in a symbolic and practical way, the equality between the Union's Member States. It also reflects the value of democratic governance, since it guarantees that legislative, executive and judicial powers transferred from the Member State level to the European level shall be exercised there in a manner which is comprehensible, literally speaking, for the citizens of all Member States. Finally, this multilingualism is a precondition for the claim, made by the European Court of Justice and accepted by domestic courts, that large parts of EC law are directly applicable without the need to be transformed into national law; such a

---

87 See P. Fraisseix, 'La France, les langues régionales et la Charte européenne des langues régionales et minoritaires', *Revue française de droit administratif* (2001), 59.

88 This part of the paper draws on an earlier publication by one of the authors: B. de Witte, 'Language Law of the European Union: Protecting or Eroding Linguistic Diversity?', in R. Craufurd Smith (ed), *Culture and European Union Law* (2004) 205.

claim would not be tenable if Community law were not enacted in the languages of each member country.

The principled choice for multilingualism is not clearly expressed in the text of the European Treaties. However, an indirect expression of that principle can be found in Article 21 EC Treaty which includes (since an amendment made by the Treaty of Amsterdam) a *right for citizens of the Union to use any of the Treaty languages* for dealing with the institutions of the European Union.[89]

This right corresponded, when it was 'constitutionalized' in Amsterdam in the late 1990s, to the existing long-standing practice of the European Union. Indeed, this rule was originally set out in the very first Regulation ever adopted under the EEC Treaty, namely Council Regulation 1/58 on the use of languages by the Community institutions.[90] The Council then adopted the principle, which is still valid today, that the national languages of the Member States were to rank equally as official and working languages of the European Communities, subject to more detailed arrangements to be adopted by each institution separately. This rule was extended later on to the national languages of all the states acceding to the Communities[91]

---

89 Article 21, third indent: 'Every citizen of the Union may write to any of the institutions or bodies referred to in this Article or in Article 7 in one of the languages mentioned in Article 314 and have an answer in the same language.' The 'institutions or bodies referred to' are the European Parliament, the Commission, the Council, the Court of Justice, the Court of Auditors and the Ombudsman; they do not include the European Central Bank, the European Council, nor the various EU agencies. Article 314, the last article of the EC Treaty, states which language versions of the Treaty are to be authentic versions. In the consolidated version of the EC Treaty after the Treaty of Accession of 2003, the languages listed are: Dutch, French, German, Italian, Czech, Danish, English, Estonian, Finnish, Greek, Hungarian, Irish, Latvian, Lithuanian, Maltese, Polish, Portuguese, Slovak, Slovenian, Spanish and Swedish (see *Official Journal of the European Union* 2006, C 321 E/180). Article 314 was again modified by the latest Treaty of Accession so as to add Bulgarian and Romanian to the list (*ibid.*, C 321 E/327). Therefore, the right of Article 21 EC Treaty today refers to 23 languages altogether.

90 *Journal Officiel des C.E.*, 1958, 385. The Regulation was adopted pursuant to Article 217 EEC Treaty (now Article 290 EC Treaty), which states: 'The rules governing the languages of the institutions of the Community shall, without prejudice to the provisions contained in the rules of procedure of the Court of Justice, be determined by the Council, acting unanimously'.

91 An exception was made for Irish. There is an authentic version in Irish of the founding Treaties, but Irish was not included among the official and working languages when Regulation No 1 of 1958 was modified upon the accession of the UK, Ireland and Denmark (Section XIV of Annex I to the Act of Accession, *OJ* 1972, L 73/122). Irish became an official language only very recently, from 1 January 2007, due to an amendment of Regulation No 1 (*OJ* 2005, L 156/3), but its use will be more restricted than that of the other 22 official languages. As for Letzeburgesch, it became an official language of Luxembourg many years after that country helped found the European Communities, and this language was not subsequently added to the list of Regulation No. 1.

and, with the Maastricht Treaty, it was also extended to the second and third pillar of the European Union.[92]

Still, the inclusion of a *right* to use these languages, as part of the citizenship rights reforms enacted by the Treaty of Amsterdam, is not insignificant. It lends an entrenched constitutional status, in part at least, to a linguistic regime that hitherto was regulated by an act of secondary Community law (although, to be true, the existing regime was already firmly entrenched before, thanks to the unanimity requirement imposed by Article 290 EC Treaty for the adoption of modifications to the relevant Council regulation). The language clause of the Amsterdam Treaty was also important because it renewed the original commitment of the Member States to linguistic diversity, at a time when the cost of the language regime had become much higher than in 1958. Recommendations for a simplification of the Union's linguistic regime have thus been ignored. Also, the Treaty of Accession of April 2003 has simply extended the existing linguistic regime to the European Union of 25 Member States, modifying Regulation No 1 of 1958 so as to add nine additional official languages including even Maltese,[93] and the most recent Treaty of Accession also added Rumanian and Bulgarian to the list. On those occasions, the exponential increase of translation and interpretation costs, and the growing danger of communication failures between actors in the European policy-making and implementation process, could not outweigh the commitment to linguistic diversity and equality among Member States.

Between 1958 and now, the commitment to linguistic diversity has, in fact, radically changed in its tone and implications. In 1958, it was a pragmatic solution adopted by the EEC, in the same way as other international organizations decide on their language regime. The rather liberal option taken then in the EEC, which did not sacrifice any of its Member States' national languages, was taken at a rather low cost, because it meant that a co-official status was being given to four languages only in the fairly limited range of activities covered, at the time, by the EEC. Today, the commitment to the equality of Europe's national languages has become a constitutional principle of paramount importance, which is extended to 23 languages, applies to a vastly expanded scope of EU activity and therefore lays a heavy burden on the Union's institutional machinery.

However, the principle does not guarantee full equality between all the EU citizens and residents irrespective of their mother tongue. Indeed, the right may well apply to all the *national* languages of the Member States, but it does not apply to their *regional* languages, some of which have more speakers than national

---

92 See the Articles 28 and 41 EU Treaty.

93 Treaty of Accession, Annex II, section 22 (document AA 2003 final of 3 April 2003, p. 2473).

languages (compare Catalan with Danish, or Welsh with Maltese),[94] nor does it include the languages of migrant communities, which are also spoken by numerous EU citizens (compare the number of EU residents speaking Turkish or Arabic with those speaking Latvian or Slovenian).

Moreover, the leeway left to each of the institutions by Article 6 of Regulation 1/58, namely that they could make practical accommodations of the equality norm, has been used very extensively. The day-to-day reality of the European Union shows a rather different picture than the principles outlined above.[95] Increasingly, policy documents emanating from the European institutions are placed on the internet site of the EU in a few language versions only. Furthermore, it is widely known that the internal working languages of the Commission services are English and French, to the almost total exclusion of the other languages (although German is formally the Commission's third working language, it is very seldom used). It is also known that the European Court of Justice has so far conducted its deliberations in French, and that much of its preparatory work takes place exclusively in French although the Court is careful to pay tribute to the multilingual nature of primary and secondary EU law when interpreting these norms of EU law.[96]

There is also a tendency to restrict the range of languages to be used in newly established bodies of the European Union, mainly in the numerous EU agencies that have been created in recent years. In the *Kik* case, both the Court of First Instance,

---

[94] Recently, in 2005, the Council of the European Union decided that Member States could conclude administrative agreements with the various EU institutions in order to arrange for the use of regional languages in communications of these institutions with the citizenry. This results from a request by the Spanish government and is now being implemented, to a limited extent, for the benefit of Spain's regional official languages such as Catalan, Basque and Galician. However, these special arrangements do not provide for genuine *rights* to use those languages. See, for the details, F. Esteve Garcia, 'El nuevo estatuto jurídico de las lenguas cooficiales en España ante la Unión Europea', *Revista de Derecho Comunitario Europeo* (2006) 439.

[95] For more detailed analysis of the current language regime of the European Union, see among others: R. Creech, *Law and Language in the European Union* (2005) chapter 1; F. Mayer, 'Europäisches Sprachenverfassungsrecht', *Der Staat* (2005) 367; A. Milian-Massana, 'Le regime juridique du multilinguisme dans l'Union européenne. Le mythe ou la réalité du principe d'égalité des langues', *Revue juridique Thémis* (2004) 211; A. de Elera-San Miguel Hurtado, 'Unión Europea y Multilingüismo', *Revista española de Derecho Europeo* (2004) 85; B. Nabli, 'Les implications de l'élargissement sur le multilinguisme institutionnel de l'Union européenne', *Cahiers de droit européen* (2004) 197.

[96] G.F. Mancini and D.T. Keeling, 'Language, Culture and Politics in the Life of the European Court of Justice', *Columbia Journal of European Law* (1994/95) 1; L. Sevón, 'Languages in the Court of Justice of the European Communities', in *Scritti in onore di Giuseppe Federico Mancini*, Vol. II (1998), 934; G. Van Calster, 'The EU's Tower of Babel – The Interpretation by the European Court of Justice of Equally Authentic Texts Drafted in more than one Official Language', *Yearbook of European Law* (1997) 363.

and later the European Court of Justice,[97] accepted the distinction between the language regime of the EU institutions and that of other 'bodies', such as OHIM, the trade mark office of the European Union, by stating that Council Regulation 1/58 only applied to the former but not to the latter. The argument was made by the applicant that the language regime of OHIM was in breach of the unwritten principle of non-discrimination, because it treated speakers of the smaller Community languages less favourably than the speakers of the five most widely spoken languages. The Court of First Instance rejected this claim and held that 'in pursuing the objective of determining the language of the proceedings where parties who do not share the same language preference fail to agree, the Council must be considered to have made an appropriate and proportionate choice, even if the official languages of the Community were treated differently'.[98] Clearly, the Court of First Instance gave precedence to the interest of ensuring the efficient functioning of the trademark office over the interest of protecting the linguistic interests of traders from smaller EU countries.

The general significance of the *Kik* judgments is that they exclude the existence of a constitutional principle of language equality, and thereby pave the way for the EU legislator to create differentiated language regimes for the various EU agencies – though not for the institutions referred to in Article 21 EC, because these must observe the constitutional right of individuals to use any of the official EU languages. The restricted scope of the fundamental right to use one's language relates uneasily to another fundamental right that is recognized by the EU legal order, namely the right not to be discriminated against on the ground of language – the right to which we turn now.

### *B. Freedom from discrimination on grounds of language*

The EU Charter of Fundamental Rights contains, in its Article 21, a list of suspect grounds of discrimination which corresponds to that of Article 14 of the European Convention of Human Rights, and includes 'language'. However, this right not to be discriminated against on the grounds of language was not newly created by the Charter. It is, rather, inherent in the general principle of equality, one of the unwritten fundamental rights which is part of the Community legal order and which is frequently used by the European Court of Justice as a standard for the control of EU legislative and administrative measures and, indeed, as a standard applying to the Member States and to individual persons when acting within the scope of EC

[97] Court of First Instance, Case T-120/99, *Christina Kik v. Office for Harmonisation in the Internal Market (Trade Marks and Designs)*, judgment of 12 July 2001; in appeal: European Court of Justice, Case C-361/01 P, *Christina Kik v. Office for Harmonisation in the Internal Market (Trade Marks and Designs)*, judgment of 9 September 2003.

[98] CFI, *Christina Kik* judgment, par. 63.

law.[99] It is settled case law of the European Court of Justice that 'the principle of equal treatment or non-discrimination requires that comparable situations must not be treated differently and that different situations must not be treated in the same way unless such treatment is objectively justified'.[100] Given this starting-point, the general principle of equality may impact on concrete situations in which the linguistic rights and obligations of EC and state authorities, or private individuals, are at stake.

In principle, EU law does not affect the power of the Member States to determine their official language regimes and to differentiate between languages which may and may not be used in communications between citizens and public authorities. However, these official language rules are not entirely immune from the impact of Community law. They must be applied without direct or indirect discrimination against citizens of other EU countries. Thus, imposing proficiency in one or more particular languages as a condition of recruitment to public employment is allowed by Community law, but only if this requirement does not indirectly lead to discrimination against EU citizens originating from other countries. The fact that linguistic conditions of employment could function as indirect discrimination against foreigners was recognized early on in the history of EC law, in the text of Regulation 1612/68 on the free movement of workers. Article 3 of the Regulation, which has not been modified since 1968, prohibits indirect discrimination resulting from actions having as their exclusive or principal aim or effect to keep nationals of other Member States away from the employment offered. To this rule, a qualifying statement is added, namely that the prohibition does 'not apply to conditions relating to linguistic knowledge required by reason of the nature of the post to be filled'. The question therefore is whether a particular requirement of linguistic proficiency is genuinely related to the function concerned or, rather, is a condition whose aim or effect is to exclude foreigners, in particular EU citizens.

This issue was addressed by the European Court of Justice in a high-profile case decided in 1989, the *Groener* case.[101] Irish law imposed the requirement that candidates for a permanent post in public education should demonstrate an adequate knowledge of the Irish language. A Dutch applicant for this job, Anita Groener, having failed the language test, alleged that this requirement effectively excluded EU citizens from applying for any of these jobs and was therefore a form of indirect

99 For a recent case in which the general principle of equality was interpreted as a source of obligations for the Member States and for individual persons, see ECJ, Case C-144/04, *Werner Mangold v. Rüdiger Helm*, judgment of 22 November 2005. In this case, the ground of discrimination was age.

100 Among the many judgments in which this phrase is repeated (sometimes with slight variations), is Case C-210/03, *Swedish Match* (2004) ECR I-11893, par. 70.

101 ECJ, Case 379/87, *Groener v. Minister for Education and the Dublin Vocational Education Committee* (1989) ECR 3967.

discrimination falling under the prohibition of Article 3 of Regulation 1612/68. There seemed to be very good reasons to hold this view given the particular facts of the case. The job for which Ms Groener applied, that of teacher painting in the College of Marketing and Design in Dublin, did not in fact require her to speak Irish at any time, and therefore knowledge of that language was not a functional necessity. However, the Court of Justice gave a remarkably wide interpretation to the language clause of Regulation 1612/68. Because Irish was an official language of the country, Ireland was allowed to require its knowledge from all teachers, even those who would not be called to use it in the course of their work, on condition that the required level was not set too high. The Court did not read Article 3 of the Regulation as laying down a purely functional test (namely: is knowledge of the language necessary for the day-to-day performance of the job?), but as leaving space for the broader constitutional background and the language policy priorities of the Member States.

There has been much speculation about the implications of the *Groener* judgment, beyond the specific case of Ireland and of employment in public education.[102] The judgment certainly expressed sensitivity from the side of the Court for the national identity concerns of the Member States. However, no blank check was given to the Member States and their regions. Whenever a language criterion is used in recruitment for a particular job, the suspicion arises that it may be indirectly discriminating against EU citizens. If litigation arose, it would be for the national court and the ECJ (if asked for interpretative guidance by the national court) to decide whether the language knowledge is actually required and, if so, whether or not it is set at a disproportionately high level. On the basis of this proportionality requirement, the Commission recently stated that the condition, which is frequently used in announcements of recruitment, that candidates should be 'native speakers' of a particular language, is a form of indirect discrimination against citizens of other EU countries which is prohibited by EC law.[103]

The scope of this prohibition of discriminatory language conditions has been extended in two directions since 1968. Its substantive scope has been extended from public to private employment conditions and its personal scope is being extended, hesitantly still, from EU citizens to other categories of foreigners. The extension of the principle of non-discrimination on grounds of nationality to private sector employment was probably not intended by the drafters of the EEC Treaty but it

102 For a detailed analysis of the implications of the judgment, see N. Nic Shuibhne, *EC Law and Minority Language Policy. Culture, Citizenship and Fundamental Rights* (2002) at pp. 80-104.

103 See Commission Communication of 11 December 2002, *Free Movement of Workers – Achieving the Full Benefits and Potential*, COM(2002) 694, at p. 7: 'The Commission considers that while a very high level of language may, under certain strict conditions, be justifiable for certain jobs, a requirement to be mother tongue is not acceptable'.

was clearly affirmed in the *Angonese* judgment of the European Court of Justice in 2000. That case had been referred to it for a preliminary ruling by an Italian court; it questioned the fact that access to employment in a private bank in Bolzano had been made dependent upon demonstration of adequate language knowledge of both Italian and German, the two official languages in South Tyrol. This, the Court found, was a direct and acceptable consequence of the minority protection regime enacted in this region of Italy (even though it concerned employment in a private bank), but the additional requirement that evidence of bilingualism could be provided only by means of a local certificate was held to be an indirect discrimination against citizens from other EU countries, and hence in breach of EC law.[104] The judgment has become famous for its sweeping statement that the right to free movement has full horizontal application, i.e. that private persons are bound to respect the freedom and must abstain from discrimination against EU citizens. So, the situation today is that, both in public and in private employment, language skills may only be imposed on citizens of other European Union countries to the extent that they are necessary for the good performance of the job.

The protection against language discrimination in recruitment and conditions of employment now arguably applies to *third country nationals* as well, on the basis of the European Community's Race Discrimination Directive of 2000.[105] Indeed, linguistic proficiency requirements that are not justified by the nature of the job could be considered as an indirect form of racial or ethnic discrimination under the terms of this Directive. This duty of non-discrimination also applies horizontally; indeed, its main concern is to combat discrimination in private legal relations and in social life in general. So, the imposition of language conditions or requirements by private employers could amount to indirect discrimination on the grounds of race and ethnic origin, and thus be in breach of the Race Directive. Similarly, employment conditions unduly prohibiting the use of minority languages during work could be indirect discrimination on grounds of race.[106]

---

104 ECJ, Case C-281/98, *Angonese v. Cassa di Risparmio di Bolzano*, judgment of 6 June 2000, [2000] ECR I-4083. See the comment by R. Lane and N. Nic Shuibhne, in *Common Market Law Review* (2000) 1237.

105 Council Directive 2000/43 implementing the principle of equal treatment between persons irrespective of racial or ethnic origin, *OJ* 2000, L 180/22. Third country nationals are within the personal scope of this directive, although only half-heartedly; see C. Brown, 'The Race Directive: Towards Equality for *All* the Peoples of Europe?', *Yearbook of European Law* (2001-2) 195, at pp. 209-212.

106 An example from practice is the decision of the Dutch Equal Treatment Commission (*Commissie Gelijke Behandeling*) of 28 March 2000. It held that the internal rules of firms that impose the use of Dutch as the language of communication among the workforce could be disproportional and therefore discriminatory. This is the case, for example, where no linguistic conditions have been formulated upon recruitment for the job (the text of the decision is on the web site of the CGB, <www.cgb.nl/oordelen/tekst/2000-15>).

The material scope of the Directive is not limited to employment but also extends to discrimination (by both public authorities and private persons) in the fields of education, housing and social protection. The Directive thus follows the model of Regulation 1612/68 which also sets a wide scope for the protection of EU citizens against nationality discrimination. In fact, the consequences of the equal treatment principle affect the official language regime of the Member States in more subtle ways than only by requiring justification of language conditions for employment. In several rulings, the Court of Justice held that, if Member States or regions provide for the right to use minority languages for public transactions (as, for example, in court proceedings), then that right should be extended to EU citizens who happen to speak that same language. Thus, an Austrian visitor in South Tyrol may use German in court proceedings, even though this right was only intended for the German speaking minority of the area.[107]

The situations considered so far involved the compatibility of *Member State* linguistic policies with European Union rights. In addition, the right not to be discriminated against on the grounds of language can also be invoked against the European Union itself. As was mentioned above, such a claim was unsuccessfully made in the *Kik* case, where the Court of Justice effectively held that the EU legislator was justified in distinguishing between 'major' and 'lesser' EU languages in organizing the work of the European trademark office. But there could be other cases in which distinctions made by the EU institutions between speakers of different languages may not be objectively justified.

[107] ECJ, Case 137/84, *Ministère Public v. Mutsch*, [1985] ECR 2681; Case C-274/96, *Criminal proceedings against Horst Otto Bickel and Ulrich Franz*, [ECR] 1998, I-7650. The second of these two Court cases, like the *Angonese* case (mentioned above) which was decided by the ECJ two years later, dealt with the complex language regime of the Italian province of South Tyrol. On the question of the EU-compatibility of South Tyrol language laws, see G. Toggenburg, 'Diritto comunitario e tutela delle minoranze in provincia di Bolzano. Due aspetti inconciliabili di un (unico) sistema?', in *L'ordinamento speciale della Provincia autonoma di Bolzano* (2001) 139.

# 13
# The Place of Cultural Rights in the WTO System

*John Morijn*

## I. Introduction

The appropriate weight to be given to cultural diversity considerations in the context of global trade liberalization continues to preoccupy many. This chapter seeks to contribute to this debate by analysing scholarly writings and international legislative activity relating to the trade liberalization/cultural diversity debate. In particular, it highlights the contribution made by the recently adopted UNESCO Cultural Diversity Declaration and Convention in this respect. Drawing on aspects of the trade/human rights debate, the chapter primarily focuses on locating a cultural rights approach to World Trade Organization (WTO) law. By way of a first application of such an approach, it comments on some suggestions for legal avenues to integrate cultural diversity concerns in the context of WTO law relating to the free movement of goods and services (GATT and GATS).

One of the main reasons why the debate about the linkage of trade liberalization and cultural diversity has not moved on a great deal in substantive terms is its sheer contextual complexity. Even if it should by now be common place that economic globalization takes various different modes, such as that of trade liberalization, privatisation and increasing corporate power, critical writings from a cultural perspective often descriptively conflate these elements to imply that 'economic globalization' represents a coherent and uncontrollable force that pushes for a 'neo-liberal'[1] agenda. Likewise, economists' and free trade proponents' responses to such critical cultural assessments often do not move beyond out of hand dismissals of such concerns as

---

1 To borrow the terminology of J. Chan-Tibergien, 'Cultural Diversity As Resistance To Neoliberal Globalization: The Emergence Of A Global Movement And Convention', *Review of Education* (2006), pp. 89-105; and of R.J. Coombe, 'Legal Claims to Culture in and Against the Market: Neoliberalism and the Global Proliferation of Meaningful Difference', in *Law, Culture and Humanities* (2005), pp. 32-55, available at: <www.yorku.ca/rcoombe/publications/Coombe_Legal_Claims_to_Culture.pdf>.

Francioni and Scheinin (eds), *Cultural Human Rights*, 285–316

mere 'conservative' or 'protectionist'. Engagement with the issue of the way in which a cultural critique may be different from other non-economic critiques, or other non-trade issues, is preferably side-stepped by both sides to this debate.

Apart from the fact that both the alarmist cultural critiques and their patronising rebuttals by free traders[2] are not usually backed by rigorous analysis[3] – thus often making for a trade/culture debate that creates more heat than light – the regular assessment by both sides are united in stating their claims in too general terms. Different forms of economic globalization make for different interfaces with cultural considerations. Each of these interfaces is in turn subject to continuous change, in particular as a result of developments in information and communication technology. Even if it is therefore evident that it is extremely difficult to disentangle cultural and technological aspects of economic globalization's impact on cultural diversity,[4] it is important to be aware of the fact that, on the one hand, criticism of economic globalization as a process is often directed in fact to matters relating to communication technology. On the other hand, praise of any of the elements of economic globalization is also often expressed (equally erroneously) with reference to what is in reality the result of the communication revolution. In this light it may be a useful general starting-point for the discussion undertaken here to acknowledge that formulating responses in general terms to the many aspects of the linkage (i.e. economic globalization is 'good' or 'bad' for culture) is impossible. In examining particular parts of the globalization/culture interface there is a need for careful analysis of the specific merits of both sides of the story[5] (and an awareness that the general validity of findings in a particular context may be very limited).

---

2 M. Hahn, 'A Clash of Cultures? The UNESCO Diversity Convention and International Trade Law', *JIEL* (2006), pp. 515-552, at p. 521 (lamenting the fact that in the trade/culture debate both sides advance their arguments 'with an unusual degree of high-handed self-righteousness').

3 Cf. R. Adlung, 'Public Services and the GATS' *JIEL* (2006), pp. 455, 456; '[M]any statements [about GATS] appear to be influenced by personal prejudice or aversion, rather than by thorough analysis or factual evidence'; and, with regard to the World Trade Organization more particularly, M.J. Trebilcock, 'Critiquing the Critics of Economic Globalization', *Journal of International Law & International Relations* (2005), pp. 213-238, available at: <www.jilir.org/docs/vol1no1-2/JILIR%201%281-2%29%20Trebilcock-Critiquing%20the%20Critics%20of%20Economic%20Globalization.pdf> (at p. 213): '... it is important to bring some measure of rigorous detachment to the evaluation of criticisms that have been widely and vehemently directed at the WTO ...'.

4 As equally observed by M. De Saint Pulgent, 'Mondialisation Et Politiques Publiques: Le Case De La Culture En France', in M. De Saint Pulgent (ed.), *Mondialisation et diversité culturelle – Le cas de la France* (IFRI, Paris, 2003), pp. 15-54, at pp. 15-16.

5 As a recent study concluded, 'critical scholarship ... is sorely needed to explore and evaluate the motives, stakes, and limitations of "culturalising" rights assertions ... and to consider the conditions in which they support and those in which they undermine [different modes of economic globalisation]'; Cf. R.J. Coombe, *cit. supra* note 1 (p. 22 of the typescript).

With regard to international economic law, it is to be noted that cultural issues are dealt with in a variety of ways in several of its different sub-disciplines. These range from elements of international trade law such as free movement of goods (e.g. in debates about the legal status of Geographic Indicators,[6] and agricultural products – with the recent tendency to stress the 'culture' in agri*culture*), services and intellectual property rights regimes,[7] to competition law and state aid law.[8] The interplay of these various forms of international economic law with cultural considerations may well vary. It is therefore important to keep in mind that concentrating on the WTO's GATT and GATS in the legal 'trade/culture debate' is a partial approach.

The UNESCO Universal Declaration on Cultural Diversity[9] and its follow-up Convention on the Protection and Promotion of the Diversity of Cultural Expressions[10] present a useful benchmark for taking stock of the global trade liberalization/cultural considerations debate. It embodies one of the few matters that proponents and opponents of the need for special measures and mechanisms for cultural diversity protection agree on: this Convention is the most recent attempt at formulating a cultural response to the precisely identified 'threat' posed by WTO governed rules dealing with trade in goods and services. Reading this text closely may reveal where the battle lines have been frozen for now, and where it is possible to move to from here.

The chapter is structured as follows: the analysis commences with a contextual formulation of the nature and specificity of cultural activists' concerns regarding GATT/GATS, and the typical response to these concerns by trade liberalization proponents (section 2). It then assesses the way in which arguments presented in terms of cultural rights protection are employed by each side of the debate to reinforce their claims, and proposes an alternative, more nuanced cultural rights approach to WTO law (section 3). On this basis, the UNESCO Cultural Diversity Declaration and Convention are subjected to a close reading (section 4). A later section explores from a cultural rights viewpoint two legal avenues in GATT/

---

6 T. Broude, 'Taking "Trade And Culture" Seriously: Geographical Indicators and Cultural Protection in WTO Law', *University of Pennsylvania Journal of International Economic Law* (2005), pp. 623-692.

7 F.M. Abbott, 'TRIPS and Human Rights: Preliminary Reflections', in F.M. Abbott (et al.) (eds.), *International Trade and Human Rights, Foundations and Conceptual Issues* (University of Michigan Press, Ann Arbor, 2006), at pp. 145-170.

8 E. Psychogiopoulou, 'EC State Aid Control and Cultural Justifications', *Legal Issues of Economic Integration* (2006), pp. 3-28.

9 UNESCO Universal Declaration on Cultural Diversity, 2 November 2001.

10 UNESCO Convention on the Protection and Promotion of the Diversity of Cultural Expressions, adopted on 20 October 2005, at: <unesdoc.unesco.org/images/0014/001429/142919e.pdf>.

GATS law that are often highlighted in trade/cultural diversity discussions for their potential, or lack thereof, for accommodating cultural diversity concerns (section 5). The conclusion wraps up the discussion (section 6).

## 2. Characterisation of the trade liberalization v. 'cultural (diversity) considerations' debate and legal framework

Discussions about safeguarding culture in the context of trade are not, of course, new. Conflicts between trade liberalization and cultural values go back to the 1920s, when a number of European countries introduced quotas in order to protect their ailing film industry from a sudden influx of films for the US.[11] The post WWII Marshall Plan for Europe's provisions linked levels of aid directly to recipients' willingness to accept imports of US motion pictures.[12] In the GATT/WTO context the trade and culture conflict first developed during the Tokyo Round Negotiations in the late 1970s, when the US complained about the subsidies given to cinema and television by a number of GATT member states.[13] Therefore it is striking that the dispute is between industrialised states, and not between the North and the South.[14]

What does the controversy essentially consist of? Cultural considerations inspired policy has been described as serving various different purposes. Amongst its objectives are (1) the protection of heritage, (2) the maintenance of cultural institutions, (3) the support of creative production and (4) access to culture. A first clarification is that not all of these aims are being seen as challenged by trade liberalization *per se*: only the last two aspects of cultural policy making.[15] According to cultural proponents, cultural products are essential instruments of social communication which convey values, ideas and meaning, and thus contribute to fashioning the

---

11 P. Sauvé and K. Steinfatt, 'Towards Multilateral Rules on Trade and Culture: Protective Regulation or Efficient Protection?' (2000), available at: <www.cid.harvard.edu/cidtrade/Papers/Sauve/sauveculture.pdf>.

12 A.J. Scott, 'Hollywood in the Era of Globalization – Opportunities and Predicaments', *Yale Global* (29 November 2002), available at: <yaleglobal.yale.edu/article.print?id=479>.

13 C.B. Graber, 'The New UNESCO Convention On Cultural Diversity: A Counterbalance To The WTO?', *JIEL* (2006), pp. 553-574, at pp. 561,fn.38.

14 J. Wouters and B. De Meester, 'UNESCO's Convention on Cultural Diversity and WTO Law: Complementary or Contradictory?', Institute for International Law, Working Paper No. 73 (April 2005), fn. 52 (referring to the analysis by B. De Witte, 'Trade in Culture: International Legal Regimes and EU Constitutional Values', in G. De Búrca & J. Scott (eds.), *The EU and the WTO* (Hart Publishing, Oxford, 2001), at pp. 237-255).

15 M. De Saint Pulgent, *cit. supra* note 4, at p. 23.

cultural identity of a given community.[16] Upon that clarification, the challenge posed by trade liberalization has been well put as follows:

> Cultural diversity is ... threatened by the impact of trade liberalisation on the capacity of States to sustain distinct cultural expressions, since it prevents them from adopting standards that directly or indirectly impede the circulation of cultural goods and services ... this threat is all the more alarming in that the creators of culture and cultural intermediaries play a crucial role in adapting cultures to change insofar as they create a space where national values and foreign values can confront one another, as can traditional values and behaviours and new perspectives ... from this vantage point, preserving the diversity of cultural expression is to preserve cultural diversity itself, since the first plays an instrumental role in achieving the second.[17]

In other words, champions of cultural considerations are concerned that WTO obligations undermine governments' ability to pursue policies often employed by cultural policy-makers, such as granting preferences to domestic suppliers, establishing foreign ownership restrictions, paying preferential subsidies, administering broadcast quotas, entering into bilateral co-production treaties, and supporting national broadcasting undertakings.[18] They therefore advocate that cultural considerations be *de facto* or *de jure* excluded from the reach of these international trade agreements.[19]

Moving to the perspective of trade proponents, it is worth stressing, at the outset, that free traders can in some sense be viewed as basing their very economic theory upon cultural diversity, although perhaps indirectly. Its founding principle is that of comparative advantage, which hinges on natural or chosen differences between countries' endowments and regulations. The fundamental cultural choices laid down in these regulations embody a codification of these differences. Therefore, (cultural) diversity is what makes economic free movement tick.[20]

---

16 I. Bernier, 'Trade and Culture', in P.F.J. Macrory (et al.) (eds.), *The World Trade Organization: Legal, Economic And Political Analysis – Volume II* (Springer, New York, 2005), at pp. 747-793, at p. 778.

17 I. Bernier and H. Ruiz Fabri, 'Evaluation of the Legal Feasibility of an International Instrument Governing Cultural Diversity', 2002, available at: <w3.a-e-r.org/PDF/CD_Meetings/etude_faisabilite_en.pdf> (at p. 23).

18 K. Acheson and C. Maule, 'Convention on Cultural Diversity', *Journal of Cultural Economics* (2004), pp. 243-256, at p. 244.

19 I. Bernier, *cit. supra* note 16, at p. 778.

20 M.G. Trebilcock, *cit. supra* note 3, at p. 215. See also J. Smiers, *Arts Under Pressure – Promoting Cultural Diversity in the Age of Globalisation* (Zed Books, London, 2003), at p. 85 (referring to the economist John Gray).

Trade proponents tend to see cultural products as entertainment products that are similar, in commercial terms, to any other product and therefore completely subject to the rules of international trade.[21] It is argued that, if anything, trade liberalization helps creative exposure to other cultures due to greater openness caused by the breaking down of trade barriers. Moreover, it is pointed out that the closing of borders to non-national cultural products would in fact impede upon the rights of those creating these products, and those wanting to receive them. On the other hand, there are also economists who take the position that the view according to which cultural diversity is best achieved through largely unfettered market mechanisms is questionable from an economic viewpoint.[22]

As a matter of WTO law, cultural products and services are not excluded, in principle, from its scope.[23] Focusing first on the GATT, it is to be noted that some aspects of cultural diversity are excluded from the full force of trade discipline. Article IV GATT stipulates that a contracting party can maintain internal quantitative regulations requiring that films of national origin be screened over a specified period of time, during a specified minimum proportion of the total screen time actually used. The clause therefore explicitly recognizes the specificity of film as a product involved in international trade. The other provision of GATT 1994 that is concerned directly with trade in cultural goods is Article XX(f), which recognizes, as exceptions, restrictions imposed for the protection of national treasures of artistic, historic or archaeological value.

Apart from this carve-out and exception, cultural products must be treated exactly like any other product from the perspective of the multilateral trade rule system. This was confirmed in the WTO Appellate Body Ruling *Canada – Certain Measures Concerning Periodicals*,[24] where provisions designed to protect Canada's periodical industry were deemed inconsistent with Article III (national treatment) and Article XI (quantitative restrictions) of GATT 1994. This has caused considerable concern among cultural champions, to the extent that the case was described as 'the decisive moment for the formal inauguration of the global culture and trade debate'.[25]

In the case of the GATS, there are no provisions pertaining specifically to culture. However, to some extent the very structure of GATS represents a sort of 1994 meta-compromise over trade/culture. This is so as 'the deal' eventually struck over GATS was a combination of a flexible method for liberalizing trade in services (states can decide individually and on a sector-by-sector basis whether to make commitments) and an agreement to the principle of progressive liberalization. This

---

21 I. Bernier, *cit. supra* note 16, at p. 778.

22 As pointed out by M. Hahn, *cit. supra* note 2, at p. 524.

23 I. Bernier and H. Ruiz Fabri, *cit. supra* note 17, at p. 38.

24 WT/DS31/AB/R, 30 June 1997.

25 R.J. Neuwirth, 'The Cultural Industries as a Regulatory Challenge for International Trade Law', Ph.D. Thesis, European University Institute, Law Department (2005), at p. 5.

can be seen as an agreement in principle on subjecting culture to trade liberalization logic, while at the same time enabling states to carve out their own exceptions by not (yet) committing.[26]

Article II:1 GATS[27] may also impact on states' leeway to accommodate cultural considerations regardless of whether or not states have made liberalization commitments in this sector. GATS stipulates further that in response to requests from other contracting parties, signatories must undertake, in addition to the general commitments, specific commitments concerning the liberalization of trade in services in sectors of their choice. Even if it is not obligatory to respond to demands which call for opening the market of cultural services, WTO Members that wish to continue to protect cultural services will have to provide compensating concessions in other sectors in a negotiating round as a result of the WTO's negotiation mantra that no *a priori* exclusions are allowed. Therefore, guarding the continued exclusion of cultural services (for which the GATS was apparently given its complicated structure) *de facto* implies having to 'move' on other types of services, the liberalization of which may equally have an impact on non-trade policy making.[28]

## 3. A cultural rights perspective of trade liberalization v. 'cultural (diversity) considerations' debates

In their effort to gain the upper hand in the ongoing debate, both trade proponents and champions of cultural diversity regularly resort to arguments couched in cultural (human) rights language. In aiming to identify the place of cultural rights in the WTO system, it is necessary to analyse this employment in detail. Can cultural human rights be resorted to simultaneously to strengthen the case of the free traders and the culture proponents? Or would an approach based on cultural rights in fact limit and/or condition claims made by either side? If so, how? After discussing the use of cultural rights language by culture proponents and free traders, some further remarks are made with regard to the functionality and urgency of approaching trade/ cultural diversity discussions and negotiations from the perspective of (cultural) human rights.

---

26 C.B. Graber, *cit. supra* note 13, at p. 555.

27 'Each Member shall accord immediately and unconditionally to services and service suppliers of any other Member treatment no less favourable than that it accords to like services and service suppliers of any other country'.

28 See *infra* section III.3 for a discussion of some of the implications of this point from a wider human rights viewpoint.

### A. Cultural rights arguments as used by culture proponents

At first sight, human rights issues and cultural considerations brought up in the context of trade liberalization appear to be united in providing a contra-trade liberalization story. Yet, no explicit efforts have been made (legally) to connect WTO/cultural considerations and WTO/human rights debates. This is particularly striking as both human rights advocates and culture proponents in academia and advocacy,[29] often claim, or at least imply, that their topic of study cross-cuts other legal disciplines and responsibilities, including states' obligations under WTO law. For example, it was recently argued that 'due to the dynamism, elasticity, and holistic aspiration in the concept of culture, the [trade and culture] debate may … be characterised as the synopsis of all separate "trade and …" pairs [including "trade and human rights"], since it focuses on the refinement of the trade order as a whole'.[30] Yet, even if there are obvious parallels in the concerns about the process of global trade liberalization that both communities seek to address, establishing the substantial relationship between the 'cultural considerations' agenda and the human rights approach to trade liberalization is not usually undertaken. It may therefore be worthwhile to take up this task here. It will be argued in the following that a *cultural rights approach* needs to be distinguished from proposals by culture proponents which seek to reinforce the capacity of states to take measures to protect and promote cultural diversity and identity – proposals that boil down to a *cultural policy approach* to trade.

A number of human rights norms have come to be understood as cultural rights (or rights with a strong cultural element) over the years, including the right to education, the right to participate in cultural life, freedom of religion and expression, the right to self-determination, the right to enjoy the benefits of scientific progress and its applications, the right to benefit from the protection of the moral and material interests resulting from any scientific, literary, or artistic production of which the person is the author, and freedom of scientific research and creative activity.[31] It

---

29 See, for example, Joint NGO Statement, 'Cancun Declaration on Cultural Diversity', September 2003, available at <www.ebu.ch/news/press_archive/press_breves_204_Cancun.php>, starting as follows: 'Recognising that expression of culture is one of the fundamental human rights …' but not mentioning them in the operative part outlining for states what to take into account in WTO negotiations.

30 R.J. Neuwirth, *cit. supra* note 25, at p. 11.

31 See, for example, B. Robbins and E. Stamatopoulou, 'Reflection on Culture and Cultural Rights', *The South Atlantic Quarterly* (2004), pp. 419-434, fn. 14; E. Stamatopoulou, 'Remarks at "The Case for Cultural Rights Workshop"', Carnegie Endowment Human Rights Initiative (23 September 2004), available at: <www.carnegiecouncil.org/viewMedia.php/prmTemplateID/1/prmID/5006>; and Y. Donders, 'The Development of the Right to Cultural Identity in International Human Rights Law', in Y. Donders et al. (eds.), *Law and Cultural Diversity* (School of Human Rights Research, Utrecht, 1999), at pp. 65-94, at p. 65; and UNESCO, 'Desirability

is clear that different forms of trade liberalization have distinct implications on different cultural rights. As a matter of narrowing the focus for our assessment of the way in which cultural diversity advocates embrace human rights language in the context of trade liberalization, we will concern ourselves with what are sometimes termed cultural rights in the narrow or restricted sense, being those specifically mentioning the word 'culture' (i.e. Article 27 UDHR, Article 15 ICESCR, and Article 27 ICCPR). This approach is further justified as these human rights norms most clearly and directly deal with support of creative production and access to culture, which were identified above as elements of cultural policy most directly challenged by international trade liberalization.[32]

It is necessary first to formulate our understanding of how culture and human rights in general (of which cultural rights form an integral part) are typically discussed in relation to one another.[33] In such discussions the denomination of 'culture' is typically used in a very broad sense. It almost always implicitly embraces such diverse matters as traditions, aspects of participation in or benefiting from cultural activities, as well as matters relating to religions and religious activities. In using 'culture' in this way, the concept is usually presented as a coherent and stable[34] whole. Potential tensions and contradictions within (for instance, minority v. majority (dominant) tradition) or between (tradition v. religion) components encompassed by the used concept of 'culture' are not often acknowledged.

This is problematic from a human rights viewpoint. Human rights law could be seen as a mechanism that actually sets out rationally to *separate* the components of 'culture' (along with other values in a society). Human rights law functions to endow these 'cultural concepts' with different and distinguishable normative meanings, and subjects the various issues to different obligations and limitations.[35] Arguably, it also establishes a (primitive) method to balance the ingredients of 'culture' with other

---

of Drawing Up an International Standard-Setting Instrument on Cultural Diversity', 32 C/52, 18 July 2003, p. 5.

32 Cf. *supra*, section II.

33 See for a more extensive discussion of this relation, in particular a rebuttal from a cultural particularist viewpoint of many of the arguments advanced to question the universality of human rights; J. Morijn, 'Universality of Human Rights and the Challenges of Cultural Particularism – Re-Grounding Universality by way of Particularist Interpretation', Submission for the Essay Competition for the Berlin Roundtable on Transnationality (June 2005), available at: <www.irmgard-coninx-stiftung.de/en/download/037%20Morijn.pdf> (presented at a Workshop in Berlin, 4-6 October 2005).

34 N.A. Englehart, 'Rights and Culture in the Asian Values Argument: The Rise and Fall of Confucian Ethics in Singapore', *Human Rights Quarterly* (2000), pp. 548-568, at p. 562; '[The] dominant approach has been to treat culture as a relatively fixed set of psychological traits, as 'values' and 'orientations' that learned early in life and are relatively stable'.

35 To take the same examples, as a matter of human rights law the provision of primary education is seen as of greater urgency than other levels of education, and non-interference with

human rights (including cultural rights *inter se*), as the exercise of human rights can be subject to the extent to which they impact on 'the fundamental rights and freedoms of others'. In any event, for relevant human rights law analysis it therefore seems necessary to indicate what aspect/component of 'culture' is being discussed. Human rights are important *conditioners* for claims about the relevance of culture used in a broad, non-specified way.

On a more substantive level, there is often confusion about the subject and addressee of cultural rights. Cultural diversity proponents in a trade liberalization context argue, or imply, that they think of states, or societies, as the rights holders of cultural rights (rather than the holders of obligations to uphold or provide these rights). Neuwirth, for example, has stated about the culture/cultural rights nexus that

> cultural diversity can only be established when there is an equality of all cultures ... To be different means first to have equal rights, especially political, cultural and economic rights as recognised in the International Bill of Rights. From this perspective ... culture and trade appear entwined in a harmonious mutual process characterised by both the attempts to provide a common framework, either in the form of a community or a market, in which interactions between individual constituents, either in form of communication or business transactions, can take place with a view of improving or refining the welfare or well-being of all its members.[36]

The implication is that the 'legal harmony' in this reasoning can only be discerned to lie in the fact that both in trade and in cultural rights *states* are the subjects of the rights. It is submitted here that positioning cultural rights in such a way is at odds with human rights theory. Only individuals can hold human rights.[37] Even if it is acknowledged that there may be a certain indispensable community aspect for some individual rights, the entitlements themselves remain individual in nature. Indeed, many 'non-controversial' human rights are logically to be constructed with reference to the presence of 'relevant other individuals', without that fact alone taking away the individual nature of the right itself. Think, for example, about the right to

---

scientific research is subject to stricter control than more positive action required from states in line with Article 15 ICESCR.

36 R.J. Neuwirth, *cit. supra* note 25, at p. 361.

37 As Professor De Witte has written: 'rights are granted ... to individuals belonging to groups or minorities, not to these groups themselves. But, of course, when individual persons exercise rights granted to them in the cultural sphere, they often interact with other persons ... The "group dimension" is therefore, quite simply, the necessary *consequence* of granting cultural rights to individual persons, and there is no point in opposing the "individual" and "collective" dimensions of rights'; B. De Witte, 'Introduction', in Y. Donders (et al.) (eds.), *cit. supra* note 31, at pp. 1-6, 4-5.

found a family, or the right to family reunification. They are individual rights, but impossible to exercise without some 'significant others'.

In analysing cultural considerations brought up in a trade liberalization context, it is therefore necessary to distinguish a cultural rights and a cultural policy angle.[38] The two perspectives can sometimes come into tension (for example, a state not defending the rights to cultural identity of the members of a minority community within its boundaries for the reason that it does not recognize its existence as a minority). Therefore the purpose and effect of a cultural rights analysis is to scrutinize and (re)direct (top-down) policy to give expression to (bottom-up) entitlements of individuals. In other words, human rights law takes as its primary focus individuals as legal subjects, rather than itself constituting a policy objective.[39] This is not only about establishing a hierarchy of legal importance to be attached to a cultural policy or cultural rights focus. It is equally a point that cultural policy protection and cultural rights protection each have a functionally distinct role to play. It is problematic – as is implicit in the way culture proponents refer to cultural rights – to present a GATS/'cultural considerations' agenda that holds both cultural policy and cultural rights aspects as internally coherent.

One further way of putting this for the discussion to come is to point out that it is erroneous to see human rights protection as a 'non-trade topic'. Responses to claims for greater leeway for the pursuit of non-trade policy-making in a GATS context tend solely to stress that states still have the *possibility* to regulate. However, from an international human rights perspective, such reference to national *autonomy* largely rings hollow. This is particularly so since, in the context of public services, what is at stake is the right of access to the service, which requires an active stance of a state.[40] In such a case, a state is not 'free' to do what it pleases, but is *bound by*

---

38 Importantly, this has, in fact, been acknowledged by UNESCO in preparatory work leading to the UNESCO Cultural Diversity Convention, without however following through on it analytically. Cf. UNESCO, *cit. supra* note 31, at pp. 2-3 (arguing that the concept of cultural diversity raises two main questions that need to be addressed in parallel. These are 'on the one hand, the links between cultural diversity, human rights and cultural rights [and] on the other, the links between diversity, creativity and cultural policies').

39 An article by the former Special Rapporteur on the Right to Education that critically addresses the intentions of some leading human rights NGOs that have recently broadened their professional focus to include economic, social and cultural rights (such as Human Rights Watch) implicitly holds this line of reasoning, K. Tomasevski, 'Unasked Questions about Economic, Social and Cultural Rights from the Experience of the Special Rapporteur on the Right to Education (1998-2004): A Response to Kenneth Roth, Leonard S. Rubenstein, and Mary Robinson' *Human Rights Quarterly* (2005), p. 709: 'economic, social and cultural rights are not about poverty but policy' (p. 713) and 'those who claim to be doing human rights work should be distinguishable from their colleagues who work in education' (p. 712).

40 Cf. C. Graham, 'Human Rights and the Privatisation of Public Utilities and Essential Services', in K. De Feyter & F. Gomez Isa (eds.), Privatisation and Human Rights in the Age of Globalisation (Intersentia, Antwerp, 2005).

*a positive obligation* to provide what is required by norms relating to a particular human right.

This is a very important point. Often one cannot escape from the impression that it is not appreciated by some trade specialists that regulatory autonomy is not only circumscribed by WTO law, but in fact by many international obligations simultaneously, including human rights law. This reality cannot be side stepped, or wished away.[41] As a result, presenting trade agreements as very flexible (and therefore – it is clearly implied – hardly capable of creating 'problems') serves to underplay the tension between the simultaneous international obligations flowing from WTO agreements, treaties dealing with non-trade matters and international human rights treaties that are all part of international law.[42] It is legally more correct to analyse the terms of the tension, and think constructively about how to solve them.

With regard to a human rights scrutiny of cultural policy advocacy in a trade context, it is worth emphasizing that it does not necessarily correspond to past practice within human rights monitoring circles. In 1993 the Committee on Economic, Social and Cultural Rights stated, in words very similar to those typically used by culture proponents, that 'there is a danger of growing standardisation of culture or the lowering of the level of culture to the lowest common denominator, generally due to the invasion of a cultural model from outside which is accepted purely because of economic factors and due to market forces'.[43] In other words, making the case for the human rights viewpoint of cultural policy as outlined above also needs to be undertaken *within human rights circles*.

All of this, of course, still leaves open the question as to what normative content an individual right to cultural identity could contain? Even if the International Covenant on Economic, Social and Cultural Rights contains in its Article 15(1)(a)

---

41 For an interesting attempt in the WTO context, see S. Cho, 'The WTO's Identity Crisis – Review of Conflict of Norms in Public International Law: How WTO Law Relates to Other Rules of International Law, By Joost Pauwelyn, 2003' Global Law Books <www.globallawbooks.org/reviews/detail.asp?id=53>, (2006), accessed 3 October 2006: '[C]ross-fertilization or reconciliation [of non-WTO norms and WTO norms] should be the WTO's call ... no other treaties should replace the WTO in that call ... after all, it is all about "trade and (...) human rights", *not* "... human rights and trade"'. (emphasis in the original).

42 For example, Krajewski presents his claim that GATS should give priority to the regulatory autonomy of WTO Members as in line both with WTO case law allowing for deference to national regulatory choices and at the same time coinciding with the OHCHR human rights approach to trade, which stresses that GATS is to be interpreted as far as possible so as not to constrain governmental action with regard to basic service provision; M. Krajewski, 'Public Services and Trade Liberalization: Mapping the Legal Framework' *JIEL* (2003), p. 341, pp. 346-347. It is argued here that a human rights focus and a non-trade agenda need not always coincide.

43 R. O'Keeffe, 'The "Right To Take Part In Cultural Life" Under Article 15 of the ICESCR', *ICLQ* (1998), pp. 904-923, 919, fn. 108, read together with fn. 4.

the right to participate in cultural life, this right has, so far,[44] been only 'declared, but not defined'.[45] Yet, as was of course correctly observed, 'giving definition to cultural rights is necessary for legal enforceability',[46] in particular in contexts not primarily familiar with human rights law and principles.[47] It is obvious that this is the hard question in this discussion. Indeed, as De Witte has written, 'whereas the concept of human rights has made triumphant progress in both international and national law in recent decades, at least at the norm-setting level, the implications of this human rights revolution for the recognition of *cultural* rights, and more specifically the right to be culturally *different* from mainstream society, are still controversial and hotly debated'.[48]

Cultural rights have in fact been defined to some extent by UN human rights monitoring bodies. A recent in-depth study concluded that even if it were 'an impossible task to examine participation in cultural life as a stand-alone right',[49] many aspects of the context and conditions for the enjoyment of this right relate to the enjoyment of other human rights which have benefited from a more developed interpretation. It was observed that in the UN human rights treaty monitoring practice 'the majority of violations with regard to access to culture ... fall into the category of failure to take action to protect the cultural rights of minorities ... the less ethnically and culturally diverse the society in the reporting State, the fewer the ... violations ... concerning cultural rights'.[50] On this basis it was argued that:

> Obligation to conserve culture requires a State to recognise the identity and existence of all cultures within its jurisdiction and to recognise that they all form and contribute to a national and global culture... this entails respecting the self-identification of individuals and groups as minorities, indigenous or tribal and guaranteeing the equal treatment of these cultures at all levels and without discrimination... States must ensure particularly that

---

44 Work on a General Comment on Article 15(1)(a) ICESCR about the right to participation in cultural life is already underway; Cf. 3D: Three -> Trade, Human Rights, Equitable Economy, 'Intellectual Property and Human Rights – Is the Distinction Clear Now?', Policy Brief (October 2006), available at: <www.3dthree.org/pdf_3D/3D_GC17_IPHR.pdf> (at p. 4).

45 As it was put by S.A. Hansen, 'The Right to Take Part In Cultural Life: Toward Defining Minimum Core Obligations Related To Article 15(1)(A) Of The International Covenant On Economic, Social And Cultural Rights', in A. Chapman & S. Russell (eds.), Core Obligations: Building a Framework for Economic, Social and Cultural Rights (Intersentia, Antwerp, 2002), pp. 279-303, at p. 303.

46 B. Robbins and E. Stamatopoulou, *cit. supra* note 31, at p. 428.

47 See, *infra*, section V for a discussion of avenues for addressing cultural rights in WTO Dispute Settlement.

48 B. De Witte, *cit. supra* note 37, at p. 2-3 (emphases in the original).

49 S.A. Hansen, *cit. supra* note 45, at p. 290.

50 *Ibid.*, at p. 302.

> minorities have full opportunities for gaining access to and participating in the national and global culture, while safeguarding their right to preserve their own cultural identities as well.[51]

To summarize the argument made in this sub-section, and to set the stage for the next: a cultural rights perspective is to be thought of and construed as distinct from a cultural (or economic) policy approach. Policy approaches focus by their very nature on the top-down capacity of the state to regulate and conceptualize individuals essentially as objects rather than subjects of this process. A human rights perspective gives an alternative perspective in that it goes about addressing issues in a bottom-up way, taking the effects on individuals as its starting point of analysis (and urging states to prioritize this aspect in their actions). As a result, a human rights law approach represents a distinct, legally relevant, and logically unified perspective of both economic (in this case trade) and non-economic (in this case cultural) claims in the context of trade liberalization/cultural considerations discussions. Human rights law is to be seen as providing a framework within which the particular cultural needs of individuals as right-holders can be formulated in a balanced way.

### *B. Cultural rights arguments as used by trade liberalization proponents*

Trade proponents also attempt to reinforce their case in the trade/cultural diversity debate with reference to cultural rights, in particular the right to freedom of expression. As was pointed out above, this has been characterized as one of the cultural rights in the broad sense. Therefore it is worth looking at this in more detail.

On the international level this human right is present in Article 19 of the UDHR and Article 19 of the ICCPR. Paragraph 19(2) ICCPR states in particular that the freedom of expression includes 'the right of everyone to seek, receive and impart information and ideas of all kinds, regardless of frontiers, either orally, in writing or in print, in the form of art, or through any other media of his choice'. This leaves us with the question as to whether this human right is unjustifiably restricted, as argued by the United States of America in particular, by national cultural policy measures subsidizing national film industries and public service television programmes. This could be seen as being the case since they limit access to programmes and films from elsewhere and therefore discriminate against foreign products.

However plausible this critique may seem at first sight, in the face of the *de facto* dominance of particularly US cultural products eventually it does not hold water. We can refer to Graber to make this point:

> the right to freedom of expression has an individual and institutional element … the institutional element entails that freedom to express one's opinion

[51] *Ibid.*, at p. 300.

> presupposes the freedom to form an opinion … logically, [this] freedom … would not be possible under circumstances where only a very limited choice regarding sources of information exists … freedom of expression presupposes a variety of sources of information … in modern societies characterised by mass communication, this ultimately presupposes media pluralism, which provides the basis for public discourse, thereby fostering free intellectual debate … Therefore governmental measures protecting and promoting cultural diversity may be necessary to guarantee the effective enjoyment of the freedom of information.[52]

In terms of human rights law, the 'institutional element' mentioned by Graber is to be guaranteed by simultaneous protection of cultural rights in the narrow sense. On a close look, single-minded stress on the cultural right of freedom of expression ends up prioritizing the importance of the cultural messenger over the interests of the cultural addressees. In doing so, this approach actually serves to deny, whether or not intentionally, the human rights nature of cultural rights in the narrow sense. Therefore, even if the cultural rights of producers of cultural products and services deserve protection, this needs to be achieved in a more appropriately balanced framework of cultural rights than that presented by trade proponents making their case in 'cultural rights language'.

### *C. Function of a 'cultural rights approach' to GATT/S*

Perhaps as a result of the 'contaminated' nature of invoking cultural rights in the context of trade liberalization v. cultural diversity considerations discussions, the most significant civil society groups focusing on the WTO from a human rights viewpoint have not yet taken an interest in scrutinizing the WTO's activities and case law from the particular angle of cultural rights.[53] Academic literature on the trade/

---

52 C.B. Graber, *cit. supra* note 13, at pp. 561-563.

53 See, for example, 3D -> Three: Trade, Human Rights, Equitable Economy, 'Practical Guide to the WTO for Human Rights Advocates', (December 2004), available at: <www.3dthree.org/en/complement.php?IDcomplement=36>, and International Federation for Human Rights, 'Understanding Global Trade & Human Rights – Report & Resource Guide for National Human Rights NGOs in View of the 2005 WTO Ministerial Conference, Hong Kong' (July 2005), available at: <www.fidh.org/IMG/pdf/wto423a.pdf>. A notable exception was a recent publication on cultural rights by the Carnegie Council on Ethics in International Affairs; The Editors, 'Institutionalization and Standardization', in Cultural Rights – What They are, why they matter, how they can be realized, Special Issue of 'Human Rights Dialogue' Carnegie Council on Ethics and International Affairs (New York, 2005), available at: <www.cceia.org/media/5131_HRD2_12.pdf?PHPSESSID=b78ea23fc350a25bbbff6a6d28638976>, 'The rising heat of intellectual property debates is reflected in UNESCO's current effort to draft a binding cultural diversity convention. This effort aims to bring better balance to the rapidly globalising system of rights of invention, access, use, and appropriation regulated by the World Trade

cultural rights issue is also notably incomplete.[54] Therefore we are largely left to our own devices in identifying a cultural rights approach to GATT and GATS, and to appreciate the trade/cultural diversity debate and norm setting and interpretation activities within UNESCO and the WTO.

What would be the point of already analysing cultural diversity issues relating to GATT/S from a human rights viewpoint at this stage? For is it not the case that there is a cultural exception in GATT and most states have chosen not to commit cultural industries in the GATS context? Why not focus exclusively on (the stage of) the settlement of legal disputes? The answer to these questions has different aspects.

Firstly, in cases where it is not yet known whether a proposed trade or non-trade policy is likely to promote or undermine human rights, it has been confirmed in the particular context of trade liberalization by UN treaty monitoring bodies that human rights law requires that a prior assessment be carried out.[55] In line with this, many human rights advocates argue that it may be more effective to think ahead in a constructive way rather than only to engage in *ex post* criticism of negotiation results. Much work is currently being done to develop a so-called human rights impact assessment. It is an analytical tool, used both *ex ante* and *ex post*, to evaluate the effects of a policy on specific human rights.[56] More institutionally, given that trade negotiations are usually the sole competence of trade officials at the domestic

---

Organization and using the language of patent, copyright, and trademark. If this system is to avoid setting one-sided standards … favouring the "free trade" of economic globalisation, it must first reconcile with existing cultural rights standards. To do so requires recognising forms of protection for traditional sources of cultural creativity that support collective cultural distinctiveness (at p. 25). Finally, also the Trade and Human Rights Partnership Project, however, can be taken to hint at least a partial cultural rights focus by referring 'gender and diversity – Women's rights, indigenous rights, minorities' rights, rights of the disabled and other oppressed groups' as of the categories of intended focus in a background paper on its research activities; at: <www.kenan-flagler.unc.edu/KI/kiWashington/humanRightsAndTrade/hrtBackground.cfm>.

54 For example, in two recent books about trade/human rights no chapter was dedicated to the interface of cultural human rights and free movement of goods and services; T. Cottier (et al.) (eds.), *Human Rights and International Trade* (Oxford University Press, Oxford, 2005); and F.M. Abbott et al. (eds.), *International Trade and Human Rights, Foundations and Conceptual Issues* (University of Michigan Press, Ann Arbor, 2006).

55 3D, *cit. supra* note 53, at pp. 71-72, referring to the Committee on the Rights of the Child.

56 International Federation for Human Rights, *cit. supra* note 53, at p. 11. See also K. De Feyter, *Human Rights: Social Justice in the Age of the Market* (Zed Books, London, 2005), p. 216: 'Human rights proponents need proactively to identify the human rights impact of economic globalisation, if human rights are to fulfil their potential as instruments of social protection … they need to do so at an early stage, when economic norms and mechanisms are being negotiated … human rights concerns must be part and parcel of the regulation of economic globalisation'.

level, a further reason for *ex ante* analysis is that it may help empower officials of other departments to have their interests heard in the domestic trade departments at a time still relevant to the formulation of positions in trade negotiations.[57] It appears that these considerations are also relevant for a cultural rights approach to GATT and GATS.

Secondly, this proactive human rights approach seems to be particularly valid for the GATS context. There is no sector, including cultural industries, that is *a priori* excluded from the current round of negotiations,[58] known in trade-speak as the 'built-in agenda'. This understanding to the effect of liberalizing trade in services through successive rounds of negotiations 'accentuates the need for ... analysts to be alert to the GATS' possible consequences for national freedoms to plan and operate collective, redistributive, citizen-based [public services]'.[59] Moreover, given the mercantilist nature of international trade negotiations, it is quite likely that requests are made with regard to one sector to compensate for a 'sacrifice' in another. Sectors, for which the implications of liberalization have remained under-negotiated and hence under-explored, are more vulnerable to be 'negotiated away' as a result,[60] particularly in the proverbial last-minute deals.

Thirdly, a human rights approach may also help identify the *most urgent* human rights concerns to be addressed in a trade liberalization context. As was pointed out above[61], the very structure of GATS can be understood as representing a meta-compromise on the trade/culture linkage. Therefore states may have the inclination not to make commitments in the field of cultural services. As Voon has written, states *a priori* excluding a willingness to commit to service sectors with a bearing

57 P. Rose, R. Carr-Hill, K. Holmes, and T. Henderson, *Education and the General Agreement on Trade in Services: What Does the Future Hold?* (The Commonwealth Secretariat, London, 29 May 2003), p. 5.

58 J.A. Van Duzer, *Navigating Between the Poles: Unpacking the Debate on the Implications for Development of GATS Obligations Relating to Health and Education Services*, in E.-U. Petersmann & J. Harrison (eds.), *Reforming the World Trading System: Legitimacy, Efficiency and Democratic Governance* (Oxford University Press, Oxford, 2005).

59 N. Yeates, 'The General Agreement on Trade in Services: What's in it for Social Security?', *International Social Security Review* (2005), p. 3, at p. 4.

60 See for this point in a different context, S. Bjarnason, 'Debate on Education and GATS: Where Do We Stand?', in P. Rose (et al.) (eds.), *Education and the General Agreement on Trade in Services: What Does the Future Hold?* (The Commonwealth Secretariat, London, 2003), p. 16: 'The fact that the education sector is one of the least actively negotiated should not give way to a sense of complacency as the negotiators have potentially much larger services on the table from a national perspective. It is possible that if the negotiators (usually departments of trade) are not lobbied persistently by education representatives to enable them to clearly understand the issues from the education sector, them the temptation might well be to make concessions in the education sector in order to gain a stronger position in what might be perceived be perceived to be some larger public issue'.

61 See *supra*, section II.

on 'culture' 'would … have to "pay" for [their] refusal to improve commitments in relation to cultural products as part of its overall negotiating package'.[62] It is important to realize that, from a human rights viewpoint, this leads to a situation in which in the GATS context the protection of human rights with a cultural aspect is implicitly viewed as more urgent than other human rights. It is obvious that according to this mindset areas of non-trade policy other than culture (and human rights other than cultural rights) are likely to be contemplated for commitment *first*. However, GATS potentially covers services of immediate and direct relevance to a much wider area of human welfare, such as water, energy, health and social care, education, and income support services.[63] Analysis based on human rights law can help assess the limits within which commitments in any area, including that of cultural services, are supportable. Consequently, it can also provide arguments for the extent to which each area, including cultural services, can be 'freed up' for negotiation. In such a way human rights that are equally (or more) urgently affected by GATS than are cultural rights can be equally safeguarded.

## 4. A cultural rights perspective of the UNESCO Cultural Diversity Declaration and Convention

In light of the WTO system's perceived threat to the continuance of cultural protection policies that were largely still possible under GATT 1947, a movement stepped up to try and bolster states' capacity to guarantee a space for cultural policy making. A UNESCO Universal Declaration on Cultural Diversity[64] was initially adopted for this purpose in 2001. The first of the 'Main Lines of an Action Plan' for its implementation was to take forward 'the consideration of the advisability of an international legal instrument on cultural diversity'. The adoption of such an international instrument was seen as facilitating a legal environment in which some countries would feel more at ease to make commitments under GATS. To put it more precisely, it would allow state parties of the Convention that are equally WTO signatories to sustain their WTO obligations but make no further commitments in areas such as audiovisual services under the GATS unless these commitments would be deemed compatible with cultural diversity,[65] or would allow states to refuse to make

---

62 T. Voon, 'UNESCO and the WTO: A Clash of Cultures?', *ICLQ*(2006), pp. 635-652, at p. 643.

63 N. Yeates, *cit. supra* note 59, at p. 7.

64 See *supra* note 9.

65 K. Acheson and C. Maule, *cit. supra* note 18, at p. 249.

such commitments.[66] It was seen as an alternative to a GATS cultural exception.[67] Moreover, the initiative was hailed by some human rights NGOs as a contribution to the advancement of cultural rights.[68] The Convention was adopted in 2005. In light of the discussions in the previous sections, it is important to assess whether the UNESCO initiatives reflect a cultural policy or a cultural rights approach to trade liberalization, or perhaps both.

With regard to the 2001 UNESCO Universal Declaration on Cultural Diversity, its Article 6, placed under the banner of 'Cultural Diversity and Human Rights', stated that '... care should be exercised that all cultures can express themselves and make themselves known'. As the title of that article reads 'towards access for all to cultural diversity', it is clear that this refers to access for all *states, or societies*.[69] On the other hand, the same section contains the wording that 'the defence of cultural diversity ... implies a commitment to human rights ..., in particular the rights of persons belonging to minorities and those of indigenous peoples' (Article 4), and a mention of cultural rights in the narrow sense (in Article 5) 'as an enabling environment for cultural diversity'. Substantively, therefore, the clauses of Articles 4-6 of the Declaration are ambiguous about whether a cultural policy or cultural rights approach to trade is favoured. On balance, even if UNESCO itself made the case that the Declaration 'demonstrated that the debate between advocates of cultural goods and services and the champions of human rights could be transcended, the two approaches being complementary',[70] it arguably favours a cultural policy approach.[71]

---

66 I. Bernier and H. Ruiz Fabri, *cit. supra* note 17, at p. 38.

67 F. Papandrea, 'Trade and Cultural Diversity: An Australian Perspective', *Prometheus* (2005) 23(2), pp. 227-237, at p. 227.

68 Fédération International de Droits de L'Homme, 'In Support of the Draft Convention on the Protection of the Diversity of Cultural Contents and Artistic Expressions', 18 October 2005, available at: <www.fidh.org/article.php?3id_article=2766>.

69 It is not possible to interpret the text as a sort of short-hand for 'care should be exercised that all *members of a culture* can express themselves ...', as the wording of Article 6 should be interpreted in light of the definition given in the preamble that 'culture is the set of distinctive spiritual, material, intellectual and emotional features *of society or a social group*, and ... encompasses, in addition to art and literature, lifestyles, ways of living together, value systems, traditions and beliefs' (emphasis added).

70 UNESCO, *cit. supra* note 31, at p. 3.

71 In this sense it is instructive to note that it was never clearly explained why a cultural rights instrument, which was considered as an alternative to a cultural diversity convention, was not found *legally suitable* for addressing the threat of trade liberalization; only *policy* reasons were given by UNESCO: 'the wisdom of a specific instrument on cultural rights is under debate ... the prospect of actually seeing one remains very remote ...'; Cf. UNESCO, *cit. supra* note 31, at p. 5.

The drafting of the UNESCO Convention was taken up in 2003, and the final version agreed upon in October 2005. As has been observed, the *raison d'être* of the UNESCO Convention was 'to create a safe haven for protectionist measures aimed at ensuring cultural diversity, read: for allowing WTO members to legally provide shelf-space for domestic productions in television programs and cinemas'.[72] It therefore reaffirms what had been previously noted in trade/cultural diversity discussions: it centred on the film and television industries, 'to the extent that the term "culture"became synonymous with the word "audiovisual"'.[73] It is easily observed from a human rights viewpoint that focusing on cultural contents and artistic expressions implies a rather narrow view of trade's effect on cultural diversity. Other aspects that could be seen as important and relevant elements, such as the sum of distinctive traits distinguishing a society or group, cultural heritage in all its forms, copyright, etc. are largely left aside as topics in themselves.[74]

Human rights protection is referred to in several places in the Convention. Article 2(1) lists the 'principle of respect for human rights and fundamental freedoms' as the first of eight 'Guiding Principles', which also include 'sovereignty' (principle 2), 'equal dignity of and respect for all cultures' (principle 3) and 'equitable access' (principle 7). The latter principle curiously proclaims both the apparently individual entitlement of 'access to a rich and diversified range of cultural expressions from all over the world' as well as 'access of cultures to the means of expressions and dissemination'. Article 5(1) of the Convention contains the second reference to human rights in the following terms: 'The Parties, in conformity with ... universally recognized human rights instruments, reaffirm their sovereign right to formulate and implement their cultural policies and to adopt measures to protect and promote the diversity of cultural expressions...'. Therefore it seems to be acknowledged, in line with the function of a cultural rights approach to trade,[75] albeit in a very ambiguous way, that human rights law circumscribes states' leeway to go about cultural policy making.[76]

Human rights assessment of the Convention has been varied. One analyst has lamented the fact that human rights are just one of the considerations listed in Article

---

72 M. Hahn, *cit. supra* note 2, at p. 533.

73 M.E. Footer and C.B. Graber, 'Trade Liberalization and Cultural Policy', *JIEL* (2000), pp. 115-144, at p. 119.

74 I. Bernier, 'Preliminary Draft of the Convention on the Protection of the Diversity of Cultural Contents of Artistic Expressions – Analysis and Commentary', 2004, at: <www.culture-quebec.com/international/diversite-culturelle/eng/pdf/draft_analysis-commentary_2004.pdf>.

75 See *supra* section III.C.

76 See, however, C.B. Graber, *cit. supra* note 13, at p. 559: 'Article 5 CCD gives *unlimited* discretion to the Parties to decide autonomously which cultural policy measures they deem appropriate for the protection and promotion of the diversity of cultural expression' (emphasis added).

2's Guiding Principles as a 'worrying lack of sensitivity for individual human rights'.[77] Another has written that Article 2(1) and Article 5(1) of the Convention 'create the possibility that a Party could object to a policy or measure of *another* Party on the grounds that it violates the fundamental rights of individuals'.[78] It could be argued that, *a fortiori*, these provisions should then also be understood as enabling states to act internally, within their own territory and with regard to their own population, when it comes to preventing the violation of cultural rights.

On balance, however, the Convention, like the Declaration, is best characterized as representative of a cultural policy approach to trade rather than a cultural rights approach, particularly as a result of the mentioned concept of 'equitable access'. As the Executive Director of the International Network for Cultural Diversity, one of the main instigating NGOs for the development of the Convention, has written: 'what began as a statement of the right of individuals to have choice in cultural products was transformed into a principle of "equitable access" … what would have been a powerful limitation on the sovereign right of states was confused and weakened ….[79]' More generally, many more tensions are to be seen between the principles listed in Article 2 of the Convention, making it hard to see how it could give much guidance to the pursuit of a cultural rights agenda in the WTO setting.[80]

In conclusion, the sort of language highlighted in the Declaration and the Convention could be seen as an attempt to widen or bolster the scope of action for national cultural policy making. The way cultural (human) rights are mentioned seems, on balance, not coherent with the *raison d'être* of cultural rights protection. In particular, as was mentioned earlier,[81] the subject of cultural rights cannot be simultaneously individuals *and* the state (or only the state or a community or

---

77 M. Hahn, *cit. supra* note 2, at p. 536.

78 G. Neil, 'How Effectively Does the Convention Respond to the Cultural Challenges of Economic Globalization?', Suisse Culture (6 March 2006), available at: <www.suisseculture.ch/doss/unesco_ccd/neil_convention0603.pdf> (at p. 18) (emphasis added).

79 *Ibid.*, at p. 12. See also R.J. Coombe, *cit. supra* note 1, at pp. 7-8 of typescript: 'critics complain that through the processes of negotiation assertions of rights have been abandoned … culture has been reduced to the content of goods and services, with special rights for minorities and indigenous peoples to benefit from the development of their traditional cultural expressions poorly integrated into a document that is primarily designed to protect public sector interventions into market economies'.

80 See for example, the critical assessment by K.A. Appiah, 'The Case for Contamination', *New York Times*, 1 January 2006: 'The UNESCO Convention affirms the "principle of equal dignity of and respect for all cultures" (what, all cultures, including those of the K.K.K. and the Taliban?) and "the importance of culture for social cohesion in general and in particular it potential for the enhancement of the status and role of women in society" (but does not 'cohesion' argue for uniformity? And would not enhancing the status and role of women involve changing, rather than preserving, cultures?)'.

81 See *supra* section III.A.

minority group), as is suggested in the text of the Declaration and the Convention (Article 2(7)), as the latter is actually the addressee of cultural rights. A state is bound to provide the mentioned protection to individuals, whether or not as part of a community. Therefore, the question of how the parallel consideration of cultural policy and cultural rights could influence the thinking about cultural diversity protection in a context of trade liberalization – an issue that, it must be remembered, was flagged by UNESCO itself in preparatory work for the drafting of the Convention[82] – remains unanswered in the UNESCO initiatives. Rather than offering a basis to legally square cultural rights protection and cultural policy making efforts, UNESCO work favours a cultural policy approach.

This may have left us with a situation that is *de facto* less favourable for cultural rights than the situation as it existed before the UNESCO initiatives. Indeed, concern has been expressed about international legislative activity aimed at enhancing cultural policy protection while at the same time being at the cost of cultural rights protection: 'policies that promote cultural diversity should give expressions of minority cultures more opportunities … unfortunately, the draft Convention on Cultural Diversity … pays hardly any attention to the promotion of minority cultures at home … The [NGO draft] suffers from a misguided concept of cultural diversity …'.[83] In other words, even if rhetorically the concerns of UNESCO initiatives relate to national cultural *diversity*, a deep reading of the texts shows a far more ambiguous motivation. In particular, following an arguably implicit state/*one* culture conflation, the regulatory aim tends towards protecting states' majority culture(s).[84] As a result, and notwithstanding the UNESCO initiatives' various references to the obligations to protect human rights, the cultural diversity concept favoured by them appears to lock in cultural protective practice that many human rights norms seek *to break*.

Eventually, then, we should not shy away from pointing out that on a deeper level a cultural rights and a cultural policy perspective may have quite fundamentally different premises and priorities. This is best illustrated by referring to the wording

82 See *supra* note 38.

83 F. Van der Ploeg, 'Comment on "Convention on Cultural Diversity" by Keith Acheson and Christopher Maule', *Journal of Cultural Economics* (2004), pp. 257-261, at p. 261 (Commenting on a draft cultural diversity convention developed by an NGO before the drafting of the UNESCO Convention was undertaken, but valid still with regard to the UNESCO Draft Convention).

84 Cf. K.R. Srinivas, 'UNESCO: Cultural Diversity Convention', Economic and Political Weekly, 11 March 2006, available at: <www.ssrn.com/>; 'In the eagerness to protect national culture from globalisation, nations may not give much importance to protect protect[ing] the local or regional *from* [the] national … while the Convention will definitely help nations in framing cultural policies to counter the threats from globalisation, it may not be very helpful in protecting and promoting cultural diversity *within* nations, unless the national governments and regional governments give equal importance to that …' (emphases added).

in Article 1 of the Universal Declaration on Cultural Diversity that reads: 'As a source of exchange, innovation and creativity, cultural diversity is necessary for humankind as biodiversity is for nature'. The value of this analytical parallelism of biodiversity and cultural diversity is apparently widely shared by culture proponents and has been acknowledged in other fora.[85] The mindset behind it has been well captured as follows: '[T]he preservation of cultural diversity implies at the outset the preservation of all existing cultures because each culture that disappears, each language that ceases to be spoken, is a loss for cultural diversity.'[86]

The problem with this statement, and the analytical conflation of cultural diversity and biodiversity, is that on reflection it makes little sense on a philosophical level, and tends to lead to a flawed focus when applied in practice. Fundamentally, there is a qualitative difference between what Man is made of, on the one hand, and what is man-made, on the other. The analytical parallelism between biodiversity and cultural diversity loses this distinction. The human species is *part of* the planet's diversity, which has inherent value for reason of its pre-human (and thus pre-cultural) Grand Design. Cultural diversity reflects different practices that humans have developed over the course of time during which they have themselves developed as a species. Unlike the biological patrimony, there is no reason why cultural practices cannot be rationally abandoned or changed.

More practically, as Sen has put it, '[t]here is a big difference between (1) valuing multiculturalism because of the way, and to the extent that, it enhances the freedoms of the people involved to choose to live as they would like (and have reason to like); and (2) valuing cultural diversity *per se*, which focuses on the descriptive characteristics of a societal pattern, rather than on the freedoms of the people involved'.[87] The biodiversity parallelism as invoked by cultural policy proponents serves as a (flawed) argument to support claims aimed at safeguarding the statement under (2). In contrast, a cultural rights approach would place much more stress on (1). As Princeton philosopher Appiah has written in his commentary on the UNESCO Convention:

> If we want to preserve a wide range of human conditions because it allows free people the best chance to make their own lives, we cannot enforce diversity by trapping people within differences they long to escape ... cultures are

---

85 See, for example, Assembly of European Regions/European Regional Ministers for Culture and Education, 'Brixen/Bressanone Declaration on Cultural Diversity and GATS', 18 October 2002 , para. 16: 'We ... concur with the recognition ... that cultural diversity is as necessary for humankind as biodiversity is for nature and that policies to promote and protect cultural diversity thus are an integral part of sustainable development'.

86 J. Smiers, 'A Convention on Cultural Diversity: From WTO to UNESCO', *Media International Australia incorporating Culture and Policy* (2004), pp. 81-96, at p. 88.

87 A. Sen, 'Elements of a Theory of Human Rights', *Philosophy & Public Affairs* (2004), pp. 315-356, at p. 336,fn. 36.

> made of continuities and changes, and the identity of a society can survive through these changes ... societies without change are not authentic; they are just dead.[88]

## 5. Exploring avenues to articulate cultural rights concerns in GATT/S law

This short section discusses, from the viewpoint of the cultural rights approach to trade, two entry-points in GATT and GATS law that have been focused on in the context of the trade/cultural policy debate for their potential (or perceived lack thereof) to integrate cultural diversity concerns into WTO law. These relate, firstly, to the extent to which the provision of services aimed at enhancing access to culture can be characterized as a public service provision and as a matter of GATS law (and thus the degree to which public cultural service provision could be construed to be excluded from the scope of GATS by virtue of Article I:3(b)/(c) GATS). Secondly, an assessment will be made of the extent to which proposals to the effect of conceptualizing public morality and public order wording in GATT and GATS general exception clauses for inclusion of cultural diversity considerations hold water from the viewpoint of cultural rights.[89]

In opting to deal with these two issues only, it is of course acknowledged that this focus is but a starting point of an analysis of the legal place of cultural rights in WTO law. Yet, in taking up these two GATT/S contexts proposed by cultural policy proponents, the discussion may also serve to illustrate the argument made in previous sections to the effect that a cultural rights approach to trade is to be distinguished from a cultural policy approach to trade. It will be shown that the

---

88 K.A. Appiah, *cit. supra* note 80. See also M.J. Trebilcock, *cit. supra* note 3, at p. 219: 'Citizens ... should be assured of the right to freely choose which traditional cultural values and practices to preserve, which to modify, and which to abandon ... this is a freedom that others have no right to deny to them' (referring to A. Sen, *Development as Freedom* (New York, Alfred Knopf, 1999)).

89 This section does not consider the technical legal details of the problem of how, as a matter of WTO law, non-WTO law such as UNESCO law or international human rights law can come to be brought up, and taken up in WTO dispute settlement. This is in itself far from an uncontroversial matter. Rather, it is presupposed here that, as a matter of legal coherence, human rights law must be relevant to WTO dispute settlement, particularly when brought up by States in defence of the interests of, or entitlements owed to, their own population. The simple reason is that states cannot be presumed to have laid off their (cultural) human rights obligations when entering an economic integration scheme. It seems only a matter of time before a state phrases legal arguments in terms of human rights in a WTO dispute. The aim of this section is to discuss a number of possibilities of GATT and GATS legal contexts in which cultural human rights arguments could, or could not be brought up.

two approaches may sometimes lead to different legal conclusions. It should be stressed that in framing the discussion thus, it is in no way a denial of the *relevance* of a cultural policy approach. On the contrary, the most effective cultural response to trade liberalization will result from a convincing linkage of a cultural rights approach and a cultural policy approach.[90]

### A. *Creating space for cultural rights through the public service exemption in Article I:3(b)/(c) GATS*

One of the arguments used by cultural policy proponents to sustain their non-committal stance with regard to cultural services under GATS is that it is seen as doubtful that cultural service provision can be characterized, as a matter of GATS law, as a 'public service'. As a result, it is presumed that the provision of cultural services cannot benefit from the carve-out in Article I:3(b)/(c) GATS according to which public services are excluded from the scope of GATS. This sub-section argues that there may be reason to be more optimistic about the possibility of accommodating cultural concerns in GATS law through the public policy exemption, and therefore that it is at least worth closer consideration. To begin such closer consideration, elements for an argument are presented to support the view that to the extent that the provision of cultural services protects cultural rights, such a provision could be construed as qualifying as a 'public service' and therefore be relieved from the full force of GATS discipline.

The 2002 Brixen Declaration on Cultural Diversity and GATS contains the following statements that seem to summarize well the convictions of many cultural policy proponents:

> we are … far from … convinced that Article I:3 [GATS] referring to 'services exercised in [governmental] authority' presents a safeguard [to the effect of] leaving the final decision to state authorities as to where to open … culture and the media to private competition, or to permit or to refuse access of private enterprises to public funding including establishment of foreign subsidiaries is essential … due to the fact that no state exists where the service structures in … culture and media are exclusively based on public authority *involvement*, the clause of exception is open to interpretation …

---

[90] The cultural policy approach to trade has benefited from renewed attention as a result of the adoption of the UNESCO Convention discussed in the previous section. As the Convention was clearly drafted with mainly (if not exclusively) the WTO Covered Agreements in mind, and as it is clear that Convention's relevance will eventually be tested in the WTO context even if it established its own dispute settlement procedure, analysis has focused on the way in which the UNESCO Convention can become legally relevant in the WTO context. See for early analysis, for M. Hahn, *cit. supra* note 2, C.B. Graber, *cit. supra* note 13, and T. Voon, *cit. supra* note 62.

> we regard this as a permanent danger for the status of public services as they could be challenged by the private sector …[91]
>
> … it is also stated [in this GATS article that the 'supply in the exercise of governmental authority'] only [relates] to 'services which are supplied neither on a commercial basis nor in competition with one or more service suppliers'[92] … the term 'on a commercial basis' … entails the notion of a consumer paying a price for a service … we therefore assume that every service, with the exception of those provided without costs, has to be regarded as provided on a commercial basis … as nearly all public services imply a price to be paid by the consumer, we would be obliged to accept the rules of GATS.[93]

The first part of this statement essentially boils down to an interpretation of the GATS wording that 'governmental authority' requires an exclusive and direct institutional engagement by states in the supply of the public service. The second part of the statement assumes that only services provided free of charge could qualify as public services. In order to engage with this position we need to analyse the text of the relevant GATS article, and how it has been interpreted and applied. Article I:3 (b) and (c) GATS reads as follows:

> For the purposes of this agreement
>
> (b) 'services' includes any service in any sector except services supplied in the exercise of governmental authority
>
> (c) 'a service supplied in the exercise of governmental authority' means any service which is supplied neither on a commercial basis, nor in competition with one or more service suppliers.

With regard to the first point made by cultural policy proponents that seems to relate in particular to the wording of 'governmental authority', it has been pointed out that the focus of GATS with regard to public services is on the *nature of particular activities*, and *not on the institution providing them*. In other words, the main concern of GATS is functional, not institutional.[94] Therefore, it was rightly observed that it is misplaced to think that once, say, a museum develops one commercial service, all its other activities provided non-commercially and non-competitively will be affected and equally considered a service (and therefore impossible to 'protect' by exclusion from the scope of GATS). As Adlung has written, 'Article I:3 refers

91 Assembly of European Regions, *cit. supra* note 85, para. 20 (emphasis added).

92 *Ibid.*, para. 20.

93 *Ibid.*, para. 21.

94 R. Adlung, *cit. supra* note 3, at p. 455.

explicitly to the conditions governing the supply of a particular service and not to [a provider's] overall role within a supplier's accounting system or to the existence of remunerative activities that might be conducted in parallel'.[95] Moreover, an analysis of WTO case law has shed further light on what Article I:3(b)/(c) GATS wording of 'authority' could be taken to mean. Leroux has found that the Appellate Body could be understood as linking this wording to a power to regulate, supervise and restrain the conduct of individuals and entities through the exercise of official legal authority.[96]

In other words, arguments can be found to support the position that an interpretation of 'governmental' implies neither exclusive nor direct[97] involvement of a state in providing a public service, and that 'authority' relates to the existence of continued official legal authority to intervene if necessary. Even in the face of the reality of more and more states opting to privatize some public services, making the applicability of the public services exemption of Article I:3 GATS harder to assess,[98] it would depend on the nature of the activity provided and the extent of public legal authority still available to intervene legally to assess whether the service would qualify for consideration for continued 'supply in the exercise of governmental authority'.

For the purpose of this chapter, it can be argued that one area in which states must by definition be understood as having reserved their official legal authority to intervene is that of human rights protection. In fact, as a matter of human rights law, the GATS terminology of 'authority' needs to be interpreted as a sort of '*noblesse oblige*' – if there exists sufficiently clear authority to intervene as a result of human rights requirements, the state is required by human rights law to invoke its authority for that purpose in trade negotiations and litigation. For that purpose, the functional rather than institutional understanding of the wording of 'governmental' in GATS can be argued to be capable of accommodating the requirement for a state to maintain this measure of control without necessarily directly or exclusively supplying a service itself. The terminology of 'authority' can be seen as sufficiently wide to facilitate state obligations that are more supervisory in nature if privatization is opted for.

---

95 *Ibid.*, at p. 463.

96 See E.H. Leroux, 'What is a "Service Supplied in the Exercise of Governmental Authority" under Article I:3(b) and (c) of the General Agreement on Trade in Services?', *JWT* (2006), pp. 345-385, at 352 (referring to *Canada-Dairy* (13 October 1999) WT/DS103/AB/R).

97 See, however, Adlung, who has argued that the 'constructive ambiguity' of Article I:3(b)/(c) GATS may effectively hides a state-centred anchoring of the exemption, namely as a result of the combination of the functional wording ('on a commercial basis/in competition') with the implicit institutional wording ('governmental'), from which he infers that 'this could prompt speculation about a third [and hidden] criterion [in Article I:3 GATS], the *direct* participation of a governmental agency'; R. Adlung, *cit. supra* note 3, at p. 466 (emphasis added).

98 E.H. Leroux, *cit. supra* note 96, at p. 385.

This still leaves us to deal with the second aspect of the statement by the cultural policy proponents to the effect that only public services provided free of charge are likely to be exempted from GATS' scope as a cultural service cannot be supplied 'on a commercial basis'. This is an issue that indeed requires further research. It is interesting, however, that experience in a different setting of economic law may evidence that there is no need to be overly pessimistic about the possibility of coming to a culturally satisfactory solution.[99] More generally, it has indeed been observed that Article I:3(c) GATS defines governmental authority in connection with the *economic* context of the supply and not on the basis of the public interest nature of an activity. As a result, given that economic circumstances change over time,[100] it is likely not possible to claim that certain services are going to be *permanently* excluded from the scope of GATS because of their nature as public or governmental services. In this regard it would need to be established whether the public service exception would be sufficiently flexible in allowing the inclusion and exclusion in the category of public services on the basis of relevant *non-economic* circumstances. In the context of cultural services, a cultural rights approach to trade could again be useful, in that it could help articulate the minimum level of continued access to culture for all individuals, which states would need to maintain and assert in the GATS context.

Finally then, it is important to point at the wider relevance of the argument presented here to the effect that there may be arguments for being less sceptical about the possibility of integrating cultural concerns into a GATS understanding of 'public services'. As explained earlier,[101] a prior 'no commitment' attitude of states relating to cultural services has a *de facto* impact on other non-trade policies (and the human rights inherent in these). If the aim is to seek a comprehensive and balanced integration of human rights into GATS it may be better to let go of the 'red line' that 'culture' now is, and consider the conditions under which commitments can be made in the cultural sector that do not imperil cultural rights protection to the same extent as in other areas. This may create greater leeway to protect other important human rights.

---

99 For example, in the context of a review of how the European Commission deals with cultural concerns in state aid, it has been found that 'in the [European] Commission's view, museums, the central purpose of which is to preserve and manage heritage assets, do not, in principle, carry out an economic activity in competition with other cultural institutions'; E. Psychogiopoulou, *cit. supra* note 8, at p. 23. The fact that the museum is not considered to carry out an economic activity is presumably notwithstanding the fact that it charges a price for an entry ticket.

100 M. Krajewski, *cit. supra* note 42, at p. 353.

101 See *supra* section III.C.

### B. Public morality/public order wording in GATT/S General Exceptions clauses

One option that has recently been tabled by commentators discussing the WTO/ cultural diversity interface, is that the 'public morals' wording present in Article XX(a) GATT and the 'public morals and public order' wording present in Article XIV(a) GATS could inspire 'cultural diversity friendly' WTO Dispute Settlement interpretation.[102] This suggestion is interesting for the purpose of the current chapter focusing on cultural rights protection due to a recent study undertaken for the OHCHR.[103] In it, a case was made for seeing the public morality and public order wording (along with that of 'human, animal and plant life or health') as entry-points for a broad range of human rights concerns into WTO law, including GATT/S. Therefore it is interesting to assess the merits of this proposal for cultural rights protection.[104]

It is submitted here that the GATT/GATS public morality and public order wording is logically problematic for the integration of human rights. Similarly worded public policy grounds are equally present in human rights treaties and are generally only invoked to restrict rather than facilitate human rights protection. Public morality, just like similar clauses such as public security and public policy, are therefore conceptually different from human rights and function as their limitation.[105] As public morality serves as a limit to individual entitlements in human rights law, it is hard to see how cultural diversity related human rights can be properly integrated into trade agreements through a legal concept that equally serves as an exception to their *own* application. Suggesting such an avenue essentially amounts to a call for invoking human rights in a trade context *through their own exception*. Therefore, seeking to integrate cultural rights concerns into GATT and GATS in such a way amounts to a *legal contradiction*. In this light it is suggested

---

[102] T. Voon, *cit. supra* note 62, at p. 647 (arguing in favour of seeing public morality as enabling cultural diversity integration); T. Broude, *cit. supra* note 6, at fn. 2 (arguing in favour of seeing public morality as enabling cultural diversity integration); J. Wouters and B. De Meester, *cit. supra* note 14, at fn. 75 and fn. 116 (arguing in favour of seeing public order as enabling cultural diversity integration); but see C.B. Graber, *cit. supra* note 13, at p. 68, fn. 62 (arguing against seeing public morality as enabling cultural diversity integration – without however explaining why).

[103] Office of the High Commissioner For Human Rights, 'Human Rights and World Trade Agreements – Using General Exception Clauses To Protect Human Rights', December 2005, available at: <www.ohchr.org/english/about/publications/docs/WTO.pdf>.

[104] It should be noted that, as pointed out above in section II, the GATT also contains a specific general exception ground for some aspects of culture, i.e. Article XX(f) GATT. It has also been proposed to give a cultural reading to Article XX(d) GATT/Article XIV(c) GATS, relating to human life and health; Cf. T. Voon, *cit. supra* note 62, at p. 648.

[105] With regard to the EU setting this point was made by me in J. Morijn, 'Balancing Fundamental Rights and Common Market Freedoms in Union Law: *Schmidberger* and *Omega* in the Light of the European Constitution', *European Law Journal* (2006), pp. 15-40, at p. 39.

that, following similar proposals made with regard to the EC context,[106] cultural rights experts may do better to push for a legislative, or a judge-made *sui generis* general human rights exception.

## 6. Conclusion

As was recently written, 'the regulation of the relationship between international trade law and cultural protection is one of the challenges that the [WTO] will be facing with greater intensity in the second decade of its existence'.[107] It is not, however, easy to identify the precise terms of this challenge. One of the problems in advancing the cause of cultural diversity protection in legal contexts not primarily dealing with it, such as the WTO, is that the concept itself raises both cultural rights and cultural policy protection concerns that need first to be distinguished and then convincingly linked to make for a coherent 'cultural response' to trade liberalization. Even if the UNESCO Cultural Diversity Declaration and Convention employ the rhetoric of (cultural) human rights, they mainly articulate the cultural policy component.

Upon characterization of the culture/trade debate and after an analysis of how cultural rights are invoked by culture proponents and free traders, it has been argued in this chapter that integrating the (cultural) human rights aspect into the cultural diversity challenge to trade liberalization would both condition and bolster the current initiatives primarily guided by cultural policy considerations. It could help articulate the concerns more precisely, with regard to more matters than just audio-visual industries,[108] and make them more balanced to take account of the cultural entitlement of all individuals in states' territories. From a cultural rights viewpoint, cultural policy measures worthy of exemption from, or special treatment within the trade law discipline, are those tailored to guaranteeing and facilitating people's equitable access to their own culture and other cultures of their own choice. In that sense it is also important to acknowledge that the openness created by trade liberalization may under certain circumstances be understood to facilitate cultural rights protection, for example freedom of expression.

A more convincing combination of the cultural rights and cultural and trade policy concerns should be undertaken on the basis of a cultural rights impact

---

106 *Ibid.*

107 T. Broude, *cit. supra* note 6, at p. 625.

108 As it was recently put, 'the application of a broader concept of culture within a human rights context, one that goes beyond the traditional focus on creativity and the arts, demonstrates the inextricability of culture from all aspects of human life ... within this context, cultural rights apply not only to aspects of creativity, but to a much wider set of human rights concerns, ranging from food procurement to intellectual property protection'; S.A. Hansen, *cit. supra* note 45, at p. 303.

assessment[109] to help guide ongoing trade negotiations.[110] As a result of the fact that human rights law is a firm part of international law, by which the WTO has acknowledged that it is bound, the linkage of cultural policy and cultural human rights would also better equip the WTO Dispute Settlement system to take on board cultural diversity concerns in their more precisely articulated terms.

Applying some of these insights to a number of suggestions made by cultural policy proponents with regard to cultural diversity integration into GATT/S law as made, it was found that cultural rights considerations could serve to start delineating the extent to which cultural service provision could be seen as a 'public service'. This could result in excluding some aspects of cultural considerations from the scope of GATS given the applicability of the public service carve-out as laid down in Article I:3(b)/(c) GATS. On the other hand, it was pointed out that cultural rights concerns are unlikely to be served by a cultural diversity-friendly reading of the GATT/S General Exception clauses public morality and public order wording. Public policy grounds equally function as exceptions to cultural rights protection, which would turn such a proposal into a call for integrating cultural rights into trade law through their own exception.

Finally, returning the trade law/culture discussion to its wider context, it must be stressed that economic globalization by no means only poses a threat to the fulfilment of the obligations to facilitate access to culture, in particular as a result of the increasing significance of enhanced communication technology. For example, it was recently argued with regard to the cultural effects of globalization that as 'the information age has moved from rhetoric to reality ... all too frequently, a narrow economic focus on globalisation misses the transformative effects of technology [and] liberalisation'.[111] It was also argued by an influential journalist that 'it is becoming clear that [the combination of globalization of enhanced communication techniques], while it has the potential to homogenise cultures, also has ... an even greater potential to nourish diversity to a degree that the world has never seen before'.[112]

Whatever the merit of these particular claims, these types of observations force us to have a wider perspective of the challenges posed. Indeed, from the perspective of cultural rights and its bottom-up concern to ensure equitable access to culture for all, the UNESCO Cultural Diversity Declaration and Convention could in some sense at least partly be seen as a (problematically ambiguous) response to yesterday's

---

109 See *supra* note 56.

110 See for suggestions with regard to the cultural right of education, J. Morijn, 'Economic Liberalisation of Education Provision within the EC & WTO: A Human Rights Perspective', *Croatian Yearbook of European Law & Policy* (2006), pp. 99-136.

111 D. Drache and M.D. Froese, 'Globalisation, World Trade and the Cultural Commons: Identity, Citizenship and Pluralism', *New Political Economy* (2006), pp. 361-382, at p. 373.

112 T.L. Friedman, *The World Is Flat – the Globalized World in the Twenty-First Century* (Penguin Books, London, 2006), at p. 506.

problem. There is a real danger that fulfilment of cultural rights will become mainly contingent on access to these new technologies (rather than the state's capacity to promote and protect cultural diversity by way of policy measures). Therefore, cultural rights proponents, apart from focusing solely on the WTO and other institutions driving trade liberalization, should equally make sure that every effort is made to prevent exclusion from the international cultural space as currently constructed by means of new technologies.[113]

[113] I. Bernier, *cit. supra* note 16, at p. 781.

# 14
# A Right to Cultural Identity in UNESCO

*Yvonne Donders*

## 1. Introduction

This chapter touches first on the idea of developing a right to cultural identity in international human rights law, in order to clarify the issues and difficulties surrounding this right. Afterwards, it will address the work of UNESCO in relation to a right to cultural identity, including the adoption of several relevant instruments and the encouragement of debate through studies and seminars. As regards UNESCO instruments, this paper focuses only on those that are most directly related to a right to cultural identity. The work of UNESCO in the field of the protection of cultural products or heritage or on the rights of cultural creators and artists is not specifically addressed.[1]

1 Instruments in these fields include: the Agreement on the Importance of Educational, Scientific and Cultural Materials (Florence Agreement, 1950); the Convention for the Protection of Cultural Property in the Event of Armed Conflict (The Hague Convention) and its Protocol (1954); the Convention on the Means of Prohibiting and Preventing the Illicit Import, Export and Transfer of Ownership of Cultural Property (1970); the Convention Concerning the Protection of the World Cultural and Natural Heritage (1972); UNIDROIT Convention on Stolen or Illegally Exported Cultural Objects (1995); the Convention on the Exchange of Official Publications (1958); the Universal Copyright Convention (1952 and revised in 1971); the Recommendation on the Status of Scientific Researchers (1974); the Recommendation on the Status of the Artist (1980); the Recommendation on the Safeguarding of Traditional Culture and Folklore (1989). These instruments are not discussed in detail, since they do not include a right to cultural identity or other cultural rights in the sense of human rights.

Francioni and Scheinin (eds), *Cultural Human Rights*, 317–340

## 2. The background of a right to cultural identity

The idea of promoting a separate right to cultural identity originated mainly in two debates within human rights discourse: on cultural rights and on collective rights.

### *A. Debates on cultural rights and collective rights*

Although the division between different categories of human rights – civil, political, economic, social and cultural – does not imply that one category is more important than another, practice shows that the different categories of human rights have not developed at an equal pace. Cultural rights have received less attention and are, therefore, less developed than civil, political, economic and social rights.[2] Relatively few states have been eager to adopt international regulations in relation to cultural rights. Most did not consider that cultural rights might imply positive state obligations. States were rather concerned that strengthening cultural rights might lead to tension and instability in society, because giving cultural communities certain rights could empower them and thereby endanger national unity.[3] It also seems that cultural rights have been considered less important than other human rights. Culture was often considered an *elite* concept, equivalent to arts and literature. Accordingly, cultural rights were seen as something 'extra'. It has been argued that other human rights need to be implemented first; and that a certain level of economic and social development should be reached before cultural rights make sense.[4] Nowadays, however, culture is generally considered a broad anthropological concept, in other words a way of life, including language, religion, customs, etc. It is a dynamic process instead of a collection of fixed products. It is clear that cultural identity represents a very important part of human dignity.[5] It has also been recognized in the 2004 UNDP Human Development Report 'Cultural Liberty in Today's Diverse World',

---

2 See, *inter alia*, 'Cultural Rights: An Underdeveloped Category of Human Rights. Conclusions of the Eighth Interdisciplinary Colloquium on Human Rights, organised by the University of Fribourg, 28-30 November 1991', *The Review of the International Commission of Jurists* (1992), pp. 51-53. See, also, J. Donnelly, *Universal Human Rights in Theory and Practice* (London, Cornell University Press, 1989), pp. 154-155; J. Symonides, 'Cultural Rights', in J. Symonides (ed.), *Human Rights – Concepts and Standards* (UNESCO Publishing, Paris, 2000), pp. 175-176.

3 See, *inter alia*, J. Symonides, *cit. supra* note 2, pp. 176.

4 UN Doc. E/C.12/1992/WP.4, Implementation of Cultural Rights, analytical study of Article 15 of the International Covenant on Economic, Social and Cultural Rights, by Mr. S.R. Konaté, 25 November 1992, pp. 12-14.

5 J.H. Burgers, 'The Right to Cultural Identity', in J. Berting et al. (eds.), *Human Rights in a Pluralist World* (Meckler/Westport/London), 1990, pp. 251-252.

among others, that not only democracy and economic growth, but also diversity and cultural freedoms, are crucial for development[6] – not only the other way around.

One of the main reasons for the underdevelopment of cultural rights and their lack of conceptualisation is the vagueness of the term 'culture'. Culture can refer to various things, from cultural products like arts and literature to the cultural process, or culture as a way of life. In between lie the cultural institutions established to transfer culture, such as museums, educational institutions and the media. Accordingly, cultural rights can refer to various human rights and freedoms. No international human rights instrument defines cultural rights, as such, so that different lists of legal provisions that could be labelled 'cultural rights' have been drawn up in international instruments. For example, cultural rights could be rights concerning creativity, such as rights to freedom of expression, artistic and intellectual freedom, as well as rights related to the protection of producers of cultural products, including copyright. Cultural rights can also refer to the protection of cultural products and cultural expressions, including cultural heritage. Cultural rights in relation to the process of cultural development could include the right to self-determination and rights to freedom of thought, religion and assembly and the right to education. Cultural rights can also concern *the right to culture or cultural identity*, in the sense of the right to preserve, develop and have access to culture and cultural identity.[7]

Because of numerous violations of cultural rights, for example the oppression of indigenous peoples and the forced assimilation of minorities and immigrants, there has been an increasing call for the clarification, promotion and protection of cultural rights over the last decades. In many parts of the world, individuals and communities have been, and still are, unable to express and preserve their cultural identity because of intolerance and discrimination. Therefore, in order to better promote and implement cultural rights, the need to elaborate a new codification of cultural rights, including a separate right to cultural identity, has been suggested.[8]

---

6 Human Development Report of 2004, 'Cultural Liberty in Today's Diverse World'. See at: <www.UNDP.org>.

7 L.V. Prott, 'Cultural Rights as Peoples' Rights in International Law', in J. Crawford (ed.), *The Rights of Peoples* (Oxford, Clarendon Press, 1988); J. Donnelly, *cit. supra* note 2, p. 155; J. Donnelly, 'Human Rights, Individual Rights and Collective Rights', in J. Berting et al. (eds.), *Human Rights in a Pluralist World* (Meckler Westport/London, 1990), pp. 54-55; P. Meyer-Bisch, 'Les droits culturels, forment-ils une categorie specifique de droits de l'homme?', in P. Meyer-Bisch (ed.), *Les droits culturels, une categorie sous-developpee de droits de l'homme, Actes du VIIIe Colloque interdisciplinaire sur les droits de l'homme* (Suisse, Editions Universitaires Fribourg, 1993), pp. 18, 24; S. Marks, 'Defining Cultural Rights' in M. Bergsmo (ed.), *Human Rights and Criminal Justice for the downtrodden – Essays in Honour of Asbjorn Eide* (2003), p. 295.

8 See J. Symonides, 'The History of the Paradox of Cultural Rights and the State of the Discussion within UNESCO', in Meyer-Bisch, *ibid.*, p. 71; J. Symonides, *cit. supra* note 2, pp. 176-177.

The second discussion behind a right to cultural identity concerns collective rights. Since the 1980s, many scholars have argued that an individualistic approach to human rights no longer meets the challenges of global issues concerning development and the environment, and the needs of communities. The codification of human rights has focused too much on an individualistic outlook of the world and of human nature. It has been asserted that communities are an important factor in creating a valuable life for individuals, and that these communities should be protected by collective rights. Apart from rights like the right to development, the right to environment and the right to peace, the right to be different, as well as the right to cultural identity were mentioned as examples. Cultural identity was thus considered so collective in nature that individual human rights norms would not be sufficient to protect it properly.[9]

### *B. Supporters and opponents of a right to cultural identity*

Supporters of a right to cultural identity emphasize that the claim for a right to cultural identity originates in the context of serious human rights violations. An individual or collective human right to cultural identity is seen as necessary to protect and promote cultural identity as an important element of human dignity. Cultural rights are underdeveloped and neglected; and a right to cultural identity could give new impetus to their development.[10] A right to cultural identity is considered by some as '... a general form of all cultural rights'.[11] Some actually argue that this right already exists in international human rights law, even though it is not specifically included in the International Bill of Human Rights.[12] The UN Commission on

---

9 K. Vasak, 'Pour une troisième génération des droits de l'homme', in C. Swinarski (ed.), *Essays on International Humanitarian Law and Red Cross Principles in Honour of Jean Pictet* (The Hague, Martinus Nijhoff, 1984), pp. 839-840. See, also, S. Marks, 'Emerging Human Rights: A New Generation for the 1980s?', *Rutgers Law Review* (1981) pp. 435-452; P. Alston, 'Conjuring Up New Human Rights: A Proposal for Quality Control', *AJIL* (1984), p. 610; J. Berting, *cit. supra* note 5, pp. 77 and 251-258; Galenkamp, for example, argues that the right to the preservation of one's cultural identity is a paradigm case of a collective right, see M. Galenkamp, *Individualism versus Collectivism – The Concept of Collective Rights*, Gouda, Quint (1998), pp. 15 and chapter 7, pp. 121-151.

10 See J. Symonides, *cit. supra* note 8, p. 71; J. Symonides, *cit. supra* note 2, pp. 176-177; J.H. Burgers, *cit. supra* note 5, pp. 251-252; P. Meyer-Bisch, *cit. supra* note 7, p. 302; R. Stavenhagen, 'The Right to Cultural Identity', in J. Berting et al. (eds.), *Human Rights in a Pluralist World* (Meckler/Westport/London, 1990), pp. 256-258; R. Stavenhagen, 'Cultural Rights: A Social Science Perspective', in A. Eide, C. Krause and A. Rosas (eds.), *Economic, Social and Cultural Rights – A Textbook* (Dordrecht, Martinus Nijhoff Publishers, 2001), pp. 97-98.

11 P. Meyer-Bisch, *cit. supra* note 7, p. 302.

12 Thornberry, for example, argues that the right to cultural identity has obtained a prominent place in human rights discourse. As an example, he refers to a statement made by the representative of the United Arab Emirates before the Human Rights Commission in 1992 in which he

Human Rights also referred to a right to cultural identity when it recognized, in subsequent resolutions, that states are responsible for the enhancement of respect for different cultural identities.[13]

Opponents of promoting a right to cultural identity point out that the existing human rights framework provides sufficient protection for cultural identity; and that a right to cultural identity would add nothing to established human rights. Instead, attention should focus on the promotion and protection of existing human rights, especially cultural rights. It is also argued that the content and scope of a right to cultural identity are obscure. The concept of cultural identity is considered too vague to be transformed into a substantive legal right. Opponents also reject the possible collective subject of a right to cultural identity. Apart from the difficult definition of 'community', special concern has been expressed about the position of the individual in relation to cultural communities. Although communities as a whole are meant to enjoy a right to cultural identity, it is probably an *elite* or leading figures within the community who decide which cultural identity needs to be promoted and protected. Another concern in this regard is the possibility of forced assimilation of individuals within a community, which could imply the 'locking up' of individuals within a community identity that may no longer be theirs. To what extent can individuals oppose cultural practices imposed by the community? And to what extent can they leave the community? A right to cultural identity could further stigmatize cultural communities, setting them apart within society and encouraging tensions such as xenophobia, nationalism and tribalism.[14]

Another argument against a right to cultural identity is that this right could be interpreted as supporting questionable cultural activities: for example, the subordinate position of women, as reflected in forced marriages, bride price, female circumcision, or lesser rights than men with regard to land ownership or inheritance. Such cultural practices are in conflict with human dignity, the protection of which is an important argument for developing a right to cultural identity. This is an important point to be briefly elaborated. It has been argued that a right to cultural identity could be in conflict with other existing human rights and could therefore not be enjoyed unlimitedly. This issue is very sensitive and difficult to answer in general

---

included the right to a cultural identity among his list of the most basic human rights. UN Doc. E/CN.4/1992/SR.7, Commission on Human Rights, 48th session, *Summary Record of the 7th meeting*, 6 February 1992, para. 21. See, also, P. Thornberry, 'The UN Declaration on the Rights of Persons Belonging to National or Ethnic, Religious and Linguistic Minorities: Background, Analysis, Observations and an Update', in A. Philips and A. Rosas (eds.), *Universal Minority Rights* (Turku/Abo and London, 1995), p. 41.

13 Commission on Human Rights Resolution 2002/26 (22 April 2002), 2003/26 (22 April 2003) and 2004/20 (16 April 2004), 2005/20 (15 April 2005) all called 'Promotion of the enjoyment of the cultural rights of everyone and respect for different cultural identities', para. 5.

14 J. Donnelly, *cit. supra* note 2, pp. 158-160; J. Donnelly, *cit. supra* note 7, pp. 58-59; M. Galenkamp, *cit. supra* note 9, chapter 7, pp. 121-151.

terms. In principle, a right to cultural identity should not be categorically rejected solely on the grounds that it could conflict with other human rights. However, the enjoyment of cultural rights, in general, and a right to cultural identity, in particular, may be limited.

First of all, human rights, including cultural rights, could be limited by law. Such limitations should be determined by law and are only permissible if they are compatible with the nature of the rights and '... solely for the purpose of promoting the general welfare in a democratic society'.[15] This limitation clause is not meant to provide states with a simple excuse not to implement the provisions of the ICESCR. Although states are allowed to impose limits on the enjoyment of rights, the possibilities for limitation are restricted by establishing criteria on the way they may be imposed. The limitations may not contradict the nature of the rights in the Covenant, otherwise the provisions would no longer have content and value. Lack of financial or other resources does not fall under the limitation clause of Article 4 and is therefore not a sufficient ground for limitation.[16]

The question remains how the state should be allowed to limit cultural rights without making it an excuse for not implementing cultural rights at all. Whether some legal limitation of cultural rights is justified depends on the concrete circumstances. The phrase 'for the general welfare' may be too broad, and therefore dangerous, if states abuse it to justify certain cutbacks. However, the unlimited exercise of cultural rights may seriously endanger the rights of others or of society. The Committee on Economic, Social and Cultural Rights, for example, has shown that it does not accept the unlimited freedom of creative activity. Creative expression should not harm the cultural life of society as a whole or of specific groups, such as children. Another example is that the right to take part in cultural life may be limited if cultural activities include discriminatory expressions.[17]

---

15 Article 4, International Covenant on Economic, Social and Cultural Rights. Similar clauses can be found in other international human rights instruments. See, for example, Article 18(3) of the International Covenant on Civil and Political Rights, which says that 'freedom to manifest one's religion or beliefs may be subject only to such limitations as are prescribed by law and are necessary to protect public safety, order, health, or morals or the fundamental rights and freedoms of others'. A similar provision can be found in Article 19(3) concerning the right to freedom of expression.

16 P. Alston. and G. Quinn, 'The Nature and Scope of States Parties' Obligations under the International Covenant on Economic, Social and Cultural Rights', *Human Rights Quarterly* (1987), pp. 193-194; Limburg Principles, Nos. 52 and 56, see 'Limburg Principles on the Implementation of the International Covenant on Economic, Social and Cultural Rights', *Human Rights Quarterly* (1987), pp. 122-135.

17 B. Toebes, *The Right to Health as a Human Right in International Law* (Antwerp, Intersentia/ Hart, 1999), pp. 297-298; R. O'Keefe, 'The Right to Take Part in Cultural Life under Article 15 of the ICESCR', *ICLQ* (1998), pp. 911-912; F. Vlemminx, *Het Profiel van de Sociale Grondrechten* [The Profile of Social Rights] (W.E.J. Tjeenk Willink, Zwolle, 1994), pp. 117-119.

Secondly, a general rule is that the enjoyment of human rights by one individual may not unjustifiably limit or violate the enjoyment of human rights by others. In other words, the enjoyment of cultural rights can be limited by the rights of others. In fact, many human rights can potentially conflict in certain situations.[18] Each of these situations should be evaluated case by case to determine which right prevails in that given situation.

The issue remains of how to deal with cultural *activities* or *practices* – not to be confused with cultural *rights* – that conflict with or limit the enjoyment of human rights. It is argued that such practices should not be protected by cultural rights. No general statement can be made on the acceptability of cultural practices and their relation to human rights, since these activities are very diverse. Their possible conflict with human rights should be treated on a case-by-case basis. However, in general, cultural practices that clearly conflict with international human rights norms cannot be justified by stating that they are protected under the category of 'cultural rights'. An appropriate criterion could be that cultural practices should not conflict with the value of human dignity. This also implies that, for example, cultural communities should guarantee and respect the rights and freedoms of individual members, including, the right to participate in society at large, for instance through education, the right to take part in the decision-making process that determines and develops the community's cultural life, as well as the right and freedom to leave the community.

Changes in cultural practices should come from the cultural community itself, and should not be imposed from outside. However, states should try to find ways to promote such changes. In this regard, it is interesting to note that, for example, the International Convention on the Elimination of all forms of Racial Discrimination (ICERD) includes the obligation that states parties adopt immediate and effective measures, particularly in the fields of teaching, education, culture and information, to combat prejudices which lead to racial discrimination and to promote understanding, tolerance and friendship among nations and racial or ethnical groups (Article 7). Furthermore, the Convention on the Elimination of All Forms of Discrimination against Women (CEDAW) states in Article 5 that 'States Parties shall take all appropriate measures: (a) To modify the social and cultural patterns of conduct of men and women, with a view to achieving the elimination of prejudices and customary and

18 One can think of the 'Danish Cartoon affair', which reflected tension between freedom of religion and freedom of expression. The answer is not to reject either one of these rights, or to privilege one *a priori* over the other. 'A human rights approach requires … seek[ing] harmony between these freedoms in practice …', see K. Boyle, 'The Danish Cartoons', *Netherlands Quarterly on Human Rights* (2006), p. 188.

all other practices which are based on the idea of the inferiority or the superiority of either of the sexes or on stereotyped roles for men and women…'[19]

### *C. Right or freedom of cultural identity?*

It should be noted that the formulation of 'a right to cultural identity' is rather strange. How can one actually have a right *to* cultural identity? The right to cultural identity implies the right to *have* or *be provided with* a cultural identity. This seems rather odd, since individuals and communities simply *have* a cultural identity, which cannot and should not be provided for by states. 'It is not a good, service or status that can be given to people.'[20] Consequently, this right has been formulated in different ways. Meyer-Bisch, for example, speaks of the right to cultural *identification*, '… *car l'identité n'est pas un état mais une acte* …'.[21] He argues that individuals acquire a cultural identity by living their life, and compose it along lines of participation in multiple communities delineated by nationality, race, family, religion, gender, etc.[22]

Another formulation refers to the right to *the protection and development* of cultural identity, or the right to preserve one's identity.[23] A right to preserve and/or develop one's cultural identity might be a good option, since it emphasizes that communities and individuals have the right to develop their cultural identity and expect its protection and preservation.

However, I would suggest another formulation: the right to *freedom* of cultural identity. It seems that one of the central claims of a right to cultural identity is the right to decide *freely* to have, develop and preserve it, as well as to change it. A right to freedom of cultural identity reflects the idea of cultural identity as a changeable process, as well as the importance of choice. In this respect, a right to cultural identity has much in common with the right to freedom of religion. Both rights have an individual as well as a collective dimension; cultural identity as well as religion is experienced both individually and collectively. Both concepts are hard to define;

---

19 The Protocol to the African Charter on Human and Peoples' Rights on the Rights of Women in Africa (in force since 25 November 2005) includes a similar provision in Article 2(2), which states that 'States Parties shall commit themselves to modify the social and cultural patterns of conduct of women and men … with a view to achieving the elimination of harmful cultural and traditional practices and all other practices which are based on the idea of the inferiority or the superiority of either of the sexes …'. See, also, S.A. Hansen, 'The Right to Take Part in Cultural Life: Toward Defining Minimum Core Obligations Related to Article 15(1)(A) of the International Covenant on Economic, Social and Cultural Rights', in A. Chapman and S. Russell (eds.), *Core Obligations: Building a Framework for Economic, Social and Cultural Rights* (Antwerp, Intersentia, 2002), pp. 288-289.

20 J. Donnelly, *cit. supra* note 2, p. 158; J. Donnelly, *cit. supra* note 7, p. 58.

21 P. Meyer-Bisch, *cit. supra* note 7, p. 35.

22 *Ibid.*, p. 281.

23 J. Symonides, *cit. supra* note 8, p. 62; M. Galenkamp, *cit. supra* note 9, p. 116.

although one generally knows what they mean, there are no unambiguous legal definitions. Cultural identity and religion both concern the meaning and significance of human activities and relations. Furthermore, religion is an important aspect of cultural identity. It has played an important role in the creation and development of almost all cultures.[24]

It is interesting to see how cultural identity as a right has been used in the different texts and instruments discussed below. Have the arguments outlined above played any role in the use of a particular formulation?

## 3. UNESCO instruments including a right to cultural identity

As argued above, UNESCO has actively promoted a right to cultural identity over the years. Three somewhat older UNESCO instruments with a direct link to a right to cultural identity are the Declaration of the Principles of International Cultural Co-operation (1966), the Recommendation on Participation by the People at Large in Cultural Life and their Contribution to It (1976) and the Declaration on Race and Racial Prejudice (1978). Two more recent instruments also touch upon issues linked to a right to cultural identity: the Universal Declaration on Cultural Diversity (2001) and the UNESCO Convention on the Protection and Promotion of the Diversity of Cultural Expressions, adopted by the General Conference in October 2005. How was a right to freedom of cultural identity included in these UNESCO instruments? To what extent do these instruments provide some clarification of the right in terms of its scope and content? How have Member States dealt with issues related to a right to freedom of cultural identity, like its individual and collective dimension, or the meaning of the concept of cultural identity and eventual corresponding state obligations?

### *A. Declaration of the Principles of International Cultural Co-operation*

In November 1966 the General Conference of UNESCO adopted the Declaration of the Principles of International Cultural Co-operation. According to the Preamble, the idea behind the Declaration sprang from the fact that ignorance of the life, customs and culture of communities was considered an obstacle to friendship among nations and to peaceful cooperation. International cultural cooperation could contribute to better understanding and, consequently, to the construction and maintenance of peace, which is the main purpose of UNESCO. The Declaration deals mainly with international cooperation in the field of culture and does not include an explicit reference to cultural identity. However, the equality of cultures and the value of cultural differences – important elements in relation to a right to freedom of cultural

---

24 See, *inter alia*, B. Parekh, *Rethinking Multiculturalism – Cultural Diversity and Political Theory* (Macmillan Press, Basingstoke, 2000), pp. 146-147.

identity – were confirmed *inter alia* in the first article of the Declaration. This provision has become well known both within UNESCO and elsewhere in relation to the promotion and protection of cultural rights. Article 1 states that:

> 1. Each culture has a dignity and value which must be respected and preserved.
>
> 2. Every people has the right and the duty to develop its culture.
>
> 3. In their rich variety and diversity, and in the reciprocal influences they exert on one another, all cultures form part of the common heritage belonging to all mankind.

The first paragraph shows the importance that Member States attach to culture as a value that must be preserved and respected. The second paragraph contains a collective right and duty to develop cultures. No further clarification was given to concepts such as 'people' and 'culture'. The Declaration is not legally-binding, as such, but reflects principles that have a moral and political force.

### B. Recommendation on Participation by the People at Large in Cultural Life and their Contribution to it

In November 1976 the General Conference adopted a Recommendation on Participation by the People at Large in Cultural Life and their Contribution to it. The Recommendation emphasizes a broad meaning of 'culture' that encompasses not only cultural products and arts, but also the way of life of communities and individuals, and includes issues like education and communication. The Recommendation was developed to give communities and individuals the opportunity not only to have access to culture, but also to participate actively in cultural life.[25] This implies specific cultural policies that are integrated into other policies in the fields of economics, social matters and education. The Recommendation further emphasizes the special position of minorities in relation to the development and preservation of their cultural identity.[26]

The adoption of the Recommendation was the result of a long process that started in 1952, when the General Conference authorized the Director-General to organise a meeting of experts on the '... practical application of man's right "freely to participate in the cultural life of the community, to enjoy the arts ...", in accordance with Article 27(1) of the Universal Declaration of Human Rights and in the light of

---

25 It should be kept in mind that the International Covenant on Economic, Social and Cultural Rights (adopted in 1966), which includes in Article 15(1) the right of everyone to take part in cultural life, entered into force that same year.

26 See for an analysis of the Recommendation, S. Marks, *cit. supra* note 7, pp. 304-306.

any further development in the United Nations concerning this right.'[27] This reference concerned the preparation of the International Covenant on Economic, Social and Cultural Rights (ICESCR), adopted in 1966. In fact, it was decided to suspend work within UNESCO on an international instrument on the right to participate freely in cultural life until the work on the ICESCR was finished.[28]

The second stage of preparing the Recommendation started in 1972, with the Intergovernmental Conference on Cultural Policies in Europe. In his opening statement to the Conference, the Director-General of UNESCO maintained that if everyone had the right to share in the cultural heritage and cultural activities of the community, then the state had a duty to provide the means for such participation. The concept of culture was widened to embrace 'the individual's whole way of life'. The Director-General stated: '[t]he recognition of the right to culture as a human right marks the end of culture as an object and of culture for the élite, quite as much as of the laissez-faire abstentionist attitude of the State in cultural matters.'[29]

During drafting, several Member States expressed their concern that this Recommendation would oblige them to adopt one uniform cultural policy, which, in their opinion, would be impossible considering the different social, economic and constitutional situations of states. Some Member States, including the United States and Italy, expressed doubts that access to, and participation in, culture could be regulated by an international instrument.[30] It was finally agreed that the Recommendation should be no more than a statement of basic principles or standards acceptable to all, without entering into too much detail. Accordingly, several interesting changes were made during the drafting of the Recommendation. For example, in the Preamble, a reference was added to respect for the sovereignty of Member States. The definition of culture was changed from 'the whole way of life' to 'all forms of creativity and expression ...' Access to culture was no longer provided for 'all groups and individuals', but instead for 'everyone', thereby taking away the collective dimension. Specific references to cultural rights and the right to culture were replaced by general references to human rights.[31] The Recommendation

---

[27] UNESCO General Conference, 6th session, 1952, Resolution 4.52.

[28] UNESCO Doc. 7C/PRG/10, *Report on the Proceedings of the Committee of Experts formed to Study the Right to Participate Freely in the Cultural Life of the Community*, Paris, 3 November 1952, pp. 3-8.

[29] UNESCO Doc. SHC/EUROCULT/4, *Intergovernmental Conference on Cultural Policies in Europe*, Paris, 30 March 1972, pp. 1-2.

[30] UNESCO Doc. SHC/MD/31, *Action to Ensure that the People at Large have Free, Democratic Access to Culture and Participate Actively in the Cultural Life of Society – Final Report*, Paris, 11 March 1976; UNESCO Doc. 19 C/27, *Draft Recommendation on Action to Ensure that the People at Large have free, democratic access to culture and participate actively in the cultural life of society*, 1976, Annex II, p. 2.

[31] *Ibid.*, p. 3.

was not unanimously adopted. Before the vote on the Recommendation, several delegations expressed their objection to the terminology and meanings used in the Recommendation, as well as to its possible implication of state control over creativity.[32]

The recommendation includes various references to (cultural) identity, for example in the Preamble:

> Considering that participation in cultural life takes the form of an assertion of identity, authenticity and dignity; that the integrity of identity is threatened by numerous causes of erosion stemming, in particular, from the prevalence of inappropriate models or of techniques which have not been fully mastered,
>
> Considering that the assertion of cultural identity should not result in the formation of isolated groups, but should, on the contrary, go hand in hand with a mutual desire for wide and frequent contacts …

The concept of cultural identity is now explicitly used in an international instrument. Although the wording of these phrases is somewhat vague, it shows awareness of the importance of cultural identity as a value and as a policy principle. It is asserted that possibilities for participating in cultural life relate to the development and maintenance of cultural identity.

Another interesting provision is Article 4(f), in which Member States are recommended to:

> … guarantee the recognition of the equality of cultures, including the cultures of national minorities and of foreign minorities if they exist, as forming part of the common heritage of all mankind, and ensure that they are promoted at all levels without discrimination; ensure that national minorities and foreign minorities have full opportunities for gaining access to and participating in the cultural life of the countries in which they find themselves in order to enrich it with their specific contributions, while *safeguarding their right to preserve their cultural identity.* (emphasis added)

The equality of cultures is the starting point of this provision. It further provides for state obligations to protect the right of national and foreign minorities to preserve their cultural identity. This is an interesting step. While the equality of cultures is emphasized, it is acknowledged that national and foreign minorities might be in a special position in wishing to preserve their own cultural identity. However, which communities are meant by 'national and foreign minorities' is not explained in any

---

32 These delegations were Belgium, Canada, the Federal Republic of Germany, France, Guatemala, Italy, Portugal, the United Kingdom and the United States. See J. Symonides, *cit. supra* note 8, p. 71.

of the drafting reports. In a comment by the UNESCO Secretariat, it is stated that foreign minorities include workers employed abroad, for example, but there is no final clarification.[33] It also remains unclear what this provision entails in concrete terms, for example, in the field of legislation or policies.

The Recommendation also contains provisions on artists and creative work, on the mass media and on the protection of cultural heritage and the environment. In one of the final articles on international cooperation, another reference is made to cultural identity. In Article 18(d), it is stated that Member States should develop cultural exchanges to promote '... an ever deeper appreciation of the values of each culture and, in particular, draw attention to the cultures of the developing countries as a mark of esteem for their cultural identity'. With this provision, the value of cultural identity for developing countries in gaining freedom from colonization is emphasized.[34]

### *C. Declaration on Race and Racial Prejudice*

The Declaration on Race and Racial Prejudice was adopted in 1978 by the General Conference, by consensus and without opposition.[35] This Declaration was meant to describe the background of differences between people, emphasizing the value of these differences. It did not intend to give certain communities or individuals specific rights. The Declaration starts in Article 1(1) with the fact that all human beings come from a common stock and continues in the second paragraph with an assertion of the right of individuals and groups to be different. For the first time, this right was officially recognized in an international instrument. According to the Preamble, the right to be different includes, *inter alia*, the right not to be excluded, humiliated, exploited or forcibly assimilated.

The Declaration contains several references to cultural identity. Article 1(3), for example, reads as follows:

---

33 UNESCO Doc. SHC/MD/31, *cit. supra* note 30, p. 7.

34 See, for example, UNESCO Doc. SHC/MD/28, *Action to Ensure that the People at Large have Free, Democratic Access to Culture and Participate Actively in the Cultural Life of Society – Preliminary Report*, Paris, 22 August 1975, p. 6, para. 19, p. 8, para. 28. See, also, UNESCO Doc. 19 C/27, *cit. supra* note 30, p. 7.

35 UNESCO Doc. 18 C/36, *Preliminary Study on the Legal and technical Aspects of a Draft Declaration on Race and Racial Prejudice*, Paris, 19 September 1974; UNESCO Doc. SS-77/CONF.201/1, *Working Paper of the Meeting of Government Representatives to prepare a Draft Declaration on Race and Racial Prejudice*, Paris, 18 August 1977; UNESCO Doc. SHC/MD/33, *Committee of Governmental Experts to Prepare a Draft Declaration on Race and Racial Prejudice, Preliminary Draft*, Paris, 14 June 1976; UNESCO Doc. 20 C/18, *Draft Declaration on Race and Racial Prejudice*, Paris, 25 September 1978, Annex, 1978; see, also, L. Lerner, *Group Rights and Discrimination in International Law* (Dordrecht/Boston/London, Martinus Nijhoff Publishers 1991), pp. 155-156.

> Identity of origin in no way affects the fact that human beings can and may live differently, nor does it preclude the existence of differences based on cultural, environmental and historical diversity, nor *the right to maintain cultural identity*. (emphasis added)

This provision implies that identity of origin – the fact that human beings come from a common stock – does not affect the right to be different or the right to maintain cultural identity. The concepts used in this provision, such as identity of origin and cultural identity, are not further clarified. An earlier draft of the Declaration included an explanatory report, which elaborated the content of several provisions. However, while adopting the final version of the Declaration, the explanatory report was removed because it was considered unnecessary for a declaration without legal obligations.[36] According to the draft explanatory report, Article 1(3) '… constitutes the assertion of cultural autonomy, an essential pre-requisite for the independence of peoples'. The different communities were supposed to decide themselves on the development and expression of their cultures, thereby denouncing policies of forced assimilation of national, religious, linguistic, cultural and ethnic communities.[37]

Article 5(1) of the Declaration also explicitly refers to cultural identity:

> Culture, as a product of all human beings and a common heritage of mankind, and education in its broadest sense, offer men and women increasingly effective means of adaptation, enabling them not only to affirm that they are born equal in dignity and rights, but also to recognise that they should respect *the right of all groups to their own cultural identity* and the development of their distinctive cultural life within the national and international contexts, it being understood that it rests with each group to decide in complete freedom on the maintenance, and, if appropriate, the adaptation or enrichment of the values which it regards as essential to its identity. (emphasis added)

According to this provision, culture makes human beings realize that they should respect the right of groups to their own cultural identity. It is interesting to note that the right to cultural identity is given to 'groups' without further specification. These groups should also have the freedom to determine which values of their identity they want to preserve and to what extent they wish to join the common culture, as described in the second paragraph of the provision. Emphasis lies on the collective protection of cultural identity.[38]

---

[36] UNESCO Doc. SS-77/CONF.201/1, *cit. supra* note 35; 20 C/18 Add., *cit. supra* note 35, p. 10 (para. 59).

[37] UNESCO Doc. 20 C/18, *cit. supra* note 35, Explanatory report, para. 5; see, also, L. Lerner, *cit. supra* note 35, p. 157.

[38] *Ibid.*, p. 158.

According to the draft explanatory report, Article 5 would have far-reaching consequences. First, it was emphasized that the preservation of cultural values by different communities does not *ipso facto* constitute a threat to the state. Second, the diversity of cultures should be officially recognized; and all cultures should receive financial support accordingly. The preservation of cultures should not, however, be imposed on any community.[39]

Article 5 has a peculiar formulation because it is not directed toward the state, but toward people in general. Although Article 6 of the Declaration lays down that states have the primary responsibility for promoting and protecting human rights, Article 5 aims for 'men and women' to respect each others' cultures.

In conclusion, the Declaration shows that, already in 1978, a right to (preserve/maintain) cultural identity was formulated in an international instrument, albeit not as a substantive right but rather as a principle or policy goal. The Declaration confirms that differences between people are worth preserving, for example, by the right to be different, which is closely related to a right to freedom of cultural identity. It further emphasizes the need to protect the cultural identity and cultural development of communities against forced assimilation.

## 4. Other developments in UNESCO in relation to a right to cultural identity

In the 1970s and 1980s, UNESCO organized various intergovernmental Conferences on Cultural Policies, at which a right to cultural identity was extensively discussed.[40] Cultural identity and cultural rights were also addressed in the study presented in 1995 by the World Commission on Culture and Development, paving the way for further standard-setting in UNESCO.

### *A. Mexico Declaration on Cultural Policies*

The second World Conference on Cultural Policies (1982) adopted a Declaration in which the concept of cultural identity was significantly present. It was, for example, determined that the assertion of cultural identity could contribute to the liberation of peoples. Forms of domination could constitute a denial or impairment of that identity.[41] The Mexico Declaration notes that:

---

39 UNESCO Doc. SS-77/CONF.201/1, *cit. supra* note 35, pp. 18-19; UNESCO Doc. 20 C/18, *cit. supra* note 35, p. 4.

40 The first World Conference on Cultural Policies took place in Venice (1970). Regional conferences were later held for Europe (1972), Asia (1973), Africa (1975) and Latin America (1978).

41 UNESCO Doc. CLT/MD/1– Mexico City Declaration on Cultural Policies 1982, pp. 41-42.

> [t]he international community considers it its duty to ensure that the cultural identity of each people is preserved and protected.[42]

This provision emphasizes the general responsibility of the international community; but what is meant by 'international community' remains unclear, as does the content and kind of obligations entailed. At state level, it was agreed that there was a need for cultural policies that would protect, stimulate and enrich the cultural identity of all peoples. It was stated that:

> [t]he equality and dignity of all cultures must be recognised, as must *the right of each people and cultural community to affirm and preserve its cultural identity* and have it respected by others.[43] (emphasis added)

It is interesting to note that cultural identity is included here as a value formulated in terms of rights. Generally, the rights enumerated in the Declaration reflect principles that should guide the cultural policies of states. However, individuals and communities cannot invoke a right to cultural identity on the basis of this Declaration; nor are any state obligations defined.

### *B. 'Our Creative Diversity' Report*

In December 1992, within the framework of the World Decade for Cultural Development (1988-1997), UNESCO and the UN jointly set up the independent World Commission on Culture and Development. The World Commission was asked to prepare a policy-oriented report on the interactions between culture and development, to serve as the basis for new cultural policies. In November 1995, the Commission presented its report, entitled 'Our Creative Diversity', to the General Conference of UNESCO and the General Assembly of the UN.

In general, the report asserts the view that development is not only about access to goods and services, but also about the opportunity of people to choose a satisfying and valuable life.[44] The report addresses various interactions between culture and development, such as global ethics, pluralism, the media, gender, young people, cultural heritage and the environment. It ends with an International Agenda consisting of a set of actions to be transformed into development strategies,

---

42 *Ibid.*, para. 7.

43 *Ibid.*, para. 9.

44 A similar conclusion was drawn in the UNDP Human Development Report 2004 (*cit. supra* note 6), which emphasises that accommodating people's growing demands for inclusion in society and for respect of their ethnicity, religion and language takes more than democracy and equitable growth. Also needed are multicultural policies that recognize differences, champion diversity and promote cultural freedoms, so that all people can choose to speak their language, practice their religion and participate in shaping their culture.

including the protection of cultural rights as human rights (Action 7).[45] According to Action 7, the following actions are needed to protect and promote cultural rights as human rights:

- The International Law Commission (ILC) should be requested to draft a list of cultural rights not (yet) protected by existing international instruments.
- Based on this list, the ILC could develop an International Code of Conduct on Culture, to condemn violations of cultural rights.
- The ILC could also examine possibilities for the establishment of an International Office of the Ombudsperson [sic] for Cultural Rights, which could deal with the complaints of individuals and communities and could negotiate with governments to search for a peaceful solution.
- A re-examination of international enforcement procedures to improve the prosecution of violations of cultural rights could include examination of the possibility of establishing an International Court, which could deal with alleged violations of cultural rights. This Court might become a part of the International Criminal Court.[46]

The report was presented to UNESCO, but was not formally adopted by its Member States.[47] Most Member States found the way in which the report dealt with the issues at hand too far-reaching. In fact, Action 7 concerning cultural rights received most of the criticism. While the suggestion to draft an inventory on cultural rights was generally supported, Member States rejected the other measures proposed, especially the establishment of an International Court for cultural rights. Member States also argued that the efforts of other international organizations, like the Council of Europe, to promote cultural rights showed how difficult it is to define such rights. They generally expressed concern that the development of new cultural rights would only increase the list of existing international provisions that are not well implemented.

---

45 The complete list of actions is: 1. The publication of an annual report on culture and development. 2. The preparation of new culture-sensitive development strategies. 3. International mobilisation of cultural heritage volunteers. 4. An international plan for gender equality. 5. The implementation of new media policies. 6. Media rights and self-regulation. 7. The protection of cultural rights as human rights. 8. Global ethics and global governance. 9. A people centred United Nations. 10. A Global Summit on Culture and Development. See World Commission on Culture and Development, *Our Creative Diversity*, UNESCO, (Paris, 1995), pp. 271-288.

46 *Ibid.*, pp. 281-284.

47 Most Member States provided the UNESCO Secretariat with an official response to the report. These comments are not published, but have been examined at the Department of Culture at UNESCO Headquarters in Paris. Additional information was obtained from interviews with Mrs. L. Arizpe, Assistant Director General, Sector of Culture and Mr. Y. Isar, Head of the Sector of Culture, in May 1998.

'Our Creative Diversity' was intended to intensify international discussion on the links between culture and development, and it did so. However, the follow-up given to the report was very cautious. As regards Action 7 on cultural rights, an inventory of cultural rights, including a right to cultural identity, was prepared on the basis of rights enumerated in international instruments like the UDHR, the ICCPR, ICESCR, ILO Conventions and the regional instruments of Europe, Africa and America.[48] Subsequently, a working group on cultural rights was to be created to examine the list and decide which cultural rights needed to be further or newly developed. However, this working group was never set up, because it did not receive sufficient support from the Member States. The report did, however, provide impetus for the elaboration of the Declaration on Cultural Diversity seven years later.

## 5. The Declaration on Cultural Diversity (2001)

At the General Conference in November 2001, the Member States adopted a Declaration on Cultural Diversity. The elaboration of the Declaration shows some interesting developments. The preliminary draft text included several references to (a right to) cultural identity, which were not kept in the final text. For example, the Preamble of the preliminary Draft Declaration included definitions for culture and cultural identity. Culture was described as '… the whole complex of distinctive spiritual, material, intellectual, and emotional features that characterise a society or social group …' including '… not only the arts and letters, but also modes of life, ways of living together, the fundamental rights of the human being, value systems, traditions and beliefs …'.[49] Cultural identity '… represents all the ethnic, linguistic, religious and other references that underpin the conscious or unconscious identification with a group.' It was also stated that '… identity is by no means essentially changeless but can evolve, draw on allegiances of various kinds, and be enriched through contact with other cultures.'[50]

The preliminary draft generally contained principles, not rights. In Article 1, however, a reference was included to the rights of groups and of persons belonging to national or ethnic, religious and linguistic minorities to have free access to the expression of their own culture and that of others.

The concept of cultural identity was present in several provisions of the preliminary draft. According to Article 2, a democratic framework promoting cultural diversity should ensure 'respect for cultural identities … fostering the ability of persons or

48 B. Leander, *Preliminary List of Cultural Rights*, UNESCO, Culture and Development Co-ordination Office (1996).

49 UNESCO Doc. 161 EX/12 + Annex, *Report by the Director-General on the Progress of the UNESCO Draft Declaration on Cultural Diversity*, Paris, 12 April 2001, Annex, p. 3.

50 *Ibid.*

groups with different cultural identities to live together (inclusiveness) and thus contributing to the development of an environment conducive to the expression of creative capacities (empowerment)'.[51]

In relation to linguistic diversity, the preliminary draft contained another reference to cultural identity. Article 7(b) stated: '[g]iven that language is one of the foundations of cultural identity, all individuals should have the right to express themselves, create, disseminate their own works and have access to information and knowledge in the language of their choice, including, among others, their mother tongue'. Finally, cultural identity was coupled with education. Article 9(b) laid down that '[e]ach individual has a right to good-quality education and training which fully respects his or her cultural identity'.[52] Member States were asked to comment on this preliminary draft; a few states did so individually and several collectively.[53]

The final Declaration adopted by the General Conference aims to promote cultural diversity in the context of respect for human rights. The final text is, however, very different from the preliminary draft. Cultural identity is no longer defined, although an affirmation is made in the preamble that '... culture is at the heart of contemporary debates about identity ...'.[54] In fact, the term cultural identity can hardly be found in the Declaration, except as a general value – and certainly not in terms of rights. Article 2, for example, laid down that, in contemporary diverse societies, it is essential to ensure '... harmonious interaction among people and groups with plural, varied and dynamic cultural identities ...'.[55]

The importance of cultural rights is stressed in Article 5 of the Declaration, entitled *cultural rights as an enabling environment for cultural diversity*. It is stated that:

> Cultural rights are an integral part of human rights, which are universal, indivisible and interdependent. The flourishing of creative diversity requires the full implementation of cultural rights as defined in Article 27 of the Universal Declaration of Human Rights and in Articles 13 and 15 of the International Covenant on Economic, Social and Cultural Rights. All persons have therefore the right to express themselves and to create and disseminate their work in the language of their choice, and particularly in their mother tongue; all persons are entitled to quality education and training that fully respect their cultural identity; and all persons have the right to participate

---

51 *Ibid.*, p. 4.

52 *Ibid.*, p. 6.

53 These were Belgium, Canada, France, the Netherlands, Turkey and the United Kingdom and two groups of UNESCO Member States, namely the Group of Fifteen (the then-EU Member States) and the French-speaking Group (Organisation Internationale de la Francophonie), in which more than fifty States participate.

54 UNESCO Doc. 31 C/44, *Draft Declaration on Cultural Diversity* (Paris 2001), Annex, p. 1.

55 Compare UNESCO, *Declaration on Cultural Diversity*, adopted 2 November 2001 with UNESCO Doc. 31 C/44, *cit. supra* note 54, *Draft Declaration on Cultural Diversity*, pp. 2-3.

in the cultural life of their choice and conduct their own cultural practices, subject to respect for human rights and fundamental freedoms.

This provision enumerates existing human rights related to culture, including the right to participate in cultural life, freedom of expression and the right to education. In relation to the latter, respect for cultural identity is added.[56] The provision also deals with limits on the enjoyment of cultural rights in terms of the conduct of cultural practices, which should respect human rights.

The Declaration on Cultural Diversity includes mainly principles to be respected by Member States. The 'main lines of an action plan' for its implementation confirm that Member States have the obligation to adopt policies to protect and promote cultural diversity. It is, *inter alia*, determined that Member States should make further headway in clarifying the content of cultural rights. However, it is interesting to see that a right to freedom of cultural identity, as such, is no longer referred to. It should be noted that several states, including the Netherlands and the UK, issued declarations that they could agree with the Declaration but not with the additional Action Plan, especially where the latter called for the development of norms and standards in the field of cultural diversity. Another striking point is that freedom of religion does not form part of the Declaration, even though it could be considered an important element of cultural identity.

## 6. The Convention on the Protection and Promotion of the Diversity of Cultural Expressions

After the adoption of the Declaration on Cultural Diversity, Member States decided to proceed with the drafting of a Convention on Cultural Diversity. Four options were identified in this respect:

- A new comprehensive instrument on cultural rights
- An instrument on the status of the artist
- A new Protocol to the Florence Agreement on Educational, Scientific and Cultural Materials
- A new instrument on the protection of the diversity of cultural goods and artistic expressions.[57]

---

56 A similar provision can be found in the Convention of the Rights of the Child, in force since September 1990. In Article 29 of this Convention, it is determined that the education of the child should be directed to 'his or her own cultural identity, language and values'.

57 UNESCO Doc. 32 C/52, *Desirability of drawing up an international standard-setting instrument on cultural diversity*, Paris, 18 July 2003, pp. 5-7, paras. 20-23.

Member States decided to proceed with a Convention on the Protection and Promotion of the Diversity of Cultural Expressions, which was adopted on 20 October 2005 by a large majority of Member States, with only 2 against and 4 abstentions.[58]

The basic idea behind the Convention is that '... cultural activities, goods and services have both an economic and a cultural nature, because they convey identities, values and meanings, and must therefore not be treated as solely having commercial value ...' (Preamble). The purpose of the Convention, as stipulated in Article 1, is to protect and promote the diversity of cultural expressions and '... to reaffirm the sovereign rights of States to maintain, adopt and implement policies and measures that they deem appropriate for the protection and promotion of the diversity of cultural expressions on their territory' (Article 1(h)).

The Convention focuses on cultural goods and expressions, and does not specifically include substantive cultural rights or a right to freedom of cultural identity for individuals or communities. However, several general references to human rights can be found in the Convention. The Preamble, for example, states that cultural diversity is important for the full realization of human rights, as proclaimed in the Universal Declaration and other universal instruments.

The Convention also contains several guiding principles, including Principle 1 concerning respect for human rights and fundamental freedoms (Article 2(1)):

> Cultural diversity can be protected and promoted only if human rights and fundamental freedoms, such as freedom of expression, information and communication, as well as the ability of individuals to choose cultural expressions, are guaranteed. No one may invoke the provisions of this Convention in order to infringe human rights and fundamental freedoms as enshrined in the Universal Declaration of Human Rights or guaranteed by international law or to limit the scope thereof.

The Convention also refers to the situation of minorities and indigenous peoples. For example, the Preamble refers to the importance of traditional knowledge systems, in particular of indigenous peoples, as a source of wealth. It also states that the vitality of cultures is taken into account, '... including for persons belonging to minorities and indigenous peoples, manifested in their freedom to create, disseminate and distribute their traditional cultural expressions and to have access thereto, so as to benefit from them for their own development'. Furthermore, Principle 3 recognizes the equal dignity of and need for respect for all cultures, including the cultures of persons belonging to minorities and indigenous peoples.

Although the Convention does not contain substantive rights for individuals or communities, but rather for states, several provisions speak of measures that

---

58 The United States and Israel voted against, while Australia, Honduras, Liberia and Nicaragua abstained. The text of the Convention, as well as the status of ratifications and background information, can be found at: <www.unesco.org>.

*may* be taken by states to protect cultural diversity. These possible measures could be considered similar to possible measures flowing from cultural rights or a right to freedom of cultural identity. For example, according to the Convention, states may take measures that '... provide opportunities for ... the creation, production, dissemination, distribution and enjoyment of such domestic cultural activities, goods and services, including provisions relating to the language used for such activities, goods and services' (Article 6(b)). This provision also speaks of measures to establish and support public institutions; to support artists and others involved in the creation of cultural expressions; as well as to enhance the diversity of the media, including through public service broadcasting (Article 6(f), (g) and (h)). Such measures could also include public financial assistance (Article 6(d)). Furthermore, states should encourage individuals and groups to create, produce, disseminate, distribute and have access to their own cultural expressions, '... paying due attention to the special circumstances and needs of women as well as various social groups, including persons belonging to minorities and indigenous peoples' (Article 7(a)). Although states may decide on the kind of measures to take, in becoming parties to the Convention they accept a responsibility to take positive measures in relation to the promotion and protection of cultural diversity.[59]

The Convention has encouraged intense international debate on the issue of cultural diversity, involving experts as well as government officials. The Convention confirms that the diversity of cultural goods and expressions is of crucial importance for development. It codifies the right of states to implement cultural policies and establishes a new foundation for future cooperation in the area of cultural diversity, with special attention for the needs of developing countries. The Convention is not a human rights instrument. It does not include rights for individuals or communities, but only for states, which is in fact contrary to the idea of limiting state power for human rights. The Convention does not, and was not meant to, further elucidate the cultural rights of individuals or communities. It mainly confirms general human rights principles in relation to the protection of cultural diversity.

The Convention does not provide new developments in relation to the right to freedom of cultural identity. The Member States of UNESCO have chosen not to pursue the path of further elaborating cultural rights or promoting the right to freedom of cultural identity.

## 7. Concluding remarks

Since its foundation in 1948, UNESCO has been active in the field of the promotion and protection of cultural diversity. Its Member States have on various occasions

[59] On 15 November 2006, 16 States were Party to the Convention. The Convention needs 30 ratifications to enter into force.

recognized the importance of a right to freedom of cultural identity. The right to the preservation and maintenance of cultural identity, though not always formulated in strict legal terms, is included in several UNESCO instruments. Most UNESCO instruments take the form of recommendations or declarations and, as such, are not legally binding on the Member States. Generally speaking, most of UNESCO's work is in the field of developing concepts and attuning policies. The instruments discussed reflect the progress made in perceptions of the concepts of culture and identity, as well as a right to freedom of cultural identity.

It appears from the above that the general concept of cultural identity is not elaborated in concrete legal terms within UNESCO. Member States did not develop a right to freedom of cultural identity as a substantive right for individuals or communities, with corresponding state obligations. The concept is rather used as a moral value worth preserving and as a political value, whereby states are held responsible for adopting cultural policies to respect and protect cultural identity.

In other words, while the value of cultural identity for human dignity is recognized, a human right to freedom of cultural identity has not been further developed in UNESCO. While the UNESCO instruments adopted in the 1970s included a right to preserve and maintain cultural identity and although the Mexico Declaration of 1982 even explicitly promoted a right to cultural identity, more recent UNESCO instruments and documents no longer refer to this right. The Declaration on Cultural Diversity, for example, speaks of Member State policies that respect cultural identities instead. In fact, Member States seem to be moving away from the further elucidation of cultural rights, including a right to freedom of cultural identity, to the promotion of more practical aspects of culture, including tangible and intangible cultural heritage, cultural goods and cultural expressions. While these issues have a clear link with human rights, they are not explicitly directed at the enhancement and better implementation of cultural rights – something that is still very necessary.

Despite varied UNESCO initiatives in the 1970s and 1980s to promote a right to freedom of cultural identity, the work of UNESCO does not provide clear-cut answers to the issues described above: namely, the content and scope of the right, its collective and individual dimension and corresponding state obligations. It appears that UNESCO has focused on cultural identity as an important value, but has not incorporated a substantive right to freedom of cultural identity into a legally binding instrument. However, this does not mean that a right to freedom of cultural identity is without any meaning. It is clear that cultural identity forms an essential part of human dignity and of cultural diversity. Many communities and individuals need promotion and protection of their cultural identity, in part through the implementation of cultural rights. A right to freedom of cultural identity, even in non-binding legal terms, could serve as a general underlying value to enhance the promotion and protection of cultural rights and cultural diversity. It would reflect the right to be different, which, as described in the Preamble of the

UNESCO Declaration on Race and Racial Prejudice (1978), implies the right not to be excluded, humiliated, exploited or forcibly assimilated. It is in this spirit that a right to freedom of cultural identity should be valued.

# 15
# Political Change and the 'Creative Destruction' of Public Space

*Sanford Levinson**

The major premise of what follows is in fact quite simple: *all* political orders are 'tutelary'. That is, all polities known to me across time and space have engaged or now engage in a variety of practices designed to inculcate in their members preferred ways of viewing the world, especially – it should go without saying – with regard to the legitimacy of the existing political order. I am also assuming that the existing political order is historically located. It did not always exist; and there is some finite possibility that it will not exist in the future, unless it takes steps to defend itself. This is most obvious in the case of expenditures for national defence against potential enemies. But it also explains many other governmental expenditures that are designed to reinforce the desired political culture.

Government-sponsored – or mandated – tutelage is most obvious with regard to education of the young. They must, after all, be socialized in a given culture if it is to endure into coming generations. But civic education certainly takes place outside the schoolroom door and also targets groups other than the young. Maintaining a given culture, particularly if there is any prospect of dissent from that culture, is a full-time job for any political regime.

My subject in this essay is a pervasive aspect of such 'tutelary politics': the management of public space. I am especially interested in the power of what I have elsewhere called 'sacred space' – that is, the grounds of capitol buildings, public cemeteries, great public squares and the like – to convey and legitimize the official ideology and the culture it instantiates.[1] Most obvious, of course, are objects, such as statues. But one should also be aware of the political dimensions that shape decisions about what to name such squares – and, for that matter, major streets more

* The arguments presented in this chapter build on my book, *Written in Stone: Public Monuments in Changing Societies* (Duke University Press, 1998).

1 See *Written in Stone*, *Ibid*., p. 8. See also the introduction to D. Chindester and E.T. Linenthal (eds.), *American Sacred Space* (University of Indiana Press, 1995), pp. 1-42.

Francioni and Scheinin (eds), *Cultural Human Rights*, 341–351

generally. Whether one is talking about the ancient monuments of the Pharaohs in Luxor, or modern events like the renaming of Washington's National Airport after Ronald Reagan or the construction of a brand new monument – albeit designed in accordance with very old, and some would say outmoded, ideals of war monuments – to the veterans of World War II in the National Mall in Washington, D.C., the attempt by political elites to manage public space on behalf of their preferred visions of politics is a constant. And, precisely because it *is* a constant, one cannot cogently criticize the phenomenon, as such, unless one can really imagine a public landscape that is truly 'neutral' with regard to political values. I take it that although one can imagine this as a logical possibility, the vision makes no 'practical sense'. One of the things politics is necessarily about, at least as an empirical matter, is who gets to control the public landscape. *No* political movement has ever promised to leave the existing landscape just as it is.

What is therefore also constant, at least in reasonably democratic politics and especially in times of political transition, is public disputation about the transformation of public space. Serious transitions, after all, involve far more than simply new faces in public office. Some offices, kingships in the most obvious example, may be eliminated while, as happened in the United States immediately after the American Revolution, statues of royal personages disappear from public view – perhaps because they have been melted down to provide metal for rebel armaments. I shall have some occasion below to discuss such great transitions. (There is a reason we often call such great transitions 'monumental'!) But, of course, transitions occur all the time, even when they are less complete than what has come to be called 'regime change'. And almost inevitably attached to such transitions are debates about the public landscape.

Indeed, once one becomes sensitive to such issues it seems almost impossible to pick up newspapers without running into examples of an ever-changing political scene. I offer three very recent examples taken from three quite different areas of the world. In London, Mayor Ken Livingston – sometimes called 'Red Ken' for his antagonism to the views of many of his erstwhile colleagues in the Labor Party – is currently attempting to add a statue of former South African President Nelson Mandela to the collection of worthies immortalized in London's Trafalgar Square.[2] Although the opposition has chosen to focus on what they view as the aesthetic demerits of the proposed statue, Livingston suggests, altogether plausibly, that resistance is based rather on reluctance to open up a square dedicated to memorializing a central hero of the saga of British imperialism to someone who stands for a quite different view of the world.

---

2 See, e.g., J. Lawless, 'Mayor Ken Locks Horns with Tory Council of Trafalgar's Nelson II', *The Independent*, 2 October 2005, available at: <www.sundayindependent.co.za/index.php?fSectionId=1042&fArticleId=2899962>.

In Tokyo, Prime Minister Junichiro Koizumi paid a number of visits to a Shinto shrine while in office. An editorial in the 19 October 2005 *International Herald Tribune* took him to task for his most recent visit, inasmuch as the shrine is viewed not only as a monument to Japan's two-and-a-half million war dead in World War II, but also as the instantiation of an 'unapologetic view of Japan's atrocity-scarred rampages' through Asia and, therefore, of 'the worst traditions of Japanese militarism'.[3] This is obviously not a brand new monument, but one increasingly invested with new political meaning because of its apparently warm embrace by the person who claims to speak for the future, and not only the past, of Japan. Koizumi's actions are certainly in line with what is widely regarded as Japan's almost total failure to own up to its past with regard to World War II. Japan, like Austria, has been able to cast itself as a 'victim nation', largely because of the fortuity of Hiroshima and Nagasaki.[4] It is no coincidence that the best known monument in Japan – at least to Westerners – is the Peace Monument in Hiroshima, although one might fear, as a practical matter, that the Shinto shrine offers greater insight into contemporary Japan.

Of course, one should not consider the Japanese unique in their unwillingness to come to terms with their own past. The United States certainly has a mixed record in this respect. For example, one of the more bizarre aspects of the 2000 presidential race was the extent to which views about flying the Confederate battle flag over the state capitol of South Carolina became a central issue in that state's presidential primary. Indeed, one could argue that John McCain would today be President if he had not been so politically unwise as to express reservations about a flag that can well be regarded as a symbol of treason (though not, of course, in South Carolina). George W. Bush's refusal even to comment on the issue, ostensibly because it was a 'local' matter for South Carolina – though one might note that the Texas capitol grounds contain no fewer than three statues commemorating the Confederate military – was a contributing factor to his being able to stave off the McCain challenge.

Finally, consider an 'editorial comment' from the 20 November 2005 *New York Times*, tellingly titled 'Ultimate Soviet Henchman Returns to His Pedestal'.[5] It concerns a statue of Felix Dzerzhinsky, aptly described as 'the father of the secret police, the founder of the gulag, the man whose people tortured and killed millions to create Lenin's dream state'. One of the iconic moments of the dissolution of the Soviet Union was the presumed destruction of that statue on 22 August 1991. As a matter of fact, it was not wholly destroyed, but rather moved, like other Communist-era statues, to 'an undistinguished patch of land behind the New Tretyakov Gallery',

---

3 See 'Provocation in Tokyo', *International Herald Tribune*, 19 October 2005, available at: <www.iht.com/articles/2005/10/18/opinion/edjapan.php>.

4 See I. Buruma, *Wages of Guilt* (1995).

5 E. Randolph, 'Ultimate Soviet Henchman Returns to His Pedestal', *New York Times*, 20 November 2005, Section 4 (News of the Week in Review), p. 11.

apparently called the 'monster's graveyard' by foreigners. According to the *Times*, however, '[e]arlier this month, with little fanfare but plenty of dreary symbolism, Mr. Dzerzhinsky was returned to a position of honour in central Moscow'. It is, in fact, not exactly the same statue or the same plinth, but that scarcely lessens the 'dreary symbolism' involved in returning him to *any* place of honour.

These recent controversies simply underscore the extent to which political figures and the movements they purport to lead must necessarily respond to their own past. The response can be critical, as was Livingston's and McCain's, or embracing, as was that of the Japanese Prime Minister and, apparently, Putin's Russia. In a sense, however, the direction of the response may be less important than the fact that such action takes place at all.

The phenomenon of what might be called 'tutelary landscaping' is most dramatic whenever a current polity self-consciously attempts to question its past and substitute a new view of the world. I find extremely useful a term offered by the economist Joseph Schumpeter to describe the dynamic of capitalist economic development. He spoke of the 'creative destruction' of traditional industries or practices and the ways of life that may be embedded in them. Perhaps it is worth noting that Karl Marx, in *The Communist Manifesto,* also famously wrote that one consequence of capitalism is that 'all that is solid melts into air'. It is banal to point out that the development of the automobile eliminated not only the need for builders of horse-drawn vehicles, but also, and probably more importantly, the particular mode of life that existed prior to the possibilities created by motorized transport. An entire culture was radically transformed by this technological development – a phenomenon we see repeated even more dramatically in an age of globalization.

It should be equally clear that, for good or ill, political development also brings 'creative destruction' of the public landscape in its wake. I titled a short book I have written on this general subject *Written in Stone: Public Monuments in Changing Societies,* both to evoke the particular solidity – and promise of Permanence – attached to stone and to suggest the paradox – or tragedy from the point of view of the creators – that these monuments often do not, in fact, endure (and not only because of the ravages of acid rain or car pollution).

Indeed, when asked by friends to describe the point of my book, I usually say that the central question it asks is whether it is 'Stalinist' to tear down public statues of Stalin. After all, one of the central symbols of the ill-fated Hungarian revolution of 1956 was precisely the tearing down of such a statue – just as the demolition by a public mob of the statue honouring Dzerzhinsky in 1991 was symbolic of the far more successful overthrow of Soviet Russia. The destruction of civic monuments has become a central symbol of revolutionary transformation. There was a reason why the United States more or less engineered the televized destruction of a statue of Saddam Hussein to accompany what was then perceived as the unequivocally victorious arrival of American troops in Baghdad in 2003. It was one thing to declare that Hussein was no longer in power; it was quite another to demonstrate this through the iconic destruction of what was itself an iconic statue.

I spend several pages of my book describing (and illustrating) change in the public landscape of Budapest since 1989. Almost all Soviet-era public monuments have been eliminated, with the exception of a monument to the Soviet soldiers who gave their lives to liberate the city from Nazi rule in 1945 – some of whom, it has been suggested, are buried beneath the memorial. However, I was recently informed that the monument no longer contains a *red* star at its top; instead, the star is now *gold*.[6] Many of the monuments formerly found in the public spaces of the city have now been moved to 'Statue Park', a remarkable collection of such statuary that at once preserves the artifacts and profoundly changes their meaning for almost all viewers. Also, one now finds near the Hungarian parliament a moving memorial to Imre Nagy, Prime Minister during the 1956 insurrection, who was executed by the Communists that kept power as a result of Soviet intervention.

I take it as a given that no serious argument supports the notion that new political regimes have a 'public duty' to preserve the public statues of hated tyrants, like Stalin (or Saddam Hussein), or the names of public spaces, including great cities, designed to memorialize such figures (or, in the case of Stalingrad, honour them in life). Consider the former Leningrad in this context. Couldn't one say that those who rename for political reasons – as was surely the case with the renaming of Petrograd by newly empowered Soviet leaders on behalf of their own Founding Father –, as it were, have no cause to complain when successor regimes engage in similar effacement of the past for their own political reasons, as in changing the name of the city to St. Petersburg? But it is equally true, I am certain, that almost all of us would wish to put limits on the 'creative destruction' allowed any new political regime, especially with regard to material artifacts that are constitutive of a now-displaced culture.

I would be quite surprised, for example, if anyone reading this essay would defend the wanton, decidedly 'uncreative' destruction of the great Buddhist monuments of Bamiyan, regarded by the Taliban as a culturally dangerous endorsement of infidels. Nor, I am sure, would there be any sympathy for a contemporary Egyptian regime that decided to demonstrate its own commitment to a culture of human rights by tearing down even one of the remarkable memorials to the Pharaohs, however much we might agree that they were tyrants unworthy of the slightest emulation in today's world. At some point, all of us would agree that 'the demands of history' or 'the claims of our collective culture' take precedence over even the most justified political opposition to the particular people or events memorialized. There is something truly totalitarian about the notion that public space must be completely 'cleansed', as it were, of reminders of past evil. But defending the non-destruction of such reminders may require considerable intellectual agility.

---

[6] I am grateful to Enikő Horváth for pointing this out to me.

One way of defending the maintenance of such artifacts is to attempt to focus on public monuments entirely through the lens of aesthetics or history, which requires, among other things, a basic turning away from the explicit political or cultural content attached to them at the time of their creation. Just as atheists can devote themselves to appreciation of the artistic achievements of Italian painters who believed that they were engaged in a common enterprise of glorifying God and, more particularly, Christianity, so we can brush off the particular characters of Pharaohs or similar tyrants by reference to the breath-taking aesthetic achievements of the ancient sculptors. I am confident that if the Roman Forum contained any public sculpture honouring Nero or Caligula, there would be passionate opposition to the suggestion that it be removed from public view merely because the particular emperors were dreadful. 'Culture' is thereby defined as aesthetic appreciation of the material achievements of past, often dead, cultures rather than any genuine engagement with the normative 'cultures' they represent.

My very examples, however, suggest that moves toward such aestheticizing or historicizing may be easier to make (tolerable) the more distant the past – though, of course, the time periods of what might be termed 'cultural states of limitation' may themselves vary across cultures. The world would surely be better off if Protestants in Northern Ireland did not remain fixated on events that occurred in the 17th century or if Kosovars and Serbs could just forget, in some sense, a 14th-century battle and its aftermath. Many might have similar views about 'the remembrance of things past' with regard to Israel and Palestine. But surely none of us believe in complete historical amnesia.

Consider in this context the controversy attached to Ronald Reagan's visit in 1986 to the cemetery at Bitburg, Germany, which contained the graves of a number of SS members. Forty – or now 60 – years does not begin to suffice to eliminate the particular valence attached to Nazism. Similarly, I suggest in my own book that the United States made a grievous error in according, even by the 1880s, equal respect and dignity to those who fought on the two sides of the Civil War. At the very last, this required overlooking the fact that the Confederacy's principal project was the maintenance of racialist chattel slavery. There are no monuments to the Confederate dead in Washington, nor, I believe, should there be. I mentioned earlier that the Texas State Capitol grounds contain three monuments to the Southern soldiers. There are none to those who fought for the Union. (It is as if contemporary Madrid had only Francoist statuary, and none for the Spanish Republicans or, indeed, Anarchists memorialized in George Orwell's *Homage to Catalonia*.)

I include in my book a series of possible responses to the domination of the Texas public landscape, or at least the state Capitol, by such monuments to the Confederacy and, therefore, implicitly to the racist culture for which it spoke. These range from destroying the monument to the Confederate dead to adding a new monument honouring either slaves or the Union soldiers whose victory liberated the slaves. A more 'moderate' solution, perhaps, would be to move the offensive statue from the 'sacred space' of the Capitol grounds to the Texas State Historical Museum.

So the dilemma is this: fidelity to the past, including what we today regard as the heritage of our common culture, may have its claims, but it cannot be the case that all pasts are worth cherishing and, even more to the point, that all pasts have a moral claim on the public spaces used to form our contemporary cultures and to create heritages that we hope to hand down to our progeny. Whatever one thinks of the present government of Zimbabwe, it surely had no duty to keep the original colonial name of Southern Rhodesia as the name of the country; or the capital's name as Salisbury; or to maintain in the space surrounding its capital statues of Cecil Rhodes and Lord Salisbury. Perhaps someone might oppose the replacement of a statue of Lord Salisbury by one of Robert Mugabe because of substantive political views about his person; but if we were speaking of South Africa, it would be as bizarre to claim that a statue of Nelson Mandela should not replace one of Mr. Rhodes or, even more to the point, statues honouring the architects of the apartheid regime, as to proclaim the necessity of keeping unchanged the name of what used to be the Daniel Malan International Airport in Cape Town. Thomas Jefferson was notorious for saying that the earth belonged to the living and that constant revolutions were useful to prevent the remnants of a dead past from limiting future possibility. But there is always a tension between claims for recognition and honour by our ancestors and the necessity to reject those claims and, in some sense, to destroy their purported heritage in the name of generating hopeful futures for ourselves and our descendants.

How, then, can we resolve this dilemma (which some may analogize to squaring the circle)? There are, as already suggested, what might be termed 'intermediate' solutions, like the displacement of public monuments from 'sacred space' in front of capitol buildings, great public plazas or national cemeteries to museums. One purpose of museums, after all, is to put such artifacts in their place, so to speak, by transforming them from tutelary objects to historicized emblems of a past that may well be viewed today as no longer in possession of a genuine normative claim on us. An especially vivid example of such a transformation may well be an exhibition organized last year in New York, by the Guggenheim Museum, of objects exemplifying the Aztec empire in Mexico. It was certainly a striking exhibit, but even the cosmopolitan and multicultural exhibit designers could not completely ignore the fact that Aztec culture was in many ways horrendous. One need not applaud Spanish imperialism in Mexico to believe that, on balance, the world is better off with the destruction of a culture based on blood sacrifice of human beings and an extraordinary class system that kept most in absolute privation while rulers lived in relative luxury. One could, then, admire the Aztec objects on formal aesthetic grounds – some of them were indeed beautiful – without real regret that the culture that supported their creation had been destroyed by the Spanish. One's feelings – or, at the least, *my* feelings – were altogether different from the lament I recently felt, when visiting museums in Athens, at the victory of Alexander the Great over the weakened Athenians and what remained of their democracy.

Obviously, there is much to be said for the preservation of past cultures in museums, even if these cultures are, from a variety of normative perspectives, dreadful. Part of becoming culturally aware is the realization that there is no particular connection between aesthetic sophistication and normative goodness. 'Culture', from an anthropological or historical perspective, is a positivist notion referring to the ways people have organized themselves and made the world meaningful, and *not* a normative notion declaring that whatever human beings have created is automatically worthy of admiration. None of us could make sense of the dynamic cultures in which we all live if we truly believed that whatever cultures existed in the past are worthy of maintenance and continued emulation. We are all the more or less grateful beneficiaries of the creative destruction of various forms of (stifling) past cultures.

What I am calling the 'museum solution' – i.e., the movement of public art from its original public space to the enclosed space of a historical (and historicizing) museum – is obviously not 'neutral'. Those who in fact share a veneration of the persons or causes memorialized will object to the quite explicit political and cultural message of such displacement. Someone who really admired Cecil Rhodes, for example, would scarcely be assuaged, upon seeing his statue removed from a central public space to the National Museum, by the response, 'Well, at least we're not completely destroying it'. And, of course, this new national museum is scarcely likely to *honour* Rhodes, even as it recognizes the undoubted role he played in the formation of what became Zimbabwe.

It should also be recognized that at least some persons on 'the other side' may wish *only* destruction, so that placing the object – and, symbolically, its honouree – in a state museum would still convey more public esteem than they feel might be merited. Would a German art museum, for example, display a portrait of Hitler, whatever its aesthetic merits might be? Many Nazi objects, of course, can be found in museums devoted to the explicit history of World War II, but those institutions I have seen leave no doubt about their disdain for the Nazis. Such museums are fully 'tutelary' in their aims.

Whatever the merits of the 'museum solution' in some instances, it is scarcely sufficient to resolve the tensions identified by this chapter. Some artifacts, after all, depend on occupying certain spaces for their power. Few would have accepted a Taliban solution consisting of moving the Buddhist statues that were destroyed to a museum in Kabul, ostensibly so that more Afghans could have the opportunity to see these important remnants of the Afghan past. (Though, if I am correct in my assumption, one should ask why the removal by Lord Elgin of the Parthenon friezes does not generate similar outrage and a demand that the British Museum return its ill-gotten goods.) Or, should someone object to the gigantic tribute to Victor Emmanuel in Rome – either because one is anti-monarchist or because one identifies its particular architectural style with fascism – it would scarcely be possible to offer as a compromise the solution of moving it to another location. There is no feasible alternative between leaving it where it is, thereby accepting its domination of the part of Rome in which it is located, or destroying it – and I presume that no one would seriously suggest the latter.

I offer as an aside that there is currently a fascinating dispute in New York City about the preservation of the building that a noted American architect, Edward Durell Stone, designed for what was then the Huntington Hartford Museum of Art at Columbus Circle; it was widely derided at the time of its creation, approximately 50 years ago. This fact has not prevented many current urban historians and cultural preservationists from arguing that it has become part of New York's 'cultural heritage' and should be preserved in accordance with Stone's vision of the building, regardless of its aesthetic merits. (Perhaps this is best conceived as the cultural equivalent of what lawyers term 'adverse possession', where long-term occupation of someone else's property operates to transfer title and to legitimize what in another context might be regarded as theft.) It may also be worth noting that before September 11 the World Trade Center was also widely (and, I believe, justifiably) criticized as America's own contribution to an inhumane aesthetic of grandiosity that expressed no concern at all for the daily lives of the New Yorkers who actually lived near it. This has not prevented calls for rebuilding the Center in order to demonstrate to the terrorists that they did not prevail. And, as could be readily predicted, there are ever more bitter fights about what should go into any museum devoted to the events of September 11.

In any event, it should be obvious that the 'museum solution', though attractive in some instances, can scarcely work in all. And even if it is a perfect solution to the dilemma of what should happen to *one* particular statue of a now-discredited public figure, it does not tell us what to do with what may be many other statues of a figure who was once pervasive in the public landscape. A museum may 'need' one statue of Stalin or Saddam, but there is no conceivable need for a dozen such artifacts. Thus, there is no escaping the question of when it is permissible to destroy a given public artifact and transform public space in the name of new cultural values.

Having set out the dilemma at some length, the obvious question is whether there is indeed a principle that will support the destruction of statues of Stalin or Saddam Hussein that does not offer aid and comfort to what we would probably regard as a crazed ideologue who would wish to do the same with Ramses II, Trajan, or one or another of the disreputable Borgias who contributed so much to the making of Florence. Perhaps it is in answering this question that I display my colours as an American lawyer, for I doubt seriously that such a helpful abstract principle exists. Instead, I am inclined to argue that decisions must always be made pragmatically – which means, in effect, the contextual balancing of interests and values that distinguishes a 'common law' from a 'civil law' sensibility.

Still, even in the absence of hard and fast principles, there remain at least two procedural points that I hope resonate with the work of our colleague, Francesco Francioni, who has spent much time over the years wrestling with just such questions as a participant and chain in the UNESCO project involving the declaration of a right involving the 'world heritage', with a special claim to be preserved against transformation. The first question is a classic lawyer's: the *burden of proof*. Should the preservationist or the transformationist bear the burden of demonstrating the advisability of maintaining or changing a particular venue? From one perspective, it may not matter much if the only purpose of a burden-of-persuasion rule is to decide who wins in case of a genuine equilibrium. One suspects that, most of the time, analysts would agree that one side has the better of the argument, even if only by a slight measure. Of course, things get more complicated if one sets a higher standard of persuasion, so that, for example, one would have to demonstrate by 'clear and convincing evidence' that the status quo should be changed or, concomitantly, that it should be maintained against the desires of those now exercising political control to reshape public space. And does it matter whether they can plausibly claim to speak on behalf of a popular majority? My own inclination would be to place the burden on those desiring change, but to limit – relatively speaking – the onerousness of the burden. 'Clear and convincing' strikes me as too demanding a standard: it asks too much from those who wish to change things. Of course, we might demand at least such a burden with regard to sites that merit the term 'world heritage'. Indeed, for such sites, we might well demand a 'beyond reasonable doubt' standard. This 'sliding scale' approach naturally makes the process of identifying 'world heritage' sites ever more important.

Thus we move to a second important question: *precisely who gets to assess the quality of arguments on behalf of labelling some sites as truly special and, in turn, to weigh arguments between preservationists and transformationists*? One can imagine possibilities ranging from democratically accountable public institutions, such as city councils or legislatures, to more detached public commissions, to citizen juries or, finally, to judges. Of course, there is also a subset of questions attached to such a decision. For example, should public commissions consist of trained professionals, including historians and art critics, or rather of 'local notables' whose legitimacy is based more on presumptive popular esteem than the possession of relevant professional training? And, finally, to what degree should such decision-making bodies be local or even national, as opposed to international? After all, if one can seriously speak of a 'world heritage' with regard to cultural sites or artifacts, then it seems ill-advised not to include 'the world' in the decision-making process in order to guard against the possibility that a given national regime will underweight this interest. Obviously, international 'representation' can be provided by lobbyists who attempt to influence those with actual decision-making power. What would be better, presumably, would be actual voting power, even if it is difficult to imagine how this would be guaranteed – especially in a country like the United States, which is currently undergoing a fit of unseemly parochialism with regard to the views of anyone outside the United States.

## Conclusion

Multiculturalism is a pervasive part of human reality. Today, we most often think of multiculturalism in a 'horizontal' dimension where living cultures interact with one another, for good and for ill, and where we necessarily wrestle with the complex questions of how sometimes antagonistic cultures make their peace with one another. But it should be obvious that there is also a 'vertical' dimension to multiculturalism, inasmuch as existing cultures are built, sometimes quite literally, on the ruins of past cultures, with ever-present questions as to what duties, if any, we – the living – owe to the material legacy of the past. Of course, the vertical and horizontal connect whenever contemporary cultures claim a connection, however attenuated, with artifacts from the past.

It is facile to suggest that there is a strong right to maintain a given culture, given the dynamism attached particularly to economic and political transformations. Creative destruction is a given. The best that can realistically be hoped for is that we become more sensitive to the costs, as well as the benefits, of such development and try to minimize the amount of unnecessary destruction. But those most committed to the cultures being swept aside can scarcely be expected to agree with those doing the sweeping on what counts as costs and benefits.

# Notes on Contributors

**Mattias Åhrén** comes from the Saami people, indigenous to northern Fennoscandinavia and the Kola Peninsula in the Russian Federation. He holds LLM degrees from the University of Stockholm and the University of Chicago. Having clerked at Stockholm City Court and worked as an associate at Mannheimer Swartling and Danowsky & Partners law firms in Stockholm, he took up the position of Head of the Human Rights Unit of the Saami Council in 2002. He has represented the Saami people in numerous UN and other international conferences. Since October 2005, Mattias Åhrén has combined this work with PhD studies at the University of Tromsö, Norway. He has published several articles on the rights of the Saami people and indigenous peoples generally, particularly within the field of cultural rights.

**William Barth** completed his doctoral studies at the University of Oxford in 2006 with a dissertation entitled On Cultural Rights: The Equality of Nations and the Minority Legal Tradition,. Dr Barth is an Associate Fellow at the University's Rothermere American Institute, and a Junior Member of St Antony's College. Dr Barth previously served as a senior lawyer and manager for the US Department of Housing and Urban Development. He received his Master's Degree in Public Administration from Harvard University, John F. Kennedy School of Government in 1986 and his Juris Doctor from Loyola University School of Law in 1979. He has been a member of the California State Bar since 1979.

**Bruno de Witte** is Professor of European Law at the European University Institute in Florence, Italy, and Co-Director of the Academy of European Law. Prior to joining the EUI faculty in 2000, he was Professor of European Law at the Universiteit Maastricht (the Netherlands). He is a member of the Board of Editors of the *European Law Journal* and the *European Human Rights Law Review*. His current fields of research interest include institutional law of the European Union – relations between EU law and national law and between international law and EU law, protection of fundamental rights, horizontal and vertical divisions of powers, sources of EU law – as well as European, international and comparative legal regulation of culture, media, education and language use, and the protection of minorities.

**Yvonne Donders** is Deputy Director of the Amsterdam Center for International Law at the Faculty of Law of the University of Amsterdam. Until May 2006, she worked as Programme Specialist on Economic, Social and Cultural Rights in the Division of Human Rights and Struggle against Discrimination of the UNESCO Secretariat in Paris. Her current research interests include general public international law, international human rights law with a particular focus on economic, social and cultural rights, and human rights and development.

**Francesco Francioni** is Professor of International Law and Human Rights at the European University Institute, Florence, and at the Law Faculty of the University of Siena. He is also Co-Director of the Academy of European Law, General Editor of the *Italian Yearbook of International Law* and member of the Board of Editors of the *European Journal of International Law*. Professor Francioni is a member of the American Law Institute and of the Executive Board of the European Society of International Law. He has been a member of the Italian delegation at many diplomatic conferences and international negotiations, particularly in the field of environmental law and cultural heritage. He has given courses at the Hague Academy of International Law (1995), Cornell Law School (1983-1986), Texas Law School (1988-2005) and Oxford University (1999-2003).

**Enikő Horváth** completed her doctoral studies at the European University Institute in 2006. Her current research interests include international human rights law, the protection of minorities and the regulation of immigration and nationality, as well as culture, education and language use in Europe. Among others, she is the author of *Mandating Identity: Citizenship, Kinship Laws and Plural Nationality in the European Union* (Kluwer Law International, forthcoming).

**Stéphanie Lagoutte** is a Senior Research Fellow and Academic Coordinator of the Research Partnership Programme at the Danish Institute for Human Rights, Copenhagen. She has published articles about the right to respect for family life, reform of the European Court of Human Rights, freedom of religion, and fair trial. She is the editor of a report on the response to Protocol 12 in the Nordic countries. She is currently working on a research project concerning the proceduralization of the jurisprudence of the European Court of Human Rights. Her fields of interest and teaching include international and regional protection of human rights, European Court of Human Rights, freedom of religion, right to respect for family life, family law, and immigration law. She has also taken part in the Danish-Iranian Dialogue on Human Rights.

**Eva Maria Lassen** is a Senior Research Fellow at the Danish Institute for Human Rights, Copenhagen. She has previously held fellowships at Lucy Cavendish College and Gonville and Caius College, University of Cambridge. Her research interests include the history of human rights; the relationship between modern human rights and religious traditions; the Holocaust and the emergence of international human rights law; Jewish contributions to the development of international human rights law; Christian values and human rights; women's rights and religious traditions; religious freedom; and Islam. She has written extensively on these subjects. She is the Danish Director of the European Master's Degree in Human Rights and Democratisation and is a member of the Executive Committee of the Master's Programme. She is a member of several national and international committees, amongst them the ODIHR Panel of Experts on Freedom of Religion or Belief (OSCE) and she has taken part in the Danish-Iranian Dialogue on Human Rights.

**Federico Lenzerini** is Professor of Public International Law, Private International Law and European Community Law at the University of Siena (Italy). He acts as Consultant to the United Nations Educational, Scientific and Cultural Organization (UNESCO) and as Legal Advisor of the Italian Ministry of Foreign Affairs at international negotiations concerning the protection of cultural heritage. He is also a member of the International Law Association (ILA) 'Biotechnology Committee'. His main research interests lie in the areas of international protection of human rights; refugee rights and right of asylum; rights of indigenous peoples; international protection of cultural heritage; international trade law.

**Sanford Levinson** is Professor at the University of Texas Law School and in the Government Department at the University of Texas. He has also taught at the Harvard, Yale, NYU, and Boston law schools, as well as the Central European University in Budapest, University of Paris II, and the Hebrew University in Jerusalem. He has written many books on constitutional law and theory, and is the author of *Written in Stone: Public Monuments in Changing Societies* (Duke U. Press, 1998). His most recent book is *Our Undemocratic Constitution: Where the Constitution Goes Wrong (and How We the People Can Correct It)* (Oxford University Press, 2006). He was elected to the American Academy of Arts and Sciences in 2001.

**Tore Lindholm** is a philosopher and Associate Professor at the Norwegian Centre for Human Rights, Faculty of Law, University of Oslo. His earlier scholarly work was in philosophy of science and social theory (Marx, Popper, Gadamer). He was lead editor of Lindholm, Durham, Bahia Tahzib-Lie (eds), *Facilitating Freedom of Religion or Belief: A Deskbook* (Martinus Nijhoff Publishers, 2004). His ongoing research addresses principles, conditions and strategies for collaboration and solidarity-building across religious and life-stance divides with respect to human rights. He co-initiated and sat on the steering committee of the Norwegian Research Council Program on Research in Ethics 1990–2001. He is Chair of the Board of the international NGO, the Oslo Coalition on Freedom of Religion of Belief and is also a member of the Church of Norway (Norway's Lutheran State Church) Human Rights Committee.

**Timo Makkonen** is undertaking doctoral studies at the University of Helsinki. He is a Deputy Judge at the National Discrimination Tribunal of Finland and a member of the European network of independent legal experts in the non-discrimination field established by the European Commission. His research interests include international human rights law, in particular a multidisciplinary approach to anti-discrimination law and minority rights. His publications include *European Handbook on Equality Data* (Office for Official Publications of the European Communities, 2007) and *Identity, Difference and Otherness: The Concepts of 'People', 'Indigenous People' and 'Minority' in International law* (Helsinki University Press, 2000).

**Susanna Mancini** is Professor of Comparative Public Law at the Faculty of Law of the University of Bologna, Italy. She has written extensively on the protection of minorities, the management of ethnic and linguistic conflicts, federalism and secession, freedom of religion, cultural diversity and gender equality. Among others, she is the author of *Minoranze autoctone e stato - Tra composizione dei conflitti e secessione* (Giuffrè, 1996).

**John Morijn** is a PhD researcher at the European University Institute, Florence. He is a graduate in law of Rotterdam Law School and holds an LL.M from the College of Europe, Bruges (Belgium) and a master in human rights from the European Master's Programme in Human Rights and Democratisation, Venice. He has also been a visiting research scholar at Michigan Law School, Ann Arbor. His research focuses on integrating non-economic and human rights concerns into EC and WTO trade law. He serves as a member of the European Social Charter Academic Network.

**Evangelia Psychogiopoulou** is a research fellow at the Hellenic Foundation for European and Foreign Policy (ELIAMEP) and attorney at law. She completed her PhD at the European University Institute on the integration of cultural considerations in EU law and policies. She has held positions at the Academy of European Law and the Directorate-General for Education and Culture of the European Commission. Her research interests lie in the field of EU/EC law, with special emphasis on EC cultural and audiovisual policies, and human rights protection.

**Martin Scheinin** is Professor of Constitutional and International Law and the Director of the Institute for Human Rights at Åbo Akademi University, Finland. He obtained his Dr.iuris degree at University of Helsinki in 1991, and has published extensively in the fields of human rights law, public international law, and Finnish and comparative constitutional law. In 1997-2004 he was a member of the Human Rights Committee acting under the International Covenant on Civil and Political Rights, and since 2005 he has served as United Nations Special Rapporteur on human rights and counter-terrorism. He is the leader of the Finnish Graduate School in Human Rights Research and of the Nordic School in Human Rights Research. He has been the chairperson of the Committee on human rights law and practice within the International Law Association since 1998. In 2003-2005 he was a member of the Expert Commission that drafted a proposal for a Nordic Saami Rights Convention.

**Ana Filipa Vrdoljak** is Marie Curie Fellow at the Law Department, European University Institute and Senior Lecturer at the Faculty of Law, University of Western Australia. She has previously been a Jean Monnet Fellow at the EUI and Senior Research Associate at the Faculty of Law, University of Sydney. She has also been a visiting scholar at the Lauterpacht Research Centre for International Law, University of Cambridge and the Global Law School, New York University. She is the author of *International Law, Museums and the Return of Cultural Objects* (Cambridge University Press, 2006).

# Subject Index

## N



## O



## P

## R



## S



## T



## U

# Index of Case Law

## Court of Justice of the European Communities



## European Commission of Human Rights



## European Court of Human Rights